Democratic Choice and Taxation

This book examines tax policies and tax systems as they arise from democratic choices, set against the background of a market economy. The authors find that democratic institutions yield complex tax systems with features that follow a varied but predictable pattern. In developing their analysis, they use formal modeling of voting behavior, emphasizing recent advances in the theory of probabilistic voting.

The analysis in this book differs from the available tax literature by relating fiscal choices directly to voting and political competition and by examining tax systems in democratic countries from a variety of perspectives. The authors originally focus on explaining observed features of tax systems, but they also devote considerable space to discussion of the welfare and efficiency effects of taxation in the presence of collective choice, and they review other models and the related literature. In addition, they use applied general equilibrium analysis and statistical research on national and state governments in the United States and Canada to link theory to empirical data.

Walter Hettich is Professor of Economics at California State University, Fullerton. He has also held faculty positions at Carleton and Queen's Universities, Canada, and visiting positions at the University of California at Berkeley and Santa Cruz, and has been a research scholar at the University of Konstanz, Germany. He is the author of articles in the *American Economic Review, Journal of Public Economics, Canadian Journal of Economics, National Tax Journal, European Journal of Political Economy,* and *Public Choice,* among other publications. A former consultant to several departments of the Canadian government, he has also been named Outstanding Professor, School of Business and Economics, California State University.

Stanley L. Winer is Professor of Economics at the School of Public Administration, Carleton University, Ottawa, Canada. He has served as a visiting professor at the Universities of Montreal and Western Ontario, Carnegie-Mellon University, and Renmin University, China, and has held research fellowships at the Australian National University, the University of Haifa, and Statistics Canada. A consultant to several agencies of the Canadian federal and provincial governments, he has published articles in the *Journal of Political Economy, American Economic Review, Journal of Public Economics, Canadian Journal of Economics, European Journal of Political Economy, International Tax and Public Finance,* and *National Tax Journal,* among other periodicals. He is a co-author (with D. Gauthier) of *Internal Migration and Fiscal Structure* (Economic Council of Canada, 1982). Professor Winer was awarded a Research Achievement Award by Carleton University in 1998.

Democratic Choice and Taxation

A Theoretical and Empirical Analysis

WALTER HETTICH and STANLEY L. WINER

CAMBRIDGE
UNIVERSITY PRESS

PUBLISHED BY THE PRESS SYNDICATE OF THE UNIVERSITY OF CAMBRIDGE
The Pitt Building, Trumpington Street, Cambridge, United Kingdom

CAMBRIDGE UNIVERSITY PRESS
The Edinburgh Building, Cambridge CB2 2RU, UK   http://www.cup.cam.ac.uk
40 West 20th Street, New York, NY 10011-4211, USA   http://www.cup.org
10 Stamford Road, Oakleigh, Melbourne 3166, Australia

First published 1999

Printed in the United States of America

Typeface Times Roman 10/12 pt.   *System* QuarkXPress [EC]

A catalog record for this book is available from the British Library.

Library of Congress Cataloging-in-Publication Data

Hettich, Walter.
    Democratic choice and taxation: a theoretical and empirical
analysis / Walter Hettich and Stanley L. Winer.
        p.   cm.
    Includes bibliographical references (p.   ) and indexes.
    ISBN 0–521–62291–3
    1. Taxation.   2. Taxing power.   I. Winer, Stanley L., 1947–   .
II. Title.
HJ2305.H525   1999
336.2–dc21   98-26458

ISBN 0-521-62291-3 hardback

To the late P. Muros and my teachers – W.H.
To Albert and Shirley, and to Amalia, Avital, and Oren – S.W.

Contents

**PART FIVE: POLITICAL INSTITUTIONS
AND TAXATION**

Preface

The foundation of this book derives from two sources. Like most writers concerned with public finance, we rely on traditional microeconomics and general equilibrium analysis to describe the economic decisions of individuals in the private sector. To this, we link formal modeling of collective choice behavior, relying in particular on recent advances in the theory of probabilistic voting. The book examines taxation as it arises on this joint foundation – as a result of the interaction of maximizing decisions in the private and public sectors.

Although the final form of the book reflects our special interests and concerns, we have attempted to present a balanced picture, one that is more comprehensive than commonly found in the literature on taxation that includes elements of collective choice. We examine taxation and tax systems in democratic countries from a positive or predictive point of view, but we also devote considerable space to discussion of efficiency and of normative concerns. In addition, we use applied general equilibrium analysis and statistical research to link theory to empirical data. We feel that taxation as it arises out of democratic choices can best be understood if examined from all these perspectives in relation to an expanded theoretical foundation that incorporates collective choice.

Although the book was written over the past four years, the material reported in several of the chapters evolved over a longer period. As our thinking developed, we benefited from the writings of many authors, whose specific contributions are acknowledged at various points in the text. We would, however, like to give special credit to the Scandinavian economists who pioneered research on the public sector, particularly to Eric Lindahl, whose later writings helped us see how the work reported in this book is linked to the Scandinavian tradition and how it extends that tradition in a new direction. Of course, we would also like to acknowledge our debts to those who encouraged us and who helped us undertake and complete this enterprise. Foremost among them are Thomas Rutherford, who carried out the analysis and co-authored with Stanley Winer the discussion paper on which Chapter 7 is based, and George Warskett, a co-author of Chapter 4. In addition, we benefited greatly from our contacts and discussions with Richard Bird, George Break, Geoffrey Brennan, Richard and Peggy Musgrave, Friedrich Schneider, and David Sewell, the late Irwin Gillespie, and the late Werner Pommerehne.

We would also like to thank those who made valuable comments on the manuscript (or portions of it) or on papers that later became chapters in the book in somewhat altered form. They include three anonymous referees chosen by Cambridge University Press, as well as Thomas Borcherding, Leonard Dudley, Stephen Ferris, and Dennis Mueller.

Others who contributed to research at various stages and in various ways include Marcus Berliant, Albert Breton, Peter Coughlin, Bruno Frey, Gianluigi Galleotti, Berndt Genser, the late Douglas Hartle, Louis Hotte, Nurul Islam, Larry Kenny, Herbert Kiesling, David Laband, Allan Maslove, Gilbert Metcalf, Jack Mintz, Claude Montmarquette, Rebecca Morton, Thomas Rymes, Pierre Salmon, Karl Scholz, Anthony Scott, Hirofumi Shibata, Dan Usher, Frans van Winden, Edwin West, Ronald Wintrobe, David Wong, Shlomo Yitzhaki, Akira Yokoyama, and Robert Young.

Some of the ideas developed in the book were presented in preliminary form at international conferences. We would like to acknowledge helpful comments by participants at Villa Colombella Conferences in Italy, France, and Canada, at International Seminars in Public Economics in Amsterdam, Linz, and Oxford, at the Workshop on International Taxation at the University of Konstanz, Germany, and at the Tax Conversations Conference in Sydney, Australia. In addition, we want to thank the members of the Faculty and Student Seminar in Economics at California State University and of the Workshop in the Evaluation of Public Budgets at Carleton University for comments on various papers related to the book.

Nothing in this book has been published before in the exact form it has taken here. We have, however, used material from previously published papers of ours. For their kind permission to do so, we wish to thank the following: *International Tax and Public Finance*, the *Journal of Public Economics*, the *National Tax Journal*, the *Osgoode Hall Law Journal*, the American Economics Association, Cambridge University Press, Elsevier Science Publishers, Kluwer Academic Publishers, and Kluwer Law International. Full citations are given in the bibliography.

While working on the manuscript we benefited from the hospitality of several universities. Stanley Winer spent three months at Australian National University in the summer of 1996 and the fall term of the same year at the University of Montreal, and Walter Hettich was a visiting research scholar at the University of Konstanz for a two-week period in 1993. He would also like to thank the School of Public Administration at Carleton University for providing office facilities during several research visits.

We are grateful to the Social Sciences and Humanities Research Council of Canada for financial support over a number of years. Walter Hettich would like to acknowledge release time from teaching obtained from the dean of the

School of Business and Economics at CSUF in connection with published research papers related to material in the book.

Thanks should also go to those who served as research assistants, particularly to Maria Javenia and Wannakan Phiryaprcunt. We are indebted to our editor Scott Parris for his unstinting support, to Kelly Donovan, who drew all the figures, and to Ted Reed and Avital Winer for their assistance with the editing. Finally we thank Amalia Winer for her understanding and support over the years. While we are grateful for all the help received, we accept full responsibility for any errors that may have crept into any part of the book.

CHAPTER 1

Introduction

Taxes are the sinews of the State.

Marcus Tullius Cicero (1st century B.C.)

It is not surprising and is indeed appropriate that fiscal policy ... should be among the most controversial of policy issues. The fiscal process, as much as any other democratic institution occupies the middle ground between anarchy and absolute rule. It provides the forum on which interest groups and ideologies may clash without resort to the barricades, and on which compromise and cooperation may be sought.

Richard Musgrave (1981, p. 1)

Taxation has been a major subject of comment and analysis throughout history. It is not difficult to understand the source of this widespread attention. Taxes directly affect the daily lives of individual citizens while also providing "the sinews of state," as pointed out long ago by the Roman writer Cicero. They give the government access to private economic resources and make possible the provision of essential public services, such as defense, police protection, and the enforcement of property rights through the courts. Their imposition influences the distribution of personal income and may alter the division of wealth among different groups. How a society employs taxation reveals much about the relation between its citizens and the state, and thus defines an important part of the nation's character.

Economists have made many contributions to the study of taxation and fiscal choices. Although our analysis falls into this broad tradition, it also represents a new departure. The book is based on a definite point of view on how to approach the study of fiscal matters in democratic states. We see tax policies as equilibrium outcomes of a collective choice process that is constrained by political as well as economic forces, and we believe that tax analysis at its best should reflect this more inclusive and complex view of the fiscal process.

A different starting point often leads to new research questions, or to a reframing of the analysis and a changed emphasis. In the following remarks we indicate in some detail how the approach we develop in this book differs from other work on taxation and public finance generally.

Public Finance and Collective Choice

The analysis in this book bridges the fields of public finance and collective choice. The traditional concerns of public finance – the incentive and incidence effects of taxation and the implications of these effects for efficiency in the allocation of resources and for interpersonal equity – all play an important role. In addition, the analysis reflects our view that a full understanding of taxation also requires examination of the process by which tax structure is determined. In most economic studies of public policy, political behavior and the public policy process lie outside the formal framework. This limited approach may be adequate from the perspective of policy makers who want to know how the status quo could be changed to achieve particular exogenously specified political or social objectives. It is no longer sufficient, however, if the objective is a full understanding of the forces that shape the fiscal system at a point in time, or its evolution over time.

Expanding the Domain of Fiscal Voting Analysis

Two elements are central to our approach: We assign an explicit role to the political process, and we interpret fiscal choices and policies as equilibrium outcomes. An emphasis on politics may not seem surprising or novel to those who agree with Richard Musgrave's view of budgetary outcomes as "compromises without resort to the barricades," or to the average taxpayer familiar with the phrase "no taxation without representation." A large part of the economic literature has not followed popular experience, however, treating taxation and politics as two distinct fields. Although we do not attempt to capture the full force of the fiscal drama alluded to by Musgrave, we take the need for collective choice seriously and treat politics as an integral part of theoretical and empirical analysis.

Despite advances in understanding of the public sector made possible by the application of rational choice models to political behavior, much remains to be done in this area. At present, a typical study of the fiscal system that incorporates voting decisions explicitly into the analysis is focused on the overall size of government, or on the determination of an average tax rate in a simple fiscal system. But the observed structure of expenditures and taxes in modern nations is much richer. If public sector analysis is to progress, it must go beyond the study of narrowly limited fiscal systems and show that it can give guidance in a more realistic setting. Although useful models must always simplify and abstract from reality – a model of the entire U.S. tax code would probably be neither feasible nor desirable – the gap between the fiscal facts familiar to most taxpayers and the tax structures found in collective choice models of the public sector remains too wide.

Unified Application of a Consistent Framework

After a review of available models, we choose the probabilistic voting framework as the most suitable one for dealing with the inherently multidimensional nature of tax policy. An important feature of this model is that equilibrium policy outcomes reflect a balancing of heterogeneous and opposing interests in the electorate. The model provides the starting point for all analysis in the book, be it theoretical, empirical, positive, or normative. The study represents the first comprehensive and unified evaluation of taxation based on a collective choice model other than the median voter framework. Because of the greater generality of the theoretical approach, we are able to raise a broader set of questions and deal with a wider set of issues than studies of taxation based on other formally developed models of collective choice.

*General Equilibrium Analysis of the Public Sector
and of the Political Economy*

Our interest in fiscal systems, rather than in the effects of selected individual policies, derives from the view that interdependence among policies is crucial. We believe that decision makers in the public sector rely on a variety of instruments to achieve their objectives, adjusting policy mix so as to equalize the marginal costs of different policies, to the extent that such costs are relevant to their aims. As a result, changes in the use of one policy tool must lead to adjustments in the employment of other major instruments. Recognition of such interdependence has important implications for theoretical and empirical analysis, as well as for understanding of government actions.

We believe that the broader view adopted in this book is valid for studying all aspects of the public sector, but our analysis is restricted to taxation. This is done to keep a large subject within manageable bounds, and in the service of constructing a theoretical framework that can be tied effectively to empirical research. Although the expenditure side of the government's budget is not treated in detail, the determination of expenditure levels is incorporated explicitly into the theoretical framework, with budget size being determined simultaneously with the structure of taxation.

The choice of policies takes place against a wider background that includes both the public and the private sectors of the economy. Several decades ago, Arnold Harberger revolutionized the study of public finance by showing how the general equilibrium effects of taxation within the private economy can be taken into account in studying the incentive or incidence effects of taxation. Contributors to the equilibrium approach to public finance since the time of his seminal work have no doubt been aware of the possibility of expanding the model further to make policy choices endogenous as well. But with few exceptions, they have chosen to widen the scope of their analysis in other directions. In this book, we redirect attention to this important aspect of equilibrium analysis. The study shows how significant aspects of the public and private sectors may be integrated into an equilibrium framework, how this more inclusive model may be used to study the political economy of fiscal structure, and why such a broader framework leads to a fuller understanding of major fiscal policies.

1.1   A BRIEF OUTLINE

Even though the study is unified by the use of a consistent theoretical approach, it still covers a wide range of topics and issues related to taxation. In order to provide the reader with an overall perspective, presentation of the material has been divided into five parts, with each part corresponding to a major topic area.

Part I provides a review of the existing literature on the positive political economy of taxation, as well as a new theoretical analysis of how tax systems and their main elements – such as rate structures, tax bases, and special provisions – emerge in democratic states. The new framework provides the foundation for the rest of the book.

Existing normative theories of taxation are reconsidered in Part II. The discussion reveals a need for a different approach to the normative evaluation of tax systems in the presence of collective choice. We take several initial steps toward reformulating normative tax analysis.

Part III serves as a bridge between the conceptual analysis and the subsequent empirical work. A computable general equilibrium version of the model developed in Part I is constructed and used to identify economic and political factors that are responsible for the evolution of U.S. fiscal history.

Part IV introduces issues and problems that face the researcher interested in statistical modeling of tax systems. Two econometric analyses, implementing the model described in Part I in different ways, are then presented. One study focuses on differences in the reliance of political jurisdictions on particular aspects of taxation at a given point in time, and on the concurrent relationship between various parts of a tax structure. The other study is concerned with modeling the evolution of a tax system as a whole over a longer period.

In Part V, we turn to the influence of political institutions that constrain political competition. We investigate the effect on tax structure of differences in the operation of parliamentary and congressional political systems. The model developed in Part I serves as a background, but testing of hypotheses is of a less formal nature.

For those who wish to focus on selected aspects of the analysis, we next present a more detailed review of research questions and chapter content.

1.2   A SURVEY OF CONTENT

What major research questions and topics does our approach to taxation suggest? A natural starting point is to ask what collective choice model is most suitable for research on multidimensional fiscal issues in an equilibrium context. After examining the best-known available models, we resolve this question in Chapter 2 by choosing a framework where voting is probabilistic, with parties maximizing expected votes or support.

The central theoretical issues raised by our approach concern the nature and characteristics of fiscal systems. What type of tax system would self-interested political decision makers create? How would fiscal instruments arise, be shaped, and be combined into an equilibrium mix of tax policies in a world where taxpayer responses, economic welfare losses, administration costs, and budget size are part of the political calculus? The answers are developed in Chapter 3, where the basic theoretical framework is presented, and they point to a complex tax system having all the essential features observed in the real world: tax bases, separate rate structures, and a variety of special provisions.

Similar issues are taken up in Chapter 4, based on joint research by the authors with George Warskett, where the model is reformulated and extended to encompass self-selection behavior by taxpayers, and where the influence of administration costs, self-selection, and inequalities of political influence is examined formally. In addition, the chapter gives conditions under which a perfectly competitive political system will lead to the creation of a Pareto-efficient tax structure. For convenience, we call this formal result the "Representation Theorem," a name suggested by the method of proof. We demonstrate that, under certain conditions, the fiscal equilibrium can be represented by solving a specific constrained optimization problem in which the objective function consists of a weighted average of the utilities of all voters and where weights reflect the sensitivities of individual voting probabilities to changes in economic welfare.

Much of the literature on public economics is written from a normative point of view and does not attempt to explain observed policy outcomes. Policy recommendations are derived in a framework that is restricted to economic variables and that excludes politics. The view adopted in this study forces one to question this approach and to ask explicitly what should be considered a valid counterfactual for judging tax systems and choices on taxation made by democratically elected decision makers.

In Chapter 5, we critically assess the three best-known normative approaches (Optimal Taxation, Equitable Taxation, and Fiscal Exchange) in the light of this question, examining the role assigned to the political process in each one of them. The discussion reveals a need for a new normative analysis that includes collective choice, while also dealing with the three basic steps underlying traditional welfare economics.

Chapter 6 uses the Representation Theorem developed in Chapter 4 to suggest a new approach to the normative study of policy outcomes in competitive political systems. The new approach is contrasted with an analysis based on Lindahl equilibrium. Further topics include the implications of political market failure for fiscal policy and the measurement of welfare losses from taxation in a more comprehensive model that accounts for collective choice.

A major question in all of public economics concerns the interdependence of the public and private sectors. Computational general equilibrium models offer an opportunity to study this connection in a more systematic way than is otherwise possible. However, such models tend to have rather simple and stylized versions of the public sector and rarely include collective choices as an integral part of the analysis.

Chapter 7, based on research co-authored by Stanley Winer and Thomas Rutherford, incorporates probabilistic voting into a computable general equilibrium model of economic and political competition in which tax rates and the size of government are determined along with private market prices and quantities. Numerical implementation of the model relies on the Representation Theorem. The framework is applied to the United States with the use of the GEMTAP model (with 19 industries), amended to include individual demands for public services and foreign capital flows. The chapter investigates the Pareto set of fiscal policies for representative members of three interest groups defined by the level and source of factor incomes, and it demonstrates the importance of taking the general equilibrium effects of public policy into account when interpreting U.S. fiscal history.

Placing taxation in the context of the larger fiscal system has important implications for the direction of empirical research. In Chapter 8, we adapt the theoretical model to serve as a basis for statistical research. We raise methodological issues that arise in formulating estimating equations that describe a limited part of a larger fiscal system as well as in distinguishing empirical results based on probabilistic voting models from results derived with the use of competing frameworks. The chapter also contains a brief survey of empirical research on fiscal structure based on different political models.

Looking at revenue systems as a whole, we notice many aspects that call for explanation yet that until recently have received only scant attention by economists. An example is the significant variation observed among the tax systems of similar political entities, such as states, provinces, or nations. The statistical analysis presented in Chapter 9 focuses on two related decisions made by state governments: how much to rely on personal income as a tax base, and whether to introduce an income tax credit or rebate for local property taxes. A system of two simultaneous equations is used to analyze pooled cross-section data for 48 U.S. states.

Chapter 10 tests the theoretical framework in an historical context. Estimating equations are specified and used to explain the development of the revenue structure employed by the Government of Canada from 1871 to 1913, a period when major revenue sources consisted of the tariff, debt, and excises. The empirical analysis distinguishes between government plans and ex post observations of public revenues and places particular emphasis on the derivation of hypotheses linking economic, political, and administrative variables to the evolution of the revenue system as a whole.

The probabilistic voting model has little explicit institutional content. It is nonetheless used by many authors as a basis for research into the effect of institutions on policy outcomes. In Chapter 11, we turn to this question by investigating whether differences in the federal tax systems of the United States and Canada can be explained, at least in part, by differences in the constitutional frameworks of the two countries. The analysis is of a less formal nature than in previous chapters, but it provides support for the significance of institutions and suggests that a more formal treatment of their effects is an important task for future work.

The final chapter reviews what has been accomplished in light of the starting point of the book's analysis. In so doing, Chapter 12 identifies topics for further research and briefly restates the case for approaching the study of taxation and other aspects of the public sector with an emphasis on collective choice and equilibrium policy outcomes.

PART ONE

THEORETICAL FRAMEWORK

CHAPTER 2

Models of Political Economy
and the Study of Taxation

> It is possible to go further and to consider the public sector in another way. One then tries to explain the actions of public authorities as determined by, for instance, such things as the various influences of social classes and pressures, the social mechanism of selection of leaders of state and municipal institutions, their knowledge or lack of knowledge when taking decisions, etc. This will be a theory about politics.
>
> Leif Johansen (1965, p. 6)

> The suitability of a model depends as much on what is left out as on what is put in.
>
> Martin Shubik (1984, p. 11)

We begin the study of the power to tax in democratic states with a review of six well-known models that have been used to investigate important aspects of the formation or evolution of tax systems. Five of them include collective choice as an integral part. Johansen's challenge to "go further and to consider the public sector in another way" has not gone unanswered in the fiscal literature during the last four decades. Many authors have attempted to explain how selected aspects of tax systems, or tax structure as a whole, emerge in an equilibrium resulting from the interaction of the private economy and the political process. The major contending frameworks include the median voter model, structure-induced equilibrium, probabilistic voting, the Leviathan model, and cooperative game theory. We provide a sketch of each of these approaches. In addition, we refer to a sixth framework, the representative agent model, which is often employed in tax analysis but does not take into account the collective nature of decisions on tax policy.[1]

The chapter then proceeds to a comparative assessment of the modeling traditions by considering how they deal with several elements that are necessary to create a collective choice analysis, and by contrasting the determination of

---

[1] References to the models provided in the text are to selected seminal contributions. Additional references are provided in surveys of the literature by Hettich and Winer (1997) and Inman (1987). A concise and readable introduction to the models is provided by Mueller (1989).

equilibrium tax rates in five of the approaches. The discussion is designed to highlight the relative strengths and weaknesses of the different models when they are used for the analysis of taxation. In a separate section, we pay particular attention to the choice between present and future taxation, an aspect of fiscal structure that raises special questions for the analysis.

We conclude the chapter by selecting the framework that appears best suited for the explanation of widely observed stylized facts on tax structure. All of the approaches contribute to the understanding of fiscal choices, but we believe that the probabilistic voting model provides the best starting point for analyzing the formation and evolution of complex fiscal policies.

2.1   A REVIEW OF ALTERNATIVE FRAMEWORKS

All predictive models in which collective choice plays an important role have three major elements: a collective choice mechanism, usually some variant of majority rule; an explicit or implied institutional structure within which collective choice takes place; and an economy of private agents whose activity is being taxed to provide public services and to coercively redistribute income. Although the models reviewed in this section all assign a similar role to the private economy, they are distinguished from each other by the collective choice process and by the political institutions assumed to govern this process. They also differ in their ability to explain stable choices in a political setting, a problem to which we drew attention in Chapter 1.

In order to make a meaningful diagramatic comparison possible, and to contrast the predictions of the different frameworks, we use a set of simple assumptions to characterize the fiscal economy. We imagine a situation where the public sector provides one public good and where the resources needed to provide it are raised by proportional tax rates imposed on two bases. Voters have preferences for the public good, as well as for the output of the private economy. Most diagrams in the chapter relate voter utility to different combinations of the two proportional tax rates, and they are best thought of as representing indirect utility functions. It is assumed that preferences result in indifference curves having circular shape. An exception is the examination of the median voter model, where the model's limitations restrict the analysis to rankings over a single tax rate.

The simple fiscal framework excludes consideration of lump-sum taxation and benefit taxation. This is in accordance with the approach taken in other chapters. We are mainly interested in exploring situations where a significant separation exists between taxing and spending, since we believe that this best describes tax policy in democratic states. Lump-sum taxation can be a useful theoretical device in certain analytical contexts, but it does not have a counterpart in most real-world situations. In a similar manner, pure benefit taxation represents a rare occurrence in most observed tax systems.

2.1.1   The Median Voter Model

The first positive model of taxation to incorporate a collective choice mechanism was based on the median voter theorem of Duncan Black (1958). This is a model of direct democracy in which any voter may costlessly propose amendments to the status quo. The institutions of representative democracy do not play any role. When applied to the choice of tax rates, the model focuses on how the fiscal system can be used by a decisive voter to achieve a most preferred outcome and to redistribute in the voter's favor when public services and taxes are not uniformly spread over the electorate as a whole. This model is successful in dealing with the difficult problem of explaining coercive redistribution because the analysis is carried out in a carefully limited framework.

Assume that a single proportional tax rate on labor income is to be chosen by majority rule, and that this choice will determine the level of output for a public good. Each voter i knows the implications of every possible tax rate for i's own welfare, and has a well-defined preference relation defined over all possible rates. Voting is in accordance with true preferences (i.e. sincere), and there is no uncertainty about how any voter's ballot will be cast. Voting continues on pairs of proposed tax rates until one rate emerges (the Condorcet winner) that cannot be defeated by any other in a pairwise majority vote.

If all voter preference relations are single-peaked, then the tax rate that emerges from the collective choice process is the one that maximizes the welfare of the median voter – the voter whose preferred rate is at the median of the rates most desired by each voter (Romer 1975, Roberts 1977).[2] This rate maximizes the decisive voter's fiscal surplus – the difference between the value of public services received and the loss in welfare as a result of taxation.

The process is illustrated in Figure 2.1 for three voters, denoted P, M, and R, who have single-peaked preferences over possible tax rates. The vertical axis shows a ranking of welfare levels while the horizontal axis measures proportional tax rates (which cannot exceed a value of unity). Any proposed rate that is higher than the median voter's most preferred or "ideal" rate t_M^* will be defeated in a pairwise vote, since the voter who would like a rate falling below

---

[2] A single-peaked preference relation is either mountain-shaped with one peak, or it reaches a maximum at an end point of the domain of possible tax rates with no turning points. Roberts (1977) relaxes the single-peak condition somewhat, provided that tax schedules are linear in income.

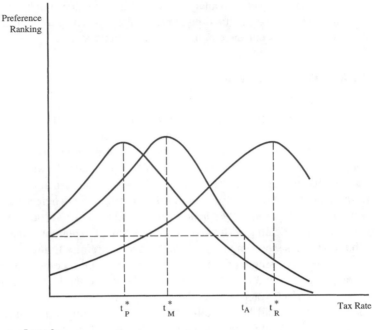

Legend

t^*_i = Most preferred or "ideal" tax rate for voter i

t_A = Maximum rate that the median voter would approve if the reversion rate were zero

Figure 2.1. The median voter model

t^*_M will support the median voter's choice over any higher rate. Similarly, any rate that is lower than the median voter's ideal one will be defeated by a coalition consisting of the median voter and the third voter who favors a rate that is higher than t^*_M.[3]

In order to proceed further we need additional assumptions about the tax system, the distribution of income, and individual behavior. It can be shown, for example, that if the tax structure consists of a single marginal rate applied to labor income above a given exemption level that is the same for all taxpayers, and if average income exceeds that of the median voter, then the median voter will demand and receive a positive marginal tax rate. Moreover, in the

---

[3] If P is interpreted as the low-income person and R as the high-income person, then one can imagine situations where R would prefer a tax rate lower than the one now identified as the median voter. This may be the case, for example, if all tax revenues are used to finance transfers to voters P and M.

linear income tax case, the equilibrium rate and thus the degree of tax progressivity depend on the elasticity of labor supply. As this elasticity increases, more substitution from work to leisure occurs at the existing rate of tax, causing a reduction in the aggregate size of the tax base and in the fiscal surplus of the median voter. The tax rate demanded by the decisive voter therefore declines.[4]

Some attempts have been made to extend the median voter theorem to explain the structure of more complex and realistic tax systems. But the application of the model encounters difficulties when the policy space is multidimensional. As long as voters' decisions are regarded as being strictly deterministic, and even when preferences are single-peaked in each dimension taken by itself, a new coalition can always be formed that will dominate an existing one under majority rule (McKelvey 1976, Schofield 1983). The result is an endless sequence of changes from one majority outcome to another, rather than the Condorcet equilibrium of the median voter theorem.

In the traditional application of the model, the median voter's preferred rate wins because all possible alternatives can be proposed for a vote. If voting choices are restricted and decision makers from outside the model can set the agenda, then a larger or smaller rate may be the outcome. Assume that voters must choose between a zero rate (called the reversion rate) and some other specified rate, while no revoting is possible. In such a situation, the median voter in Figure 2.1 will approve a rate as high as t_A, the maximum rate that leaves him or her just as well off as a zero tax rate, implying no provision of the public good. If those who control the agenda desire to maximize the budget, they will set t_A (or a rate just below it) as one of the two rates from which voters must choose. If a different reversion rate is assumed, we obtain a new maximum tax rate that will be offered to voters.

The median voter model with agenda setters was originally proposed by Thomas Romer and Howard Rosenthal and is reviewed in Rosenthal (1990). While the analysis makes clear that institutional assumptions are crucial, it does not determine the degree of agenda-setting power within the model. A similar limitation also affects the next framework to be reviewed.

2.1.2   Structure-Induced Equilibrium

That deterministic models of pure majority rule appear to predict *unstable* policy outcomes has led some political economists to ask why policy outcomes are so rarely reversed in practice and why vote cycling seems an infrequent

---

[4] Model assumptions in which these results were derived differ somewhat from those underlying the diagrams in the book. For example, the government may provide pure redistribution rather than a public good. See the work by Romer (1975), Roberts (1977), and Meltzer and Richard (1981) for a discussion of particular models. A further example providing a more complex context is provided by Atkinson (1995, Chap. 4).

occurrence in the real world. A possible answer concerns the role of institutions. Some analysts argue that equilibria are enforced by the political rules of the game or by the accepted context within which alternatives can be offered for collective choice (Shepsle and Weingast 1981). Those who adopt this view analyze the workings of legislative institutions and then relate particular legislative rules of procedure, committee systems, and other aspects of institutional design (the "structure") to the nature and stability of policy outcomes.

Applications of the idea in the context of taxation involve an institutional structure that effectively separates each dimension of the tax policy space, thus limiting challenges to each proposal (Meltzer and Richard 1985). It is assumed, for example, that each parameter determining the nature of the tax system is decided upon in a separate legislative committee that has enough agenda power to implement its preferred choice on the floor of the legislature. In each committee the median voter theorem applies, given the median choices of other committees.

Figure 2.2 shows the preferences for three voters over proportional tax rates imposed on income from capital (t_K) and income from labor (t_L).[5] In the figure, each person's preferences are represented by circular indifference contours. The most preferred or ideal point for the high-income individual (R), labeled R^*, shows a low tax rate on capital combined with a high rate on labor, reflecting R's income sources (it is assumed that this individual receives a relatively large proportion of income from capital). The ideal point for the low-income individual (P), given as P^*, reflects preferences that are opposite – this person would like to tax capital income much more heavily than labor income. The median voter (M), with a more balanced mix of income sources, prefers the intermediate combination indicated by M^*. The diagram assumes that the same individual has median preferences with regard to both tax rates.

If voting on each rate is carried out separately, then M^* represents the equilibrium outcome for the system. Voting over rates on capital income will result in the choice of the median voter's most preferred rate t_K^M. Similarly, voting over proportional rates on labor income will yield t_L^M.

It is important to note that for M^* to be a stable equilibrium, voting choices on one of the rates must be fully isolated from those on the other rate, except for the special case (illustrated in Figure 2.2) in which indifference curves are circular. In other words, participants who decide on the tax rate on capital cannot do so with the expectation of voting later on the tax rate applied to labor, as this violates the spirit of the model. Such an implied connection would lead to the re-emergence of the vote cycle as choices on the first issue are carried out in anticipation of the consequences of voting behavior for the outcome of the

---

[5] Utility functions and their indirect counterparts for a median voter are discussed by Mueller (1989, pp. 327–31) and Atkinson (1995, pp. 81–2). See also Meltzer and Richard (1981, 1983).

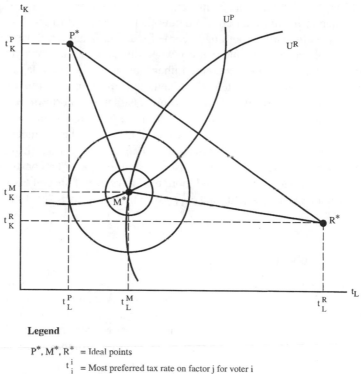

Legend

P^*, M^*, R^* = Ideal points

t^i_j = Most preferred tax rate on factor j for voter i

U^i = Indifference curve for voter i

Figure 2.2.   The structure-induced equilibrium model

next round, effectively bypassing the institutional rules intended to separate the two issues. Only if indifference curves are circular will a voter's ideal preference on one issue be independent of what prevails on the other (see e.g. Ordeshook 1992, p. 283).

The point M^* is a structure-induced outcome that is stable only because of institutional arrangements. Note that a majority would favor a different rate combination: any point falling in the area bordered by indifference curves U_P and U_R would be preferred over M^* by both P and R. One must also note that no agenda-setting power exists in this version of the model. If alternatives and the number of votes are restricted for one or both rates, the final outcome will differ from M^*.

If the model is applied to legislative actions, then the assignment of legislators to committees and the institutional arrangements that create agenda power for each committee are key issues in explaining the final outcome (Weingast and Marshall 1988). A major challenge in using the framework lies in identifying actual institutional arrangements that correspond to those required to induce a particular equilibrium outcome for a significant fiscal variable.

The challenge is met more easily when the approach is employed to study specific features of a tax structure rather than as a way of explaining the formation of an entire tax system. One example is the work by Robert Inman and Michael Fitts (1990), who focus on universalism as a norm of behavior that emerges to overcome political instability in legislatures, with each legislator agreeing to support the allocations preferred by every other member of the legislative body. As long as benefits are concentrated within particular districts while costs are spread through the fiscal system over a wider constituency, the norm leads to larger budgets and more extensive use of special tax provisions than would occur if benefits and costs were matched more closely within each district.[6]

2.1.3   Probabilistic Voting

The probabilistic voting model starts from the assumption that political institutions exist that allow for regular elections and free entry of new political parties. Voters choose between parties on the basis of the policies that they propose to implement, while continual pressure from the opposition forces each party to adopt a fiscal platform that it believes will maximize its expected plurality or expected vote in the next election.

As suggested by the model's name, and in contrast to the median voter theorem, parties do not know with certainty how voters will cast their ballots.[7] This assumption opens up the possibility that an equilibrium exists even if the tax system is multidimensional (Hinich, Ledyard, and Ordeshook 1973, Hinich 1977, Coughlin and Nitzan 1981a, Enelow and Hinich 1989, Coughlin 1992). When voting is strictly deterministic, each voter will abruptly switch support from the incumbent to the opposition (or vice versa) if promised a sufficiently favorable policy outcome. The points at which voters switch their support from one party to another become the objects of a bidding war between the parties, leading to vote cycling over alternative platforms. However, if voting behavior is probabilistic, then a small change in a policy platform directed at any voter will lead at most to a small change in the *probability* of support from that voter, not to a total loss of support.

---

[6] In addition, there are several interesting explorations of U.S. tax reform in the structure-induced equilibrium tradition. These include Stewart (1991) and McCubbins (1991), who concentrate on the implications of a divided Congress for the politically feasible set of tax proposals.

[7] The model may also allow for uncertainty on the part of voters concerning what the parties propose to do if elected.

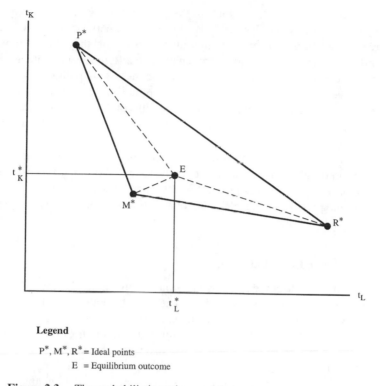

Figure 2.3. The probabilistic voting model

In this setting, and under constant pressure from the opposition, each party chooses a fiscal platform – a level and pattern of expenditures and taxes – so as to continually maximize its total expected plurality or expected vote while constrained by the structure of the private economy. (Parties believe that the provision of public services will increase the utility and hence the probability of support from any voter, and that an increase in the tax levied on any voter with a given level of services will reduce it.) Equilibrium platforms are the outcome of a (Nash) game between parties and are defined by the conditions for the choices of politically optimal strategies.

Figure 2.3 illustrates the determination of tax rates for the same three individuals represented in the previous diagram when voting is probabilistic. For convenience, indifference curves have been omitted, with only the ideal points P^*, M^*, and R^* shown. The straight lines connecting the three ideal points represent contract curves between pairs of voters, reflecting the assumption that indifference contours are circular. As a result of political competition, the equilibrium combination of tax rates, shown as E, will fall somewhere within the area bounded by the contract curves.

The solution illustrates that, in the probabilistic voting framework, each voter counts to some degree. This must be so; otherwise, the vote cycle will reemerge.[8] However, even though all voters count, they do not have equal influence on outcomes. Parties are sensitive to differences in political behavior, giving greater weight in accordance with the increase in political support that is expected from each voter in response to a policy change. Differences in influence are reflected in the diagram by the lengths of the lines connecting E to P^*, M^*, or R^*, with distance being inversely proportional to the effective political influence of the respective voter.[9]

In Chapter 3, we demonstrate in detail how tax structure emerges in the equilibrium of such a model. The analysis will show that governments that maximize expected votes respond to voter demands by creating fiscal systems containing all the major elements currently observed in the tax systems of democratic nations.

2.1.4   The Leviathan Model

In the models discussed so far, taxation is constrained by the institutions of direct or representative government. The Leviathan model, as reformulated by Geoffrey Brennan and James Buchanan (1980), is based on the radically different assumption that the state has unlimited power to tax private activity. The reason for the use of this power is to redistribute income toward government. The politics of majority rule are irrelevant in determining tax structure. Presumably, administration costs are also unimportant, since Leviathan would not care about the level of public services that could be financed from a given level of tax revenues.[10] Only the adverse effects of taxation on the level of taxable economic activity are of concern, because this determines the maximum size of total revenues.

Figure 2.4 shows the relationship between proportional tax rates on a particular base, such as labor income, and total tax revenues collected from that base. The shape of the curve is determined by the ability of taxpayers to avoid or to evade taxation by altering their economic behavior, and the diagram is

---

[8] If it is certain that a group of voters will never vote for the government no matter what, they will be taxed very heavily. Such voters then have nothing to lose by appealing to the opposition, even if they are only slightly better off as a result. The government will then respond with a somewhat better proposal, and so on.

[9] A more formal development of the probabilistic voting model is presented in Chapter 4, where the meaning of weights and the Pareto optimality of equilibrium outcomes are examined in the context of a mathematical model.

[10] Brennan and Buchanan do not formally consider administration costs. Further work on the Leviathan model may lead to a different conclusion concerning the role of such costs from that suggested here.

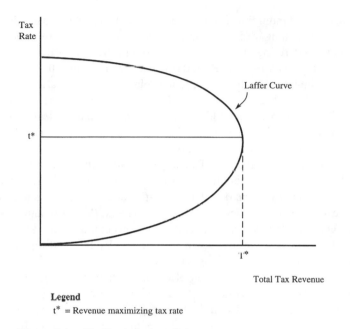

Legend
t^* = Revenue maximizing tax rate

Figure 2.4.   The Leviathan model

drawn under the assumption that taxpayer adjustments to a particular tax are independent of what other types of taxes and tax rates are imposed in the economy. Leviathan will pick t^*, the revenue-maximizing rate. If more than one tax base is available, a similar figure must be developed for each base. In a more general analysis of rate–revenue relationships for different bases (often referred to as Laffer curves; see Laffer 1981), it would be acknowledged that such relationships may not be independent since consumers and investors may respond to increased taxation of a particular activity by reallocating resources to a competing income source.

The Leviathan model was originally proposed as a normative framework for thinking about how the power of governments could best be limited.[11] It has since been used by others as a positive model, ostensibly in situations where the costs of controlling the behavior of the authorities are substantial.

The tax structure chosen by Leviathan is multidimensional, consisting of elements such as bases, rate structures, and special provisions, though there is no explicit analysis of how each of these elements arises endogenously.

---

[11] The Leviathan model is also reviewed in Chapter 5 together with other normative approaches to taxation.

Manipulation of a multidimensional structure can be used to expand the ability to discriminate among taxpayers and thereby to increase total revenues.

The logic underlying Leviathan's choice of tax structure is that of price discrimination. Broad bases are preferred because they minimize the possibility of tax evasion, thus leading to rate–revenue relationships or Laffer curves that turn backward at a higher level of total revenues than if narrow bases were employed. Leviathan will levy higher rates on bases that are less elastic with respect to tax rates, since the extent of substitution away from taxed and into nontaxed activities will thereby be reduced.[12]

Rate structures are regressive. This is analogous to the statement that a perfectly discriminating monopolist maximizes profit by charging prices that decline at the margin of market demand. Special provisions are used to discriminate further among heterogeneous taxpayers. A combination of high nominal tax rates and extensive special provisions could yield maximum revenue to the state by permitting even more carefully targeted distinctions in accordance with economic responses to taxation.

A more sophisticated application of the Leviathan model would acknowledge the possibility of constitutional constraints on Leviathan's access to tax bases and on the power to discriminate, though the source of these constraints – like Leviathan's power to tax – would remain exogenously specified.[13]

2.1.5   Cooperative Game Theory

Our discussion of this approach will be rather brief, reflecting the limited ability of the approach to deal with the formation of tax structure. The emphasis in the cooperative game theory model is almost exclusively on coercive redistribution. Coalitions form and the numerically largest coalition determines taxes and transfers. Voters can influence the outcome only by joining a coalition. They may, if they wish, destroy part of their endowments, though in equilibrium nothing is in fact destroyed. The ability to destroy endowments can be viewed as a rough approximation of the ability to escape into leisure when income is taxed.

Once voters have formed into two coalitions, they play a cooperative bargaining game with threats. The solution concept is the bargaining solution of John Nash (1950), which yields a compromise in which the aggregate utility that remains after the threat points are guaranteed is split evenly between the coalitions. The Shapley value (1953) of the game to each voter is then used to divide up a coalition's aggregate utility among its members, assuming utility is

---

[12] Those readers with a background in optimal taxation will recognize this as the inverse elasticity rule, which in this context becomes a revenue-maximizing rule.

[13] Wintrobe (1990) suggests how the power to tax may be endogenized in a more general model of authoritarian power.

transferable through transfers of income (see Shubik 1982; 1984, Chap. 20) for a discussion of the technical ideas).

In the original paper by Robert Aumann and Mordechai Kurz (1977), the interesting implications for tax structure are that marginal tax rates are above 50 percent for all voters and are equal to 50 percent if utility functions are linear, and that those voters with the greater absolute risk aversion toward small bets and greater aversion to risking total ruin in the redistribution struggle end up facing the higher marginal tax rates. The new element introduced in this approach is the attitude of voters toward risk.

Extensions of the basic model incorporate changes in the political power required to effectively tax the minority and in the ability of voters to conceal or destroy their endowments.[14] Not surprisingly, redistribution and the tax rate decline with the size of the majority required for effective political power, and tax rates on goods which can be concealed are lower than on those which cannot.

2.1.6   The Representative Agent Model

The final model in our discussion is the representative agent framework. Here it is assumed that a benevolent government adopts the fiscal system that maximizes the welfare of a representative or average citizen. Although the simple version of the model refers to a single agent and does not deal with heterogeneous preferences, the framework can be expanded to accommodate differences in tastes by assuming that the government's objective is to maximize social welfare or to minimize the sum of individual welfare losses. Analysis in this approach (still widely used) does not address collective choice issues. Instead, emphasis is placed on how the structure of the private economy influences the determination of a socially optimal tax system.

The technical nature of the analysis in this framework is familiar from consumer theory and welfare economics, where the analytics of welfare maximization have been worked out in detail. Since collective choice is not explored, the more difficult questions concerning the existence and stability of equilibrium for the fiscal system do not arise. The model can accommodate a varied tax structure, but the political reasons that lead to a multidimensional tax system in models where the struggle for votes is important do not play a role in the analysis.

2.2   COMPARATIVE EVALUATION
OF FORMAL MODELS

To increase the understanding of the nature and operation of the different models, it is useful to look at them from a comparative point of view. In this section, we consider how the six frameworks use essential analytical elements and

---

[14] See Gardner (1981), Osborne (1981), and the discussion in Shubik (1984).

confront important theoretical problems that arise in the study of political economy. In addition, we combine some of the diagrams introduced earlier to provide a comparison of equilibrium tax rates yielded by the different approaches.

Table 2.1 singles out six issues that must be addressed in any complete political economy framework and summarizes how they are dealt with in each of the models under review. The table begins with an entry referring to the nature of participation in collective choices. All models of the public sector deal with nonmarket institutions and with the policy outcomes produced by them. Such institutions are governed either by collective choices made according to some set of voting rules or by dictatorial decisions imposed on the collectivity. This means that explicit assumptions concerning the source and nature of authority conferred on government are necessary. With respect to the treatment of the source of authority for taxation, the models can be separated into two categories. The median voter model, expected vote maximization, structure-induced equilibrium, and cooperative game theory are all approaches where individuals affect the formulation of collective decisions. Leviathan, on the other hand, represents an approach where decisions are dictatorial. The representative agent model fails to address the question of just where decision-making authority originates.

If we start from the assumption that individuals count, we must specify the manner in which their votes are aggregated into a collective outcome. This provides the second dimension of our comparison. In the median voter model, each eligible person has one vote, and choices are made by direct democracy using simple majority rule. When votes are counted, each one is treated the same. Expected vote maximization also starts with one vote per eligible person, but the nature of the collective choice process is broader and is able to encompass the institution of representative government. Political parties formulate policies so as to maximize their total expected vote, an objective that is intended to capture the behavior of politicians continually engaged in the competitive struggle for power and unsure of the identity or characteristics of their opposition in the next election (Denzau and Munger 1986, Mayhew 1974).[15] The model assumes that the probability of a voter supporting either party is positive, implying that the preferences of all voters – and not just those of the median voter – are taken into account in the formulation of policy proposals, although not all are given equal weight. It is assumed that the party winning the election forms the "government," but the exact nature of the governing structure is left somewhat vague. Although consistent with the general framework,

---

[15] Maximization of such an objective also captures the behavior of a party that expects the benefits from holding office to be an increasing function of its margin of victory (Stigler 1972, Kramer 1977).

Table 2.1. Basic structure of the formal models

Essential Modelling Elements	Median Voter	Probabilistic Voting	Structure-Induced Equilibrium	Cooperative Game Theory	Leviathan	Representative Agent
Rights to participate in collective choices	One vote per eligible person	One vote per eligible person	One vote per eligible person	Equal right to join coalition	Those outside government have none, or rights are worthless	Not treated
Nature of collective choice process	Simple majority rule. Equal influence	Government maximizes expected plurality or votes. Possibly unequal influence	Majority rule subject to specific institutional constraints	Majority coalition enforces its preferences. Possibly unequal influence	Government maximizes total revenue subject to existing Laffer curves	Not treated
Assumed individual behavior in collective choices	Voters support alternative yielding highest utility. Non-strategic behavior	Voters maximize net benefits from public sector	Voters support alternative yielding highest utility. Behavior may be strategic	Join voting coalition yielding highest utility. Behavior depends on risk aversion	Not modelled for those outside government	No collective choice mechanism
Information	Voters may have complete or limited information	Voters may or may not have complete information. Parties are uncertain about voting behavior	Legislators may have complete or limited information about voters	Complete	Different assumptions about information will affect economic behavior	'Government' has complete information on voter preferences.
Equilibrium a.existence and stability b.nature of outcome	Stable for one-dimensional issue space and single-peaked preferences. Alternatives preferred by median voter wins	Existence & stability if voting probabilistic. Preferences of all voters count to some extent	Stability depends on specific institutional arrangements. Outcome may be anywhere in the issue space	Nash bargaining solution	Stable for given Laffer curves. Government operates at inflection point of Laffer curves	Stability assumed. Outcome maximizes welfare of representative agent
Problems of delegation and agent control	None for agenda with unlimited alternatives in one dimension. Can be introduced via agenda control by bureaucracy	Problems of delegation in representative government acknowledged informally	Explicitly represented in particular cases	Not treated	Extreme problem. No control over government	Implicitly assumed to be unimportant or solved
Unresolved questions	Generation of agenda not explained. Stability for multi-dimensional issues	Modelling of political process underlying government behavior	Stability of institutional arrangements or constraints. Representation of institutions in model-equivalent form	Link to observed institutions. Special solution concepts	Shape of Laffer curves depends on government policy. Formation of government not explained	Collective choice issues

the institution of representative government is not generated from the model's assumptions.

Structure-induced equilibrium models also fail to derive collective choice institutions as the outcome of model assumptions, but this approach does explicitly incorporate legislative arrangements – unlike the median voter and expected vote maximization models, where institutions are implicit or hidden constraints on political optimization. Cooperative game theory provides the most general theoretical approach among the models, since it proceeds from simple assumptions about individual participation and attempts to generate redistribution as part of the solution to the aggregation of preferences into an actual decision. On the other hand, the very generality of the approach makes it difficult to relate the results to observed reality and to use the model for empirical work. As pointed out earlier, Leviathan assumes imposed outcomes, but how or why government comes into existence is not explained as part of the theoretical framework. The representative agent model simply bypasses the role of elections and the institutions of government.

The third and fourth essential ingredients in modeling are assumptions concerning individual behavior and the information available to those who make relevant choices. In the median voter model, voters support the alternative that yields the highest utility to them; they do not form coalitions or behave strategically. Information on alternatives may be complete or limited, depending on specific model assumptions. In expected vote maximization, voters similarly maximize their own expected net benefits from public policies in casting their votes. It is possible to assume either perfect or imperfect information for voters about policy proposals, but uncertainty by politicians about individual voting behavior is essential to the establishment of an equilibrium in the model.[16] Structure-induced equilibrium is similar to expected vote maximization with respect to information assumptions, but also allows for strategic behavior by legislators in the determination of policy outcomes. Cooperative game theory as applied to taxation emphasizes risk aversion as an important component of individual behavior influencing the formation of coalitions, and it generally assumes that participants have perfect information. With Leviathan, the motivation of individuals outside the government is confined to attempts at escaping taxation by adjusting private economic behavior. The model is consistent with different assumptions concerning information that will influence outcomes, primarily by yielding different Laffer curves. The representative agent model can encompass any behavioral assumption about the nature of an individual economic agent that is consistent with rational behavior.

---

[16] See Austen-Smith (1991) for extensive discussion of the information assumptions in an expected vote-maximization framework.

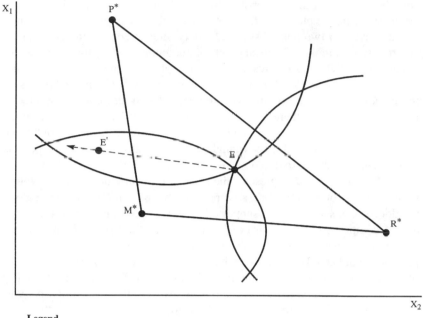

Legend

P^*, M^*, R^* = Ideal points

E = Status quo

E' = Outcome that dominates E with deterministic voting

Figure 2.5. The stability of equilibrium with uncertainty about voter behavior

In introducing the different models, we have emphasized the need for stable equilibria. Most theoretical analysis in economics depends on the application of equilibrium concepts. As pointed out, special assumptions are needed to establish the existence and stability of equilibrium in noncooperative games with deterministic voting, such as the median voter model. Unless the issue space is one-dimensional and preferences of voters over that issue space are single-peaked, cyclical majorities will result. Correct use of the model is therefore limited to situations where voting decisions are made on one policy parameter at a time and where single-peakedness with respect to that parameter can legitimately be inferred. However, if voting behavior is probabilistic or, more generally, if the objective pursued by political parties is a continuous function of party platforms, then existence of an equilibrium can be demonstrated even when policy platforms have many dimensions.

Figure 2.5 illustrates the absence of equilibrium policy outcomes under deterministic voting and provides the intuition behind the establishment of an equilibrium when voting is probabilistic. Like Figures 2.2 and 2.3, it depicts an electorate of three voters: P, M, and R. Each voter has an indirect utility function defined over two policy issues x_1 and x_2. Indifference contours are again assumed to be circular. The ideal points of maximum welfare for the three voters are at P^*, M^*, and R^*, respectively. The straight lines joining the ideal points are contract curves for the corresponding pairs of voters, and points on these lines and inside the triangle constitute the Pareto set for the committee of three (where the term "Pareto set" is interpreted in relation to unanimous decision making.) If choices were made under a unanimity rule, the committee would choose a point within the triangle or on its borders. Once such a point is picked, unanimous consent to deviate from it can no longer be reached.

Suppose that point E represents the status quo. Under deterministic voting in the median voter framework, a proposal to move from E to any point along the dotted line, such as E', is supported by a majority, since the welfare of P and M is improved and only that of R is reduced by the move.[17] In this case, E cannot be a stable equilibrium. When voting behavior is probabilistic from the perspective of candidates for office, however, movements along the dotted line produce continuous reductions in the probability that R will vote for the party making the proposal and also continuous increases in the probability that voters P and M will support that party. If the total expected vote for the party proposing a platform like E' is concave (for each platform chosen by the opposition) as well as continuous in the policies that it adopts, with a maximum at E, then its total expected support will decline if a policy like E' rather than E is adopted.[18] This is illustrated in the diagram for a situation where the welfare of R, and with it the probability of R's electoral support, declines substantially with the party's move to E', while the welfare and expected support of P and M increase only a little. In that case, E remains the optimal political strategy for the party.

We can look at the same question from a second perspective. The lack of a unique equilibrium for majority voting in the face of multiple policy dimensions arises because the decision context does not allow any further Pareto improvements, and there is no mechanism to weigh and compare the utility levels of voters to make progress toward a unique solution. In the probabilistic voting model, the government's expected vote function provides a device to aggregate utilities and thus to transform the problem of multiple dimensions into a one-dimensional decision problem, where maximization that takes

---

[17] An additional assumption being used here is that voting behavior is positively related to economic well-being.

[18] Assuming that the objective functions of political parties are concave amounts to saying that each party can define an optimal policy platform for each platform announced by the opposition. On this point, see also Hinich and Munger (1994, p. 210).

account of all opposing interests in the electorate is possible. As a result, a stable equilibrium outcome can be reached.

In the structure-induced equilibrium approach, stable outcomes are created by the interaction of legislative or other institutional constraints with deterministic voting behaviour. Using Figure 2.5 to illustrate this in a somewhat simplified manner, we may think of voters P, M, and R as representatives of three parties in a legislature, where committees that reflect the distribution of interests in the legislative body as a whole are assigned to deal with one, and only one, of the issues shown on the axes. (In other words, voter M represents the median voter in each committee.) If no amendments to the decisions taken in committees are permitted on the floor of the legislature, then the final legislative outcome will be at M^*, reflecting the median voter equilibrium on each issue that emerges from a particular committee. The structure-induced equilibrium model can thus provide a framework for investigating the interaction of various legislative rules with the preferences of elected representatives in determining equilibrium outcomes.

As pointed out earlier, cooperative game theory requires special solution concepts. Equilibrium represents the bargaining solution of Nash, while the Shapley value is used to assign the payoff within coalitions. The final distribution of payoffs depends on differences in risk aversion among participants.

The literature applying the Leviathan model to taxation does not formally deal with the question of equilibrium. It is assumed that a multidimensional equilibrium will exist and be stable if Laffer curves are stable for every aspect of the tax structure, with the government operating at the maximum revenue point on each of the curves. The representative agent model also ignores the question of whether policies can represent stable equilibrium outcomes in a collective setting.

A prevailing theme in economics is that the enforcement of contracts is costly, creating a problem of agent control in both the public and private sectors. Table 2.1 identifies the need for such control as the sixth central issue. The simplest version of the median voter model does not deal with agent control; it is simply assumed that all relevant alternatives in one dimension will be available for potential or actual voting. The recognition that bureaucrats who present alternatives to voters may have an interest in manipulating and restricting the agenda has given rise to more complex versions of the model. Decision makers are assumed to set voting agendas so as to maximize public budgets, subject to the constraint that the outcome must win the support of the pivotal or median voter (see e.g. Romer and Rosenthal 1979b).[19] Since it is not explained endogenously how bureaucratic agenda setters arise, nor what defines and limits their power, this approach does not fully resolve the theoretical issue.

---

[19] Rosenthal (1990) provides a comprehensive review of work on the agenda-setter model.

The literature on expected vote maximization deals informally with problems of agent control arising for voters from the existence of representative government, but it generally neglects such problems with regard to bureaucracy.[20]
The structure-induced equilibrium approach deals with principal–agent problems arising within legislatures and between legislative bodies and the bureaucracy. Politicians may manipulate agendas within the legislature and may
influence bureaus by the choice of appointees and assignment of policy respon-
sibilities. A group of legislators may, for example, attempt to delegate power to
a particular regulatory agency if they think it acts in a predictable and desirable
manner.[21] If the decision to delegate may be contested, the outcome will be stable only as long as the rules of procedure allow a majority choice on the delegation issue in isolation from decisions on other related matters.

The theoretical framework in cooperative game theory does not lend itself
to the analysis of principal-agent problems. In the Leviathan model, they are
avoided; it is assumed that those outside the government cannot constrain government behavior. (At a deeper level, one may ask what determines property
rights in a dictatorship and what the costs and limits are of enforcement in such
an environment.) The representative agent model involves an implicit assumption that is at the other extreme from that made in the Leviathan model; in the
former, government is assumed to act benevolently and so the control issue is
disregarded.

A final entry in the table raises unresolved questions for each tradition.
Some of these have already been alluded to. For the median voter model, the
main unresolved concern is the theoretical necessity of assuming the existence
of a one-dimensional issue space. In the expanded framework including
agenda setters, the context of voting choices no longer derives strictly from the
collective choice rule, adding adhoc elements to the theoretical structure. In a
probabilistic voting model, the process of political competition generating
"government" is not explicitly modeled. Structure-induced equilibrium cannot
explain why vote cycling does not occur with respect to institutions, even if
slowly, when outcomes under existing institutional rules are repeatedly unfavorable to some voters. It should also be noted that the representation of institutions in model-equivalent form is difficult, being confined in most
applications to a narrow set of legislative procedures such as those governing

---

[20] A few attempts have been made to formally incorporate the role of the bureaucracy into the vote-
maximization framework. See for example van Winden (1983), who includes the bureau as
another interest group that the government must deal with, and Holtz-Eakin (1992), who has
proposed a model in which the government maximizes the welfare of bureaucrats subject to a
reelection constraint.

[21] On this point see, for example, McNollgast (1990).

operations of the U.S. Congress. As far as cooperative game theory is concerned, the main problem lies in its abstractness – direct connections to existing institutions have not yet been made. Leviathan depends heavily on given Laffer curves. This seems unsatisfactory since government can encroach on private behavior to quite different degrees. Ultimately, the shape and position of Laffer curves is endogenous, depending on enforcement, scope of private activity, and prevailing property rights. A theory of how the government is formed would be necessary to deal with these deeper issues. Choice of a dictatorial model does not absolve the theorist from confronting the problem of equilibrium directly, since questions of existence and stability arise also in a world with dictatorship or oligarchy. The problem with the representative agent framework is obvious: ignoring the existence of collective choice is not conducive to guiding the researcher in studying collective decision processes and outcomes.

It is clear from the discussion related to Table 2.1, as well as from the graphic analyses, that the various frameworks have quite different implications for equilibrium tax structure. To complete the comparative examination, we show how model differences affect the determination of equilibrium tax rates. We do this by constructing a single composite diagram based on the preceding figures. As before, we consider the situation where all tax revenues must be raised by levying proportional tax rates on labor (t_L) and capital incomes (t_K), and where there are three voters differentiated by the sources of their income.

Figure 2.6 illustrates the tax rates and revenues predicted by the different models (except for cooperative game theory, where solutions cannot be shown in the same graphic context). Voters are assumed to have the same type of indirect utility functions as in earlier figures. As before, voter R, the high-income taxpayer, enjoys a substantial income from capital and has an ideal point at R^*, where the tax on labor income is relatively high and that on capital relatively low. Voter P, the low-income taxpayer, has an ideal point with the opposite mix of tax rates, since P's income is primarily a result of supplying labor services. The ideal point for voter M, the middle-income voter, lies in between the other ideal points, reflecting the diversified nature of his or her income.

The rate–revenue or Laffer curves that embody the structure of the private economy, including individual responses to taxation, are given in the upper left and lower right quadrants of the diagram. It is assumed for convenience that these curves can be drawn independently of each other. The total revenue implied by any pair of tax rates is recorded by a line of constant total revenue in the lower left quadrant, with lines farther to the left indicating larger totals.

The same quadrant also indicates revenue composition. If we draw a line starting from the origin and bisecting the quadrant, then the points on this line represent an equal division of revenues from the two tax sources. Points to the

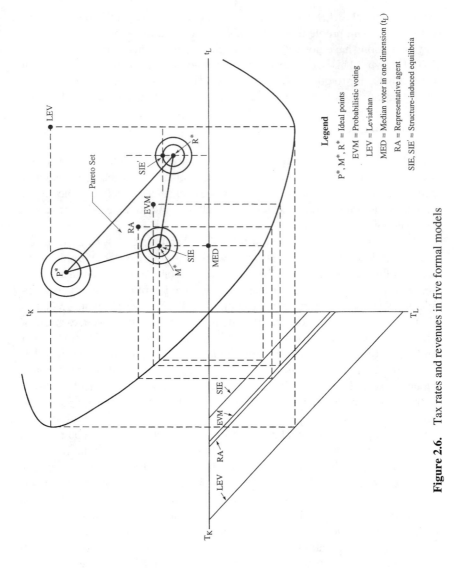

Figure 2.6. Tax rates and revenues in five formal models

left or the right of such a line indicate that a larger proportion of the total budget originates from the tax on capital or on labor, respectively.

The median voter model applies only if we restrict policy dimension to one instrument – say, the rate of tax on labor incomes. In this case the outcome is the median of the ideal points projected onto that axis, which in the figure happens to coincide with M's ideal point in that dimension, labeled MED on the horizontal axis in the upper right quadrant (P prefers a lower tax on labor, while R would like a rate that is much higher). The outcome for the probabilistic voting model is labeled EVM, an obvious acronym for the objective of political parties in the model. This equilibrium must lie within the Pareto set, since it involves a weighting of the interests of the three voters.[22] Moreover, tax rates here must be lower than the rates at which Laffer curves bend backward toward the axes. Otherwise, it would be possible for the incumbent party to lower tax rates, raise more revenue, and supply more public services – actions that lead to a higher expected vote.[23] In the case shown, the EVM outcome favors voters M and P, who are assumed to be relatively more influential than voter R.[24]

The outcome consistent with the representative agent framework is given by the unweighted average of the ideal points, the point that maximizes the welfare of the synthetic average citizen. In the figure, this point is shown as the balancing point of the Pareto set. For the same reason as in the probabilistic voting model, the representative agent outcome must also lie in the Pareto set at rates below those where revenues from either base begin to decline. But the actual rates and size of government will be different from those in the expected vote maximization framework, depending on the extent to which political influence is unequally distributed throughout the electorate.

Two possible structure-induced equilibria are shown in Figure 2.6. If legislative procedure leads to each rate of tax being decided upon separately in a committee of the whole, with each committee member having the right to propose amendments at any time, then the outcome coincides with M's ideal point in two dimensions. On the other hand, if R, acting strategically, is able to set the agenda with respect to the taxation of labor incomes and if t_K is set in a committee of the whole, where no agenda-setting power is exercised, then the final outcome is at point SIE′, which lies outside of the Pareto set. One may note that this outcome depends on a somewhat arbitrary assumption concerning the conditions and nature of agenda-setting power. Many other such assumptions would also be possible, each yielding a different equilibrium outcome.

---

[22] In the probabilistic voting model, voters R, M, and P may be regarded either as individuals or as representatives of a group of relatively homogeneous voters.

[23] See section 3.4.1 for a more detailed analysis of this point.

[24] If voters are regarded as representatives of groups then political influence also will depend on the number of voters in each group, and we could say that the outcome in the figure reflects the numerical superiority of the M and P groups.

Finally, the Leviathan fiscal system is represented by point LEV, corresponding to the maximum revenue points on the Laffer curves. The tax system at LEV involves the highest tax rates and the largest public sector; as illustrated by the diagram, it need not lie inside the Pareto set.

Figure 2.6 implies that the models surveyed here yield differing outcomes, and that variations in predicted rates or budget composition should be reflected in empirical work based on the competing frameworks. At the same time, the discussion shows that particular predictions depend on the underlying assumptions and institutional arrangements specified. We shall return to this point in Chapter 8, which contains a review of empirical research. When the difficulties of deriving estimating equations are added to those of capturing a particular collective decision context theoretically, distinguishing among the predictions of alternative models becomes a rather challenging task.

2.3   TAXING THE FUTURE

In the survey of approaches to the political economy of taxation, the time profile of taxes has not been an explicit concern. This section provides a brief overview of attempts to incorporate the time dimension into the literature on fiscal structure.

Generalizing the analysis of taxation to deal with intertemporal issues adds substantial complexity: intertemporal preferences of voters and of politicians become relevant, and the consistency over time of tax policies by successive governments becomes a concern. Even though the time profiles of *all* revenue sources are of interest to voters and politicians, the treatment of intertemporal issues can be simplified by separating revenue sources into (i) public debt, having an explicit intertemporal character, and (ii) taxation of current activity, connected to debt finance primarily through the government budget constraint (which now includes the deficit as a source of funds and interest payments on outstanding debt as a use of funds).

Because it has developed in a rather different context, the extensive literature on debt finance cannot readily be classified according to the six modeling traditions discussed in this chapter. However, it can serve to identify a set of issues with relevance for the construction of collective choice models of fiscal systems in any of the approaches. A review of the literature on debt suggests the following major points relating to the choice between current and future taxation.[25]

Any government concerned with the welfare of its citizens may want to use debt to smooth current tax rates over the business cycle (Barro 1979, 1986).

---

[25] For more extensive discussion of these issues and additional references to the literature, see, Ingberman and Inman (1988), Persson and Tabellini (1990), and Alesina and Tabellini (1992).

Since the excess burden of current taxation rises with the square of tax rates, issuing debt when current tax revenues temporarily decline, and retiring debt when revenues are high, results in lower overall excess burdens than a policy of adjusting rates to balance the budget in every period.[26]

Similar reasoning suggests that the government will increase reliance on deficit financing if growth is expected to increase in the long run. Shifting the composition of revenues toward a more rapidly growing tax base – in this example, future economic activity – permits the government to raise the same total revenue with a lower overall excess burden. At the same time, spreading the tax as widely as possible will allow it to reduce opposition to taxation, since the costs of organizing opposition are more difficult to overcome if many taxpayers are affected to a small degree than if payments are concentrated among a few (Hettich and Winer 1984, Winer and Hettich 1991a)

Other writers have emphasized that voters cannot be sure whether future majorities will share their preferences for public goods. This, coupled with the difficulty of committing future governments to a policy chosen in the present, provides a complementary explanation for debt finance (Persson and Svenson 1989, Persson and Tabellini 1990, Tabellini and Alesina 1990).[27] For example, voters in a presently dominant coalition who favor a small public sector, and who anticipate that more liberal governments will be elected in the near future, may vote for more public borrowing today to constrain the size of the public sector in the future.[28]

This motivation for debt finance introduces an explicit link between the revenue and expenditure sides of the budget. Incorporating the rationale into a fiscal model requires the introduction of heterogeneity in preferences for public goods. In addition, a more sophisticated definition of equilibrium is needed, one where all agents behave rationally given current *and* expected future policies and where, in each period, the equilibrium policy satisfies the government's objective in that period.[29]

Conflict between generations reflects another aspect of heterogeneity among voters relevant for debt policy. Voters who do not plan to leave any positively valued bequests may support deficit financing (Buchanan and

---

[26] Consideration of the time profile of consumption may also explain the use of debt finance. Politicians may issue debt when undertaking public investment to smooth current tax payments and hence the disposable income of taxpayers. A government may also find it politically profitable to use its greater borrowing power in bad economic times to help the liquidity-constrained voter smooth his or her consumption over time.

[27] For further discussion of the commitment problem and the time consistency of revenue structure, see for example Fischer (1980) and Lucas and Stokey (1983).

[28] Tabellini and Alesina (1990) suggest that reliance on debt finance will increase with the likelihood of disagreement between current and future voters.

[29] For further discussion of the definition of an equilibrium, see Persson and Tabellini (1990, p. 155).

Roback 1987, Cukierman and Meltzer 1989). Assuming that debt obligations are honored, such voters can use debt finance to increase their own consumption while reducing their bequests below zero by the present value of the future tax liabilities.[30] Even in the absence of bequest constraints, a coalition of current voters may appropriate resources from future generations in a similar fashion (see e.g. Tabellini 1991 and references cited therein). The conditions under which governments do or do not honor debt obligations inherited from the past are a central issue in this context.

A relationship between debt finance and the degree to which political power is fragmented has also been suggested (Roubini and Sachs 1989, Alesina and Drazen 1991).[31] When fragmented systems are subjected to unfavorable economic shocks, politicians may find it difficult to agree on the increases in current taxation required to prevent large deficits.

A quite different argument centers on the consequences of voter myopia for the choice among revenue sources (Buchanan and Wagner 1977). A balanced budget policy of cutting taxes and issuing debt involves immediate benefits for taxpayers, whereas raising taxes to retire debt involves short-run costs. Hence democratic systems may contain an inherent bias toward deficit financing when voters are myopic about the longer-term consequences of public financing decisions.

The literature on debt adds further complexity to the study of tax systems. When the time implications of fiscal choices are recognized, it becomes even more difficult to reduce to a single dimension the issue space over which collective decisions are made. Nor is it readily apparent how all issues raised in the debt literature could be incorporated into a single framework that would also deal with other major aspects of tax structure. Available work usually focuses on one or two relevant points in order to keep the analysis tractable and to explore that particular aspect of intertemporal choice in more detail. Such an approach is chosen in Chapter 10, where tax smoothing and tax spreading are emphasized in empirical research that focuses on the choice between current taxation and debt creation in nineteenth-century Canada.

2.4   CHOOSING AMONG MODELS

In carrying out specific work on tax structure, the researcher must choose among alternative approaches. We believe that this choice should be made in the light of essential stylized facts about the nature of policy outcomes that are

---

[30] Cukierman and Meltzer (1989) argue that reliance on debt finance is greater the larger the fraction of individuals with a relatively small part of total wealth, since in this case the fraction of the population that wishes to leave negative bequests is larger.

[31] Fragmentation may involve dispersion of power across branches of government as in the United States, or across members of the governing coalitions that typically exist in countries that use proportional representation.

widely observed in democratic countries. In our opinion, the preferred model should be consistent with the following facts, even if it cannot explain them completely.

> *Fact 1*: Tax structure is inherently multidimensional, consisting of tax bases, rate structures, and numerous special provisions.
>
> *Fact 2*: Vote cycling over feasible tax systems is not a general or widespread characteristic of representative democracies.
>
> *Fact 3*: Several important changes in a tax system are often debated and enacted simultaneously. Even where the debate focuses on one major aspect, choices involve several policy dimensions.

To encompass these stylized facts, it is necessary to choose a model with an equilibrium in the face of multidimensional policy issues, ruling out use of the median voter model. A structure-induced equilibrium framework can deal in principle with the complexity of tax policy, but the specific models available at this time are not capable of yielding a detailed equilibrium tax structure, except under the unrealistic assumption that voting on each important component is effectively separated from (or occurs independently of) voting on any other significant aspect. Such separation of policy issues does not conform to actual decision patterns; even a cursory review of major tax reforms in democratic countries indicates that it is common for several aspects of a tax system to be debated and altered more or less simultaneously. Moreover, it is not certain that institutional constraints are the fundamental reason why an equilibrium exists, as this approach assumes. In the long run, institutions may only slow down vote cycling, as legislators who understand the importance of institutionalized rules attempt to change them in a way leading to more favored policy outcomes. The stylized facts also rule out cooperative game theory as a framework for research. Its orientation toward the emergence of redistributive coalitions and its level of generality prevent this approach from explaining commonly observed features of actual tax systems.

A fourth stylized fact precludes adoption of the Leviathan model as an effective basis for research on tax systems in democratic societies.

> *Fact 4*: Public policy is normally influenced by many opposing interests in the electorate.

This model generates well-defined predictions when the issue space is multidimensional and details of relevant Laffer curves are known; however, it bypasses the question of how the collective choice process in a *democratic* society aggregates differing preferences.

The representative agent model also appears to conflict with the fourth stylized fact in not allowing for compromise among different and conflicting interests in the electorate. It is true that heterogeneity of preferences can be incorporated into the analysis by assuming that the government's objective is to maximize welfare or to minimize the excess burden of taxation across all taxpayers, but this does not answer the more basic methodological point. The extended version of the model, like its simpler counterpart, fails to confront the possibility that what governments *should* do (maximize social welfare) is not what they do in actual practice. As Joseph Schumpeter (1950) commented more than forty years ago:

> In observing human societies we do not as a rule find it difficult to specify, at least in a rough commonsense manner, the various ends that the societies under study struggle to attain. These ends may be said to provide the rationale or meaning of corresponding individual activities. But it does not follow that the social meaning of a type of activity will necessarily provide the motive power, hence the explanation of the latter. If it does not, a theory that contents itself with an analysis of the social end or need to be served cannot be accepted as an adequate account of the activities that serve it. (p. 282)

We follow Schumpeter in believing that politicians, like agents in the private sector, pursue their own objectives and that social welfare is achieved only indirectly (if at all) as a by-product of the competitive struggle for power.

The arguments made so far point to probabilistic voting as the most appropriate framework for research on tax systems.[32] Unlike the median voter model, it can be used to describe the formation of a complex, multidimensional tax structure in a political equilibrium. It does not require special rules of procedure separating decisions on different aspects of the tax system as structure-induced equilibrium analysis, and it does not bypass the aggregation of heterogeneous interests through a collective process as do the Leviathan and representative agent models. Moreover, equilibrium in an expected vote-maximization model reflects an important aspect of democratic politics; it is a balancing of opposing interests in society, with some interests being more influential than others in the final outcome.

Some authors have recently objected to expected vote maximization on the grounds that the assumption of probabilistic voting does not fully resolve the problem of vote cycling, or that it may be inconsistent with rational behavior. Dan Usher (1994) argues that polarization of party platforms may be so great that the probability of a significant number of voters supporting at least one of the parties drops to zero. In that case, the continuity of the expected vote function is lost, and a vote cycle (and the associated coercion of minorities) can reappear when disaffected voters are successfully appealed to by the opposition.[33] If one accepts the view that such polarization is a normal occurrence, one is again faced with the problem of explaining the apparent stability of policy outcomes. Usher goes on to argue that this problem is implicitly dealt with

---

[32] See also Lafay (1993) for an interesting and sympathetic assessment of what he refers to as the "silent revolution" of probabilistic voting.

[33] Hinich and Munger (1994, p. 211) have made a similar point.

in democratic societies by restrictions on the range and nature of issues that are placed in the public sector, with particularly contentious issues being excluded from public debate.

We would not deny the possibility that an equilibrium in a probabilistic voting model can break down because of polarization – for this reason at least, the vote cycle always lurks beneath the surface of electoral politics.[34] But we think it reasonable to regard such polarization as the exception to the rule, given the range of issues usually dealt with by public policy, and to proceed to the study of tax systems in "normal" times. It must be admitted that this answer does not explain how institutional limits on the scope of the public sector are determined. Yet this is not a unique shortcoming. A similar limitation also affects models of the private economy that require property rights as a precondition but do not explain the emergence of such rights endogenously.

David Austen-Smith (1991) suggests that probabilistic voting may not be consistent with rational behavior. In a game-theoretic framework, rational voters behave probabilistically (i.e., use mixed strategies) only if they randomize their vote over the available choices; this requires that they be indifferent between the policies offered by various parties. Such indifference will occur only if all parties propose identical platforms at all times, which is quite unrealistic and rules out smooth expected vote functions defined over the entire range of feasible policy proposals. The answer to this objection, acknowledged by Austen-Smith, is that the uncertainty generating the continuity of a party's objective function with respect to the range of feasible policy proposals must involve uncertainty by the party about the effects of its policies on voting behavior; this approach is taken by Enelow and Hinich (1989) and by Coughlin, Mueller, and Murrell (1990a,b), among others.[35] Such candidate or party uncertainty about voters is not generated from within the model, but is a statement about the nature of the world in which political competition is carried out. In our view, it is reasonable to assume that parties do not know with certainty what voters will do, even though they may be trying to learn more about

---

[34] Slutsky (1975), among others, has drawn attention to the more general point that the existence of an equilibrium in a probabilistic voting model depends on the nature of individual voting densities.

[35] For additional discussion of this issue, see Coughlin (1992) and Hinich and Munger (1994). Peter Howitt (1990) shows how an equilibrium can be obtained even when voting is not probabilistic. The key is that there is a great deal of heterogeneity in the characteristics of voters relative to the ability of government to adapt public policy to these characteristics. In such situations, a small change in any policy instrument (e.g., in some aspect of tax structure) will at most allow the government to fit policy more carefully to the characteristics of only a small number of voters, and it will therefore generate only a small change in the number of voters who will support the party. Hence in this framework the number of votes for any party is a continuous function of its proposed policy platform, and consequently an equilibrium rather than a vote cycle may exist.

the characteristics of the electorate. Indeed, one may ask from where uncertainty arises in the usual empirical investigation in the social sciences if it is believed that parties are fully aware of how voters will act, or if analogous assumptions are introduced into other similar analytical contexts.

It should be acknowledged that most models of political economy contain some elements that are not fully explained or that may not be completely consistent with the assumptions of rational behavior. As already mentioned, for example, the structure-induced equilibrium framework postulates the existence of stable institutions despite the fact that individuals have an incentive to alter existing rules when policy outcomes are repeatedly unfavorable to them. Nevertheless, the approach remains of interest in the study of legislative decisions. Similar shortcomings can also be found in other collective choice models and in many other areas of economics.

2.5   THE NARROW AND THE BROADER INTERPRETATIONS OF POLITICAL INFLUENCE

At various points in the investigation, we shall employ either a narrow or a broad interpretation of political influence in the probabilistic voting model with expected vote-maximizing political parties. The narrow view, which is more recent and more formal, has emerged from probabilistic spatial voting theory. As noted earlier, the assumption that voting is probabilistic from the perspective of parties is a critical element in a formal proof that an equilibrium policy platform exists. Interest groups do not play an essential role in this formulation.

The broader view acknowledges the activities of special interest groups; this view is both richer in its depiction of political life and less precise with respect to its theoretical foundations. The approach has its origins in the work of Anthony Downs (1957), George Stigler (1970), Albert Breton (1974), Sam Peltzman (1980), Gary Becker (1983), and others. In the broader view, political competition generally involves the exchange of policies favored by special interests for resources (money, information, or time) that these interests make available to political parties for generating electoral support.[36]

---

[36] Some authors have attempted to incorporate interest groups into a probabilistic voting model by having exogenously determined groups of relatively homogeneous voters explicitly represented in the expected vote function (e.g., Coughlin et al. 1990a,b). Austin-Smith (1987), Mayer and Li (1994), and Hinich and Munger (1994), among others, have attempted to formally incorporate the exchange of policies for political resources into a probabilistic voting framework. There is also a smaller body of work that tries to endogenize the size of interest groups along with policy outcomes (e.g., van Winden 1983), but here the issue of the existence of an equilibrium remains to be more fully explored.

We make reference to the broader model in the empirical investigations of tax structure reported in Chapters 9 and 10. In a similar manner, we introduce institutions into the discussion in Chapter 11, although the formal probabilistic voting model does not explicitly account for them. Models play a useful organizing role in most scientific investigations, but they must remain deliberate abstractions that generally cannot give a full account of all important aspects of a broadly conceived subject. We believe in expanding the formal framework in an exploratory manner where this suggests new directions, or where it adds to the understanding of important observed features of reality.

The narrow version of the probabilistic voting model provides the basis for the theoretical examination of tax structure in the following two chapters. Although interest groups and institutions may be important in many contexts, it is not necessary to appeal to their role to explain the essential characteristics of tax systems or to understand how they are shaped by the interaction of political and economic decisions. On the other hand, we must abandon the restrictions on tax structure introduced in this chapter in order to carry out the diagrammatic comparison of different models. What is required now is an analysis that allows emergence of the complex nature of taxation that we observe in democratic societies.

CHAPTER 3

Foundations of Democratic Tax Systems

Why should public finance theory only be allowed to investigate the effects of various tax proposals, but not be permitted to analyze the factors which determine the form they take and the choice between different proposals which is then made by the political authorities? In both cases the question is one of clarifying factual causal relationships.

Eric Lindahl (1959, p. 8)

It depends upon social structure and upon ... political constellations whether ... personal taxes or taxes on objects, income and profits taxes or land, investment, property and death taxes are to be chosen, whether the tax screw should be tightened or relieved, what groups of the population are to bear the heavier or the lighter burden, ... whether expenditure is to be reduced or revenue raised, how taxation is to be combined with economic incentives, and so on.

Rudolf Goldscheid (1925, p. 207)

Actual tax systems are complicated and often elaborate. Underneath their rather baroque appearance lies a simple skeleton, however, consisting of a limited number of parts. The main elements in all tax systems are tax bases, rate structures, and special provisions such as exemptions, credits, and deductions. A theoretical analysis of tax structure must explain how these elements arise as a result of private and public choices and also what determines their design and importance within the system as a whole.

We show in this chapter that the essential nature of the tax skeleton can be understood as the outcome of rational behavior in a probabilistic voting model where competing political parties maximize expected votes or plurality, and where opposition to taxation depends on the loss in full income (defined to include the excess burden or deadweight costs of taxation). Our analysis treats the level of expenditures as endogenous and integrates the influence of administration costs with that of political and economic factors. Revenue structure is shown to be a system of related components in a political–economic equilibrium.

The emphasis here is on the reasons for the emergence of the tax skeleton with a given set of political institutions. As pointed out in the preceding chapter, an alternative approach to positive tax theory – initiated by Thomas Romer (1975), K. W. S. Roberts (1977), and Allan Meltzer and Scott Richard (1981) – is to assume the existence of one particular aspect of tax structure and to allow voters to choose relevant parameters through majority rule. Although focusing on one feature permits more detailed analysis of that component, it avoids the broader questions of why tax structure as a whole exists and how different parts of the tax skeleton are related.

We begin with the informal presentation of a simple probabilistic voting model in which a governing party maximizing expected electoral support sets unique tax rates for N individuals who have different economic and political responses but who all engage in the same type of economic activity. (A more formal version of the model is presented in the next chapter.) The optimal electoral strategy of the government or incumbent party in this framework serves as a reference solution for analysis of a more general situation that includes many activities by taxpayers and accounts for the creation of bases, rate structures, and special provisions.

3.1 A MODEL OF EQUILIBRIUM STRUCTURE

Explaining the creation of tax systems is part of the broader question of how governments choose policy instruments and policy outcomes. There are four essential elements in this process: the goals pursued by the government or governing party; the reactions by the voters to the impact of the policies; the framework of political competition within which the government's strategies are determined; and the constraints imposed on the government and on taxpayers by the general equilibrium structure of the private economy.

All of these elements are present in the probabilistic voting model introduced in Chapter 2. Let us assume here that competition for office forces each party to choose a multidimensional policy platform, denoted s, so as to continually maximize expected plurality or expected votes, EV, with EV depending significantly on the consequences of policies for the economic welfare of voters. The electoral support for each party can be expressed generally as $EV_j = EV_j(s_i, s_o, x)$, $j \in \{i, o\}$, where subscripts refer to the incumbent or government (i) and opposition party (o) respectively, x represents exogenous factors, and where a government budget restraint and relationships representing the resources and behavioral responses in the private economy are part of the model's structure and have been substituted into the expected vote function.

For existence of a Nash equilibrium in the electoral game, it is necessary that objective function EV_j be continuous in $\{s_i \times s_o\}$. Otherwise, as pointed out in Chapter 2, vote cycling over alternative policies may occur. As we also noted there, the continuity condition may be satisfied if we treat voting as probabilistic. Continuity is not enough to guarantee the existence of a Nash equilibrium by itself, however. Given that the set of feasible policies is well-behaved (i.e., convex, closed, and bounded), a Nash equilibrium in pure strategies will exist provided that, in addition to being continuous, each EV_j is also quasi concave in s_j for every policy platform chosen by the other party. The equilibrium will be unique if the expected vote functions are strictly concave rather than just quasi concave (see e.g. Fudenberg and Tirole 1991, p. 34; Owen 1995, p. 72).[1]

In the development of a theory of tax structure, our aim in this chapter is to characterize the nature of fiscal policy choices made by participants in a competitive electoral system of voters who have heterogeneous tastes and interests, rather than to elaborate on the conditions required for the existence of a solution to a particular electoral game. Our aim can best be achieved by examining in detail how the government or incumbent party creates tax instruments and shapes the revenue system to maximize expected votes or political support. In order to simplify exposition, we refer only to the government in the following discussion since opposition parties pursue an analogous process in designing their competing fiscal platforms. Moreover, since we assume that policies are chosen by each party given the platform of the opposition (the usual Nash behavioral assumption), the platform of the opposition may be suppressed in describing the government's optimal choices.

3.1.1   Taxation in a Basic Model

Imagine a fiscal system where the government provides one public good G and imposes H proportional tax rates t_h, one for each voter, applied to the activity representing that voter's tax base B_h. Assume that the probability π_h, that individual h votes for the government can be written as a function of the difference I_i between component b_h, reflecting the voter's valuation of public services, and a second component c_h, representing the individual's loss in full income from taxation including the excess burden of taxation. Hence

$$\pi_h = f_h(I_h) \quad \text{for} \quad h = 1, 2, \ldots, H, \tag{3.1}$$

where $I_h = b_h - c_h$ and $c_h = T_h + d_h$, with $T_h(T_h = t_h \cdot B_h)$ being the tax payment of voter h and d_h the dollar equivalent of the excess burden that

---

[1] General discussions of the assumptions required for the existence of an equilibrium in a probabilistic voting model are provided by Calvert (1986), Enelow and Hinich (1989), Coughlin (1992), and Hinich and Munger (1994). Wittman (1987) shows that the equilibrium may exist even if there are more than two parties. The multiparty case is also discussed by Anderson, Katz, and Thisse (1994). We recall that the role of concavity in establishing an equilibrium was illustrated in the previous chapter.

results from h's attempts to avoid and evade taxation.[2] We also stipulate that b_h depends only on G, and that c_h is independent of G. This assumption reflects the separation of taxes and expenditures characteristic of most modern fiscal systems, and for this reason it is a good starting point in constructing a positive theory of tax structure. (The assumption also helps to simplify a rather complex theoretical problem.) We shall explore the implications of links between spending and taxing for tax structure in a later section of the chapter.

The total expected vote for the government can be written as

$$EV = \sum_{h=1}^{H} \pi_h = \sum_{h=1}^{H} f_h(I_h), \tag{3.2}$$

where the subscript on EV referring to a specific political party has been omitted for convenience.

The structure of the private economy enters through B_h and d_h. Assuming that activities of different taxpayers are independent and that G does not affect any tax base, for each activity h we can write

$$B_h = B_h(t_h, x_h), \quad \partial B_h / \partial t_h < 0, \tag{3.3a}$$

$$d_h = d_h(t_h, x_h), \quad \partial d_h / \partial t_h > 0, \tag{3.3b}$$

where x_h represents exogenous factors such as the voter's taste for leisure and the costs of tax avoidance and evasion activities.

In the absence of administration costs, the government's problem is to choose tax rates $t_1, t_2, \ldots, t_H$ and the level of the public good G to maximize expected total support (3.2), subject to the budget constraint

$$G = \sum_{h=1}^{H} t_h \cdot B_h. \tag{3.4}$$

If all available fiscal instruments are used, the first-order conditions include

$$\frac{\partial f_h / \partial I_h \cdot \partial c_h / \partial t_h}{B_h(1 + \varepsilon_h)} = \lambda \quad \text{for} \quad h = 1, 2, \ldots, H, \tag{3.5a}$$

where $\varepsilon_h = \partial B_h / \partial t_h \cdot t_h / B_h$ is the elasticity of base B_h with respect to t_h and λ is the Lagrange multiplier associated with the government budget constraint, and

$$\sum_{h=1}^{H} \frac{\partial f_h}{\partial I_h} \cdot \frac{\partial b_h}{\partial G} = \lambda. \tag{3.5b}$$

---

[2] The model is a modification of Hettich and Winer (1988). In the present formulation, $f_h(I_h) = f_h(b_h - c_h)$ equals the probability of voting and is explicitly incorporated into the model. Note that f_i now translates the net fiscal surplus I_h into a probability of voting.

Condition (3.5a) indicates that, whatever the level of public services may be, the government adjusts tax rates among voters until the marginal political cost (MPC), or reduction in expected votes, of raising an additional dollar as given by the left side of (3.5a) is equalized across taxpayers. In other words, the politically optimal tax structure minimizes total political costs for any given level of revenues collected. Conditions (3.5) show that the resulting tax structure is complex, with as many different tax rates as there are individuals. Furthermore, as indicated by (3.5b), the governing party will adjust the aggregate size of government until the marginal political benefit (MPB) of spending another dollar on public services is equal to the marginal political cost (λ).[3]

The solution for the optimal policy platform of the government is presented in Figure 3.1 for the case with two taxpayers. This figure is drawn on the assumption that the political cost of (or opposition to) taxation is independent of the level of the public good. We imagine that the taxable activity for both taxpayers is gainful employment and that they differ in their tastes for leisure and in the ease with which they can trade off leisure for work. As a result, they have different "Laffer curves" or rate–revenue relationships, shown in the lower part of panels a and b. They also vary in political tastes – that is, in the intensity with which they react to the loss of a dollar in full income by reducing expected support (depicted by differently shaped marginal political cost functions). Their unequal economic and political responses to taxation result in two quite different tax rates.

Panel c shows the determination of budget size. The MPC curve is the horizontal addition of marginal political cost functions, while MPB equals the vertical sum of individual marginal political benefit functions expressed per dollar of expenditure. The desired budget is $R*$ and must be raised jointly from the two individuals.[4]

These first-order conditions integrate economic and political behavior, but they yield only a very simple tax structure that still misses essential elements of

---

[3] Second-order conditions for the solution of the first-order conditions to be a unique maximum are that the objective function (3.2) be strictly concave and that the government budget constraint defined by (3.4) be strictly convex. Assuming that all functions are twice continuously differentiable, these conditions are assured if, in addition to the assumptions made in the text, for each voter h: (1) $\partial^2 f_h/\partial G^2 < 0$; (2) $\partial^2 f_h/\partial t_h^2 < 0$; and (3) $\partial^2 B_h/\partial t_h^2 < 0$. Condition (1) requires that the marginal vote productivity of G decline with the size of the public sector, and (2) requires that the marginal reduction in expected political support from any citizen increase with the tax rate levied on that individual. Condition (3) is also plausible, requiring that each tax base become more sensitive to taxation as tax rates increase. Note that cross partial derivatives (with respect to any tax rate and G, and with respect to different tax rates) do not appear in these second-order conditions because the effects on voting behavior of expenditures and taxes are assumed to be independent, and because taxable activities are assumed to be independent across taxpayers.

[4] Drawing the MPB and MPC curves independently implies that G does not enter into (3.5a).

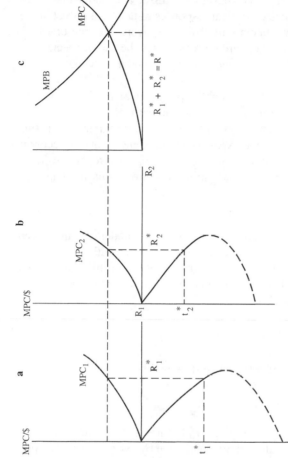

Legend

MPC = Marginal political costs

MPB = Marginal political benefits

R_i^* = Tax revenues raised from taxpayer or base i

t_i^* = Eqcuilibrium tax rates

Figure 3.1. Tax structure in political equilibrium

observed tax systems. The tax structure defined by equations (3.5) consists of *H* rates on one activity, with each taxpayer being taxed at a unique rate depending on his or her economic and political responses to taxation. As yet, there is no indication that the government will group taxpayers into rate brackets or activities into tax bases, and there are no reasons for the use of special provisions. In subsequent sections we extend the basic model to account for these additional elements.

We are interested primarily in establishing a set of minimal conditions under which a stylized tax structure is part of the optimal political strategy of the government. Since we can accomplish this without relaxing the assumptions that (i) activities of different taxpayers are independent and (ii) economic and political responses to taxation by individuals are known to the government without cost, we shall maintain these assumptions throughout the chapter.

3.1.2   Taxation of Many Activities

Complexity is further increased over that in the basic model just introduced if we allow each taxpayer h to conduct j taxable activities, with $j = 1, 2, \ldots, J$ and $B_{hj} = B_{hj}(t_{h1}, t_{h2}, \ldots, t_{HJ}, x_h)$. Note that activities of different taxpayers are still assumed to be independent in this formulation. In this case, the government budget restraint (3.4) becomes

$$G = \sum_{h=1}^{H} \sum_{j=1}^{J} t_{hj} \cdot B_{hj}, \tag{3.4'}$$

and the revised first-order condition corresponding to (3.5a) is

$$\frac{\partial f_h / \partial I_h \cdot \partial c_h / \partial t_{hj}}{B_{hj}(1 + \varepsilon_{hj}) + \sum_{k \neq j} t_{hk} \cdot \partial B_{hk} / \partial t_{hj}} = \lambda \tag{3.5a'}$$

with $h = 1, 2, \ldots, H$ and $k, j = 1, 2, \ldots, J$. The new solution involves $H \times J$ tax rates, one for each separate activity conducted by every different taxpayer. We can use Figure 3.1 to illustrate the differentiated treatment of activities by reinterpreting the diagrams as referring to a single taxpayer h and two of h's taxable activities, each of which associated with a different rate–revenue relationship and marginal political cost function. To raise any fixed amount of revenue at minimum political costs, the government equalizes MPC per dollar of revenue, imposing two different tax rates that reflect the factors shaping the curves in each of the two panels.

Equation (3.5a′) generalizes the conditions stated in (3.5a). It implies that the politically optimal tax structure equalizes marginal political opposition per dollar of tax revenue across taxable activities for each taxpayer, and across taxpayers for each activity. This condition and the foregoing argument indicate that the evolution of tax structure is closely related to economic change and development and to changes in political margins. Minimizing opposition to taxation requires the adjustment of tax structure when the nature of economic activities conducted by taxpayers changes and when the nature of political behavior is altered.

The same argument also explains why tax simplification in competitive political systems remains elusive, although it appears to be universally endorsed as a good idea – disregarding differences in economic and political behavior across taxpayers increases opposition to taxation and thus increases the possibility of electoral defeat. This can be understood by reconsidering the first-order conditions (3.5a′) when all political margins across voters are the same. In that case, the numerator of the revised condition becomes $(\partial f/\partial I) \cdot (\partial c_h/\partial t_{hj})$. We may then simplify further by moving $\partial f/\partial I$ to the right side of the equation, because that term does not have a subscript. Since the denominator of (3.5a′) remains the same, we can rewrite this equation as

$$\frac{\partial c_h/\partial t_{hj}}{B_{hj}\left(1 + \varepsilon_{hj}\right) + \sum_{k \neq j}t_{hk} \cdot \partial B_{hk}/\partial t_{hj}} = \frac{\lambda}{\partial f/\partial I}$$

$$\text{for} \quad h = 1,\dots,H \quad \text{and} \quad k,j = 1,\dots,J.$$

The revised equation shows that when only economic responses to taxation differ, the politically optimal tax system equalizes the loss in full income per dollar of revenue across taxpayers and, as a consequence, minimizes the total economic burden of taxation for a budget of given size. Exogenous constraints on a government's power to implement such a complex tax system must therefore increase opposition by increasing the burden of taxation for at least some voters.

The importance for political success of taking differences among voters into account can be seen in a second way. If we assume instead that all economic responses to taxation in (3.5a′) are the same and focus on differences across taxpayers in political margins $\left(\partial f_h/\partial I_h\right)$, it follows that overall political opposition to taxation must increase if these margins cannot be fully addressed.

Condition (3.5a′) thus indicates that complexity in tax structure is politically rational. Indeed, it implies even greater complexity than is usually observed. The task is thus not only to explain the existence of complexity but also to delineate its limits.

3.2   ADMINISTRATION COSTS AND THE CHOICE OF RATE STRUCTURES AND BASES

In the solution to the government's problem just outlined, we have N taxpayers, J activities, and $J \times N$ tax rates. This is unrealistic in two respects. First, activities are generally grouped into bases that consist of similar or related activities. In addition, taxpayers are sorted or grouped into rate brackets where, despite interpersonal differences, they pay the same tax rates.

Deviations from unique treatment of activities or of taxpayers will cause a loss in political support. What must be explained is why the government decides to accept such losses, for instance, what offsetting advantage can be gained in exchange for the grouping. The answer lies in reduced administration costs. Resources released in this way can then be used to provide more public goods and thus increased popular support. The government's problem is to balance the marginal loss in support from grouping with the marginal gain in support from spending resources not used in administration.

Since we developed the model in this chapter using a framework of H taxpayers and one activity, it is convenient to begin the analysis by considering the sorting of taxpayers into rate brackets for the case of one activity. We shall indicate later how the solution can also be interpreted as the rationale for combining different activities into bases.

Creation of rate brackets will mean that groups of individuals with differing levels of economic activity will be subject to the same tax rate. The government's problem is (i) to establish the politically optimal number of such brackets; (ii) to assign or sort individuals into these brackets in a manner that is consistent with its political objective; and (iii) to choose the rates of taxation that are to be applied to each group. We shall leave explicit investigation of the last problem for the next chapter and consider the first two problems here, beginning with the sorting of taxpayers into a given number of groups.

Let the number of rate brackets or groups be fixed at some number $N < H$, the number of individual taxpayers. Levying the same rate on all members of a given group, rather than taxing them at their unique politically optimal rates defined by first-order conditions (3.5a′), must result in a loss in expected support since it is no longer possible to equalize marginal political costs or opposition to taxation across individuals. The task for the government is to sort taxpayers into the given number of groups so as to minimize the loss in electoral support stemming from the grouping of voters for the purpose of taxation. We investigate the nature of the solution to this sorting problem at some length in the next chapter. We show that if it is possible to linearize the H first-order conditions in the absence of grouping, then the loss in support from grouping H unique individuals into N rate brackets is minimized when taxpayers are sorted so as to minimize the within-group variation in politically optimal rates defined in the absence of administration costs.

By considering solutions of the sorting problem for different values of N, it is possible to construct curve AA, the *marginal tax discrimination curve* in Figure 3.2. For each N, this curve shows the maximum reduction in opposition possible from increasing the number of groups by 1 while simultaneously resorting individuals among the $N + 1$ groups so as to minimize the total loss in support

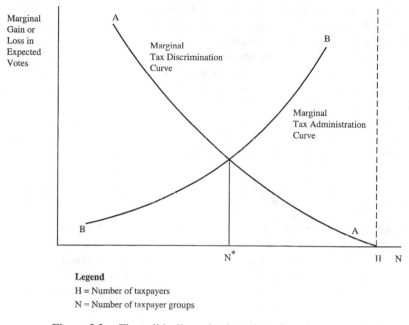

Marginal
Gain or
Loss in
Expected
Votes

A

B

Marginal
Tax Discrimination
Curve

Marginal
Tax Administration
Curve

B

A

N^*

H   N

Legend

H = Number of taxpayers

N = Number of taxpayer groups

Figure 3.2. The politically optimal number of rate brackets (or bases)

from grouping. The curve *AA* lies above the horizontal axis when $N < H$ and intersects the horizontal axis at $N = H$, where all taxpayers are treated uniquely. It is shown here to decline continuously as N approaches H. (The shape of the tax discrimination curve is also investigated in the next chapter.)

The optimal number of rate brackets N^* is determined in Figure 3.2 by the intersection of the tax discrimination curve and the curve *BB*, the *marginal tax administration curve*, reflecting the opportunity cost to the government of increasing the extent to which individuals are treated differently when this creates administration costs. For each N, the curve *BB* shows the fall in political support resulting from an increase in the number of tax rates from N to $N + 1$ and a reduction in public services by an amount equal to the corresponding growth in administration costs. It is reasonable to expect *BB* to slope upward since administration costs tend to increase with the complexity of the tax system (measured here by N, the number of brackets).[5] The types of administration costs that usually increase with the number of elements in the tax system

---

[5] It is possible that administration costs depend on the nature of the tax instruments employed, as well as on their number; see Heller and Shell (1974). We do not explore that possibility here. We shall also ignore possible discontinuities and nonconvexities introduced by administration costs.

include the costs of determining the individually correct (politically optimal) tax rates, the costs of measuring economic activity applicable to each element, and enforcement and collection costs.

A more general solution for the optimal number of brackets when each taxpayer is taxed on all of his J activities involves four elements: the maximum reduction in votes lost (i.e., the maximum marginal gain in electoral support) when the number of rate brackets k_j on any activity j is increased (written as $\partial EV/\partial k_j$); the resulting increase in administration costs $\partial A/\partial k_j$ and in total revenue $\partial R/\partial k_j$; and the additional support from spending one more dollar on public goods λ. The optimal solution for the government requires

$$\frac{\partial EV/\partial k_j}{\partial A_j/\partial k_j - \partial R_j/\partial k_j} = \lambda \quad \text{for} \quad j = 1, 2, \dots, J; \tag{3.6}$$

that is, the marginal reduction in opposition per "net" dollar of administration costs must be equal across activities.

The analysis has a second important application to the grouping of activities into tax bases. Consider a model with one representative taxpayer who engages in J different activities. The government can save on administration costs by combining related activities into a limited number of bases, such as occurs when incomes from different labor activities are included in the same tax base. Grouping leads to an increase in political opposition in this case since it will raise a taxpayer's deadweight loss associated with any given tax payment. On the other hand, the government receives additional support by spending resources saved in administration on the provision of public goods. The solution illustrated in Figure 3.2 again describes the nature of the equilibrium, where N^* now refers to the number of bases for each individual rather than to rate brackets.[6]

The preceding analysis integrates, for the first time, administration costs into political optimization.[7] In doing so, it provides a new basis for understanding the evolution of tax systems. In his pioneering work on fiscal systems, Richard Musgrave (1969) argues that *tax handles* are crucial for explaining the formation and growth of tax structure. If we conceive of the term "tax handles" in a broad sense that includes opportunities to tax and to escape taxation as well as administration costs, the theory presented here formalizes what so far has mainly been implicit. In an analysis over time, changes in economic activities and in the conditions under which they are carried out will be of crucial

---

[6] Yitzhaki (1979) uses a similar analysis of tax bases in an optimal tax framework.

[7] See also van Velthoven and van Winden (1991), who consider tax reform rather than the formation of tax structure. For a consideration of administrations cost in an optimal tax setting, see for example Yitzhaki (1979), Slemrod (1990a), Mayshar (1991), and Wilson (1989b).

importance (together with administration costs), since the nature of such activities and conditions determines the characteristics according to which the government sorts taxpayers to create bases, rate structures, and (as will be argued) special provisions. Hence the development of tax structure results from an interaction between (i) the changing ways in which people work, transact, and consume, and (ii) the cost of administering the collection of revenues. To this is added a third element – namely, the influence of those factors that determine how benefits from public goods and losses in full income from taxation are translated into political action.

3.3 SPECIAL PROVISIONS

The final feature of the skeleton that remains to be explained is the existence of special provisions such as exemptions, deductions, and tax credits. Consider the grouping of activities into tax bases in the case with H taxpayers, each of whom engages in J activities. According to the preceding analysis, the government will create separate bases for each of the H taxpayers. The composition of bases will differ among taxpayers unless there is an additional cost, not considered so far, in administering different bases for each individual. Such costs introduce a further constraint on the grouping process, leading to bases that coincide for large numbers of individuals and in rate structures that are defined on bases rather than on separate activities.

The argument is illustrated in Figure 3.3, which is drawn for two taxpayers, each of whom engages in four activities. When there are no additional costs in having separate bases for each taxpayer, the grouping process results in person 1 being taxed on two bases consisting of activities 1 and 2 and activities 3 and 4, respectively. For person 2, the two bases will consist of a combination of the first three activities and of activity 4. When there are costs to having separate bases for each individual (an additional base generally requires a new set

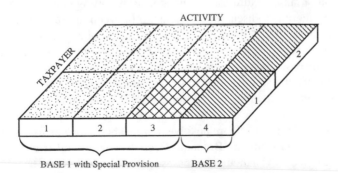

Figure 3.3. Special provisions in the equilibrium tax structure

of collection points and separate administrative arrangements), it may be preferable to define the first base for both individuals to include activities 1, 2, and 3 while making activity 4 into a second base. However, it will be politically undesirable to tax activity 3 in the same way for both taxpayers. A special provision such as an exemption or a deduction in the first base will allow the government to differentiate tax treatment of activity 3 depending on the taxpayer involved.

The argument can also be approached from a second angle. The general solution in (3.5a′) specifies a different rate structure for each activity. This, no doubt, would be administratively costly. It may be preferable to define rate structures across bases comprising several activities, but to introduce some differentiation in the tax treatment of each activity in any base by having special provisions that are specific to particular activities.

We have now shown that the government's optimizing behavior generates all essential elements of tax structure. The skeleton is complete. The analysis also demonstrates that all the parts are interdependent. This is an important point, since tax policy or tax reform often focuses only on one aspect of the system without taking account of the repercussions that must follow intervention in other parts. Rate structures, bases, and special provisions are all determined jointly. The government will furthermore try to establish a new policy platform each time there are shocks to the system such as changes in the factors (x_h) determining the supply of taxable activities, or in the nature of heterogeneity among taxpayers. The analysis suggests that tax systems should be studied as integrated systems of essential elements and not merely as collections of unrelated or ill-designed components.

3.4   EXTENSIONS OF THE SORTING PROCESS

3.4.1   The Relationship between Tax Rates and Tax Revenues

The idea that a tax structure can be thought of as sorting equilibrium throws new light on the much discussed relationship between tax rates and tax revenues. In the basic model, this relationship will differ for each individual. Each long-run Laffer curve may have a backward-bending portion, but political optimization in the basic model precludes tax rates which push taxpayers onto that portion, provided that political opposition increases continuously with tax rates and that the vote productivity of additional public expenditure is positive.

Opposition to taxation will increase with tax rates if both terms in the numerator of (3.5a) or (3.5a′) are positive. It appears reasonable to assume this to be the case – as Geoffrey Brennan, Cecil Bohanon, and Richard Carter (1984) have noted – even though increases in tax rates may lower tax revenues beyond some point. Under this assumption, and as long as λ and B_h are both positive, first-order conditions (3.5a) require that ε_h exceed -1. In other words, choice of a tax rate placing a voter on the backward-bending portion of his Laffer curve would imply that the government is forgoing revenues which could be used to generate further support, and that the affected voter is at the same time opposing the government more strongly than he would at lower rates.[8]

In a world of heterogeneous taxpayers and positive administration costs, where sorting of taxpayers is a rational political strategy, this conclusion may no longer hold for some individual taxpayers. When grouping occurs, the original optimal conditions like (3.5a') no longer apply; as a result, some individuals may become subject to a group rate placing them on the backward-bending portion of their individual rate–revenue curve. This will occur if assignment to any other group would lower the government's overall expected support.

Figure 3.4 illustrates the argument. Here we have drawn the Laffer curve for some taxpayer, say H. In the absence of administration costs, H's politically optimal tax rate is t_H^* which must lie on the increasing part of the function. Assume now that the government groups taxpayers as described earlier, and that the two group rates closest to t_H^* are t_N and t_{N-1}. If taxpayer H is assigned to the Nth group then the government faces both increased opposition from H and reduced revenue. If H is assigned to group $N - 1$, her opposition decreases and revenues will decline by an additional amount $T_N - T_{N-1}$. She will be placed in the Nth group, and therefore on the backward-bending portion, if this extra loss of revenue leads to a greater reduction in support than does her assignment to the Nth group.[9]

The argument shows that we may expect to observe some individuals whose tax payments would increase if *they alone* faced lower tax rates. One should note, however, that the same conclusion does not apply to groups. In a competitive political equilibrium, no group will be on the backward-bending part of its aggregate rate–revenue relationship. Otherwise, the government could collect more revenues from the group as a whole by lowering the group's rate and could simultaneously reduce opposition from all of its members.

3.4.2   Links between Tax and Expenditure Structure

In the discussion of Figure 3.1, the tax and expenditure sides were linked only through the budget constraint and the endogenous determination of budget size, and opposition to taxation does not depend on the level of the public

---

[8] It should be pointed out that there is no difference in the time horizon of voters and the government in the model. For a discussion of the Laffer curve that focuses on such a difference, see Buchanan and Lee (1982).

[9] The argument is intuitive. Strictly speaking, the placement of taxpayer H and the choice of group tax rates will occur simultaneously.

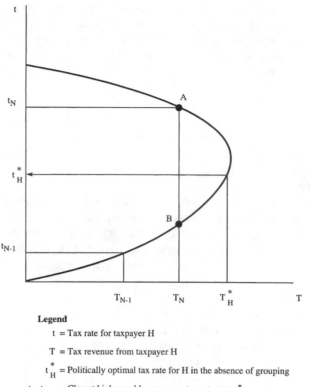

Legend

    t = Tax rate for taxpayer H

    T = Tax revenue from taxpayer H

    t_H^* = Politically optimal tax rate for H in the absence of grouping

    t_N, t_{N-1} = Closest higher and lower group tax rates to t_H^*

Figure 3.4.   The revenue-rate relationship for taxpayer H

good. A further connection is created if we make tax bases and welfare losses
from taxation dependent on public expenditures by including G in equations
(3.3), as has been suggested by Herbert Kiesling (1990). In this case, the first-
order conditions for vote maximization depend on G. The amended condition
corresponding to (3.5b), for example, is

$$\frac{\sum_{h=1}^{H} \left\{ \frac{\partial f_h}{\partial I_h} \cdot \frac{\partial b_h}{\partial G} - \frac{\partial f_h}{\partial I_h} \cdot \frac{\partial c_h}{\partial G} \right\}}{1 - \sum_{h=1}^{H} t_h \cdot \frac{\partial B_h}{\partial G}} = \lambda, \tag{3.5b$'$}$$

where the numerator equals the gain in support from spending another dollar
on G (net of the decline in political costs due to the effect of G on the burden
of taxation), and the second term in the denominator accounts for the effect on

the size of tax bases (and hence on tax revenue) of complementarities and substitutabilities between public and private goods. This condition tells us that the political costs of raising tax rates to finance another dollar of G are now less in the case of a public good that is complementary to the private activities on which the additional taxes are imposed, that is, where $\partial B_h/G > 0$. Such complementarities reduce opposition by reducing the excess burden of taxation and by maintaining tax revenues.[10]

It can be argued that the original formulation of the probability of voting, when accepted in its full generality, already implies an explicit connection between the size of the public sector and the choice of tax structure. Since voters' net evaluations of the public sector I_h depend on G, the numerator of the left side of (3.5a) will in general be a function of G. The formal implications of this for the sorting process and the resulting tax structure have not yet been established.

One can imagine how the link between expenditures and taxes may operate in practice. Assume two groups of individuals having low and high evaluations of the public good. Holding other things constant, the low demanders pay a lower tax rate than the high demanders, whereas in the simpler case shown in Figure 3.1, differences in such evaluations do not influence tax rates since only the sum of marginal evaluations is of importance. In the more complex world, the government trades off the gain in support from discriminating according to net evaluations against the loss in support resulting from lower public goods output caused by higher administration costs. As before, unlike individuals are grouped together and discrimination is imperfect in equilibrium.

Although the formal analysis assumes that the government knows the characteristics relevant for sorting, in practice considerable cost differences may exist in discriminating effectively among heterogeneous individuals on the two sides of the budget. Information on individual characteristics on the tax side is easier to acquire than knowledge of benefit evaluations. One can therefore imagine a government initially creating a tax structure on the assumption that support is independent of the level of G and subsequently amending it for certain broad classes of individuals having similar evaluations of public output. For example, persons over 65 may be given a special exemption to acknowledge a lower evaluation of expenditures on physical and human capital. We expect that the cost of reformulating tax bases to distinguish between classes of taxpayers will often exceed the cost of creating new special provisions. As a result, the direct link between expenditures and taxes via the influence of net evaluations of the fiscal system on voting behavior may appear primarily through the introduction of special provisions.

---

[10] For a related discussion in the context of an optimal tax analysis, see Atkinson and Stern (1974).

3.5   AN INITIAL APPLICATION:
THE CONCEPT OF TAX EXPENDITURES

In this section we illustrate some implications of our approach by using it to reconsider the meaning of "tax expenditures," a concept that is often relied upon in tax policy analysis.[11]

Starting with Stanley Surrey (1973), who introduced the idea into the literature, writers on tax expenditures have distinguished between an underlying "correct" tax structure and provisions in the tax system that represent deviations from this structure.[12] In identifying the standard of reference, they have drawn primarily on the Schanz–Haig–Simons approach to the definition of the comprehensive income tax.[13] Deviations from the comprehensive income tax base are viewed as implicit subsidies, hence the term "expenditures." Proponents of the concept furthermore argue that such indirect subsidies are less efficient than direct public payments in support of particular policy purposes, and that tax expenditures can rarely be justified on policy grounds. The tax expenditure concept has assumed importance in policy discussions primarily because of the development of tax expenditure budgets as a means of providing information about tax structure. These budgets consist of measures of the size of revenues forgone because actual tax bases deviate from the ideal base.

The probabilistic voting model of tax structure presented here provides an alternative way of understanding special provisions. Once this perspective is adopted, tax systems can no longer be considered as a combination of correct and incorrect elements. Tax structure, including special provisions, represents an equilibrium result of the political process where all components have been rationally chosen by governments engaged in the struggle to maintain office. The tax expenditure concept thus loses a major underpinning.

Moreover, special tax provisions are not always (or even usually) equivalent to implicit subsidies in such a political world. A complex tax system will arise for the reasons analyzed earlier even when the government provides a single pure public good and has no alternative policy objectives such as redistribution toward the poor, regional equity, or the encouragement of economic growth – objectives that are often used in the tax expenditure literature to explain the existence of special tax provisions that are, it is claimed, equivalent to public expenditures. (The voting model can be expanded to accommodate such additional goals if they generate political support for the government, but

---

[11] Further discussion of tax expenditures, together with an evaluation of the concept in a normative context, is given in Chapter 5.

[12] See also Surrey and McDaniel (1985).

[13] The primary expression of this approach to taxation is found in the report of the Royal Commission on Taxation (1966).

they are not needed to explain the complex nature of tax systems in democratic countries.)

It also follows that tax expenditure calculations of revenues lost via special provisions are incorrect. In a democracy, the enforced closing of special tax provisions may well lead to lower levels of revenue rather than higher levels as is implicitly assumed in existing tax expenditure budgets. By reducing the degree to which the government is able to discriminate among heterogeneous voters, the closing of special provisions tends to increase overall opposition to taxation.

A final judgment about the effect on government size of eliminating special provisions must take account of the change in demand for public services that may occur if such provisions alter relative after-tax prices of private substitutes for public services, though this is not the argument that Surrey seems to have in mind.[14] Closing a deduction for a favored private activity may in some cases lead to increased demands for publicly provided substitutes. As a result, and despite the increase in opposition to taxation, it is possible that the public sector may grow in size after elimination of certain special provisions.

3.6 CONCLUDING REMARKS

Existing tax systems are composed of a limited number of basic elements that have been combined to form complicated structures. To understand why tax systems have the appearance and characteristics that we observe, we must explain why the basic elements are used as building blocks and why they are combined in particular ways. We have demonstrated that the essential stylized facts of observed tax systems can be viewed as the outcome of optimizing political and economic behavior in a competitive political system. The argument further shows that the way in which these elements are combined into different structures depends on administration costs and on the nature of political and economic responses to taxation among individuals.

Tax structure is a system of related parts in equilibrium, not merely a collection of separate and ill-designed components. This has important implications for the understanding of tax policy. Changes must pass a political as well as an economic test, and reforms in one part of the system may lead to unexpected repercussions elsewhere as the government attempts to establish a new platform in its quest for electoral success. The analysis also suggests that the evolution of tax systems can be viewed as a sequence of responses to changing

---

[14] On the effect of closing loopholes on the size of the public sector, see also Anderson, Martin, and Tollison (1987).

economic, administrative, and political factors. Empirical work on the development and growth of tax systems should account for the systematic influence of these determinants.

The reader of this chapter may have noted that we did not use the term "rent seeking" in explaining the creation of tax structure. In a probabilistic voting model, the governing party is constrained effectively by political competition; it cannot seek rents for its own agents in the process of policy making. However, voters may spend resources to offer stronger opposition to particular types of taxation and, in doing so, may succeed in receiving special tax treatment. Such actions will be reflected in any equilibrium tax structure. Because the focus of our analysis has been on the government's actions in response to the given political behavior of voters, we have not paid special attention to the ways in which individuals may attempt to alter the influence that they or others exert on government policy.

Much of the literature on rent seeking emphasizes the failure of political competition. Yet it is important to understand policy equilibrium under politically competitive conditions before turning to the implications of shortcomings in the political process.

The foregoing analysis shows how any tax system can be understood as a part of a broader political equilibrium, but it does not imply that the tax system will be a well-designed part of that equilibrium when judged against an appropriate normative standard. The question arises as to whether and under what circumstances an equilibrium tax structure will be consistent with efficiency in the social allocation of resources. We consider this question, along with some extensions of the basic framework, in the next chapter. Readers with a particular interest in political market failure may also want to turn to Chapter 6, where the implications of such failure for tax structure are discussed in detail.

CHAPTER 4

Tax Structure in Equilibrium

A More Formal Model
Co-authored with George Warskett

> The power to make distinctions exists with full vigour in the field of taxation.
>
> Stanley Reed (quoted by Yablon 1994)

> If we assume that tax decisions are made by simple majority, the problem becomes a different one from Wicksell's.
>
> Eric Lindahl (1959, p. 17)

In the preceding chapter we argued that multiple tax bases, separate rate structures, and a variety of special provisions can be understood as a set of related policy instruments that are shaped and used by the government in the course of its continuing struggle to maintain itself in elected office. In this chapter we explore this idea further, using a model that is more formal than the one presented in Chapter 3. The model is also more detailed with respect to individual behavior, allowing for the possibility that voters may reduce their tax liabilities by "self-selecting" their level of work effort in order to alter their tax liabilities. Allowing taxpayers to mimic the behavior of others who face lower tax rates is a way of acknowledging that some characteristics of taxpayers that would be a useful basis for taxation, such as potential work effort or intellectual ability, cannot be directly observed by tax collectors.[1] This means that the government must levy taxes according to surrogate characteristics that are correlated with the basis upon which it would prefer to impose taxes, while allowing for the fact that taxpayers may choose to misrepresent themselves in response to

---

[1] Characteristics that cannot be altered by taxpayers in response to taxation would be a useful basis upon which to levy taxes – if these characteristics could be accurately measured and were not rejected by voters as a basis for taxation on the grounds of equity, justice, or fear of exploitation by the government. The reason any government in a competitive political system would be tempted to levy taxes according to such characteristics is that this would allow it to raise the same revenue from each individual as was collected under a tax system that was not based on such characteristics, while removing the incentive for individuals to engage in tax avoidance and evasion.

taxation based on these surrogate characteristics.[2] We use the reformulated model to investigate the manner in which administration costs, inequalities in relative political influence, and the ability of taxpayers to self-select interact in determining the nature of the equilibrium tax system.

While our concern in the chapter is primarily with the question of why tax systems look the way they do, we also consider conditions under which the equilibrium tax system will be Pareto-efficient, a result we summarize as the Representation Theorem.[3] As well as setting the stage for a more extensive consideration of normative issues in Chapters 5 and 6, this theorem provides us with a convenient method of characterizing the nature of equilibrium tax systems in competitive political systems – a method that we employ extensively in this and subsequent chapters.

The formality of the analysis allows additional insights, but at some cost in terms of the generality of the model and the degree of analytical difficulty. It is necessary to work with a framework that does not explicitly contain all of the elements of the tax skeleton. We consider the choice of proportional effective tax rates in a model with only one potentially taxable activity (labor income). In addition, the argument is more mathematical in nature. Readers who are not interested in the details of the mathematical exposition may prefer to focus on the relevant intuition that we present at each stage of the discussion.

We begin with the specification of a basic model in which neither administration costs nor self-selection behavior are present. This model is analogous to the basic model introduced in Section 3.3. All taxpayers engage in only one type of taxable activity – they sell labor services – but differ with respect to preferences for leisure and consumption, and the government is restricted to proportional taxation. In this world, political competition forces political parties to offer platforms that include a separate effective rate of tax for each voter according to that voter's unique economic and political characteristics.

We prove the Representation Theorem concerning the efficiency of the equilibrium for the basic model, though it applies as well to subsequent versions where administration costs and self-selection are present. The theorem shows that when the "power to make distinctions" among taxpayers is driven by political competition, its exercise will result in efficient policy outcomes under some circumstances. The name we have chosen for the theorem is suggested by the nature of the proof, which involves using a particular optimization problem to characterize or represent equilibrium policy outcomes. (This is

---

[2] The extensive literature on self-selection and taxation is surveyed by Cooper (1984), Stiglitz (1987), and Boadway (1997).

[3] We refer to this result as the Representation Theorem for convenience, although the name was not used in the original work by Coughlin and Nitzan (1981a).

the technique used repeatedly in the chapter to characterize political equilibria.) Of course, it has not escaped us that this name also alludes to the political setting in which we apply the theorem in this and later chapters. As far as we are aware, the first formal proof is due to Peter Coughlin and Shmuel Nitzan (1981a), who employed the theorem in a somewhat different context.

The Representation Theorem may be what Eric Lindahl had in mind when he stated in 1959 that one of the purposes of his dissertation (published forty years earlier) was to relax Knut Wicksell's (1896) requirement for unanimity in collective decision making as a way of ensuring efficient policy outcomes.[4] In any event, as will become apparent, Lindahl appears to have understood the intuition behind the theorem, a result that would not be a surprise to other authors such as Leif Johansen (1965). We are particularly interested in what Lindahl had to say about the efficiency of the equilibrium in a democracy because his dissertation work has been influential in the literature on the normative foundations of fiscal systems, and because his work – both as it is traditionally understood and as we interpret it – plays a role in the investigation of normative tax theory presented in Chapter 6.

Although the discussion of the efficiency of the equilibrium is normative in character, the chapter deals primarily with aspects of the positive theory of tax structure as we have pointed out. We continue with this investigation by next introducing administration costs into the basic model without as yet allowing for the possibility of self-selection. As in Chapter 3, a tax structure rather than a set of individualized tax rates emerges in a sorting equilibrium. We then consider how changes in relative political influence of different groups of taxpayers alters the nature of the sorting equilibrium. Self-selection behavior is then introduced into the model, and the effect of the interaction of administration costs and self-selection in determining an equilibrium tax structure is considered.

It turns out that the analysis we present bears in an interesting way on the issue of tax complexity, an issue that is often discussed in heated tones by tax policy analysts, politicians, and the general public without, it seems, much effect; tax systems remain complex despite the admonition of tax reformers. We draw out the implications of our analysis for this issue at several stages of the discussion. Before concluding the chapter, we deal briefly with the question of how tax complexity should be measured.

---

[4] The foregoing and later quotes from Lindahl's 1959 paper are taken from the 1960 English translation by T. L. Johnson. The quote in the headnote is from page 17. This quote may be surprising to some readers since Lindahl is widely regarded for his formalization of Wicksell's idea that unanimity in decision making would ensure Pareto efficiency. (Under unanimity, any policy making even one person worse off than the status quo may be blocked.) The English translation of the part of Lindhal's dissertation that deals with Wicksell's model is found in Musgrave and Peacock (1967, pp. 168–76).

4.1 A BASIC MODEL WITHOUT ADMINISTRATION COSTS OR SELF-SELECTION BEHAVIOR

The electoral game represented by the basic and subsequent models is similar to that presented in Chapter 3, and it has the following general structure. Economic and political responses to taxation are assumed to vary across taxpayers who vote for the party that promises to leave them with the highest level of economic well-being. Voters are fully aware of both the content and the implications for their welfare of party platforms. But the parties, who announce their platforms before a vote is taken, are uncertain about how particular individuals will cast their ballot, having (common) information only about individual voting densities.[5] Given this information, knowledge of the budget restraint they face if elected, and the anticipated platform of the opposition, each party chooses a platform that it thinks will maximize its total expected vote. In the resulting Nash equilibrium, the fiscal platforms of both parties converge, all taxpayer-voters make rational consumption–leisure choices, and the government budget is in balance.

4.1.1 Individual Taxpayers and Voting Behavior

We assume that there are H unique taxpayer-voters, $h = 1, 2, \ldots, H$, each of whom has a utility function $U^h(G, x_h, L_h)$. Here G is a pure public good, x is a private consumption good, and L is leisure. Marginal utility for any commodity is positive and declining with consumption of that good.

In the basic model, people do not disguise themselves for the purpose of taxation. However, it is convenient to allow for this possibility in setting up the basic framework. Following Joseph Stiglitz (1982), we therefore assume that individuals differ in ability or level of effort as indicated by their wage rate w_h and we consider income y_h, which depends on the wage rate and hours of work, to be the base on which taxation is levied. When allowance is made for self-selection behavior in a subsequent version of the model, the wage will be assumed to be unobservable by the tax authorities.

In all cases, taxation is proportional to labor income with a unique rate, t_h, for each taxpayer, and lump-sum taxation is excluded. Thus, for $1 - L_h$ hours of work, taxpayer h who earns a wage w_h receives $y_h = w_h(1 - L_h)$ as income before tax and an after-tax income of $x_h = w_h(1 - t_h)(1 - L_h)$.

Since the base on which taxes are levied is income y_h, it is useful to write $U^h(G, x_h, L_h) = u^h(G, x_h, y_h)$, where income instead of leisure is considered to

---

[5] Of course, neither parties nor voters have perfect information about the structure of the economy. Moreover, voters do not know with certainty what the parties will do once elected. These types of uncertainty are not formally integrated into the analysis, except that allowance is made for self-selection behavior by voters.

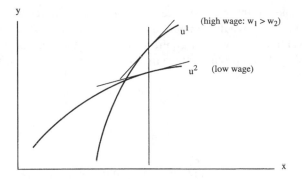

Figure 4.1.   The single crossing property

be chosen by taxpayers. Figure 4.1 shows indifference curves for $u^h(G, x_h, y_h)$ in the (x, y) plane for a high-wage individual labeled 1 and for a low-wage taxpayer 2. The curves are positively sloped, since an increase in income requires more labor or less leisure and thus reduces welfare (with x fixed).

The slope of the indifference curve for the high-wage person, given by the ratio of partial derivatives of utility $u^1_x/(-u^1_y)$, is shown in the figure as always being steeper than that for the lower-wage person for a given x. In this case, which we assume always holds, the indifference curves in the (x, y) plane cross at most once, a feature of preferences that helps to simplify the analysis when self-selection behavior is allowed for in a later section.[6] When preferences vary across individual taxpayers, the single crossing property of indifference curves must be imposed directly. To sharpen results it is necessary at various points to simplify further by assuming that preferences are identical so that individuals differ only with respect to their wage rate and their political influence. When preferences are identical, a sufficient condition for indifference maps to exhibit the single crossing property is that consumption be a normal good (Seade 1977, p. 206).[7]

As noted earlier, taxpayers are assumed to know what the parties propose to do if elected, and to vote for the party whose proposed platform would, if

---

[6] The single crossing property of indifference curves is also referred to as "agent monotonicity" (see Seade 1982, p. 638). The single crossing property leads to a monotonic relationship in equilibrium between wages, incomes, and (proportional) tax rates that is of help in characterizing the nature of tax structure when taxpayers may self-select their (unobservable) level of work effort.

[7] The slope of the indifference curve of individual h at a point in the income–consumption plane shown in Figure 4.1 is $(u^h_x/-u^h_y) = w \cdot (U^h_x/U^h_L)$, where L is leisure. Consider two individuals who are at the same point in the plane. If consumption is a normal good, then the person with the higher wage who consumes more leisure at that point will have a marginal rate of substitution of consumption for leisure that is lower (i.e., U_x/U_L is higher). It follows that the slope of the indifference curve for the higher-wage person must be steeper at the given point.

implemented, generate the highest level of individual welfare. In order to assess how well off they would be under any proposed fiscal system, individuals take as given both the level of public services and their personal rate of taxation implied by the proposal and then maximize their own utility subject to their budget restraint.

Given tax rates and the size of government, individual utility maximization requires that

$$\frac{u_x^h}{-u_y^h} = \frac{1}{1 - t_h} \quad \text{for} \quad h = 1, 2, \ldots, H, \tag{4.1}$$

where $u^h\big(G, (1 - t_h)y_h, y_h\big)$ is expressed as u^h and the subscripts x and y again denote partial derivatives of the utility function with respect to these variables.

Whereas voters know what the parties propose to do if elected, political parties do not know with certainty how each voter will respond at the polls. The parties do have common knowledge of the probability densities f_h describing individual voting behavior. We assume that f_h as seen by the parties depends only on the *difference* in utilities that would result from the adoption of the proposals of the incumbent (i) and the opposition (o).[8] Thus the probability that h votes for the incumbent may be written as $\pi_{hi} = f_h\big[u_i^h - u_o^h\big]$, where u_j^h refers to the utility of voter h under the proposal of party j and where $\partial f_h / \partial\big(u_i^h - u_o^h\big) > 0$.[9] The probability π_{ho} is equal to $1 - \pi_{hi}$ and has the analogous properties.

We must also assume that the probability that each taxpayer votes for either party is always positive even though that probability may at times be very small. Otherwise, as discussed in Chapter 2, vote cycling may reemerge when voters who provide no support for an incumbent, and who therefore are very heavily taxed, lend support to any new proposal that offers them even a small increase in welfare.

Probabilities of voting $\big($such as $f_h\big)$ may be derived in various ways (see e.g. Coughlin et al. 1990a and b and Coughlin 1992). A specific derivation is given in Chapter 7, where a probabilistic voting model is implemented in a computable general equilibrium setting using real data. However, at this point, the formulation just given is sufficient for our purposes.

4.1.2   The Platforms of the Parties and the Political Equilibrium

Each party chooses a fiscal platform $s = \{t_1, t_2, \ldots, t_H, G\}$ consisting of a set of proportional tax rates and the level of a public good so as to maximize its total expected vote. The expected vote for the incumbent, EV_i, is the sum of

---

[8] For alternative formulations, see for example Coughlin (1992).

[9] We could write f_h as depending on indirect utilities, but it is convenient to use the direct utility functions instead. We ensure that the model is consistent with rational consumption–leisure decisions by including (4.1) as a constraint on political optimization.

individual vote probabilities $\sum_h f_h[u_i^h - u_o^h]$, and the expected vote for the opposition is $EV_o = H - EV_i$.[10] The parties have common knowledge concerning voting densities and, in the basic model, are constrained in their choice of platforms only by individual economic responses to taxation as represented by (4.1) and by the government budget restraint that every party faces if elected.

Given the nature of individual consumption–leisure decisions and the government budget restraint, all of which we represent generally for the moment as $F(s) = 0$, an optimal strategy for the incumbent (analogously for the opposition) consists of tax rates t_{hi} and the level of the public good G that maximize EV_i subject to $F(t_{1i}, t_{2i}, \ldots, t_{Hi}, G) = 0$. The first-order conditions for the choice of tax rates are

$$\left[\frac{\partial f_h}{\partial u^h} \cdot \frac{\partial u^h}{\partial t_{hi}}\right] \bigg/ \frac{\partial F}{\partial t_{hi}} = \alpha \quad \text{for} \quad h = 1, 2, \ldots, H, \qquad (4.2)$$

where α represents the Lagrange multiplier associated with the constraint. A similar condition for the choice of G also applies. Political optimization requires the adoption of a platform in which the net marginal vote productivity of each policy instrument is equalized.

We recall from the previous chapter that, if the possible values of policy instruments constitute a convex and compact set, then a pure strategy Nash equilibrium in fiscal policy platforms is assured if, after substitution of the constraints, the following conditions on the expected vote functions are satisfied: For each party j, EV_j is continuous in the policy space $\{s_i \times s_o\}$ and quasi concave in each s_j. The equilibrium will be unique if the expected vote function for each party is strictly concave in its own policy platform.[11] Again, we assume that all previous conditions for a unique Nash equilibrium are satisfied. (We note that, in the computable general equilibrium version of the model implemented in Chapter 7 for the United States, there is sufficient concavity for an equilibrium to exist in the neighborhood of the actual fiscal structure to which the model is calibrated.)

Before proceeding to characterize the equilibrium tax structure in the basic model, it is important to note that the platforms of the two parties converge in the equilibrium. (A proof of policy convergence based on that by Enelow and

---

[10] In the absence of abstentions that are affected by policy choices, policies consistent with expected vote maximization are equivalent to those under expected plurality maximization, since a plurality for i is: $EV_i - EV_o = EV_i - (H - EV_i) = 2EV_i - H$, where H is the number of voters. When the size of the electorate approaches infinity or when the electoral contest is a symmetric game, these two objectives are equivalent to (yield the same policy choices as) maximization of the probability of winning. See for example Ledyard (1984) and Aranson, Hinich, and Ordeshook (1974), as well as the discussion in Ordeshook (1986, Chap. 4).

[11] The factors determining the concavity of the expected vote function are extensively analyzed by Enelow and Hinich (1989).

Hinich 1989, is provided in the Appendix to this chapter.) Convergence of platforms results from the strict concavity of the expected vote functions and the assumption that the probability of voting depends only on the difference in utilities under the platforms of the opposing parties.[12] Under these conditions, neither party can gain an electoral advantage by deviating from a common equilibrium platform, since doing so allows the other party to establish a candidate utility differential that increases that party's expected vote relative to that of the other party. Since convergence occurs, we may cease using the subscripts i and o to distinguish between the fiscal choices of the incumbent and opposition parties.

Our reliance upon a model in which convergence of policy platforms occurs does not mean that we think that party platforms are, in fact, always identical. (For evidence on this matter concerning the United States, see e.g. Alesina and Rosenthal 1995, Chap. 2.) Nonetheless, it is convenient to work with a model in which convergence occurs, for two reasons. First, it is worthwhile to deal with nonconvergence only if this feature can be explicitly related to specific aspects of tax structure; this does not seem possible at this time. Second, and perhaps more importantly in our view, the main features of tax systems are for the most part quite stable across electoral periods in democratic countries, even though the opening and closing of some special provisions may be related to changes of government. (This is the case, for example, in the empirical study presented in Chapter 10.) Thus we think that it is possible to use a model in which platforms converge without at the same time omitting features that are crucial to the understanding of the main features of democratic tax systems.

4.1.3   The Representation Theorem

It is convenient that an equilibrium policy platform in the model just outlined can be characterized by optimizing a function that is a particular weighted sum of taxpayer utilities (Coughlin and Nitzan 1981a, Coughlin 1992). The synthetic problem that can be used to replicate or represent an equilibrium involves choosing a fiscal platform $s = \{t_1, t_2, \ldots, t_H, G\}$ subject to the constraint $F(s) = 0$ to maximize what we shall call a *political support function*

$$S = \sum_h \theta_h u^h(h), \tag{4.3}$$

where $\theta_h = \partial f_h / \partial u^h$ is the sensitivity (of an individual h's probability of voting for any party) to changes in h's welfare at the Nash equilibrium.

---

[12] Platforms may not converge if voting depends in part on how policy choices interact with voter assessments of party competence or credibility (see e.g. Enelow, Endersby, and Munger 1993), or if each party uses a different set of instruments (Coughlin et al., 1990ab). Also, as discussed by Wittman (1990), convergence may not occur if politicians have a preference for particular policy outcomes.

It is easy to see that the solution to this problem can be used to describe equilibrium policy choices. Ignoring subscripts that refer to the incumbent, it is evident that the first-order conditions for the problem of choosing rates t_h to maximize S subject to $F(t_1, t_2, \ldots, t_H, G) = 0$ are given by equations (4.2) after substitution of the equilibrium values of the θ_h. But these equations are exactly the ones that characterize the vote-maximizing tax rates adopted in equilibrium by both the incumbent and the opposition.[13] An analogous argument applies to the choice of G. (A more formal statement and proof of the theorem is provided in the Appendix.)

We shall refer to the demonstration of equivalence between the Nash equilibrium fiscal platform and the fiscal system that optimizes the political support function (2.3) as the Representation Theorem, though the term was not used in the original work by Peter Coughlin and Shmuel Nitzan.[14] The intuition behind the theorem can be stated as follows. Unless the support function S is maximized, marginal changes in expected political support are not equalized across voters. It would then be possible for the opposition to increase its overall level of electoral support by adopting a platform that increases the welfare of (and support from) some voters, especially those whose political sensitivity θ_h is relatively high, even if this requires a reduction in the welfare of and support from others. Political competition ensures that, in equilibrium, no such support-improving policies remain to be proposed.

We shall use the Representation Theorem to characterize the equilibrium in the basic model as well as that of subsequent models that include administration costs and self-selection. In the basic model, where the specific constraints on political optimization consist of the government budget restraint $\left(\sum_h t_h y_h = G\right)$ and the conditions for rational consumption–leisure choices given in (4.1), the theorem indicates that the equilibrium fiscal system maximizes the support function (4.3) subject to the budget restraint and conditions (4.1). The equilibrium fiscal system thus solves the first-order conditions for the Lagrangean

$$\mathcal{L} = \sum_h \theta_h u^h(t_h) + \lambda \left[\sum_h (t_h y_h) - G \right]$$

$$+ \sum_h \phi_h \left[\frac{-u_y^h}{u_x^h} - (1 - t_h) \right], \quad (4.4)$$

---

[13] The assumption that the expected vote functions are concave is sufficient to ensure that a fiscal system that satisfies the first-order conditions for the problem of maximizing S also satisfies the second-order conditions for maximization of the expected vote functions. The nature of assumptions required for the maximization of support functions like S to replicate or represent a Nash equilibrium are discussed further by Coughlin (1992).

[14] For development of alternative versions of the result, see Ledyard (1984), Coughlin et al. (1990ab), Coughlin (1992), Chen (1994), and Yang (1995).

where again $\theta_h = \partial f_h / \partial u^h$, $u^h(t_h)$ refers to the utility function $u^h(G, (1 - t_h)y_h, y_h)$, subscripts on utility denote a partial derivative with respect to the indicated variable, and λ and ϕ_h are Lagrange multipliers.

The first-order conditions for G and t_h are[15]

$$\sum_h \theta_h u_G^h - \lambda + \sum_h \phi_h \left[\frac{\partial}{\partial G} \left(\frac{-u_y^h}{u_x^h} \right) \right] = 0 \quad \text{and} \tag{4.5a}$$

$$-y_h \theta_h u_x^h + y_h \lambda + \phi_h \left[\frac{\partial}{\partial t_h} \left(\frac{-u_y^h}{u_x^h} \right) + 1 \right] = 0 \tag{4.5b}$$

for $h = 1, 2, \ldots, H$. In implementing the fiscal system described by these equations, the government balances the heterogeneous and conflicting interests of the electorate by choosing tax rates according to individual economic and political characteristics. The tax system is complex, with a separate effective rate being levied on each distinct taxpayer. Any simpler system would allow another party to increase its chances for electoral success.

We also note for further use that, in the equilibrium described by equations (4.5a) and (4.5b), an increase in the weight θ_h on the utility of voter h in the political support function leads to a reduction in t_h and to an increase in other ts, so that (4.5b) remains satisfied through the decrease in u_x^h that results from the improvement in h's welfare and through an increase in other u_xs. Since an increase in θ_h leads to an improvement in voter h's welfare, we may use this weight as an indicator of the effective political influence exerted by voter h on the equilibrium outcome.

4.1.4   Some Comments on the Efficiency of the Political Equilibrium

Although our concern in this chapter is primarily with the positive theory of tax structure, it is of some further interest at this point to consider the normative character of the equilibrium revealed by the Representation Theorem. This discussion also serves as a prelude to the more lengthy consideration of related normative issues in Chapter 6.

In the first place, it is important to point out that reliance on the Representation Theorem does not carry the implication that we are engaged in some sort of optimal tax analysis. Tax rates in the model are not part of an optimal tax blueprint chosen by a social planner pursuing exogenously specified social goals. Rather, they are part of a political and economic equilibrium that can be

---

[15] The government budget restraint, which is also part of the first-order conditions, is omitted for the sake of brevity here and in what follows.

characterized by solving a particular synthetic optimization problem. The linear form of the function that is optimized, as well as the values of the influence weights applied to individual utilities (the θ_h) in the political support function, are determined by the structure of the electoral game. The similarity to optimal tax reasoning of the explanation for the Representation Theorem given earlier arises because voters care about their economic welfare, and because political parties are forced by competition for votes to take the consequences of taxation for both economic welfare and voting behavior into account.

Because the political support function is a weighted sum of individual utilities, it follows immediately from the Representation Theorem that the equilibrium fiscal system lies in the Pareto set of policies for the electorate.[16] Thus, while reliance on the theorem does not mean that the resulting analysis is an exercise in optimal taxation, as we have just pointed out, it could be said that there is an "invisible hand" in the political system we are investigating in this chapter. We could also say that we are here exploring the nature of the equilibrium tax system in a perfectly functioning competitive political system.

Two features of the model presented in this chapter are crucial to the "invisible hand" result. First, individual voting decisions are based on correct assessments of how tax and other policies proposed by the parties affect individual economic welfare.[17] Individual voting decisions are not biased by incorrect or purposively misleading information. Second, political competition leads each political party to continually maximize its expected plurality or vote defined over all voters. (Recall that the probability of support from any voter can never fall to zero if a majority-rule equilibrium is to exist.) As discussed in Chapter 6, relaxation of these and other conditions may result in a tax system that leads the economy to an allocation that is economically inefficient.

We pointed out in the introduction of this chapter that earlier writers were aware of the possibility that political competition could lead to efficient outcomes even without the unanimity rule advocated by Knut Wicksell. Before returning to our positive analysis, we briefly acknowledge two of these earlier views.

---

[16] Pareto efficiency is a necessary condition for a support-maximizing platform, but it is not sufficient. Some points on the Pareto frontier will be politically more advantageous than others, depending on the influence weights $(\theta_h s)$ in the support function.

[17] Implicit in this statement is the assumption that voting decisions are based on an assessment of how party platforms, if implemented, would affect individual well-being. In this sense, voting behavior is instrumental (concerned with the links between voting, electoral outcomes, and individual welfare). Brennan and Lomasky (1993) analyze expressive voting, which occurs when people cast their ballots to express feelings and desires that are independent of the potential electoral consequences of the voting act and hence may involve voting decisions that are not closely connected to the economic consequences of proposed policy platforms. We leave the analysis of the effects of expressive voting on equilibrium tax structures for future research.

Eric Lindahl (1959), who first formalized Wicksell's idea that unanimity in collective decisions would result in efficient policy outcomes, showed his awareness of the role of political opposition in the adoption of tax policies. The quotation that follows indicates his belief that successful government policy takes the heterogeneous and opposing interests of all voters carefully into account. Such a balancing of individual interests is also a prerequisite for efficient policy outcomes. In Lindahl's view, the majority may use benefit and ability-to-pay principles in designing taxation since these principles reflect the views of voters, including those in the minority, and lead to an accommodation that allows a higher budget than would otherwise be possible.

> That the taxation forced on the minority is also influenced to some extent by the benefit and ability principles can most readily be explained on the basis of the concept of "political cost." ... The resistance of the minority to taxation which it considers unjust can be assumed to be less if the minority can discover a certain measure of justice in the injustice. ... In other words, the amount of taxation which the majority can force upon a minority is greater, given the political cost, the greater is the attention which the majority pays to the interests of the minority. (p. 22)[18]

Leif Johansen (1965), who was a leading interpreter of Lindhal's work, was even more explicit than Lindahl about the possibility for efficiency in policy outcomes under majority rule:

> It is clear that by majority decisions it should be possible to arrive at a Pareto-optimal solution; for, assuming that we consider a proposal which is such that it is possible to arrive at another proposal, which improves the situation for one or several parties, without making it worse for any other party, then no-one would have any motive for preferring the first-mentioned proposal in preference to the second. There would be a unanimous transition from the first proposal ... to the second solution. ... Thus, in using majority decisions we would not acquiesce in a solution that is not Pareto-optimal. (p. 141)

4.2 ADMINISTRATION COSTS AND TAX STRUCTURE IN A SORTING EQUILIBRIUM

We continue our investigation of equilibrium tax structure with the observation that, in the face of substantial administration costs, no party would ever propose a tax system like that described by the first-order conditions (4.5) of the basic model. Relevant administration costs include the costs of determining the individually correct (politically optimal) tax rates and the costs of measuring

---

[18] The page reference is taken from the 1960 translation of the 1959 paper. In a footnote (note 25 of the 1960 translation), Lindahl attributes the term "political cost" to Carlo A. Conigliani in a public finance treatise published in 1894.

economic activity for each individual, as well as enforcement and collection costs. The reason for rejecting the system described by equations (4.5) is that – in order to economize on administration costs, which are a wedge between tax revenues and the public services demanded by voters – political parties will be forced to group or sort taxpayers into rate bands within which different individuals are taxed at the same rate. In this section we characterize in some detail the tax structure that emerges in what was referred to in the last chapter as a "sorting equilibrium." We also consider how this tax structure is affected by changes in political influence.

Grouping of taxpayers for the purpose of economizing on administration costs requires the government to simultaneously solve three related problems: (i) choosing the optimal number of groups or rate bands; (ii) correctly allocating or sorting taxpayers among these groups; and (iii) choosing the rates of taxation that are to be levied on the members of each group of voters. We begin a more formal inquiry into the nature of the sorting equilibrium with the second and third problems of sorting and taxing, for the moment taking the number of groups as given.

4.2.1   Sorting and Taxing with a Given Number of Groups

Suppose that all taxpayers are grouped into N rate bands $(n_1, n_2, \ldots, n_N)$ with associated tax rates $(t_1, t_2, \ldots, t_N)$, and that N is less than the number of taxpayers $\sum_i n_i = H$. Since voters are not taxed on an individual basis, opposition to taxation will generally be greater than in the basic model where everyone is treated differently. The loss in support from grouping H voters into N groups for the purpose of taxation (instead of taxing all individuals uniquely) is given generally by

$$\Delta S = \sum_{i=1}^{N} \sum_{h \in I_i} \theta_h \, du^h(t_i), \tag{4.6}$$

where $I_i = \{h | t_h = t_i\}$ and where the total differential $du^h(t_i)$ refers to the change in utility resulting from use of the group tax rates t_i instead of the support-maximizing individual rates, say t_h^*, defined in the absence of administration costs by equations (4.5). This expression is deceptively simple in appearance, and we shall have to resort to specific examples in order to investigate further the loss in support from grouping.

Before proceeding, however, we write down the Lagrangean expression and resulting first-order conditions for the (third) complementary problem of choosing G and group tax rates t_i that are to be applied to the N groups of taxpayers so as to maximize expected votes. The Lagrangean for this problem is

$$\mathscr{L} = \sum_{i=1}^{N} \sum_{h \in I_i} \theta_h u^h\big(G, (1 - t_i)y_h, y_h\big)$$

$$+ \lambda \left[\sum_{i=1}^{N} \left(t_i \cdot \sum_{h \in I_i} y_h \right) - G \right]$$

$$+ \sum_{i=1}^{N} \sum_{h \in I_i} \phi_h \left[\frac{-u_y^h(t_i)}{u_x^h(t_i)} - (1 - t_i) \right], \tag{4.7}$$

where the index i refers now to a group of taxpayers rather than to the incumbent party, and where we have explicitly indicated the group tax rate t_i applying to each rate band or group of taxpayers. The index sets I_i are mutually exclusive and cover the set $(1, 2, \ldots, H)$. The corresponding first-order conditions for G and the ts are, for $i = 1, 2, \ldots, N$,

$$\sum_{h=1}^{H} \theta_h u_G^h(t_i) - \lambda + \sum_{h=1}^{H} \phi_h \left[\frac{\partial}{\partial G}\left(\frac{-u_y^h(t_i)}{u_x^h(t_i)} \right) \right] = 0 \quad \text{and} \tag{4.8a}$$

$$-\left(\sum_{h \in I_i} y_h \right)^{-1} \sum_{h \in I_i} y_h \theta_h u_x^h(t_i) + \lambda$$

$$-\left(\sum_{h \in I_i} y_h \right)^{-1} \sum_{h \in I_i} \phi_h A^h + \left(\sum_{h \in I_i} y_h \right)^{-1} \sum_{h \in I_i} \phi_h = 0, \tag{4.8b}$$

where $A^h = \partial\big[-u_y^h(t_i)/u_x^h(t_i)\big]/\partial t_i$ for each $h \in I_i$. Here, in contrast to equations (4.5b) of the basic model, the marginal utilities of private consumption are no longer considered on an individual basis. In (4.8b) what matters is a weighted average of the marginal utilities of consumption within each taxpayer group or rate band. It is also clear from equations (4.8) that changing the nature of the grouping $\big($the index sets $I_i\big)$ must alter the solution for the optimal group tax rates.

As we stated earlier, and as will become apparent in the course of discussion, investigating the sorting of taxpayers formally is a difficult task, even in the simple model we have constructed. We therefore proceed by considering two specific cases. In the first of these, all first-order conditions can be linearized as a function of tax rates and, as a result, the sorting problem turns into a problem in the analysis of variance. In the second example, all voters share the same preference function and differ only with respect to their wage rates and political influence.

Case 1: The first-order conditions may be linearized. In the linear case it is useful to begin by rewriting the first-order conditions (4.5b) of the basic model to acknowledge that each voter h will be placed in some group i:

$$y_{hi}\theta_{hi}u_x^{hi}\left(t_{hi}\right) - \phi_{hi}\left[\frac{\partial}{\partial t_{hi}}\left(\frac{-u_y^{hi}\left(t_{hi}\right)}{u_x^{hi}\left(t_{hi}\right)}\right) + 1\right] = y_{hi}\cdot\lambda$$

$$\text{for} \quad h = 1, 2, \ldots, H, \quad i \in I_i, \quad\quad (4.5b')$$

where the dependence of terms on t_{hi} is explicitly noted. The left side of (4.5b′) may be thought of as the marginal political cost, in terms of expected votes, resulting from an increase in the rate t_{hi} levied on taxpayer h in group i. The right side can be regarded as the marginal political benefit that is generated by spending the extra revenue y_{hi} on public services.

Let us then assume that, in the absence of administration costs, the marginal losses and gains in support from changing t_{hi} depend linearly on tax rates as follows, where each side of the next equation corresponds to the same side of (4.5b′):

$$\alpha_{hi} + \beta\cdot t_{hi} = \delta_{hi} - \gamma\cdot t_{hi} \quad \text{for} \quad \beta > 0 \quad \text{and} \quad \gamma > 0. \quad\quad (4.5c)$$

Heterogeneity in economic and political behavior is captured in this linear version of the first-order conditions by constant terms that vary across taxpayers, and marginal political costs (benefits) are assumed to rise (fall) continuously with the tax rate.[19] This is illustrated by Figure 4.2. The optimal tax rate, t_{hi}^*, for voter h in the absence of administration costs is shown in the figure as the rate where marginal political cost and benefit curves, representing (respectively) the left and right sides of (4.5b), intersect.

Now suppose that the group rate for voter h in the presence of grouping is the rate $t_i > t_{hi}^*$, as determined by equations (4.5). Relative to the situation with costless tax administration, the levying of this group rate instead of the optimal rate results in a loss in support from taxpayer h measured by the area between the marginal political cost and benefit curves over the interval from t_{hi}^* to t_i. This area, shown as the shaded triangle in Figure 4.2, can be expressed as an integral equal to $v\cdot\left(t_i - t_{hi}^*\right)^2$, where $v = (\beta + \gamma)/2$. Thus the loss in support from taxing all members of group i alike at rate t_i is equal to $v\cdot\sum_h\left(t_i - t_{hi}^*\right)^2$, where the summation is over all $h \in I_i$. The rate t_i that minimizes this loss is the least-squares solution $t_{\cdot i} = \sum_i\left(t_{hi}^*/n_i\right)$; this implies that, for a given assignment of taxpayers to groups, the total loss in support from grouping taxpayers into N rate groups can be reduced to $v\cdot\sum_i\sum_h\left(t_{\cdot i} - t_{hi}^*\right)^2$, where the second sum is essentially the variance of optimal rates within a given

---

[19] As t_{hi} increases, the marginal utility of consumption u_x^{hi} on the left side of (4.5b′) increases as the individual's consumption $x_h = \left(1 - t_{hi}\right)y_{hi}$ declines. Therefore, it is reasonable to assume that the marginal political cost of taxation increases with the tax rate. Since the marginal utility of the public good u_G^{hi} declines with the size of the public sector, it is also reasonable to assume that the marginal political benefit of raising t_{hi} and using the extra revenue to provide public services declines with the tax rate.

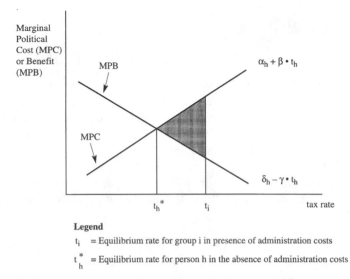

Figure legend text:

Marginal Political Cost (MPC) or Benefit (MPB)

MPB

$\alpha_h + \beta \cdot t_h$

MPC

$\delta_h - \gamma \cdot t_h$

t_h^* t_i tax rate

Legend

t_i = Equilibrium rate for group i in presence of administration costs

t_h^* = Equilibrium rate for person h in the absence of administration costs

Figure 4.2.   The loss in political support due to grouping

group. This loss can be made as small as possible if taxpayers are distributed among groups so that the variance of the t_{hi}^*s within each group is minimized and the variance in these ts between groups is maximized, a classic analysis of variance solution. Thus, in the linearized case, those with similar t_{hi}^*s would be grouped together and taxed according to the within-group average of these optimal rates.

Case 2: Identical preferences.   Without resorting to the strong linearity assumption, one that is not suitable for the analysis in the chapter as a whole, the nature of the groups into which taxpayers are sorted can be described if we are prepared to restrict the way in which taxpayers differ. For example, if utility functions are identical so that the only characteristics distinguishing taxpayers are income and political influence $\left(\text{as measured by the } \theta_h\right)$, then the government will sort people so that the variance in incomes within each group is as small as possible, again setting group tax rates according to a certain within-group average characteristic. This case is illustrated in Figure 4.3. For convenience in drawing this figure, we consider a group of taxpayers with two members, $h - 1$ and h, who are identical in all respects except that person h has a higher income than person $h - 1$.

To proceed further with this example, we also make the following three simplifying assumptions. (i) We assume incomes are fixed so that the terms in ϕ_h in (4.5b) and (4.8b) may be ignored – in this case the optimal tax rate, t_h^*, for person h in the absence of sorting is given in the figure by $\lambda = \theta_h u_x^h\left(t_h\right)$,

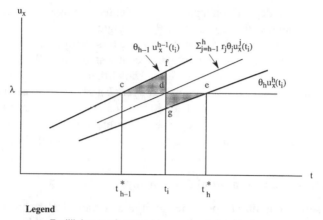

Legend

t_i = Equilibrium rate for group i in presence of administration costs

t_h^* = Equilibrium rate for person h in the absence of administration costs

Figure 4.3. A sorting equilibrium

and the equilibrium condition corresponding to (4.8b) for the two-person group can be depicted in Figure 4.3 as the solution to

$$\lambda = r_{h-1}\theta_{h-1}u_x^{h-1}(t_i) + r_h\theta_h u_x^h(t_i),\qquad(4.8b')$$

where r_h denotes each individual's relative group income $y_h/\Sigma_h y_h$ for $h \in I_i$. (ii) We assume that λ, the marginal political benefit from spending another dollar on public services, remains the same before and after grouping, so that we can use (4.5b) and (4.8b) as amended to compare tax rates with and without grouping.[20] (iii) We assume that the common utility function has the constant elasticity of substitution (CES) form, in which case $u_{xt} > 0$ and $u_{xy} < 0$.[21] Assumption (iii) ensures that each person's weighted marginal utility of consumption curve shown in the figure has a positive slope $\left(\text{since } u_{xt} > 0\right)$, and that person $h - 1$'s curve lies above that of person h $\left(\text{since } u_{xy} < 0\right)$.

In Figure 4.3 we can see that, owing to grouping, person $h - 1$ pays a higher group rate t_i than if the government discriminated fully among taxpayers, while h pays a lower rate. The group tax rate is set as in the linearized example considered earlier – that is, according to an average group characteristic, although here it is not the same characteristic as in the previous case. As

---

[20] Neither this nor assumption (i) is required for the earlier analysis of variance example.

[21] In the CES case, after dropping the h superscript, $u(x, G, y) = \left(G^\rho + x^\rho + \left(1 - yw^{-1}\right)^\rho\right)^{1/\rho}$ where $y = w(1 - L)$. Thus, $u_x = (u/x)^{1-\rho}$ for $\rho < 1$. Since $x = (1 - t)y$, it follows that $u_{xt} > 0$ and $u_{xy} < 0$.

the figure shows, t_i depends on a particular weighted average of marginal utilities of consumption with the r_h and the θ_h as weights.

As shown in the Appendix to this chapter, the loss in support from grouping under these conditions, is conveniently represented in Figure 4.3 by the sum of the shaded triangles *cfd* and *deg*. The figure shows that the loss in support from grouping will be smaller the closer are taxpayers h and $h - 1$ to each other in the income distribution, since the shaded triangles will be smaller in that case (recall that $u_{xy} < 0$ in the CES case). The government will then sort taxpayers so that the variance in incomes within each group is minimized.[22]

4.2.2   The Equilibrium Number of Groups

In the two sorting equilibria represented in Figures 4.2 and 4.3, the nature of heterogeneity within the electorate is limited in particular ways. In the real world, where responses to taxation depend on several important factors besides income (including age, family status, health, occupation, type of investment income, place of residence, and other characteristics), the sorting problem is much more complicated. We should expect that party strategists and tax policy analysts in government will be continually challenged as they try to find a solution to this problem in the face of changing circumstances. The task they face is complicated even further by the need to decide upon the equilibrium number of rate bands, in addition to solving the sorting problem for a given number of groups.

Our analysis of the equilibrium number of groups relies on the graphical solution presented in Figure 3.2, since we are not able to formally solve all three of the listed problems at the same time. We recall from Chapter 3 that adding more groups or rate bands reduces the net loss in support associated with grouping individuals for tax purposes, while at the same time raising the costs of administering the tax system and hence reducing the benefits that government can deliver with any given total level of tax revenues. The marginal increase in support as the number of rate bands is increased is given by the marginal tax discrimination curve *AA* in Figure 3.2, while the marginal loss in support due to the increased administration costs associated with greater complexity is shown as the marginal tax discrimination curve *BB*.

The equilibrium degree of tax complexity – that is, the number of rate bands that emerges in a political equilibrium – is given by the intersection of the two curves at $N^* < H$. The equilibrium tax structure is less complex than in the

---

[22] It may be helpful to note that if the two members of the group shown in the figure had the same income, their weighted marginal utility curves would coincide with each other, with both lying on top of the dotted line. In that limiting case, $t_{h-1}^* = t_i = t_h^*$, and only one appropriately chosen group rate would be needed to maintain tax rates at their optimal levels in the absence of administration costs.

basic model where there is one unique rate for each distinct taxpayer. This is a sorting equilibrium in which dissimilar taxpayers are grouped and taxed alike. As pointed out in Chapter 3, a similar analysis could be used to explain why different activities conducted by different taxpayers will be grouped into what we could call tax bases and taxed in the same manner even though each activity makes a unique contribution to each taxpayer's welfare.

In the rest of this chapter we investigate the shape and position of the tax discrimination curve in some detail. This turns out to be a useful way of inquiring into the nature of the equilibrium tax structure.

4.2.3   The Shape of the Tax Discrimination and Tax Administration Curves

The equilibrium number of rate bands defined by the intersection of the marginal tax discrimination curve and the marginal tax administration curve is well-defined if the former slopes downward continuously, and the latter is horizontal or continually upward sloping. (We have shown the tax administration curve as upward sloping in Figure 3.2.)

As noted earlier, we assume that administration costs do not decline at the margin with the number of distinctions among individuals that are embedded in the tax system. Given the marginal political benefit of another dollar of public services, this implies that the marginal tax discrimination curve – which shows the marginal loss in support as tax complexity is increased and revenues are diverted away from the provision of public services – is horizontal or upward sloping. (The marginal loss in support as the complexity of the tax system is increased is equal to the product of the increase in administration costs and the marginal political benefit of spending another dollar on public services.) In future work it may be possible to relate the costs of enforcement and collection, and thus the shape of the tax administration curve, to individual optimizing behavior in an explicit fashion. This would require an analysis of how audit and penalty structures emerge (along with the structure of taxes) in response to the costs of discriminating between taxpayers with respect to tax auditing, enforcement, and collection.

To see why it is reasonable to draw a marginal tax discrimination curve in Figure 3.2 that is downward sloping, we note first that there is indeed a political benefit to be derived from the addition of a further bracket. At worst, the new rate, say t_h, can be used to place one individual, h, at the point where the first-order conditions (4.5) of the basic model are satisfied. This particular individual would then no longer contribute to the net loss in support from grouping and political support would rise accordingly. But the government can do better than this since the new arrangement with t_h violates the optimality conditions in the presence of sorting given by equations (4.8). The government is in a suboptimal yet improved situation when one rate band is added but re-sorting has not been carried out; re-sorting of taxpayers can further enhance its position.

Although each additional rate band leaves the government with a higher level of support, it is reasonable to suppose that the benefit of adding another rate band declines with the number of bands. Consider the case of four individuals whose politically optimal rates t_h^* (in the absence of administration costs) are uniformly distributed over a given interval. Starting with one rate band and going to two, the loss from grouping will be reduced substantially as the distances $|t_i - t_h^*|$ between group rates t_i and individually optimal rates, which determine the size of the loss triangles in Figure 4.3, are greatly shortened. On introducing a third rate band the loss is reduced further, but by a smaller amount since the differences between group and optimal rates do not decline as much.[23] The introduction of a fourth rate reduces the loss from grouping to zero, though from an already low level, so that the reduction in loss is always smaller with each new band.

From these considerations we may informally conclude that the marginal tax discrimination curve slopes downward everywhere. A formal proof (provided in Warskett, Winer, and Hettich 1998) is complicated by the fact that each additional rate band involves a finer partitioning of the same taxpayers and thus the emergence of a new, *finite*-sized, group in addition to a reduction in the size of all previously existing groups.[24]

4.2.4   Political Influence and Administration Costs

How is the equilibrium tax system affected by changes in the relative political influence of different groups? This is an interesting question that can be asked only within the context of a model in which collective choice plays an explicit role.

We have in mind a situation where lower-income taxpayers become politically more active for some reason, a situation we represent by a rise in the relative size of the weights (the θ) attached to members of this group in the political support function. In order to investigate this situation, we must again assume that gross labor incomes are exogenous and that all preferences are identical and have the CES form. In addition, we shall also assume that political influence *within* any group of taxpayers is equal.

Under these circumstances it is possible to show that, when the political influence of lower-income taxpayers rises substantially relative to that of

---

[23] The argument can be made somewhat more formal by considering the limits of integration in the expression for the total loss in support from grouping given by equation (4A.4) of the Appendix to this chapter.

[24] The formal proof makes use of the assumptions that there is a continuum of taxpayers with identical CES preferences and fixed labor incomes.

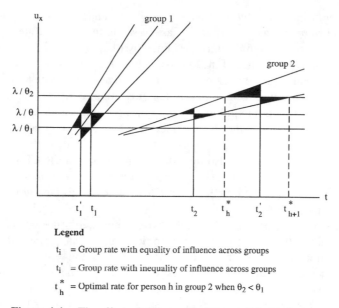

Legend

t_i = Group rate with equality of influence across groups

t_i' = Group rate with inequality of influence across groups

t_h^* = Optimal rate for person h in group 2 when $\theta_2 < \theta_1$

Figure 4.4. The effect of changes in relative political influence on a sorting equilibrium

higher-income taxpayers (as measured by the relative size of the θs for the different groups), the tax discrimination curve shifts to the right and, as a result, the equilibrium number of rate bands rises. In order to proceed with the argument, consider the situation depicted in Figure 4.4, which shows weighted marginal utility of consumption curves like those in Figure 4.3 for two groups of taxpayers, each with two members, as well as equilibrium tax rates before and after grouping. The figure shows that members of group 2 face higher tax rates before and after grouping than do the members of group 1. We shall refer to group 1 as the lower-income group and to group 2 as the higher-income group although, strictly speaking, it is necessary to prove that incomes and tax rates are positively related in the model depicted in the figure. Although it is hard to establish such a relationship in general, it turns out that if self-selection behavior is allowed then it is possible to demonstrate that proportional tax rates do increase with income in equilibrium. The language in the remainder of this section foreshadows this result.

To see how the tax rates for each group in the figure are determined when θs *within* each of the two groups are equal, (4.8b$'$) can be rewritten as

$$\frac{\lambda}{\theta_i} = r_{h-1}u_x^{h-1}(t_i) + r_h u_x^h(t_i) \quad \text{for} \quad i = 1, 2. \tag{4.8b$''$}$$

If equality of influence *across* groups also obtains and $\theta_1 = \theta_2 = \theta$, the sorting equilibrium tax rates are t_1 and t_2, as shown in the figure. Rates t_1' and t_2' represent the sorting equilibrium determined by (4.8b″) when $\theta_1 > \theta_2$, that is, when the relative influence of the lower-income group has increased.

The implications for the tax discrimination curve of increasing the relative influence of the lower-income group depends importantly on the fact that, within each income group in Figure 4.4, the weighted marginal utility of consumption curve for the higher-income individual in each group lies below that for the lower-income member. This is because $u_{xy} < 0$ in the CES case depicted in the figure. It is also important to note that, in the CES case, the vertical distance between any two curves increases with t so that the curves "fan out" as shown in the figure. (A proof that these curves fan out is given in the Appendix.)

We may now use a comparison of the two sorting equilibria $\left(\text{when } \theta_1 = \theta_2,\right.$ and when $\left.\theta_1 > \theta_2\right)$ shown in the figure to determine what happens to the tax discrimination curve when the relative influence of the lower-income group of voters is increased. Starting (without loss of generality) from a situation where influence weights are equal across groups, it is apparent from the figure that members of the lower-income group are taxed more lightly when their relative influence increases while the members of the higher-income group, with their now smaller relative political weight, are taxed more heavily as compared to the initial situation. From the figure it can be seen that the net loss in support from grouping higher-income voters, represented by the sum of the corresponding shaded triangles (analogous to those in Figure 4.3), increases when θ_1 rises relative to θ_2. Similarly, the loss in support from treating both members of the lower-income group alike declines in the equilibrium where the relative influence of the lower-income group as a whole has increased. The reason for the changes in the loss in support from grouping richer as opposed to poorer taxpayers is that the weighted marginal utility curves in the figure fan out as tax rates increase.

Since for the given number of rate bands, the loss in support from grouping is increased, it will be advantageous for the government to add another rate band as compared to the initial situation with equality of influence across groups. Thus, the marginal tax discrimination curve in Figure 3.2 for a situation where $\theta_1 > \theta_2$ will lie to the right of the same curve when $\theta_1 = \theta_2$.

We may conclude that, under the conditions presupposed by Figure 4.4 (fixed incomes, identical CES utility functions, and equality of political influence within groups), an increase in the relative political influence of lower-income voters leads to an increase in the equilibrium number of rate bands.[25] Or, to put this in another way, we can say that when the voting behavior of

---

[25] We are not able to characterize the extent of the shift in the marginal tax discrimination curve.

lower-income voters becomes relatively more sensitive to changes in economic welfare, the equilibrium tax system becomes more complex.

4.3   SELF-SELECTION IN THE BASIC MODEL WITHOUT ADMINISTRATION COSTS

Before proceeding with an analysis of how administration costs and self-selection behavior interact to shape the equilibrium tax system, it is useful to consider the situation in which self-selection is added to the basic model without administration costs.[26]

By assumption, politicians and tax administrators can now observe neither the work effort nor wage rate of individuals but only their earned incomes, so some taxpayers may choose to lower their work effort and earn a reduced income in order to be eligible for a lower tax rate – provided that the increase in leisure that results more than compensates for the loss in after-tax earnings.[27] Thus, if individual h, say, is to be taxed at a rate t_h, then the party in power must ensure that this person will not find it advantageous to effectively reduce his or her earned income in order to be eligible for a lower tax rate. Each tax rate must therefore be chosen subject to an appropriate self-selection or "incentive compatibility" constraint, which for person h can be written as

$$u^h\big(G, \big(1 - t_{h-1}\big)y_{h-1}, y_{h-1}\big) \;\leqq\; u^h\big(G, \big(1 - t_h\big)y_h, y_h\big). \tag{4.9}$$

To use the Representation Theorem to characterize an equilibrium in the presence of self-selection behavior, we must add one constraint like (4.9) for each voter to the optimization problem used for the basic model without administration cost.[28] Imposing one such constraint for each taxpayer when optimizing the political support function ensures that, in the equilibrium no taxpayer has any incentive to avoid taxation at the assigned rate in favor of a

---

[26] We could say that this part of the chapter analyzes a type of administration costs not so far considered. These are the costs associated with acquiring information about the characteristics of taxpayers, which are to be distinguished from the levels of economic and political activity that they engage in. Such costs are not included explicitly in the model, however. As is customary in the literature, only the resulting self-selection behavior is formally acknowledged.

[27] If the tax authorities could determine the ability or potential for work of each individual, then they could tax each individual accordingly so that the taxpayer could do no better, after tax, than to work to his or her maximum capability.

[28] The problem is written out explicitly in Warskett et al. (1998). We note that the self-selection constraint for the lowest-wage individual is not present in this problem, since this person has no lower wage rate to consider. The possibility that taxpayers may adopt higher wage rates (or levels of work effort) is ruled out in this formulation on the understanding that individuals can work at less than their full capacity but not at more.

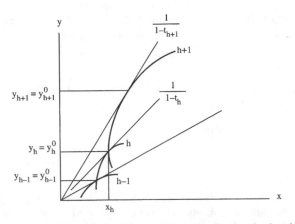

Figure 4.5. An equilibrium with self-selection in the absence of administration costs

lower rate by altering his or her level of work effort. (Otherwise, the government could not be sure that each taxpayer would be subject to the intended tax rate.)

Because the support function is optimized subject to an additional set of constraints, it follows immediately that equilibrium tax rates in the model with selectivity will not be the same as in the basic model. However, in the absence of administration costs, there will still be as many distinct tax rates as there are individuals. This perfect discrimination for purposes of taxation will occur since an appropriate optimizing decision can still be made by politicians in the case of each individual.

An equilibrium with self-selection is illustrated in Figure 4.5, which is drawn on the assumption that self-selection constraints for all individuals are binding and that preferences are identical. This diagram also illustrates a useful way to think of the problem facing the government when self-selection is added to the basic model, one that we shall rely upon in the next section where the effects of the interaction of selectivity and administration costs are considered more formally. In constructing the figure, we may think of the government's problem as that of choosing a set of threshold incomes $y^0 = \{y_1^0, y_2^0, \ldots, y_{H-1}^0\}$, as well as tax rates and a size of government, such that an income y in the interval $\{y_{h-1}^0 < y \leq y_h^0\}$ is subject to the rate t_h. This is useful because, after administration costs are added to the model with selectivity, sorting of taxpayers into groups will once again occur. Viewing the sorting process as a choice of threshold income levels between which all income is taxed at the same rate allows the use of calculus in a straightforward manner to optimize an appropriately defined political support function subject to appropriate constraints, as will be shown in the next section. Otherwise, we should have to tackle the sorting problem directly (as in the two special cases studied earlier), and in the presence of self-selection behavior this would be a difficult task.

We assume that indifference curves of different voters cross only once. Hence, as shown in Figure 4.5, the choice of thresholds in the absence of administration costs will be such that, in equilibrium, individual $h - 1$ paying taxes at rate t_{h-1} has income $y_{h-1} = y_{h-1}^0$ while an individual with income y_h such that $y_{h-1} < y_h \leq y_h^0$ pays a rate t_h and has income $y_h = y_h^0$.[29] To deal with self-selection behavior, tax rates and threshold income levels are set so that $u^h(G, (1 - t_{h-1})y_{h-1}^0, y_{h-1}^0) = u^h((G, (1 - t_h)y_h^0, y_h^0)$.[30] In equilibrium, the unique position of each individual must also be consistent with the tangency between a tax line with slope $1/(1 - t_h)$ and an indifference curve with slope $u_x^h/(-u_y^h)$, as indicated.

Given that preferences are identical, tax rates and incomes in the equilibrium depicted in Figure 4.5 can be ordered in the same way; this justifies our labeling groups by income level in the previous discussion of the effect of changes in relative political influence. The positive monotonic relationship between these variables results from the combination of binding self-selection constraints, the single crossing property, and the concavity of indifference curves in the (x, y) plane.[31] To see that this is so, consider, for example, taxpayers h and $h + 1$ where $t_h < t_{h+1}$. Individual h is shown in the figure to be consuming x_h at income y_h. Since all self-selection constraints are assumed to be binding and since preferences are identical, the utility of person $h + 1$ paying the higher rate t_{h+1} must be equal in equilibrium to that of person h if $h + 1$ were to earn income y_h and pay tax at the rate t_h.[32] This is so regardless of differences in political influence. Otherwise taxpayer $h + 1$ would choose to take more leisure, earn the lower income, and be taxed at rate t_h. Since the single crossing property is assumed to hold, the indifference curve for person $h + 1$ passing through the point (x_h, y_h) is steeper than that for person h for all $x > x_h$. Concavity of indifference curves in the (x,y) plane then ensures

---

[29] Because threshold income levels and tax rates are in a one-to-one relationship in the equilibrium, it is not necessary to explicitly include the thresholds as instruments to be chosen as part of the solution to the optimization problem used to characterize the equilibrium tax system. See Warskett et al. (1998).

[30] As preferences are identical in Figure 4.5, it is also the case that $u^{h-1}(G, (1 - t_{h-1})y_{h-1}^0, y_{h-1}^0) = u^h(G, (1 - t_{h-1})y_{h-1}^0, y_{h-1}^0)$.

[31] The single crossing property also ensures that wage rates are monotonically related to tax rates and income levels.

[32] The self-selection constraint ensures that $u^h(t_{h-1}) = u^h(t_h)$. If preferences are identical, it is also the case that $u^h(t_{h-1}) = u^{h-1}(t_{h-1})$.

that the equilibrium for person $h + 1$ must involve a consumption–income bundle such that $x_{h+1} > x_h$ and $y_{h+1} > y_h$, as shown.[33]

Before proceeding to reintroduce administration costs, it should be noted that even though the political influence weights (the θ_hs) do not appear in Figure 4.5, this does not mean that relative political influence has no affect on tax rates. Political influence weights do indeed appear in the optimization problem that, as the Representation Theorem indicates, can be used to characterize the equilibrium, as can be seen in the following section. Changes in the θ_h will affect both the x_h and the y_h and thus the position of indifference curves and the tax-rate lines in the figure.

4.4   THE INTERACTION OF ADMINISTRATION COSTS AND SELF-SELECTION

We now turn to a consideration of what happens to the sorting equilibrium when self-selection constraints are added to the model *with* administration costs discussed earlier. In this investigation we assume that administrative expenditures are not directed toward reducing the lack of information (about the characteristics of taxpayers) that underlies the self-selection constraints. We take these constraints as given, leaving aside the more general case in which the incentive compatibility constraints themselves are endogenously determined along with the level of resources used to administer the tax system.

Suppose, then, that tax administration is costly, that the possibility of self-selection exists, and that the number of rate bands is arbitrarily fixed at N so that tax rates $t_1, t_2, \ldots, t_N$ are to be chosen. The problem faced by the government (and the opposition) then consists not only of selecting the level of G and the tax rates t_i. It must also appropriately partition the set $\{1, 2, \ldots, H\} = \cup I_i$ in order to deal with self-selection, where the subsets I_i contain adjacent individuals with respect to income and are mutually exclusive.

---

[33] It is of some interest to note that the marginal tax rate of the person with the highest income is not zero as in Seade (1977) and other optimal tax analyses, as illustrated in the figure. This can be seen analytically in the first-order conditions for the choice of t_H in Warskett et al. (1998). The reason is that all tax rates in the model we are exploring are proportional to income. In the optimal tax models in which the top marginal rate on the person with the highest income is zero, tax schedules are nonlinear so that the incentive of this highest-income person to work can be enhanced without affecting tax revenues. No revenue is collected on the marginal dollars not earned by this person when the marginal tax rate applying to the next dollar earned of this person is positive, and so no tax revenue is lost when this marginal rate, and this one alone, is set to zero. In the present model, however, if t_H were reduced to zero so as to eliminate the tax on the marginal earnings of the highest-income person H, then all tax revenue from the nonmarginal earnings of this person H would also be eliminated.

As we pointed out previously, in order to express the problem in the differential calculus we suppose that – instead of attacking the partitioning problem directly – the government sets threshold levels of income (y_i^0) corresponding to the boundaries of rate bands, so that an individual h with income $y_{i-1}^0 < y_h \leq y_i^0$ is taxed at rate t_i. Given the y_i^0, the relevant Lagrangean for characterizing equilibrium choices of G and the t_i can be expressed as

$$\mathcal{L} = \sum_{i=1}^{N} \sum_{h \in I_i} \theta_h u^h \big(G, \big(1 - t_i\big)y_h, y_h\big)$$

$$+ \lambda \left[\sum_{i=1}^{N} \left(t_i \cdot \sum_{h \in I_i} y_h \right) - G \right]$$

$$- \sum_{i \neq 1}^{N} \mu_i \big[u^i \big(G, \big(1 - t_{i-1}\big)y_{i-1}^0, y_{i-1}^0\big)$$

$$- u^i \big(G, \big(1 - t_i\big)y_i, y_i\big)\big]. \qquad (4.10)$$

The sum over incentive compatibility constraints, the third term in (4.10), omits the first group since members of that group have no possibility of self-selecting into another (lower) rate band. The labor–leisure choices represented by the terms in ϕ_h in equations (4.7), but not the self-selection constraints, are omitted here for simplicity because they do not affect the qualitative nature of the discussion.

As a consequence of the single crossing property, it is necessary to consider self-selection constraints for only one individual in each of the N rate bands and, in particular, for the individual with the lowest income in the band. If the government selects rate bands and associated threshold income levels y_h^0 such that the person with this income will not self-select into a lower tax-rate band, no individual with a higher income will wish reduce work effort sufficiently to be taxed at a rate lower than that levied on the person at the "bottom" of the rate band.[34] For this reason, we have ignored all but $N - 1$ of the self-selection constraints in the Lagrangean (4.10).

Letting $i = \min\{h \mid h \in I_i\}$, the first-order conditions for the previous problem are[35]

---

[34] This is also a necessary condition for taxing members of a group at the rate specified. If the rate chosen does not effectively constrain the lowest-income member of a group, then that individual will find it advantageous to take advantage of a lower tax rate and the rate chosen will no longer apply to the group for which it is intended. It may also be noted that, in the presence of self-selection, bunching may occur at the top of each rate band as richer individuals within any group try to avoid being taxed at the next highest tax rate.

[35] If we set aside the fact that taxation is part of a political equilibrium by ignoring the weights θ_h, then equations (4.11) are analogous to conditions (2)–(4) of Boadway and Keen (1993, p. 469).

$$\sum_{i=2}^{N} \sum_{h \in I_i} \theta_h u_G^h(y_i^0) - \lambda = \sum_{i=2}^{N} \mu_i \left[u_G^i(y_{i-1}^0) - u_G^i(y_i) \right] \quad \text{and} \quad (4.11a)$$

$$-\sum_{h \in I_i} y_h \theta_h u_x^h(y_i) + \lambda \sum_{h \in I_i} y_h$$

$$= \left[\mu_i y_i u_x^i(y_i) - \mu_{i+1} y_i^0 u_x^{i+1}(y_i^0) \right] \quad \text{for} \quad i = 1, 2, \ldots, N - 1; \quad (4.11b)$$

$$\mu_i \left[u_x^i(y_{i-1}^0) - u_x^i(y_i) \right] = 0 \quad \text{for} \quad i = 2, 3, \ldots, N; \quad (4.11c)$$

$$\mu_i \geq 0 \quad \text{for} \quad i = 2, 3, \ldots, N, \quad (4.11d)$$

where we have noted the specific income level at which each marginal utility is evaluated. We again assume that all $\mu_i > 0$ for all i, so that all of the self-selection constraints are binding. Then $(1 - t_{i-1})u_x^{i-1} + u_y^{i-1} = 0$ and $u^i(G, (1 - t_{i-1})y_{i-1}^0, y_{i-1}^0) = u^i(G, (1 - t_i)y_i, y_i)$ at the lower boundary of the ith rate band y_{i-1}^0. Figure 4.5 can again be used to illustrate this situation, on the understanding that the threshold income levels shown in the figure apply to the person at the bottom of each rate band.

The terms on the right side of (4.11b) provide a convenient representation of the role of self-selection over and above that of administration costs. In the presence of administration costs alone, as in equation (4.8b′), all the μ_i are zero and the right side of (4.11b) vanishes.

Condition (4.11b) can be further simplified by dividing through by $\Sigma_h y_h$ and using the definition $r_i = y_i/\Sigma_h y_h$ for $h \in I_i$, which is the relative within-group income of the person at the bottom of the ith rate band. Thus

$$-\sum_{h \in I_i} r_h \theta_h u_x^h(y_i) + \lambda = r_i \left[\mu_i u_x^i(y_i) - \mu_{i+1} \frac{y_i^0}{y_i} u_x^{i+1}(y_i^0) \right]$$

$$\text{for} \quad 1, 2, \ldots, N - 1. \quad (4.11b′)$$

Condition (4.11b′) indicates more clearly what happens in the presence of self-selection when a new rate band is added to the tax system. Given the total number of taxpayers H, the population density H/N within each band decreases, as the number of rate bands N increases, causing the within-group income share r_i of individual i, to rise in value. As a result, the political benefit of adding a new rate band is accompanied by an extra "cost" – in addition to increased administration costs – that is represented by the increased weight of the right-hand side. This extra cost arises because, in the presence of self-selection behavior, adding another rate band gives rise to an additional incentive compatibility constraint on the government's ability to discriminate between taxpayers.

Condition (4.11b′) also indicates that the self-selection behavior has more influence on group tax rates when administration costs are low than when they

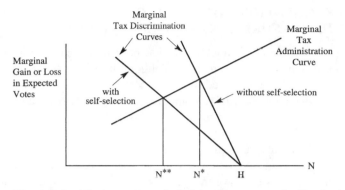

Figure 4.6. The interaction of administration costs and self-selection

are high. When administration costs are low and the equilibrium number of groups N^* (as in Figure 3.2) is close to H in the absence of self-selection, each income share r_i on the right side of (4.11b′) is relatively large. Hence adding self-selection to the model with administration costs when N^* is large compared to H leads to a substantial change in the solution for group tax rates. Intuitively, if administration costs are low then a sorting equilibrium involves many groups of taxpayers, and the introduction of self-selection behavior leads to the imposition of many additional constraints on policy choices. On the other hand, if N^* is small relative to H in the absence of self-selection, the r_i will all be small and self-selection will not play as substantial a role in the determination of group tax rates.

The self-selection constraints influence the equilibrium number of rate bands as well as the tax rates applying to each group. For any given number of rate bands, the gain in political support from adding another band must be less in the presence of self-selection than in its absence, for as we have seen, adding a rate band adds another constraint on political optimization when self-selection behavior is taken into account. This implies that the marginal tax discrimination curve in the presence of self-selection, which shows the maximum gain in support from adding another rate band, must lie everywhere below the same curve drawn for a situation with administration costs alone.[36] As Figure 4.6 illustrates, the result is an equilibrium in which tax structure is coarser, with fewer rate bands (equal to N^{**}) than would be observed if administration costs were the only impediment to the government's ability to discriminate among heterogeneous voters.

[36] Note that although the two marginal tax discrimination curves in Figure 4.6 meet where $N = H$, the *total* amount of support obtainable with self-selection must be less than that obtainable in the presence of administration costs alone.

4.5 A SUGGESTION CONCERNING THE MEASUREMENT OF TAX COMPLEXITY

The emphasis in the preceding analysis has been on formalizing ideas about how a tax structure emerges in a political equilibrium. In the course of this investigation, we have discussed several factors that play an important role in determining the complexity of an equilibrium tax system, especially administration costs and self-selection behavior. In this section we briefly draw out an implication of the analysis for the measurement of tax complexity.

The complexity of a tax system is usually associated with the numbers of tax rates, bases and special provisions it includes. Often a complex system in this sense is pointed to as evidence that taxation has been corrupted by politics or bad public management. However, the analysis of tax complexity presented in this chapter does not rely upon imperfections in the operation of the public sector. In the view we have developed here and in the preceding chapter, complex tax structures emerge as a by-product of the struggle for office, in the course of which political parties are forced to propose and implement policies that discriminate or distinguish as carefully as possible among heterogeneous voters.

In this framework, tax complexity is appropriately measured by the number of effective distinctions among taxpayers that is made by the tax system. Tax complexity in this sense corresponds to the number of equilibrium tax rates. Tax complexity is at a maximum in the basic model where a separate rate is levied on each voter. If we define a flat tax as applying the same proportional rate to everyone, such a tax would show minimum complexity. A lump-sum tax system, on the other hand, would be as complex as our basic proportional tax system, since each person would be assessed an individually specific tax payment.

The number of effective distinctions made by a tax system may be used as the basis for an index of complexity. In the equilibrium described by the basic model *with* administration costs, where the tax system distinguishes between individuals in one dimension only (income), the number of effective distinctions made between taxpayers is equal to the number of rate bands minus 1. In this case, one index of complexity that reflects the number of distinctions made by the tax system is:

$$C = (\text{number of rate bands} - 1)/(\text{number of taxpayers} - 1).$$

For example, if there are 10 effective rate bands and 1,000 taxpayers, then $C = 9/999 = 1/111$.

When the tax system distinguishes between taxpayers in many dimensions besides income – such as age, family status, health, occupation, and so on – and when different taxpayers are treated differently in each dimension, the situation is considerably more involved. Additional complications arise when acknowledging that, in the real world, special provisions and the choice of tax bases are also used to further differentiate the treatment of taxpayers. Further work is needed to devise an index of the number of effective distinctions among taxpayers made by a tax system as a whole that consistently ranks alternative systems. We shall leave development of such an index of complexity for future research, while emphasizing that our analysis suggests that such an index should be designed to measure the effective number of distinctions made among taxpayers.

4.6   CONCLUSIONS: EXERCISING THE POWER TO MAKE DISTINCTIONS

The exercise of the power to make distinctions is an essential part of politics in a competitive political system. The reason is that differentiated treatment of heterogeneous taxpayers improves political fortunes by allowing decision makers to take account more fully of differences in voting behavior and in the margins along which voters make economic adjustments. If it were possible, the parties would offer each unique taxpayer distinct treatment for each separate activity that taxpayer conducts.

Real tax systems are less complex than the one in the basic model that we have constructed, however, because of the costs of administering complexity and because of the incentive and ability that taxpayers have to disguise themselves for the purpose of reducing tax burdens. Administration costs and self-selection behavior limit the ability and the desire of any government to discriminate fully between taxpayers.

In this and the previous chapter we have argued that, in order to economize on the costs of tax administration, the successful party in a democratic state implements a tax structure in which heterogeneous taxpayers are grouped for the purpose of taxation. We described this outcome as a sorting equilibrium. In the specific examples we explored, taxpayers are grouped so as to minimize the variance of the characteristics distinguishing individuals within each group, with tax rates being chosen according to relevant average group characteristics. The number of taxpayer groups in a sorting equilibrium – represented here in stylized form by the number of proportional rate bands within which similar (but not identical) voters pay the same tax rate – depends on the gain in expected votes from distinguishing between taxpayers who have different economic and political characteristics on the one hand, and on the loss in votes that results from diverting resources away from public services and toward tax administration on the other.

Changes in the relative influence of different groups of voters may affect the net gain from further tax discrimination and thus alter the equilibrium tax system. Given the nature of administration costs, we showed how an increase in the influence of lower-income voters, which leads to an increase in taxes levied on higher-income taxpayers, creates an incentive for governments to alter the pattern of tax discrimination and, in the case examined, to increase the complexity of the tax system. This incentive arises because additional complexity allows the government to partially offset increases in opposition to taxation by the voters for whom taxation has become more onerous.

Self-selection behavior interacts with administration costs to produce a tax structure that is coarser than would be observed in the presence of administration costs alone, while also affecting the rates that are levied on each group of taxpayers. When tax administration is costly and grouping voters for the purpose of taxation occurs, adding another rate band in the presence of self-selection leads to an additional incentive compatibility constraint on the ability of the government to discriminate between voters, a constraint that does not exist in a world with administration costs alone. As a consequence, the marginal political payoff to tax complexity declines at every level of administration costs, and in equilibrium the degree of tax complexity is reduced.

Despite the grouping that occurs as governments attempt to economize on administration costs and to deal with self-selection, tax structure may still be quite complicated in the model we have explored. Though it does not rule out equilibrium systems as simplistic as some of the flat-tax proposals that have emerged in recent years (surveyed e.g. by Bernstein, Fogarasi, and Gordon, 1995), our analysis suggests that such schemes are not compatible with vigorous political competition. Moreover, declines in the costs of administering a tax system, such as may occur with advances in computer technology, can be expected to lead to further complexity. In short, we may say (perhaps somewhat provocatively) that – barring some sort of extraordinary constraint on political behavior of a type not previously observed in democratic countries – it is possible to have a flat tax, or to have democracy, but not both.

No doubt there are other important factors besides those we have investigated in this chapter that play a role in determining the nature of tax structure in a sorting equilibrium, including its degree of complexity. One such factor that comes to mind concerns taxpayer views about fairness. The fact that we have not explored the notions of horizontal and vertical tax equity and the opinions of voters about these and similar concepts within our framework may deserve some comment. Notions of equity or fairness will be reflected in equilibrium tax structure as long as the governing party and the opposition believe that voters consider them important when judging government performance. This applies regardless of whether people accept the versions of fairness advanced by economists, or whether they subscribe to different ideas that imply unequal treatment for tax purposes because of the type of income and of certain personal characteristics (such as family status, particular infirmities, or special occupations). In positive analysis, one is led to the view that concerns about fairness in taxation may be treated like tastes that vary among the electorate. As such, they may lead governments to implement particular patterns of tax discrimination and can be studied in empirical research concerned with the influence of voter opinions on tax policy.

Equity among taxpayers can also be interpreted in relation to the adminis-tration of tax systems. Legal conventions that constitute the "rule of law" con-cerning taxation and that prevent individuals from being singled out by name at the discretion of governments may be required to limit public power over citi-zens and to prevent internecine rivalry among different groups in the popula-tion (Usher 1995, Weingast 1997). In this deeper sense, equity is a feature of the institutional background for the positive model of tax structure that we have presented. As pointed out in Chapter 2, we do not explain constraints of this nature on the behavior of democratic governments, just as most models of private markets do not explain the emergence of property rights.

The emphasis in this chapter has been on formalizing important aspects in the positive theory of tax systems. However, parts of the investigation also bear on the foundations of the normative theory of taxation. The apparent incom-patibility of simple tax systems with political competition that we have high-lighted presents a serious challenge for normative views that are not cognizant of how democracies actually work. This applies most notably to the theory of equitable taxation due to Henry Simons and others, a point that we take up in some detail in the next chapter where existing normative theories of taxation are assessed. We also recall that the Representation Theorem, that we relied upon to characterize an equilibrium tax structure, demonstrates that the power to discriminate among taxpayers results in efficient tax policy outcomes under certain conditions. We shall return to this theorem and its implications for nor-mative tax theory in Chapter 6.

We conclude the chapter by noting two topics for further research that are suggested by the analysis in this and the preceding chapter. In a sorting equi-librium, taxpayers that have been grouped by the government for the purpose of taxation have an incentive to act in unison with other members of their tax group, since it will be difficult for them to get the government to alter only their own personal tax liability. Since sorting evidently alters the incentives of people to join with others in influencing the government, it can be regarded as an important aspect of a more complete theory of the formation of interest groups, an aspect that has not been previously explored. We believe that it would be of considerable interest to study the formation and role of interest groups at the same time as one investigates the nature of sorting equilibria in democratic countries.

A second topic deserving further study concerns the question of how gov-ernments actually solve the sorting problems they face in choosing a tax struc-ture, or, for that matter, the structure of policy instruments in any field. It may well be that the nature of tax structures, as well as the ultimate limits to tax complexity, are affected significantly by the ability of policy makers to cope with such problems. If so, a complete understanding of why tax systems look the way that they do will require the study of how bureaucratic organization affects actual policy choices.

APPENDIX TO CHAPTER 4: SOME FORMAL RESULTS

4A.1   The Convergence of Party Platforms

The following proof of convergence is based on that by Enelow and Hinich (1989, p. 107). Another proof is given by Coughlin (1992, p. 71).

Let w^* and z^* be the equilibrium strategies for parties i and o, respectively, and assume that $w^* \neq z^*$. Then, since $EV_o(w, z)$ is assumed to be strictly concave in z and $EV_i(w, z) = H - EV_o(w, z)$, it follows that i can only do better if o adopts w^* and i sticks with w^*, so that i's expected vote in the equilibrium must be less than $EV_i(w^*, w^*)$. Similarly, party i can only do worse if it adopts z^* and o stays with z^*, so i's expected vote in equilibrium is greater than $EV_i(z^*, z^*)$. But $EV_i = \sum_h f_h[u^h(w) - u^h(z)] = \sum_h f_h[0]$ when $w = z$, where $u_h(\cdot)$ refers to the arguments of the utility function under the indicated policy. Thus, party i's expected vote is both greater and less than $\sum_h f_h[0]$, contradicting the assumption that $w^* \neq z^*$.

4A.2   The Representation Theorem

It is of substantial convenience that the equilibrium policy platform in the model of political competition outlined in this chapter can be described by optimizing a function that is a particular weighted sum of taxpayer utilities (Coughlin and Nitzan 1981a, Coughlin 1992).

Theorem. Let a policy platform $\mathbf{s}^* = \{t_1^*, t_2^*, \dots, t_H^*, G^*\}$ be a solution to the problem of maximizing the *political support function*

$$S = \sum_{h=1}^{H} \theta_h \cdot u^h\big(G, (1 - t_h)y_h, y_h\big)$$

subject to $F(\mathbf{s}^*) = 0$, where θ_h is the value of $\partial f_h / \partial u^h$ at the Nash equilibrium in the electoral game described in Section 4.1. Then $(\mathbf{s}^*, \mathbf{s}^*)$ is the Nash equilibrium.

Proof. The first-order conditions for the problem of choosing a policy platform s to maximize S subject to $F(\mathbf{s}) = 0$ are identical to first-order conditions for the choice of policies by either party that must be satisfied at the Nash equilibrium – namely, equations (4.2) (without the index denoting party i) with each $\partial f_h / \partial u^h$ set equal to its Nash equilibrium value. Thus, if $\mathbf{s}^*$ maximizes S, then it also solves the first-order conditions for expected vote maximization by both parties at the Nash equilibrium. Second-order conditions for maximization of the expected vote functions at the Nash equilibrium are also satisfied by $\mathbf{s}^*$ since these functions are assumed to be strictly concave over the set of all feasible policy choices. QED

Our statement of the Coughlin–Nitzan result differs from that in Coughlin and Nitzan's work because they use a different specification of voting densities, and because they are interested in conditions under which $(\mathbf{s}^*, \mathbf{s}^*)$ is a Nash equilibrium *if and only if* $\mathbf{s}^*$ optimizes an appropriate function of voter utilities.

4A.3 Demonstration that the Loss in Support from Grouping Is Represented in Figure 4.3 by the Sum of the Shaded Triangles

The loss in support from grouping (4.6) can be written more fully as

$$\Delta S = \sum_{i=1}^{N} \sum_{h \in I_i} \theta_h \left\{ \left[u_G^h \frac{\partial G}{\partial t_h} + u_x^h \frac{\partial x_h}{\partial t_h} + u_y^h \frac{\partial y_h}{\partial t_h} \right] dt_h \right.$$

$$\left. + u_G^h \left[\sum_{j \neq h \in I_i} \frac{\partial G}{\partial t_j} dt_j \right] \right\}, \qquad (4A.1)$$

where dt_h refers to the difference between person h's group tax rate and his or her politically optimal tax rate in the absence of administration costs. For each $h \in I_i$, θ_h times the first square-bracketed term in this expression reflects the effect on support of the change in welfare of each voter as a result of being taxed at the group rate t_i rather than at his or her optimal rate t_h^*, holding constant the implications for total revenue and the size of G of changes in the rates faced by other taxpayers in this group. The second square-bracketed term arises because of the implications for support from voter h that follow from the change in G produced by taxing *other* voters in his group at the group rate rather than at their individually optimal rates.

When y_h is held fixed, $\partial y_h / \partial t_h = 0$ and the loss in support from grouping (4A.1) becomes

$$\Delta S = \sum_{i=1}^{N} \sum_{h \in I_i} \theta_h \left\{ \left[u_G^h \frac{\partial G}{\partial t_h} - u_x^h y_h \right] dt_h + u_G^h \left[\sum_{j \neq h \in I_i} \frac{\partial G}{\partial t_j} dt_j \right] \right\}. \qquad (4A.2)$$

Equation (4A.2) can be further simplified by observing that when y_h is fixed, the government budget restraint implies that $dg/dt_h = d(t_h y_h)/dt_h = y_h$, and also by observing that, in general, the effect on support and spending another dollar on public services can be written as

$$\lambda = \sum_{i=1}^{N} \sum_{h \in I_i} \theta_h u_G^h.$$

Substituting into (4A.2) and collecting terms leads to the following simplified expression for the loss in support from grouping:

$$\Delta S = \sum_{i=1}^{N} \sum_{h \in I_i} (\lambda - \theta_h u_x^h) y_h (t_h^* - t_i), \tag{4A.3}$$

where $y_h dt_h = y_h(t_h^* - t_i)$ is the change in the tax revenue collected from person h as a result of the grouping process.

Equation (4A.3) is appropriate for small differences between t_h^* and t_i. For discrete changes, the analog to (4A.3) is

$$\Delta S = \sum_{i=1}^{N} \sum_{h \in I_i} \int_{t_i}^{t_h^*} (\lambda - \theta_h u_x^h(t)) y_h dt. \tag{4A.4}$$

Expression (4A.4) shows that, for the group in Figure 4.3 consisting of the two voters h and $h - 1$, the net loss in support from grouping is equal to the (weighted) sum of the shaded triangles cfd and deg (with weights equal to corresponding incomes y_{h-1} and y_h).

4A.4   Proof that the Weighted Marginal Utility Curves in Figure 4.4 "Fan Out"

The fan shape of the curves can be confirmed in the following way. Consider the situation where $u_x^h = u_x^{h+1}$ for two taxpayers, h and $h + 1$, where $y_{h+1} > y_h$. We show that where these marginal utilities are equal, $u_{xt}^{h+1} < u_{xt}^h$ – that is, the person with higher income has a marginal utility of consumption curve with lower slope with respect to t, as shown in Figure 4.4. Since $u_x = (u/x)^{1-\rho}$ in the CES case, where the subscript h is omitted for convenience, it follows that $u_{xt} = -(1 - \rho)u_x(u/x)^{-\rho}(y/x)$.

Now we add the label h and note that $(u^h/x_h) = (u^{h+1}/x_{h+1})$ at $u_x^h = u_x^{h+1}$. Then, using $y_h/x_h = (1 - t_h)^{-1}$, we have that

$$u_{xt}^{h+1} - u_{xt}^h = (1 - \rho)u_x^h \left(\frac{u^h}{x_h}\right)^{1-\rho} [(1 - t_h)^{-1} - (1 - t_{h+1})^{-1}]. \tag{4A.5}$$

Since $t_{h+1} > t_h$, the last term in square brackets in (4A.5) is negative and we can see that $u_{xt}^{h+1} < u_{xt}^h$.

PART TWO

COLLECTIVE CHOICE AND THE NORMATIVE ANALYSIS OF TAXATION

CHAPTER 5

An Assessment of Normative Tax Theory

> If the economist were to accept any kind of political constraint on the tax system as true constraints on economic policy, much of the prescriptive power of welfare analysis would clearly be lost.
>
> Agnar Sandmo (1984, p. 116)

> Students of political economy make an error in defining their point of departure in such a way that they rule out as illegitimate any political survival strategies. It is analytically misleading ... to define the study of political economy in terms of some supposed set of errors in economic policy that are then attributed to politics. ... That is, by taking politics as bad compared to some ideal counterfactual policy, we will always discover that policy has been corrupted by politics.
>
> John Woolley (1984, p. 184)

Is tax policy improperly limited, or even corrupted, by politics? What is a valid counterfactual for judging tax systems and choices on taxation made by public decision makers? What steps are needed to define the elements and characteristics of a desirable or "good" tax system?

So far we have not directly confronted issues of this nature. Although the concept of Pareto efficiency was introduced in Chapter 4 in connection with the discussion of the Representation Theorem, the previous chapters have focused primarily on the presentation and development of theories that explain the structure of tax systems observed in democratic nations without evaluating outcomes in relation to a particular standard. This emphasis on what is often called "positive" analysis has been deliberate, since we believe such analysis to be of major importance. On the other hand, the positive approach is not designed to deal with the questions raised by Agnar Sandmo and John Woolley in the introductory quotations, a task requiring normative or prescriptive analysis.

In this chapter, we turn our attention to normative issues. First, we give a brief survey of the three most important normative theories of taxation that have influenced policy in recent decades, placing particular emphasis on how they deal with different aspects of tax structure. Second, we critically examine the treatment of political economy in this literature. The chapter ends with several suggested steps toward creation of a more inclusive normative analysis.

5.1   THREE NORMATIVE THEORIES OF TAXATION

There has been considerable disagreement among economists in recent decades on what constitutes a good tax system. As often happens in the development of academic disciplines, the lack of consensus has been linked to the rise of new traditions of analysis. The 1970s witnessed the rapid development of an approach to tax problems known as the theory of optimal taxation (OT). It is based on different normative assumptions and provides a different emphasis from so-called equitable taxation (ET), the predominant theory in the 1950s and 1960s. More recently, a revival and reformulation of the fiscal exchange (FE) approach has provided another competing point of view from which to consider problems of tax design and reform.[1]

Since ET, OT, and FE all influence the discussion of tax policy, it is important to understand how the three traditions differ and what assumptions are responsible for the often conflicting advice offered by economists taking them as their starting points. Furthermore, it is essential to realize that each tradition has a well-developed analytical and philosophical basis that cannot be readily rejected as inappropriate or logically deficient. In fact, careful analysis reveals elements in each approach that are missing from the competing traditions but may need to be included in any successful synthesis to be developed in the future.

5.1.1   Equitable Taxation

The theory of equitable taxation derives primarily from the work of Henry Simons (1938), who developed it as part of a broader framework for economic policy. Simons had his philosophical roots in classical liberalism; he emphasized individual liberty as the primary value, together with equality as next in importance. His economic program called for institutions and policies that minimized political interference in economic life. The public sector had an important role; among other functions, it had to provide services that the private sector could not supply effectively and to create greater equality through redistribution. Since benefit taxation was not practical, a way of taxation had to be developed that raised money according to principles of fairness and that also limited the interference of the political process in the market economy. Drawing on the work of Haig and Schanz, Simons formulated the concepts of comprehensive income and of the comprehensive tax base.

There are several basic ideas essential to an understanding of ET. The approach deals separately with the tax and expenditure sides of the budget. Taxation is imposed in accordance with ability to pay, which is measured without reference to utility theory. In proposing his own measure (i.e., the change

---

[1] Section 5.1 draws primarily on Hettich and Winer (1985), where a more detailed discussion of the three normative theories and additional references can be found.

in net wealth plus consumption defined over an appropriate accounting period), Simons argued against the use of utility analysis and for a concept having a direct counterpart in measurable dollar flows (Hettich 1979a).

More recently, several authors working in the ET tradition have advocated consumption expenditures as the most appropriate measure of ability to pay.[2] However, the majority of writers follow Simons in accepting comprehensive income. Equitable taxation makes an important distinction between horizontal equity (the equal treatment of taxpayers with the same ability to pay) and vertical equity (the taxation of those in different economic positions). The main focus is on horizontal equity and the definitional questions that it raises; ET has little to say about vertical equity, the determination of which is left to the political process. Equitable taxation does not formally integrate other objectives, such as efficiency, into the analysis. As a result, those making use of the ET framework cannot deal systematically with the trade-off among policy goals.

There is an extensive literature on the problems associated with implementing the comprehensive income tax base.[3] Major questions concern whether to base tax liability on nominal or real income, whether to tax capital gains when they accrue or when they are realized, how to deal with various types of imputed income, and how to treat income that fluctuates over time. Another question that has occasioned much debate is the definition of the taxpaying unit. All these issues pose problems of tax administration and raise the question of how to determine the desirable trade-off between administrative costs and the comprehensiveness of the tax base.

Some opponents of the ET tradition have argued that comprehensive income can never be measured adequately because the value of important components such as leisure and government services cannot be estimated at reasonable cost. It is, however, questionable whether any index of ability to pay can ever be measured in a way that is theoretically acceptable. Recent advocates of expenditure taxation have argued that a cash-flow tax would offer fewer problems of implementation, but this claim is disputed elsewhere.[4]

---

[2] See Musgrave (1976, 1983) for an evaluation of the arguments.

[3] The most detailed and authoritative treatment of such problems can be found in the (Canadian) Royal Commission on Taxation (1966) report. Other useful sources are U.S. Department of the Treasury (1977, 1984), Government of Ireland (1982), and Lodin (1978).

[4] A cash-flow expenditure tax may be implemented as a combination of two taxes, one on business income net of all business-related purchases including capital and labor services, and another on wages after allowance of deductions for personal net saving. In this scheme, loans may also be treated on a cash-flow basis, with proceeds taxable to the borrower and deductible to the lender and with interest expense and repayment of principal deductible by the borrower. It is claimed that the immediate and full expensing of capital purchases (among other features) would make this type of taxation simpler than the current form of income taxation. Zodrow (1997) outlines the various types of cash-flow consumption taxes that have been discussed in the literature.

Though administrative difficulties are considerable, the gap between theory and reality is probably smaller in ET than in the other normative traditions.

Although special provisions are frowned upon as deviations from the ideal base, the consensus does not encompass elimination of all exemptions, deductions, or exclusions. Major items that are treated differently in various sources include capital gains, owner-occupied residences, private savings for retirement, charitable contributions, depreciation of capital assets, exploration and development costs of mining and oil companies, and expenditures on research and development. Where retention of special treatment is advocated, it is generally justified with an appeal to secondary goals such as efficiency, economic growth, or administrative simplicity, although such appeals raise the unresolved question of how a systematic trade-off between multiple goals is to be determined.

5.1.2   Optimal Taxation

The roots of optimal taxation (OT) can be traced to the "sacrifice" doctrines first proposed by classical writers. J. S. Mill argued, for example, that justice in taxation required each taxpayer to suffer an equal sacrifice (*Principles*, 1817). Modern welfare economics, following Edgeworth and Pigou, interprets sacrifice as loss of utility, and advocates equalization of marginal utility as the proper rule for minimizing the aggregate sacrifice caused by taxation. Contemporary OT, following Frank Ramsey (1927), James Mirrlees (1971), and Peter Diamond and Mirrlees (1971), among others, also investigates the idea that tax structure should involve the least aggregate sacrifice, but defines sacrifice more broadly as a reduction of social welfare rather than simply as a loss in individual utilities.[5]

The social welfare function used by OT theorists is utilitarian in nature, depending on individual ordinal utilities. But it also incorporates cardinal distributional weights, which are the weighted sum of individual utilities. This permits vertical equity norms to be integrated explicitly into the analysis. Such norms may include the standard vertical equity criteria as well as special cases such as the "maximin" criterion of John Rawls (1971) (i.e., maximize the welfare of the least well-off individual). Although this is done only occasionally, horizontal equity norms may be incorporated into the analysis as constraints on the choice of tax instruments.

In maximizing the social welfare function, OT theorists make several important assumptions about the nature of the economy that constrain the choice of tax structure. First, they assume competitive markets in a general equilibrium setting that includes both production and consumption. The

---

[5] A recent textbook treatment of the optimal tax approach is found in Myles (1995).

emphasis on general equilibrium makes the OT approach theoretically interesting and mathematically sophisticated. However, it also imposes large information requirements on OT analysis.

Second, it is assumed that the structure of the economy does not permit the use of lump-sum taxation that would leave relative prices unaffected. Hence the design of tax structure always involves problems of the second best, since it is not possible for a social planner to collect a given level of revenues and achieve the specified equity goals without imposing a deadweight loss on society. Third, government is generally assumed to be exogenous to the economy, except in the restrictive sense that tax liabilities are influenced by the responses of private agents to a given tax structure.

Optimal tax analysis proceeds formally by constrained optimization of a social welfare function. Substantively, the focus of analysis is on the trade-off between equity goals and the deadweight costs of taxation facing the social planner given a revenue target, available tax instruments, and the influence of these instruments on private behavior.

In the ET tradition, the efficiency costs from pursuit of any equity norms are a secondary concern. But OT, by integrating equity and efficiency goals into a single welfare function, makes the deadweight loss resulting from pursuing any equity goal an explicit part of tax design. This has the virtue of requiring tax designers to be precise about distributional preferences in order to determine the tax structure resulting in the socially optimal equity–efficiency combination. On the other hand, the insistence on an explicit mathematical statement of the social welfare function comes at the expense of social values, such as freedom and justice, that are hard to formalize — values that nevertheless play a vital role in the formulation of tax policy. Indeed, for Henry Simons, these values were the raison d'être of equity norms (Bradford 1977, Hettich 1979a).

Precise specification of the general equilibrium structure of the economy is required for OT analysis, since the size of deadweight losses cannot be determined otherwise. Debate in the OT tradition therefore emphasizes analysis of key parameters influencing private sector responses to taxation, such as the size of various income and substitution effects, in addition to concerns over the nature of distributional weights in the social welfare function.

Precise rules for OT tax structures are almost as complicated as the underlying economic structure. On a less formal level, the idea that tax structure ought to minimize deadweight losses for given distributional goals has led to a presumption in favor of taxing consumption rather than income to avoid distortion in the intertemporal allocation of resources, and to a preference for broad-based taxes in order to avoid inducing substitution between activities that are taxed at different rates. There is also a presumption in favor of taxation by higher rather than lower levels of government to reduce elasticities of taxable activity with respect to tax rates.

These presumptions or rules of thumb are not based on a formal analysis of the OT problem. They are, rather, general statements about the nature of more efficient tax structures than exist currently, using intuition based on first-best welfare economics. As Joseph Stiglitz and Michael Boskin (1977) and many others have noted, however, the argument that fewer rather than more distortions are better is correct only under certain conditions. In the face of second-best situations, the use of first-best welfare economics may be seriously misleading. A detailed analysis incorporating other distortions in the economy is often necessary.

The OT literature has not been as concerned with special provisions as ET. The conventional wisdom that special provisions are undesirable because they distort relative prices and create vertical inequities is unconvincing if the OT problem allows for sufficient detail and variation in the characteristics of taxpayers. Stiglitz and Boskin (1977), for example, demonstrate the optimality of tax deductions for medical expenses. The existence of this deduction in their OT structure stems from the basic screening problem in OT analysis of taxing individuals according to characteristics that are most closely related to the arguments in the social welfare function when these characteristics cannot be observed directly, and when the surrogate characteristics that can be taxed are imperfectly correlated with the characteristics of direct interest and are to some extent under the control of the taxpayer.[6]

It is clear that the information requirements of OT theory are very large. For a complete analysis, it is necessary to trace the efficiency and distributional effects of a tax change through a complex economy consisting of a complicated network of markets, productive relationships and activities, and exhibiting many kinds of market imperfections. In theory, every distinct transaction should be taxed at a separate rate that takes into account all relevant direct and indirect effects on efficiency and distribution.

As noted in the Meade Report (IFS 1978, p. 27), such discrimination is not feasible in practice: "All that can be hoped is to take account of a few of the most obvious and most probable direct and indirect effects of any given tax change." The Meade Report, like Anthony Atkinson and Joseph Stiglitz (1980, pp. 423, 546), regards the results of OT theory as qualitative rather than quantitative, and as an important guide to tax design rather than as a practical basis for tax reform. In this vein, it is often argued that the principal virtue of OT is its ability to single out key parameters for the analysis of tax design – for example, the relevant distributional weights and the size of particular substitution effects.

---

[6] The incentive compatibility constraints considered in Chapter 4 represent one formal method of acknowledging the fact that many characteristics of taxpayers are only imperfectly known to the government, and that those characteristics upon which taxation can be levied are to some extent under the control of the taxpayer.

The Meade Report goes on to point out that there are important differences of emphasis in the search for feasible OT-based tax reforms. One approach is to search for new and better information regarding responses to taxation and to use this information to make possible more tax discrimination, taking account of a greater variety of general equilibrium effects of taxes on efficiency and distribution. The applied general equilibrium tax modeling pioneered by John Shoven and John Whalley (1973, 1977) and others (reviewed by Shoven and Whalley 1992a) represents perhaps the best hope yet for this sort of refinement.

A second approach to the problems of defining feasible OT reforms has been taken by the Meade Report (IFS 1978, p. 44):

> To base a tax structure on the principle of considering each rate of tax on each specific type of transaction separately is to invite distortions through the influence of pressure groups of particular interests, each obtaining some specific exemption or other advantage until the whole structure becomes a shambles of irrational special provisions. A complex system which was devised and administered by a committee of wise philosopher kings, advised by a group of omniscient economists and subject to no democratic pressures from well organized special interests, might be preferable to any one more simple system which was debarred from making many specific and detailed provisions and exceptions which would in fact be improvements. But the latter would also be debarred from making many undesirable special provisions, and in the world as it is the acceptance of a simple system based on one or two easily understood, clear rules (provided, of course, that they were well chosen rules) would almost certainly be preferable. There will, of course, inevitably be some special exceptions and exemptions; but it is desirable to start from some simple, reasonable, clearly understood general set of rules, from which only a limited number of very special exceptions are permitted.

The line of argument leading to the granting of more flexibility for tax authorities is clearly rejected here, for reasons strikingly similar to those put forward by Simons and, as shown in the next section, for reasons that are also compatible with normative fiscal exchange.

It is interesting to note that one recent branch of OT theory stemming from application of the time-inconsistency literature (Kydland and Prescott 1977) also suggests the desirability of simple constitutional rules over discretionary taxing power for the government. The idea here (see e.g. Fischer 1980, Kydland and Prescott 1980, Sheffrin 1983) stems from the view that government policy will not normally be "time consistent." Tax policies that are optimal for the government at one point in time are generally not optimal at future times. For example, in a dynamic context an efficient policy involves taxation of both labor and capital in all periods, in accordance with their supply elasticities and other relevant factors. However, once the policy has been announced and carried out for one period, it is efficient for the government *from the perspective of the second period* to tax only capital, since a tax on fixed capital bequeathed from the previous period involves no efficiency loss.

Time-inconsistent tax policies of this sort are undesirable because a history of broken promises will destroy the belief of private investors in the government's statements, causing private saving and investment to dry up and aggregate welfare to be reduced sharply along with the capital stock. Policy based on rules rather than discretion may represent a way of preventing such time-inconsistent and inefficient government behavior. However, arguments for implementation of rules must be based on careful analysis of the political context in which they will operate. The introduction of rules, such as those referred to in the Meade Report, may require a quasiconstitutional reform of the political system. Moreover, the logical steps leading to this conclusion may also lead one to reject the types of tax rules most favored by OT analysis.

5.1.3   Normative Fiscal Exchange

The fiscal exchange (FE) approach to taxation derives primarily from Knut Wicksell's voluntary exchange theory of the public economy (Wicksell 1896) and from the contemporary work in this tradition by James Buchanan (1976) and Geoffrey Brennan and Buchanan (1980).

The philosophical roots of this work lie in writings from the eighteenth and nineteenth centuries on the appropriate structure of representative government. The central problem addressed in the early literature was how to design institutions of government responsive to the electorate and at the same time ensure that electoral processes did not lead to exploitation by organized interest groups.

In their much discussed addition to the fiscal exchange literature, *The Power to Tax* (1980), Geoffrey Brennan and James Buchanan pose the question: Should the government's power to tax be limited and what form should this limitation take? Their approach provides a marked contrast to the ET and OT traditions, which ask: What is the best way to raise a budget of given size? The earlier fiscal exchange literature (e.g., Wicksell 1896, Lindahl 1919, Buchanan 1976), as well as later work by Brennan and Buchanan (1985), focused on electoral processes rather than on direct constraints on the power of government. Here the question simply was: What electoral process is most desirable?

Since the central problem in the version of FE theory developed in *The Power to Tax* – what may be called the outcome-oriented approach – concerns the possibility of malevolent government behavior, a model of such behavior is essential to their analysis. As J. S. Mill put it in his *Considerations on Representative Government*: "The very principle of constitutional government requires it to be assumed that political power will be abused to promote the particular purposes of the holder; not because it always is so, but because such is the natural tendency of things, to guard against which is the special use of free institutions" (quoted by Brennan 1981, p. 135). It is for this reason that Brennan and Buchanan start with the view that the state is a Leviathan attempting to maximize its extractions from the citizens. In other words, they take a minimax approach to the design of social institutions in order to limit the possibility of excessive government authority.

While one may object to the specific model chosen by Brennan and Buchanan, one can readily accept their insistence on the need for a model of the state. They make their point rather amusingly by discussing the best policy for restraining their dog, which likes to run onto an adjoining property:

> It is costly to build a fence or to purchase a chain. It is possible to prove that the no-fence, no-chain solution is more efficient than either *provided* that we model the behavior of our dog in such a way that he respects the boundaries of our property. As we put this example from personal experience, the exercise seems, and is, absurd. But is it really very different from that procedure which argues that tax structure X is more "efficient" than tax structure Y provided that we model the behavior of government in such a way that it seeks only to further efficiency in revenue collection? (1980, p. 193)

In *The Power to Tax*, the focus of analysis is on constitutional constraints designed to limit Leviathan-like tendencies of government. Restrictions on the ability to tax must be constitutional because Leviathan will never give up powers granted previously unless it is forced through constitutional revision to do so. Tax design is therefore a question of constitutional design, and tax reform is presumably a matter for constituent assemblies or other groups of taxpayers but not a matter for government itself. If it is carried out in the regular political context, it becomes a negative-sum game where tax reform advocacy largely takes on the pattern of mutually offsetting attempts to shift tax shares among groups. Brennan and Buchanan ask formally what tax structure would be favored at the constitutional level by a risk-averse taxpayer who decides behind the Rawlsian "veil of ignorance" or in a situation with limited information on his own future economic circumstances.

The concern in the early work of Wicksell (and Buchanan 1976) is predominantly with the ability of special interest groups to use majority rule in order to redistribute income in their favor. The focus of analysis is therefore on the choice among feasible electoral processes and not on specific limits on outcomes. Wicksell envisioned a process in which expenditures and taxes were voted on simultaneously and where public budgets were chosen in accordance with "approximate" unanimity. Such a process minimizes coercion and produces outcomes approaching Lindahl equilibrium – an equilibrium that is Pareto-efficient and that will receive unanimous support. This version of the FE tradition is not concerned with the correct degree of equity and efficiency in tax structure.[7] The desirable political process will, in this view, create whatever trade-off is appropriate in the circumstances. Nor is it concerned with structural features of the tax system per se. As James Buchanan (1976, p. 29) notes, the exchange-contractarian finds relatively little to disturb him in the presence of tax loopholes if he conceives these to reflect plausible outcomes of an acceptable political bargaining process.

In the outcome-oriented FE analysis initiated by Brennan and Buchanan, on the other hand, the problem is to choose bases and rate structures that limit Leviathan to a desirable level of total tax revenues. Analytically, assignment of a tax base to the government is equivalent to the assignment of an exclusive franchise for the sale of the output from the taxable economic activity. Since Leviathan will levy the profit or revenue-maximizing rate structure on every available base, adding bases simply increases the total deadweight loss and increases the size of government. Narrowly defined bases restrict Leviathan's power, the size of total revenues, and deadweight losses. This conclusion is in direct contrast to those reached by OT, which holds that broader bases are superior since, *given* total revenue, broadly based taxes distort relative prices to a lesser extent.

Brennan and Buchanan are also led to advocate abolition of capital taxation, since fixed capital cannot escape Leviathan's grasp. Bases such as labor income or consumption, which are more elastic, are more suitable because they allow taxpayers to escape more easily. In outcome-oriented FE, therefore, large economic responses to increases in tax rates may be the desirable result of a correctly designed tax structure.

Constitutional limitations on the nature of bases that Leviathan can exploit are also useful in ensuring that the level and type of public services provided are in accordance with the wishes of the electorate. If it is possible to assign tax bases that are strongly complementary with particular public goods, there will be an incentive for Leviathan to wield its power for the "common good." For example, a constitutional provision requiring that roads be financed exclusively by taxes levied on automobiles and associated inputs (gas, oil, tires, etc.) will encourage Leviathan to spend a large part of its revenues on road construction and maintenance. This is because automobile tax revenues will grow with the "supply" of automobile usage, while this supply, in turn, is a positive function of the size and quality of road networks.

In the work of Brennan and Buchanan, OT prescriptions become rules for maximum revenue extraction. The "multiplant" Leviathan will maximize revenues by levying higher tax rates on those bases that are less elastic with respect to changes in tax rates. Hence, the inverse elasticity rule of OT

---

[7] The Wicksellian approach to public finance is analyzed by Breton (1996) and is considered further in the next chapter.

becomes a revenue-maximizing rule in the context of FE – a rule that also maximizes deadweight losses which are a positive function of the size of government (Brennan and Buchanan 1980, pp. 80–1). As Brennan and Buchanan note, "a change in the political model may stand many of the orthodox precepts for tax change on their heads" (1980, p. 194).

Whether tax loopholes are good or bad depends on whether they are opened up at the constitutional stage or at a later time. The individual will seek deliberately to build certain "escape routes" into the tax structure at the constitutional stage. These provide the protection or guarantees against undue fiscal exploitation that he wants the constitution to embody. Post-constitutionally, loopholes are bad to the extent they represent attempts by Leviathan to discriminate among heterogeneous taxpayers. A combination of high nominal tax rates and extensive special provisions could yield maximum revenue to the state. Presumably, the constitutional convention is to decide which loopholes are good constitutional restrictions and which represent tax discrimination.

5.1.4   Implications of the Three Traditions for Tax Reform and Tax Design

The ET, OT, and FE approaches yield different implications for tax design and tax reform. All three traditions have been used as starting points for the creation of blueprints describing an ideal tax system. It should not be surprising that conceptions of what is ideal differ significantly depending on the particular point of departure.

Equitable taxation has exercised the most pronounced impact on actual tax reform and design. Its influence reached an early peak with the massive *Report of the Royal Commission on Taxation* (1966), which proposed extensive revisions in the tax system of Canada with the goal of bringing the Canadian federal tax base as close as possible to Simons's concept of income. The impact was not confined to Canada, however, nor limited to the 1960s. A similar effort to base individual income taxation more fully on a comprehensively defined base is found in the U.S. Department of the Treasury's *Blueprints for Basic Tax Reform* (1977) and *Tax Reform for Fairness, Simplicity and Economic Growth* (1984). The latter report served as a background for *The President's Tax Proposal* (U.S. Government 1985) and for the policy discussions leading to the Tax Reform Act of 1986, the most recent major revision of U.S. income-tax law.[8] Other examples of officially sponsored reform proposals include the Swedish report *Progressive Expenditure Tax – An Alternative?* (1978), issued

---

[8] For an analysis of the reforms and their economic effects, see Musgrave (1987) and Slemrod (1990b).

under the name of Sven-Olof Lodin, and the Irish *First Report of the Commission on Taxation* (Government of Ireland 1982). The book by George Break and Joseph Pechman (1975), written at a time when ET was the predominant normative approach, presents a judicious academic discussion of the meaning and feasibility of reforms derived from this tradition.

The Swedish and Irish proposals depart from the orthodox ET tradition by advocating expenditure taxes as complements to the income tax. Henry Simons firmly believed that horizontal equity required a single base and wanted to abolish all taxes not levied on income, with the exceptions of the property tax (which in his opinion had already been capitalized) and gasoline taxes (which he regarded as benefit taxes). This ideal was never achieved, or even attempted in practice, even though the Canadian Royal Commission on Taxation made proposals that would have moved the country far in this direction.

Optimal taxation has exercised a less pronounced impact on official policy proposals in recent decades. Its approach is reflected in the analysis of the Meade Report (IFS 1978), mentioned in Section 5.1.2, although the report's authors chose to recommend an income tax with a broadly defined base for implementation, rather than an OT blueprint, in order to counter the political difficulties associated with the greater complexity of an OT tax system. On the other hand, OT has influenced the academic discussion of tax reform in a far-reaching manner and has led to a renewed emphasis on consumption and expenditure taxation while lending support to the lowering of tax rates on the returns from capital assets.[9]

The influence of FE on tax policy has been more indirect than the influence of the other two traditions. This should not be surprising since the authors of major writings on FE have been more interested in raising cautions, and in emphasizing the need for constitutional limits on government, than in making detailed proposals for reform. The most immediate impact of FE analysis may have come from the intellectual support that it provided to movements for constitutional limits on the power to tax at the local and state levels in the United States.[10]

Given the policy impact of the three normative traditions, it is useful to summarize implications for tax design arising from each type of analysis. The broad differences are summarized in Table 5.1, which focuses on the main ele-

[9] Regarding consumption taxation, see the volume edited by Manfred Rose (1990), as well as Charles McLure and George Zodrow (1996) and Zodrow (1997). William Gale (1995) provides a brief overview of the debate on replacing income with consumption taxation. Regarding tax reform and capital costs, see Dale Jorgenson and Ralph Landau (1993).

[10] For material on tax revolts and tax limitation movements, see George Kaufman and Kenneth Rosen (1981), Terry Schwadron and Paul Richter (1984), and Arthur O'Sullivan, Terri Sexton, and Steven Sheffrin (1995).

Table 5.1.   Tax structure in three normative approaches

Normative Approach	Elements of Tax Structure		
	Bases	Special Provisions	Rate Structures
ET	Broad and single base, consisting of comprehensive income. Implies equal treatment of income from any source, including capital. Integration of personal and corporate taxes, no indirect taxes. (Minority of authors supports comprehensive expenditure tax)	None in principle. Measurement problems may require special provisions such as income averaging	Horizontal equity: same rate for same comprehensive income. Vertical equity: indeterminate (left to political process)
OT	*Formal Analysis* — Each transaction taxed at unique rate, depending on its weight in the social welfare function and the general equilibrium structure of the economy.		
	Informal Analysis (Rules of Thumb)		
	Single base: Broad personal consumption tax, possibly with flow of funds corporate income tax. Reduce emphasis on capital taxation. Other bases: (e.g. commodity, sales or income) if government restricted to these bases. Rely more heavily on more inelastic bases	No general rules, but favored examples, e.g., immediate expensing of investment. Complex structure of exemptions, deductions and credits may result from the interaction of particular policy objectives and screening problems if income tax is used	Hump shaped marginal rate structure
FE	Narrow, multiple bases, preferably elastic with regard to rates, e.g., restricted or selective income tax and reduced emphasis on taxation of capital	At constitutional level: Exclude inelastic portion of bases	Nonregressive. Use equity rules to limit tax discrimination

ments of tax structure. For OT, the table presents results drawn from less formal analysis – analysis that is influenced by the OT vision but does not fully implement the general theoretical model.

Depending on tradition, a single broad base (ET, OT) or multiple narrowly defined bases (FE) are preferred. The traditions supporting a single base disagree on its definition, with the majority position supporting income in ET and consumption in OT. Rules for other bases in OT (which may be necessary for reasons determined outside the OT model) conflict strongly with similar rules derived from FE. Whereas OT suggests heavier reliance on bases that are

Table 5.2. Problems of implementation emphasized by three normative traditions

ET	Measurement of comprehensive income
	Realized versus unrealized gains and losses
	Real versus nominal income
	Estimation of imputed income
	Definition of tax paying unit
	Treatment of fluctuating income
	Integration of personal and corporate income tax
OT	Information on behavioral responses of all agents required
	General equilibrium structure of the economy must be modeled (for given behavioral characteristics of agents)
	Screening problems
FE	Organization of constitutional convention
	Nature of decision making behind Rawlsian veil (or other formulation of veil of ignorance)
	Enforceability of constitutional restrictions

relatively inelastic with regard to changes in tax rates, FE recommends that the taxation of such bases be constitutionally restricted.

Disagreements also extend to the choice of special provisions. While ET argues strongly against the existence of most such provisions, FE makes their use part of its strategy to limit the power of the state. Recommendations derived from OT are less clear-cut. Depending on the government's objectives, the restrictions placed upon it, and the screening problems faced by policy makers, such features as exceptions, deductions, and tax credits may be appropriate elements of a good OT tax system.

Proposed rate structures are also at variance. Optimal taxation suggests a hump-shaped progression of marginal rates together with initially rising average rates for a broad personal consumption tax. The FE approach also argues for progressive or proportional taxation to counter Leviathan's taste for discrimination and therefore regressivity. Equitable taxation leaves vertical equity indeterminate but insists that persons with the same comprehensive income must pay the same amount of taxes regardless of the sources from which their incomes are drawn, an argument that runs counter to the recommendations of OT.

Table 5.2 summarizes the different problems of blueprint implementation emphasized in each of the three traditions. Writers on ET have devoted most of their efforts to problems of measuring comprehensive income. Questions of whether to tax real or nominal income, and realized or unrealized capital gains, are a major concern in this regard. Other problems frequently raised in this literature relate to the definition of the taxpaying unit, the treatment of fluctuating income, and the practical steps needed to integrate the personal and corporate income taxes. One should note that, among the three traditions, ET provides by far the most detailed and practical guidance on actual implementation. This, as well as its greater age, may help to explain ET's profound impact on actual tax design in recent decades.

Although OT writers take pride in the greater generality of their arguments, they must face the costs of much more extensive data requirements. In principle, information is needed on the general equilibrium nature of the economy, as well as on the behavioral responses of all affected agents. An OT analysis emphasizes screening problems as well as the study of tax incidence in a general equilibrium context. One should note, however, that policy recommendations by OT writers are related only in an approximate fashion to the empirical results obtained with general equilibrium models, and that such models are based on restrictive assumptions about the structure of the economy.

Among the three traditions, writers on FE have shown the least interest in problems of implementation. Since they emphasize constitutional revision, relevant questions center around the organization and composition of a constitutional convention, the information that should be available to convention delegates, and the enforcement mechanisms that would have to be included in any tax constitution.

5.2 NORMATIVE THEORIES OF TAXATION AND POLITICS

The three traditions represent different analytical approaches, with each having valid elements, but they are not capable of fully answering the questions posed at the beginning of this chapter. The role of politics in normative tax design and the proper counterfactual for judging public policies on taxation remain open questions.

Ideas about the political system play a part in the policy recommendations arising from all three traditions. In laying the foundations for ET, Henry Simons was searching for a way to neutralize political interference in the economy. He believed that a comprehensive tax base would accomplish this goal while also creating the basis for clear political choices on vertical equity. He expressed this forcefully by declaring: "It is high time for Congress to quit this ludicrous business of dipping deeply into great incomes with a sieve" (1938, p. 219).

Simons provided no formal analysis of how the political system works, nor of the imperfections in the system that were to be countered. As in research on economic change, comparative static analysis of political changes requires a theory of existence and stability of equilibrium, as well as a means to evaluate the efficiency of equilibrium policies. In a formal framework containing these elements, it would be possible to assess whether the introduction of a comprehensive income tax would represent a stable change and whether it would lead to an improvement in welfare. In addition, one could compare the effects of such a policy with the results of other tax regimes. Unless an appropriate formal framework is provided, however, these questions must remain largely unanswered.

The implications of a comprehensive tax base and of horizontal equity for tax structure can be illustrated with a simple example.[11] Let us assume that there are only two tax bases, B_1 and B_2, representing different components of income, such as wage earnings and capital gains, and that the two components add up to comprehensively defined income. Assume also that taxation is proportional at rate t, and that each base includes one exemption, s. Equal treatment of equals would then require that

$$\frac{s_1}{B_1} = \frac{s_2}{B_2},$$

(5.1)

where total tax payments from either base are given by

$$t_1 = t_2$$

(5.2)

and

$$T_i = t_i \cdot (B_i - s_i) \quad \text{for} \quad i = 1, 2.$$

(5.3)

Unless these conditions are satisfied, taxpayers with equal comprehensive incomes, drawn from the two sources in different proportions, will not incur equal tax liabilities.

The same formulation can also be used to bring out a second implication. We can interpret B_1 and B_2 as referring to comprehensive income and to some other possible tax base that differs from income, such as sales receipts for consumer goods. Since ET specifies income as the only correct base, the ET ideal can be satisfied only if taxation is restricted to B_1, except in the unlikely case where consumer expenditures make up the same proportion of comprehensive income for all taxpayers in the same economic circumstances and thus represent a direct proxy for income.

There is no a priori reason why a tax structure consistent with political equilibrium should satisfy these conditions, as the analysis in previous chapters demonstrates. Political costs associated with different components of comprehensive income appear to vary widely in practice, with the result that income from various sources is generally treated quite differently. In a similar fashion, there is no obvious political reason why a government should restrict itself to taxing only income, or even to deriving a sizable proportion of total revenues from income taxation. (There are, for example, several states in the United States that have no income tax at all.)

---

[11] The discussion of ET and tax expenditures in this section draws on Winer and Hettich (1988).

The discussion implies that tax reform will fail to achieve the objectives of ET unless political cost functions are changed in just the right manner. The tax reform literature in the ET tradition does not approach the problem in this way, contenting itself with proposing changes in tax laws necessary to implement the comprehensive base, or with suggesting changes that would bring the existing base closer to the comprehensive one. It should not be surprising, therefore, that such proposals are rarely implemented in the form in which they are made. One should also note that moves toward a comprehensive tax base may set off political adjustments in the tax system as a whole that may reduce rather than enhance horizontal equity.

Similar conceptual problems also arise in the literature on tax expenditures, which represents a more recent outgrowth of ET. We recall from the discussion in Chapter 3 that tax expenditures are defined as revenues forgone from granting special treatment, such as the application of lower rates to selected components of income. In other words, the existing situation is compared to a hypothetical tax system that uses a comprehensive base and does not include any special provisions $(s_i = 0)$ or rates. The difference in revenues raised by the two systems is then identified as total tax expenditures.

Whenever we define a theoretical counterpart to the existing situation, we face certain logical difficulties. In this instance, it is not immediately clear what tax rates should be applied under the hypothetical tax regime. One possibility is to assume that existing tax rates on all components of income remain unchanged at actual rates t_i. In the context of our simple example, with a single exemption on each base and proportional rates, this implies the following definition:

$$E_1 = R^*(s_i = 0, t_i) - R(s_i, t_i) \quad \text{for} \quad i = 1, 2, \tag{5.4}$$

where E_1 stands for total tax expenditures and where the expressions R^* and R on the right-hand side represent total revenues collected in the hypothetical and actual situations, respectively. The value of E_1 can be calculated as long as we either disregard likely economic adjustments to the expansion of the base (the procedure generally adopted in so-called tax expenditure budgets) or estimate R^* subject to predicted economic adjustments. Although the second course would determine the E_1 consistent with economic equilibrium, it would not ensure the existence of political equilibrium. There is no reason why the government, in the face of given political cost functions, should choose the pre-existing rates t_i as the solution to its problem of staying in office. An alternative definition avoids this lack of reality:

$$E_2 = R^*(s_i = 0, t_i = t_i^e) - R(s_i, t_i) \quad \text{for} \quad i = 1, 2, \tag{5.5}$$

where t_i^e represents the tax rate that would be chosen by a self-interested government restricted to the use of a single proportional tax rate for all components of income. Unfortunately, E_2 can only be determined if it is possible to predict rates t_i^e as well as economic adjustments to these rates. While we might expect a lower total budget if the government's objective function must be maximized subject to more severe constraints $\left(\text{i.e., } s_i = 0 \text{ and } t_i = t_i^e\right)$, it will be difficult to predict the exact extent of the decrease.[12]

Our analysis indicates that the concept of tax expenditures is theoretically unsatisfactory or, if redefined in the manner suggested, non-operational without an empirical model of equilibrium fiscal structure. It is generally understood that tax expenditure budgets are of restricted value when they fail to take account of general equilibrium effects in the private economy, but it is only rarely acknowledged that they also fall short by neglecting readjustments in the political equilibrium underlying the tax structure. This problem with the tax expenditure concept is in addition to those discussed in Chapter 3.

The theory of optimal taxation abstracts from politics by assuming a social planner who is implementing an exogenously given social welfare function. Politics is brought in, if at all, as a mere ex post adjustment of recommendations derived from a model that excludes them. The dangers of such an approach are illustrated by the quotations from the Meade Report presented in the previous section. Although the Report derives its theoretical basis from OT, it advocates a comprehensive tax base. Complexity in the tax system that would be an integral part of any blueprint in the OT tradition is rejected in order to preclude anticipated political responses. The Report's authors develop recommendations based on what they perceive as simple rules, yet they fail to consider why such rules would be consistent with the operation of existing political institutions. Nor do they explain whether their proposals represent the most efficient choice from the available set of possible rules or institutions. The analysis of tax structure in a world with expected vote maximization suggests that equilibrium tax systems in democratic societies are of necessity complex and that they are not likely to be governed by simple rules.

It may also be useful to point out briefly how the absence of a public choice analysis qualifies the conclusion of the recent OT literature on time inconsistency. This literature shows some concern with government, arguing like Simons for policy (or tax) rules rather than discretion. It is assumed that inelastic tax bases (such as capital equipment) will be taxed in an inefficient manner, since they become "sitting ducks" for the government once they have been created by private activity. The argument fails to recognize the possible adjustments by taxpayers and voters to the possibility of time-inconsistent government action. Investors who anticipate such action will spend political

---

[12] As pointed out in Chapter 3, whether the public sector increases or decreases in size in the new equilibrium also depends on the substitutability in consumption of public and private goods.

resources to protect themselves against the possibility of loss. Though the result may still be a lower capital stock than would exist if time-inconsistent behavior could not occur, it is no longer clear that policy rules that are hard to change (and impose costs of their own) represent the most efficient way of dealing with the problem.

Unlike OT, FE is concerned with politics from the start. Here the analytical gap is of a different nature. Brennan and Buchanan pay a heavy price for the use of a malevolent model of government in which voters have control only at the constitutional stage. The possibility of Leviathan-like behavior can influence the design of institutions, but it is not clear that this possibility should be the dominant consideration. Presumably, the price that people are willing to pay for insurance against Leviathan depends on the likelihood that abuse may actually occur (as well as on the tastes for liberty). Moreover, since their model excludes the interaction of partially constrained government with voters and taxpayers, which is a dominant feature of democratic systems, Brennan and Buchanan have no framework to estimate the costs of adopting rigid tax constitutions. (Such costs would have to be estimated by comparing allocation of resources under the proposed constitution with allocation under conditions closer to what now exists.) One should also note in this context that the Leviathan model is incomplete as a theoretical framework because it does not explain how dictatorship arises and under what conditions such government represents a stable outcome.[13]

Neither process-oriented nor outcome-oriented FE offers advice to existing governments. Advice is offered to those citizens attempting to institute constitutional limitations on the power to tax. Implementation therefore requires the organization of constitutional conventions or initiatives. Furthermore, information must be developed that helps convention participants make appropriate choices, including knowledge of the problems of enforcement that may arise from different legal limitations on the government. This information must be sufficient to permit decision making behind the Rawlsian veil of ignorance, a problem emphasized by Alan Hamlin (1984). In this respect, process control emphasized by Wicksell may be preferable to direct or indirect control of outcomes. The information required to undertake the appraisal of alternative processes consists of the characteristics of the various processes, the values of the members of the constituent assembly, and a description of imaginable issues. But constitutional reform directed at outlawing bad outcomes or encouraging good ones also requires that individuals be able to classify outcomes as good or bad in all possible states of the world. Otherwise, outcomes cannot be restricted to a set that dominates all alternatives in all states of the world. Given the likely degree of uncertainty about the future, this set may be very small, and it may even be empty (Hamlin 1984, p. 180).

---

[13] Wintrobe (1990) has pursued this issue further.

A further set of problems concerns implementation of a tax constitution. The distinction between the choice of constitutional rules and of policies within an existing framework is mainly a conceptual convenience. One can envisage the political system as consisting of contracts of varying duration and comprehensiveness. Constitutional rules lie at one end of the spectrum, being long-term in nature, with broad coverage and high costs of recontracting. Other components, such as rules governing legislative committees, may be shorter-lived, more partial in coverage, and easier to change. Finally, there are many temporary conventions or agreements that influence the operation of the system at a particular point in time.

Viewed in this manner, constitution making becomes an ongoing process, where the current participants must be convinced that it is in their interests to adopt particular contracts or rules. Considerations relevant to choices behind a veil of ignorance may become merely a secondary influence in such a context. One may note that this view is supported by recent developments in Canada, where protracted constitutional negotiations have taken place over the past fifteen years and where far-reaching constitutional change has been enacted. A similar picture also emerges in Eastern Europe, where fundamental political change is occurring, and with regard to the current developments within the European Union.

5.3   ESSENTIAL ELEMENTS IN AN EXTENDED NORMATIVE FRAMEWORK

The review of normative theories suggests a major criticism applying to all three approaches. A complete normative framework should encompass an analysis of political as well as economic equilibrium, making it possible to evaluate proposals systematically from a more inclusive perspective than either ET, OT, or FE alone is able to accomplish.

An examination of the foundations of normative theory in economics points to three analytical steps needed to construct an expanded framework. These are the same basic steps found in the literature on traditional welfare economics. To begin, an analysis is required that plays the role of the first theorem of welfare economics ("invisible hand" theorem) in the context of political economy. Put differently, a set of ideal conditions must be formulated that serves as a counterfactual, and a proof must be provided that, under these conditions, equilibrium tax policies will be efficient. The second necessary step is development of an analog to the analysis of market failure. Cases where the basic theorem does not hold must be identified, and an examination of such cases must be developed to give guidance to policy analysts. Third, measurement is required to make the analysis complete. It is necessary to formulate ways of assessing the consequences for welfare (or other specified social objectives) of

Table 5.3.   Normative theories of taxation and essential steps of welfare analysis

THREE STEPS	ET	OT	FE
"Invisible hand" in political economy	Concern with politics but no concept of political equilibrium	Politics a *deus ex machina*	Tax constitution not an equilibrium outcome
Market failure of political and economic markets	Comprehensive base as solution to political market failure incompatible with political equilibrium	Analysis of economic markets only	Extreme political market failure and risk aversion assumed
Measurement of policy effects	Rejects utility theory	Measured economic effects exclude political costs	No measure of costs from limiting government

suggested policy reforms, so that comparisons across alternative proposals become feasible.

To gain intuition concerning the implications of such a broader approach, it is useful to summarize briefly how ET, OT, and FE relate to an expanded analysis. Table 5.3 gives a capsule summary and a critical evaluation of the three theories from the more inclusive perspective.

None of the three approaches provides an analysis fully accomplishing the purpose of the first step. Although ET shows a concern with the political process, there is no analysis of political equilibrium and only limited attention to the operation of market forces. While OT puts a careful focus on adjustments in private markets and economic efficiency, it treats politics as a *deus ex machina*, one whose motives may be criticized but whose decisions are not subject to systematic examination. Fiscal exchange proposes a set of ideal conditions formulated with the help of a constitutional convention. However, these conditions cannot be interpreted as equilibrium policies, since the political process underlying such a convention, as well as the process leading to adoption of the recommendations by convention delegates, is not spelled out.

Market failure in an extended framework must refer to the operation of political as well as economic markets. Equitable taxation appears to view special provisions in the tax system as arising from political failure, yet its proposed solution – the comprehensive tax base – seems incompatible with competitive political markets. Optimal taxation analysis suffers from a similar shortcoming, proposing tax programs chosen by a planner that may contradict the choices arrived at through democratic institutions. Fiscal exchange assumes that political markets fail completely except at the constitutional stage, where delegates make choices behind a veil of ignorance and are extremely risk-averse to possible future actions by governments.

As emphasized earlier, ET rejects utility analysis, thus precluding the path to measurement of policy effects most commonly adopted in economic theory. The OT approach offers a sophisticated treatment of welfare effects defined within a strictly economic framework. Yet measurement may be applied to the "wrong" policies (i.e., to tax programs not compatible with democratic choices) since the costs of arriving at political decisions are not part of the analysis. The FE focus is primarily on methods of constraining Leviathan, but it does not provide ways to estimate the costs of imposing specific limits on government action.

Although the table assembles criticisms of the three normative theories, it should not be misinterpreted as a rejection of the existing literature. The ET, OT, and FE traditions represent an extensive intellectual effort, containing ideas and concepts that continue to influence policy and to provide a valuable background for theoretical and empirical work. The purpose of the table is to bring relevant issues into sharper focus and to pave the way for an extended normative approach to taxation. Review of existing theories makes clear that development of a new approach represents a major intellectual task. In the next chapter, we propose some initial steps toward creation of a more inclusive normative theory.

CHAPTER 6

Welfare, Politics, and Taxation

The problem of efficiency, however, is so vital that we cannot
ignore it merely because our answers to it are not complete. Welfare
economics, despite its limitations, provides partial answers; and I
feel that to provide partial answers to vital problems is at least as
important as it is to provide complete answers to lesser questions.

Tibor Scitovsky (1951, p. xi)

This chapter represents an exploration of a more inclusive welfare economics
of taxation. Its nature, like that of any new enterprise, is of necessity somewhat
tentative. The emphasis is on presenting an outline of ideas and illustrating
them with relevant examples. Whereas some sections develop a formal analysis, others take a more intuitive approach. The organization of the material is
based on the conclusions reached in the preceding chapter, where we sketched
three steps required for a comprehensive welfare analysis in the presence of
collective choice. (See Section 5.3.)

We begin here with the selection of the standard of reference against which
to judge collective choice outcomes. This, together with a consideration of the
conditions under which equilibrium policy outcomes will achieve the standard,
constitutes the first step. Economists have devoted much effort to working out
such an analysis for an economy with private markets, and it has been one of
the important achievements of the discipline to show that an economic system
with competitive markets will yield optimal (Pareto-efficient) outcomes under
carefully defined conditions. The question is whether such an approach can be
extended successfully to encompass public goods and collective decision making. Knut Wicksell (1896) and Eric Lindahl (1919) recognized the existence of
this theoretical problem long before others realized that difficult questions had
to be faced. We consider the answer proposed by Lindahl as well as one provided by a different (and perhaps less familiar) normative framework that
acknowledges the transaction costs incurred in actually reaching an equilibrium solution in a democracy. This latter approach makes use of the Representation Theorem to specify conditions under which the ideal outcome will be
achieved. We refer to this ideal outcome or normative standard as an "optimal
representative tax (ORT) system."

The second step involves the study of why actual political equilibria depart from the chosen (ORT) standard of reference – that is, the reasons for political market failure. We investigate this issue by considering situations in which the Representation Theorem fails to hold.

We then turn to the measurement of deviations from the preferred standard, which is the third step required for a complete welfare analysis. We inquire into the meaning of welfare losses relative to the ORT standard and consider the usefulness of the excess burden of taxation (as usually calculated) as a measure of such losses. In the light of this discussion, we reassess the rule that tax reform should lead to the equalization of marginal excess burdens per unit of revenue collected from alternative tax sources, a rule that is often relied upon in applied tax policy analysis.

We conclude the chapter by comparing the suggested approach to optimal taxation and commenting on some of the essential features of the proposed framework.

6.1   STEP ONE: THE STANDARD OF REFERENCE AND THE CONDITIONS FOR AN IDEAL EQUILIBRIUM OUTCOME

Whereas collective choice analysis has exercised an important influence on the predictive and empirical study of taxation, the search for what constitutes a "good" tax or an "optimal" tax system has been dominated by optimal taxation (OT). As pointed out in our review of the approach in Chapter 5, OT assumes that the aggregation of preferences across the electorate has already been solved in some unspecified manner, and that the resulting social judgments can be formally expressed through a social welfare function.

Normative analysis with a collective choice component provides for a rather different emphasis from analysis based on the actions of a social planner. It requires a focus on the functioning of the political mechanism and its failures, even when primary attention is given to specific outcomes. In the same manner that welfare economics of the private sector revolves around private market failure, welfare analysis for the public sector must relate to failures of political markets and the resulting consequences for economic policies. The difficulty for the analyst lies in identifying the relevant deviations from the operation of an ideal political system and in linking them to the choice of particular tax policies.

Judgments of this nature must proceed from a standard of reference. As we argued in the previous chapter, two components are needed to fully describe this standard. First, we must define the meaning of efficiency. Next, it is necessary to describe a set of institutions that produces efficient or optimal outcomes. Moreover, the ideal system must yield stable equilibria; otherwise, optimality will be only a fleeting experience, even in an ideal world.

6.1.1   Two Possible Collective Choice Standards

Can we formulate a standard of reference for a system that includes the provision of both private and public services?

Lindahl (1919) described a bargaining process for deciding collectively upon public expenditures and taxes that is analogous to the role played by competitive markets in the analysis of the private sector.[1] The process he suggested involves joint quantity adjustment by all consumers of a public good. Unanimous agreement on the good's output level and the associated tax sharing must be reached simultaneously by participants. If there is more than one public good, the process must be applied separately to each one. For each public good, output level and tax shares are adjusted until all consumers of the good are in a utility-optimizing equilibrium, where each one faces an implicit, unique "tax-price" for an additional unit of the public good that is just equal to his or her marginal valuation of it. Moreover, enforcement of the government budget restraint ensures that the sum of individual tax-prices is just sufficient to cover the marginal cost of public good production. As a result, the sum of marginal evaluations is equal to the marginal cost of the public good, and the outcome of the process is Pareto optimal.[2]

As does the operation of competitive markets in traditional welfare analysis, Lindahl bargaining leads to one point on the Pareto frontier; it does not define the best of all possible Pareto efficient allocations of resources. Collective quantity adjustment occurs for a given distribution of income. A different decision procedure would have to be used if the collectivity wanted to make choices concerning redistribution of existing income or wealth. (If redistribution is considered a pure public good then it falls within the purview of Lindahl bargaining; however, few analysts would characterize all redistribution in this manner.)

In the actual world, decisions about the provision of collective goods are usually reached through a political process based on voting. Different voting rules are possible, with majority voting being the most common one. This raises the question of how Lindahl bargaining is related to choices by voting.

[1] For a good exposition of Lindahl's model, see Johansen (1965, pp. 129–40). The work of Wicksell and Lindahl is also discussed in Escarraz (1967) and Head (1974). A recent textbook treatment of the technical literature is given by Myles (1995).

[2] Foley (1967) specifies the technical conditions under which any Lindahl equilibrium will be Pareto efficient.

In theoretical analysis, Lindahl processes have been linked to political mechanisms that require unanimous consent of participants. Unanimity, or near-unanimity, was advocated as a voting rule by Wicksell (1896) in his discussion of budget determination in Sweden.[3] He envisaged voting by the legislature on different proposals linking possible expenditure levels with specific tax-sharing agreements. Part of Lindahl's work was an attempt to formalize important aspects of this discussion.

A unanimity rule would preclude any involuntary redistribution of income, such as may occur under less restrictive voting mechanisms. Moreover, if all possible alternatives are considered in a costless manner and all participants vote their true preferences, unanimous decisions must be Pareto optimal for the group. Lindahl's bargaining model operates in this context when decisions are limited to provision of a single public good.[4]

In practice, unanimity rules can result in high decision costs and create the possibility of strategic behavior on the part of individuals who use their veto power to exact significant concessions from the majority. As a result, less restrictive voting rules may be preferable as allocation mechanisms.

Decision costs associated with different collective choice mechanisms fall into the larger category of transaction costs. The existence of such resource costs raises difficult problems for the normative theorist, who must decide whether to include them in the definition of the standard of reference or whether to treat them as deviations from the ideal world. In traditional welfare economics, transaction costs are generally treated as deviations.[5] Efficient solutions minimize such costs in relation to an ideal situation where they do not exist. Use of a Lindahl process as the counterfactual in normative analysis that includes collective choice corresponds to this approach.

Transaction costs play a more explicit role in a probabilistic voting model such as the one used in Chapters 3 and 4, where they serve to explain the nature of tax instruments and of tax structure. (They may also be used to explain why voters elect representatives rather than decide upon every issue directly.)

Given the existence of such costs, can majority choices be Pareto optimal in this framework? The answer suggested by the Representation Theorem is: Yes. Assuming that voters cast their ballots strictly on the basis of how a political platform affects their utility, competition for office forces political parties – in

---

[3] Wagner (1985b) argues that Wicksell's discussion must be understood within the context of Swedish political institutions of the time.

[4] Wicksell and Vilfredo Pareto (whose work lead to the concept of Pareto optimality) were contemporaries. For an interesting comparative discussion of their rather different approaches to public economics, see Hennipman (1982).

[5] Quirk and Saposnik (1968), one of the earliest textbooks to give a rigorous statement of welfare economics and general equilibrium theory, gives no formal treatment of transaction costs.

order to maximize their chances for electoral success – to adopt any fiscal platform that is likely to make some voters better off without making any other voter worse off. We shall label the tax structure that emerges in such a perfectly functioning representative democracy an *optimal representative tax* (ORT) system.

How do outcomes in an ORT system compare with outcomes reached through Lindahl bargaining? A Lindahl equilibrium results from a process linking the output level of a public good specifically to the tax or cost share applying to each participant, whereas voting choices in a probabilistic voting model reflect a more general political mechanism. Because of transaction costs, party platforms may include second-best arrangements that lead to separation between spending and taxing decisions on the part of consumers.

If voter-consumers no longer link quantity adjustments to changes in cost per unit of public good, taxation will create welfare or efficiency losses that do not occur in a Lindahl equilibrium, and such losses will persist even in the face of political competition. In this broader setting, efficiency merely implies that welfare losses are minimized by the political process, not that they vanish altogether. We shall return to the measurement of such losses in a later section.

6.2   STEP TWO: ANALYZING POLITICAL MARKET FAILURE

Observed political markets, like their economic counterparts, may suffer from imperfections when compared to their ideal description. Welfare analysis has traditionally focused on such imperfections, trying to assess their implications for choices by decision makers and for the well-being of individual actors in the system. Although the examination of economic market failure has a long history in the literature, less attention has been paid to formally analyze the failure of political markets. The economic analyst who attempts to carry out an inquiry of this type faces two challenges. First, she must identify and characterize a possible market failure within a formally specified political context.[6] In addition, she must link the operation of political markets to the choice of particular economic policy instruments. In this section, we illustrate such an analysis by examining three contexts in which the Representation Theorem may fail to hold. The first case concerns a situation where government choices follow those of a special interest group; the second relates to the use of tax

---

[6] There is an existing literature on "nonmarket" failure. However, though of interest for our investigation into political market failure, this literature does not establish a normative standard of reference in the presence of collective choice.

policy information in a decentralized setting. In a third illustration, we investigate the effect of contributions for political advertising on the efficiency of political markets.

To set the stage for the analysis of political market failure, we begin with a brief restatement of the probabilistic voting model employed in Chapter 4 and of the Representation Theorem used to characterize the policy platform in Nash equilibrium. In such a framework, political parties know the probability density f_h describing the voting behavior of each individual voter h. We assume that f_h as seen by the parties depends on the difference in utilities that would result from the adoption of the proposals of the incumbent (i) and the opposition (o). The probability that individual h votes for the incumbent is given by $\pi_{hi} = f_h[v^h(s_i) - v^h(s_o)]$, where v_h is the indirect utility function of voter h and s_j refers to the set of policy proposals of party j.[7] The probability π_{hi} is assumed to be increasing in $v^h(s_i)$ and decreasing in $v^h(s_o)$; π_{ho} is equal to $1 - \pi_{hi}$ and has analogous properties.

Each party chooses a platform consisting of K policy instruments $s_j = \{s_{kj}; k = 1, 2, \ldots, K\}$ so as to maximize its total expected vote, with the number of instruments K being less than the number of voters H. For the incumbent the expected vote EV_i is equal to the sum of the individual vote probabilities $\sum_h f_{hi}$. Each party's choice of a policy platform is informed by knowledge of voting densities and is constrained by the general equilibrium structure of the economy, including the government's budget restraint, which we represent in the general form $F(s) = 0$.

The first-order conditions for the optimal strategy of the incumbent (and analogously for the opposition) are

$$\sum_{h=1}^{H} \left[\frac{\partial f_h}{\partial v^h} \cdot \frac{\partial v^h}{\partial s_{ki}} \right] \Big/ \frac{\partial F}{\partial s_{ki}} = \alpha \quad \text{for} \quad k = 1, 2, \ldots, K, \tag{6.1}$$

where α represents the Lagrange multiplier associated with the constraint. The equilibrium platform is the outcome of the Nash game defined by the first-order conditions for the incumbent and opposition parties.

Note that, in contrast to conditions (4.2), the numerator in equations (6.1) includes the summation over all H voters. This acknowledges in a simple manner that, since there are only $K < H$ instruments due to sorting, each instrument will directly affect more than one voter.

According to the Representation Theorem, the equilibrium policy platform can be described by optimizing a function that is a particular weighted sum of

---

[7] In Chapter 4 we used the direct utility function u^h in the definition of the probability of voting. Consistency with individual optimization was ensured by appropriately constraining political optimization. Here it is convenient to work with the indirect utility function v^h.

taxpayer utilities. The synthetic optimization problem that replicates the equilibrium in the model just described involves choosing a fiscal system, subject to the general constraint $F(s) = 0$, so as to maximize the political support function

$$S = \sum_h \theta_h v^h(s),$$
(6.2)

where $\theta_h = \partial f_h / \partial v^h$ is the sensitivity of person h's probability of voting to changes in his or her welfare at the equilibrium. The first-order conditions for this problem have the same form as those in (6.1) defining the optimal strategies of each party. Hence the Nash equilibrium in the electoral game and the solution to the problem of maximizing S are identical, provided that the θ_h in (6.2) are fixed at their equilibrium values.

One may want to recall the underlying intuition in this connection: Unless the political support function is maximized, marginal changes in expected support across voters are not equalized. In that case, it would be possible for the opposition to increase its total expected vote by proposing policies that increase the welfare of some voters, especially those whose voting behavior is particularly sensitive to changes in utility, at the cost of some support from others. Political competition ensures that, in an equilibrium, no such support-improving policies remain to be proposed.

Among the assumptions underlying the Representation Theorem, the following have been identified as critical: (i) competition forces political parties to continually maximize expected votes defined over all voters while taking the general equilibrium structure of the private economy fully into account; and (ii) the predictable aspects of individual voting behavior, and thus expected votes for any party, depend only on how policy platforms affect individual economic welfare. When these (and other) assumptions of the model do not hold, policy makers may not take all of the relevant consequences of their actions into account, and the equilibrium of the political system may not result in Pareto efficient resource allocation.

6.2.1   Subordinate Government

Since the demonstration that policy choices in equilibrium are consistent with Pareto efficiency depends on the existence of political competition, it is essential to ask what happens to policy choices when such competition is weak. Imperfect or weak political competition must ultimately derive from a lack of free entry into the political marketplace, but it is not readily apparent how limits to entry (or their implications) can most effectively be modeled in a framework that includes both political and economic elements. A possible consequence of weak political competition is that the government may not be under sufficient pressure to resist the demands of certain interest groups, and that it may give in to their demands without taking into account the implications of doing so for all voters. Such a case has recently been characterized by Dani Rodrik (1992) as "subordinate government."

Introducing subordinate government amounts to amending our critical assumption (i) so that the constraint on the objective of the governing party includes not only the structure of the economy but also the demands of certain powerful interest groups. As we shall see, this leads the government to take actions that deviate from Pareto efficiency.

To characterize political market failure in the presence of special interests, we simplify the model of equilibrium policy choices reviewed here (and outlined in more detail in Chapter 4) in four ways. First, given the lack of knowledge concerning the influence of public expenditures on individual preferences and on the magnitude of private taxable activities, we suppose that the size of the public sector G cannot be chosen so as to influence the level of taxable activities. Second, we assume that it is possible to distinguish short-run, mainly distributional, impacts of changes in tax policy from longer-run effects that involve substantial induced changes in private behavior. Third, we assume for purposes of the following discussion that the definition – though not the level – of each tax base is exogenous, and that there are $K < H$ tax bases and rates, where H is again the number of voters.[8] Finally, we assume that the relationship between policy instruments, tax bases, and individual welfare imposed by the general equilibrium structure of the private economy are appropriately substituted into utility functions and the government budget restraint.

These simplifying assumptions suggest the following restatement of the political support function (6.2):

$$S = \sum_h \theta_h v^h(t, B(t), G), \tag{6.3}$$

where v^h represents the indirect utility of voter h, $\theta_h = \partial f_h / \partial v^h$, $t = (t_1, t_2, \ldots, t_K)$ is a vector of proportional tax rates, and $B = (B_1(t), B_2(t), \ldots, B_K(t))$ represents a vector of the corresponding tax bases that explicitly acknowledges the possibility that each tax rate may affect a large number of tax bases. The use of the indirect utility function signifies that the equilibrium structure of the private economy has been substituted into the model.

Using the Representation Theorem in the context of the simplified model in order to characterize equilibrium policy outcomes, we maximize political support (6.3) subject to the government budget restraint, $\sum_k t_k \cdot B(t_k) = G$.

---

[8] In a completely general model, the formation of tax bases would be endogenous as in Chapters 3 and 4.

The first-order conditions describing equilibrium tax rates for this problem are, for $k = 1, 2, \ldots, K$,

$$-\left\{ \frac{\partial S}{\partial t_k}\bigg|_B + \frac{\partial S}{\partial B_k} \cdot \frac{\partial B_k}{\partial t_k} + C \right\} = \lambda_k = \lambda \cdot \left\{ B_k(1 + \varepsilon_k) + D \right\}, \quad (6.4)$$

where

$$C = \sum_{j \neq k} \left[\frac{\partial S}{\partial B_j} \cdot \frac{\partial B_j}{\partial t_k} \right], \qquad\qquad (6.4a)$$

$$D = \sum_{j \neq k} \left[t_j \cdot \frac{\partial B_j}{\partial t_k} \right], \qquad\qquad (6.4b)$$

Here, explicit differentiation of the v^h with respect to t and B is suppressed. The Lagrange multiplier λ associated with the government budget restraint represents the marginal political benefit of raising another dollar of tax revenue and spending it on public services, and $\varepsilon_k = \partial B_k / \partial t_k \cdot t_k / B_k$ is the general equilibrium elasticity of base B_k with respect to tax rate t_k. An analogous condition holds for the level of public services G.

The first term on the left side of (6.4) captures the direct effect of rate t_k on political support, holding constant the size of all tax bases. The second term on the left reflects the political consequences stemming from induced changes in the tax base to which rate t_k is applied. The cross effects summarized by C capture the political consequences of interdependencies between tax bases. The right side of (6.4) represents the gain in support from raising rate t_k and spending the resulting revenue given by the expression in brackets. The terms included in D measure the effect on total revenue that occurs because a change in rate t_k causes adjustments in other bases B_j.

In equilibrium, the successful party has adjusted tax rates until the resulting "political cost" given by the left side of (6.4) is just equal to the "political benefit" summarized by the right side of the first-order conditions. Since the political support function in (6.4) is a weighted sum of taxpayer utility functions, the equilibrium in the simplified model is a Pareto-efficient one.

In order to investigate the consequences of subordinate government, it is convenient to simplify the model further by supposing that there are just two tax bases, domestic production B_1 and imports B_2. (We shall return later to the more general formulation reflected by equations (6.4).) Following Rodrik, we model subordinate government as acting like a Stackelberg follower of domestic producers who, as a group, seek protection against foreign competition but who are not strong enough to dictate actual tariff and other tax rates to the government directly. In acting like a Stackelberg follower, the government sets tax rates while accepting the behavior of domestic producers $\left(\text{represented by } B_1^*\right)$ as given, where

$$B_1^* = \underset{B_1}{\text{argmax}} \; v^1\left(B_1, t_1(B_1), t_2(B_1), G(B_1)\right) \tag{6.5}$$

is the level of activity chosen by domestic producers when they take account of the government's likely reaction to their "demands." The situation is opposite to that described by conditions (6.4), where it is implicitly assumed that the government acts as a leader in setting policy while taking the effects of taxation on each individual's private behavior fully into account.

To compare results with the efficient political equilibrium, defined in the present case by equation (6.4) with $K = 2$, we continue to assume that the government seeks to maximize expected support. Application of the Representation Theorem then requires solving the following problem:

$$\underset{\{t,G\}}{\max} \; S\left(t_1, t_2, B_1, B_2, G\right) \tag{6.6}$$

subject to

$$B_1 = B_1^*, \tag{6.7a}$$

$$t_1 \cdot B_1 + t_2 \cdot B_2 = G. \tag{6.7b}$$

Because the optimization of political support is now subject to the additional constraint (6.7a), equilibrium will differ from the situation defined by (6.4) with $K = 2$, where the government does not cater to special interests.

The first-order condition for rate t_1 on domestic production in the foregoing problem is given by

$$-\left\{\frac{\partial S}{\partial t_1}\bigg|_B + C''\right\} = \lambda_2'' = \lambda \cdot \{B_1 + D''\}, \tag{6.8}$$

where

$$C'' = \frac{\partial S}{\partial B_2} \cdot \frac{\partial B_2}{\partial t_1}, \tag{6.8a}$$

$$D'' = t_2 \cdot \frac{\partial B_2}{\partial t_1}. \tag{6.8b}$$

The first-order condition for tax rate t_2 on imports is

$$-\left\{\frac{\partial S}{\partial t_2}\bigg|_B + \frac{\partial S}{\partial B_2} \cdot \frac{\partial B_2}{\partial t_2} + C'\right\} = \lambda_2' = \lambda \cdot \{B_2(1 + \varepsilon_2) + D'\}, \tag{6.9}$$

where (6.7a) implies that

$$C' = \frac{\partial S}{\partial B_1} \cdot \frac{\partial B_1}{\partial t_2} = 0, \qquad (6.9a)$$

$$D' = t_1 \cdot \frac{\partial B_1}{\partial t_2} = 0. \qquad (6.9b)$$

A comparison of (6.4), the fully efficient case, with (6.8) shows that a subordinate government will set rate t_1 on the protected domestic market at a level that does not take into account the *direct* incentive effects of t_1 on domestic production B_1, a result that mirrors the conclusion reached by Rodrik. (The second term that appears on the left side of (6.4) is missing from (6.8), as is the elasticity ε_1 from the right side.) Thus a subordinate government chooses an inefficient policy because it disregards the incentive effects of tax policy for the activity of special interests and the consequences of these effects for the welfare of individual voters.

In addition, equations (6.9a) and (6.9b) imply that the interaction terms C' and D' will be ignored in the setting of t_2. Thus, the tax rate on the activity not directly controlled by powerful interests is set independently of the economic (and political) consequences that arise because of the interdependencies of tax bases, making the equilibrium inefficient when compared to a situation where all consequences of fiscal policy on individual voters have been taken into account.

6.2.2 Information and Decentralization in the Choice of Tax Systems

The model used so far does not include an explicit treatment of information costs in policy making. As in much of traditional welfare economics, the ideal standard has been defined for a world where policies are chosen by decision makers who have full knowledge of all alternatives. This leaves the question open of how policy makers design and implement complicated tax systems, such as the one described by equations (6.4), when it is costly to accomplish their aims.

We show here that the costs of acquiring information and of coordinating decision makers at lower levels lead to the implementation of tax systems that deviate from those adopted in a frictionless world. We then return to the case of subordinate government and reinterpret the previous results in this more general context.

A possible strategy to deal with information costs is to decentralize fiscal choices.[9] This permits decision makers to economize on information collection and processing costs and to benefit from specialization of knowledge required for the use of particular tax instruments.[10] But decentralization leads to the problem of coordinating decision makers so as to account for the general equilibrium effects of separate choices on tax rates.

To explore the problems inherent in such decentralization, we return to the general case with K tax bases in (6.4), and introduce decentralization in a simple manner by thinking of each tax base that appears in that equation as being under the control of a separate group of decision makers who can determine the tax rate levied on that base only.[11] In developing this argument, we shall assume that all the terms on the left side of (6.4) are negative. The intuitive justification is that an increase in the kth tax rate will cause a loss in support for three reasons: (i) the impact effect on support of a small increase in the kth rate, the first term on the left side of (6.4), will be negative; (ii) there will be a further loss of support because of the direct negative effect of the kth rate on the size of the kth base, hence the second term on the left side of (6.4) should also be negative; and (iii) the cross-effects of t_k on other bases B_j will, on balance, lead to yet further losses in support, represented by $C < 0$. We shall also assume that each of these three terms is decreasing with t_k.

In addition, we make the assumption that all of the terms on the right side of (6.4) are positive. This implies that (i) increasing the level of public services generates additional support (hence $\lambda > 0$); (ii) as the kth rate increases, revenue from the kth base does as well, so that $B_k(1 + \varepsilon_k) > 0$; and (iii) the substitutions away from the kth taxable activity as t_k increases lead on balance to additional revenues, represented by $D > 0$. As before, we shall suppose that the three terms just mentioned are declining with the kth rate. We note that both C and D will tend to be smaller in the short run than over longer horizons because tax elasticities tend to grow with time.

---

[9] A decentralized tax policy process can be described as a piecemeal policy process. An interesting discussion of the advantages of piecemeal policy making in the tax field is provided by Bird (1970, pp. 455–57). Bird also remarks on the connection between piecemeal policy making and Lindblom's (1969) argument for incrementalism.

[10] In setting up a decentralized system, use would be made of the near decomposability (in the sense of Simon 1981, Chap. 7) of the economy and political system into semi-independent segments in order to group taxable activities into bases that are largely independent – economizing thereby on the need for coordination in making tax policy. Decentralization of economic policy making along these lines has been advocated by Tinbergen (1954), among others.

[11] Our discussion does not allow for the principal–agent problems that often arise when the policy process disperses decision-making power. We assume that all decision makers employed by the government have the same basic objective in mind – the maximization of expected votes – and leave the study of the interaction between decentralization of tax policy making and principal–agent problems for future research.

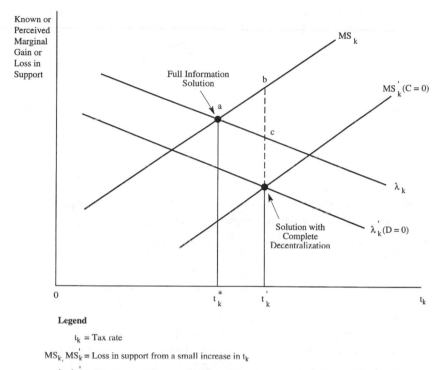

Known or
Perceived
Marginal
Gain or
Loss in
Support

Full Information
Solution

Solution with
Complete
Decentralization

Legend

t_k = Tax rate

MS_k, MS'_k = Loss in support from a small increase in t_k

λ_k, λ'_k = Gain in support from spending the additional revenue raised with a small increase in t_k

Figure 6.1 Decentralization and tax policy in political equilibrium

If information and coordination costs – especially those that arise in connection with the interaction terms C and D – are negligible, an exact and full solution of equations (6.4) is possible. Such a solution is represented in Figure 6.1 by t_k^*. In the figure, which is a partial equilibrium representation of the solution to the complete set of first-order equations, the curve MS_K reflects the left side of the first-order condition (6.4) as the kth rate changes. It thus represents the known or perceived loss in support from raising the kth rate. In the figure, this loss is shown as increasing in absolute value with t_k, in accordance with our assumptions. The right side of (6.4) as t_k changes is represented by the curve labelled λ_k, showing the perceived increase in support from spending the extra revenue from a small rise in t_k. In the figure, again in accordance with our assumptions, this increase in support declines with t_k. Note that when information for voters and politicians is costless, the perceived curves also represent actual losses and gains in support.

At the other extreme from a world of complete and costless coordination is full decentralization, where each fiscal instrument is assigned to a separate group of decision makers with the instruction that the interaction terms in (6.4) are to be disregarded. In this world, the government perceives the costs of acquiring information about C and D as prohibitive, or it perceives co-ordination costs as so high that using any information about C and D does not increase net support. Thus, each tax rate t_k is chosen according to (6.4) with C and D set to zero. All decision makers take into account only the distributional and incentive effects associated with their own instrument and ignore the effects of their decisions on the tax bases assigned to other decision makers. Since information about the C and D terms is lacking or not used, the resulting tax rate in Figure 6.1 equals t_k'. It is set where the line $\text{MS}t_K'$, representing the left side of (6.4) with C set equal to zero, intersects the line λ_k', which reflects the right side of (6.4) with D equal to zero.

Neither t_k^* nor t_k' is economically or politically efficient. The first solution presupposes that information is costless, and the second would be optimal only if there were no benefits to information acquisition or coordination across decision makers. A competitive government facing positive information costs will set a tax rate falling somewhere between those indicated in the figure, implying that some interdependencies among bases or general equilibrium effects will be disregarded as part of economically efficient decision making. On the other hand, given our results in the previous section, a subordinate government will totally ignore *all* interaction terms relating to the base identified with the dominant special interest, as implied by equations (6.8). If placed in a setting where decision making on tax bases is decentralized, subordinate government will thus use information in a biased manner, resulting in choices that deviate systematically from optimal allocation decisions.

6.2.3   Contributions for Political Advertising and Efficiency

Many observers of the public sector have drawn attention to the impact of financial contributions on the functioning of political markets, and particularly on the exchange of economic favors by the government in return for contributions received from a special interest group (see e.g. Mueller 1989, Palda 1989, and Baron 1994). It is therefore of interest to inquire into the possible adverse welfare effects of funds obtained for political advertising in the context of our framework.

For the purpose of this discussion, we leave aside the version of the support function used to discuss the problems associated with subordinate government, where the effects of policies are separated into impact and general equilibrium components. Instead, we return to a more general formulation in (6.2), where political support is a weighted sum of taxpayer (indirect) utilities $v^h(s)$ and s is a general fiscal platform $s = \{s_1, s_2, \ldots, s_K\}$. We continue to hold the definition of fiscal instruments fixed throughout the analysis.

If the individual probability of voting for the incumbent (i) over the opposition (o) is given by $\pi_{hi} = f_h[v^h(s_i) - v^h(s_o)]$, and if parties continually maximize expected votes $\sum_h f_h$ subject to the structure of the economy including the government budget restraint $F(s) = 0$, then the Representation Theorem indicates that the equilibrium satisfies the first-order conditions (6.1). For convenience we repeat these conditions here (without subscripts denoting the political party):

$$\sum_{h=1}^{H} \left[\frac{\partial f_h}{\partial v^h} \cdot \frac{\partial v^h}{\partial s_k} \right] \Big/ \frac{\partial F}{\partial s_k} = \alpha \quad \text{for} \quad k = 1, 2, \ldots, K, \tag{6.10}$$

where $\theta_h = \partial f_h / \partial v^h$ and α represents the Lagrange multiplier associated with the constraint. These conditions are exactly the same as those describing the vote-maximizing strategies of the parties, and hence they can also be used to characterize the Nash equilibrium. Since a weighted sum of utilities is maximized in this equilibrium, policy outcomes are efficient.

If we now allow resources available to political parties, denoted here by T, to have an effect on voting behavior independently of the consequences of advertising for economic welfare, and if the ability to generate such resources depends on the choice of a fiscal platform *but not on the welfare of voters*, then it is appropriate to write the probability that voter h supports the incumbent as $\pi_{hi} = f_h[v^h(s_i) - v^h(s_o), T]$, where $T = T(s)$. In this case, maximization of expected votes requires

$$\sum_h \left[\frac{\partial f_h}{\partial v^h} \cdot \frac{\partial v^h}{\partial s_k} + \frac{\partial f_h}{\partial T} \cdot \frac{\partial T}{\partial s_k} \right] \Big/ \frac{\partial F}{\partial s_k} = \alpha \quad \text{for} \quad k = 1, 2, \ldots, K, \tag{6.11}$$

where subscripts identifying the party have been dropped for convenience. These conditions indicate that when T affects the density function f directly and $\partial T / \partial s_h \neq 0$, maximization of expected votes and of the support function (6.9) are no longer equivalent. In this case, policy choices in equilibrium will not be Pareto efficient.

To see that policies are no longer efficient, it suffices to note that the first-order conditions (6.11) can be replicated by maximizing a support function S^* that is a weighted average of voter utilities *and* advertising resources:[12]

$$S^* = \sum_h \left(\theta_h \cdot v^h + \theta_h^T \cdot T \right). \tag{6.12}$$

Here $\theta_h^T = \partial f_h / \partial T$ and, as before, $\theta_h = \partial f_h / \partial v^h$. The problem is that parties find it useful to implement policies that increase T even if economic welfare is

[12] Grossman and Helpman (1994) used such a function to represent the government's objective but did not fully motivate their choice. The argument here provides justification for use of such a function.

lower as a result. They do this as long as T can also be used as a direct way of enlarging expected support.

If advertising affects economic welfare directly, perhaps by reducing information and search costs, then it would be more appropriate to include T in the indirect utility function and to specify the probability of voting as $\pi_{hi} = f_h[v^h(s_i, T(s)) - v^h(s_o, T(s))]$. In this case, maximization of the corresponding political support function $S = \sum_h \theta v^h(s, T(s))$ subject to $F(s) = 0$ will lead to the same first-order conditions as does maximization of expected votes subject to these constraints. Hence, in this case, the equilibrium is Pareto efficient.[13]

The equilibrium may also be efficient even if T affects voting behavior independently of voter utilities, provided that the level of contributions depends on the welfare of the donor, as in $T = T(v^H(s))$, where it is assumed for convenience that voter H is the sole contributor. In this case, the first-order conditions for the maximization of expected votes are

$$\sum_h \left[\frac{\partial f_h}{\partial v^h} \cdot \frac{\partial v^h}{\partial s_k} + \frac{\partial f_h}{\partial T} \cdot \frac{\partial T}{\partial v^h} \cdot \frac{\partial v^h}{\partial s_k} \right] \Big/ \frac{\partial F}{\partial s_k} = \alpha \quad \text{for} \quad k = 1, 2, \dots, K,$$

(6.13)

Conditions (6.13) can be replicated by maximizing the following weighted average of utilities subject to the same constraints:

$$S^{**} = \sum_{h \neq H} \theta_h v^h + \left(\theta_H + \sum_{h \neq H} \theta_h^T \frac{\partial T}{\partial v^h} \right) \cdot v_H.$$

(6.14)

Thus, as long as θ_h^T and $\partial T / \partial v^H$ are positive, the contributor has a larger weight placed on his or her welfare by an appreciative government. The contributor therefore faces a lower tax rate and enjoys a higher level of welfare than in the absence of contributions. But the equilibrium is not inefficient.

The preceding discussion indicates that inefficiency arises from the exchange of tax policies for advertising resources only when the level of such resources does not depend solely on the welfare of those voters who are contributors. One must therefore ask: Under what circumstances will campaign contributions be unrelated to the welfare of contributors who are bonafide members of the electorate? A possible answer may lie in the existence of a principal–agent problem in the organization of contributors or in the fact that contributors may not be legitimate members of the electorate.[14] In these cases, choices of political decision makers will involve trade-offs between policies

---

[13] There is an obvious parallel here to the debate about consequences for welfare of advertising in private markets. See for example Nelson (1976) and Staaf (1978).

[14] The Appendix to this chapter gives a discussion of the principal–agent problem in the probabilistic voting framework.

that are efficient and policies that generate contributions, with the result that outcomes depart from Pareto efficiency.

6.3   STEP THREE: MEASURING WELFARE IMPROVEMENTS

It is important to identify imperfections in political markets and to link them to the use of specific policy instruments, but the normative framework remains incomplete until measurement of welfare changes is achieved. Only such measurement will allow us to assess the quantitative significance of particular political market failures and to compare different policy situations with respect to the magnitude of their impact. It is useful to begin a discussion of the measurement issue in a representative democracy by inquiring into the meaning of the welfare loss from taxation if a Lindahl equilibrium is used as the standard of reference. We then compare welfare losses defined with respect to the Lindahl solution with those that occur if the ORT system is adopted as the standard. In this discussion, we pay particular attention to the question of whether the excess burden of taxation as usually calculated can be used to measure departures from a collective choice standard.[15]

6.3.1   Welfare Losses in Relation to Lindahl Equilibrium

In order to understand the meaning of welfare losses from taxation in relation to a Lindahl standard of reference, it is useful to ask why there are no such losses when consumers purchase private goods in a free market. Consider a situation where a consumer purchases a private good (x) in a world with other private goods (y) and leisure (l), but with no public goods. Assume that x and y are produced and sold competitively. A consumer who maximizes welfare will adjust consumption of x, y, and l until the marginal utility of the last unit consumed per dollar of expenditure is equal across x, y, and l. There is no welfare loss in this world, provided prices reflect the marginal social cost of production, since the consumer pays the marginal valuation for the last unit of each good. If the consumer chooses not to buy another unit of any commodity, it is because the marginal evaluation of that unit exceeds its price or social cost. One should note in this context that the choice of how much x to buy does affect both the amount of y and the amount of l that are consumed.

We next ask whether there are welfare losses if we introduce a social good into the analysis. Assume that x is transformed into a public good. A consumer who participates in a Lindahl process with regard to x will pay the marginal

---

[15] Usher (1991) reviews the definition of the excess burden of taxation. See Pfahler (1988) for a summary of related theoretical research.

valuation for the last unit of x consumed. Note that, as before, choices concerning x affect the trade-off between leisure and work, since they are made in a general equilibrium setting. There are no welfare losses because the consumer makes marginal adjustments that are logically equivalent to the adjustments in the world with only private goods.

The situation differs if the consumer does not participate in Lindahl bargaining. As before, we have a public good (x), a private good (y), and leisure (l). However, the amount of x is determined by a non-Lindahl process and x is paid for by a tax – say, a tax on wages. Even though a collective choice process is used to determine the amount of x to be produced (which will be consumed equally by everyone) and to determine the nature of the wage tax, the process does not yield Lindahl outcomes.

If we compare the consumer's equilibrium in this world to the position in a Lindahl equilibrium, he or she will have a different utility level. Since the consumer no longer adjusts consumption of all three goods until the marginal evaluation of the last unit consumed is equal, there are distortions and welfare losses. Note that the distortions occur throughout: the consumer will now choose different amounts of x, y, and l. A true measure of welfare costs would have to capture the combined welfare loss arising from all three margins.

The essential problem is that, in the absence of a Lindahl bargaining process, the consumer does not treat the tax as a price to be paid for another unit of the public good; instead, he or she will react to the wage tax as if it were an exogenous change in the price of leisure. In response to this change, the consumer will generally find it desirable to reduce work effort in order to lower tax payments. The shift from work to leisure will continue until the real income or output forgone from one less hour of work (equal to the before-tax wage) is just equal to the value of the additional leisure gained *plus* the savings in tax that result from switching from work (which is taxed) to leisure (which is not). The tax thus saved is essentially a transfer from the government to the taxpayer and is not lost to society as a whole. However, the excess of the output forgone over the utility gained from more leisure represents the deadweight cost, or excess burden, of the tax to society as a whole.

One should note that the connection that existed in the previous example (where a Lindahl process was used) between marginal evaluations of x and private goods y is also disrupted, and that marginal adjustments between y and l are now made as if the cost of another unit of x did not matter to the individual.

How could we determine the dollar equivalent of the net loss in welfare caused by these distortions? A widely used device to isolate excess burdens due to taxation is the lump-sum tax of equal yield. Because such a tax would reduce the consumer's income without changing the relative price of leisure (which remains equal to the wage both before and after the lump-sum tax is levied), it provides a basis or counterfactual against which to compare the net impact on economic welfare of a price-distorting levy such as a wage tax.

Would comparison of the wage tax with a lump-sum tax give a correct estimate of the excess burden of taxation relative to a Lindahl solution? If we were to raise the same amount that we collect with the wage tax from the consumer with a lump-sum tax, the relative price of leisure would not change. Thus the choice between leisure and other goods would not be distorted. Note, however, that the margins between x and y and between x and l remain distorted, since the consumer no longer regards x as a commodity for which quantity can be adjusted. In addition, the quantity of (and thus the amount spent on) x differs from what it would be in Lindahl equilibrium. This means that the amount of tax collected is also non-optimal.

Since they do not apply to all margins, welfare losses measured in comparison to a lump-sum tax of the same amount as the wage tax can capture only a part of the welfare costs of distorted margins. In addition, they do not reflect the welfare costs of non-optimal budget size. For these reasons, they can only give an approximation of true welfare losses if Lindahl equilibrium is used as the ideal basis or counterfactual to establish such losses.

6.3.2   Welfare Losses in an Optimal Representative Tax System

It has recently been argued by Albert Breton (1996) that political competition will eliminate excess burdens defined with respect to a Lindahl equilibrium because of its tendency to create a closer link between the benefit and cost sides of the budget.

In a perfectly functioning representative democracy, where parties compete for office and where the government pursues reelection as its main goal, political competition will work to bring about a closer relation between voters' evaluations of public goods and their tax payments. Much information about individual preferences will be revealed in the course of political contests, as Breton and Leif Johansen (1977) point out, since citizens have an interest in forming politically useful and influential coalitions with each other and with politicians. As long as voters make political choices based on net benefits from the public sector, it is in the interest of politicians to acquire knowledge of such evaluations and to adjust the structure of taxes and of public sector benefits in a way that takes net benefits across voters into account. This will be done while also taking account of the relevant transaction costs, which will be considerable, involved in acquiring information about individual preferences and in tailoring the fiscal system to such preferences. We have seen earlier that Lindahl (1959) held a similar opinion.[16]

However, it is difficult to see how such political competition could generate the same marginal choices on the part of consumers as a Lindahl bargaining

---

[16] Recall the quote from Lindahl's 1959 paper in Section 4.1.4.

process.[17] Imagine the work–leisure choices of an individual in such a society. Political competition at the party level, however vigorous, cannot alter the fact that a tax levied on wage changes the individual's relative price of leisure in a manner that has no counterpart when choices are made with a Lindahl process, even if wages are closely correlated with individual evaluations of the public good. Rational consumers will respond to what they see as an exogenous change in relative prices, and make adjustments that give rise to economic distortions.

As long as the costs of the public sector are paid for by taxes that are levied against private sector activities, rational maximizing behavior of consumers will generally lead to work–leisure trade-offs as well as to other marginal adjustments that differ from those in a Lindahl world. The resulting net welfare losses will persist even in an equilibrium that is based on effective political competition.

Comparison of excess burdens in an existing or proposed fiscal system with those in an ideal representative democracy requires that we measure the size of the excess burdens that will persist in the ideal system, a task of considerable complexity. An analogous problem is faced by economists who insist that transactions costs must remain part of any realistic standard of reference and who want to judge the efficiency of a private market using a standard that incorporates such costs.

6.3.3   Measuring Welfare Losses without Using a Standard of Reference

The welfare measures considered in the preceding sections involve calculation of the total loss in welfare from distorting taxation relative to an ideal or first-best situation. However, if the objective is merely to compare proposed tax systems to each other and to the status quo, measurement of the loss from each alternative relative to an ideal standard may not be required. It may be possible to develop rules that simply indicate directions of Pareto improvement relative to the existing tax system.

There is always a risk of moving in the wrong direction when measurement relative to an ideal standard is not used. Optimization over a neighborhood of

---

[17] Many authors have raised doubts about whether or not a Lindahl bargaining process could be made to work. The problem pointed to is that, in a Lindahl process, each voter faces a separate tax-price, and these prices might be altered depending on what voters say about their own evaluation of public services. Hence all voters have an incentive to falsify their announced marginal evaluations of the public good in an attempt to lower taxes paid while still receiving the public good (Myles 1995, p. 279). The difficulty raised here is of a different nature and applies whenever it is not possible to implement a Lindahl solution.

the status quo or in a restricted part of the set of feasible reforms may lead one further away from a global optimum rather than closer to it. However, since operationalizing the Lindahl and ORT standards – or, indeed, any ideal standard – is not an easy task, comparison of "nearby" alternatives to the status quo is of practical importance to politicians and policy makers.

For example, when marginal tax changes that preserve the size of total revenues are considered, it is possible to define a measure of the marginal excess burden of taxation for each individual that does not involve the problems just discussed. One way of doing this is to use the fact that a rational taxpayer will alter his activities in response to a tax increase until the marginal loss in welfare from doing so (measured in monetary terms) is equal to one dollar, which is the amount of tax thus saved. Hence, for a small increase in the tax rate, the marginal loss in welfare for the individual (over and above that due to the tax revenue collected) is approximately equal to one times the revenue lost through avoidance and evasion, which can be estimated (Slemrod and Yitzhaki 1996, p. 186).[18]

It does seem possible to measure excess burdens for marginal tax changes without measuring welfare losses relative to an ideal standard, but individual losses must still be aggregated in order to compare the overall impact of a policy proposal. In the next section we consider a widely used rule for tax reform based on the measurement of excess burdens; we argue that this rule may be misleading and (in any event) of limited interest to political parties, since it does not deal adequately with the problem of aggregating welfare losses across individuals in a democratic society.

6.3.4   Implications for Tax Policy Analysis

It is often argued that tax reform should be designed to equalize the marginal excess burden of taxation per unit change in revenue across tax sources, since only then will the total unweighted sum of excess burdens for a budget of given size be minimized. In this section we consider whether this rule of thumb for applied tax policy analysis is appropriate if the ORT standard of reference is adopted, or if a ranking of tax systems is attempted without calculation of the total welfare loss from each alternative (relative to the ORT standard).

One interesting study that makes use of this rule is by Dale Jorgenson and Kun-Young Yun (1991). These authors carefully calculate the marginal change in excess burden per dollar change in revenue, or marginal efficiency cost

---

[18] Here we assume that private and social costs are equal, and we ignore compliance and administration costs. However, these issues can also be dealt with, as Slemrod and Yitzhaki (1996, pp. 186–91) point out.

(MEC), associated with each major part of the U.S tax system.[19] They do this by computing the reduction in the unweighted sum of excess burdens across individuals that would occur if each distorting tax were lowered slightly and the lost revenue replaced with a nondistorting lump-sum tax.[20]

Jorgenson and Yun conclude that the U.S. system could be improved by reducing reliance on income taxes, which have a relatively high MEC, and by increasing reliance on sales and property taxes, where the MECs are lower. Concerning income taxation, their estimates indicate that social welfare could be increased by shifting from levies on corporate and individual capital incomes to larger levies on labor incomes (1991, p. 505).

In another, similar study, the same authors (1990) conclude that larger gains than were achieved by the U.S. Tax Reform Act of 1986 could have been obtained by transferring part of the tax burden on business capital to house-hold capital by eliminating the deductibility of mortgage interest and of state and local property taxes.

But is it appropriate to follow advice to equalize MECs across tax sources in a representative democracy? There are at least two issues that must be addressed before an answer can be given. The first one concerns correcting measures of excess burdens to allow for the role played by the valuation of public services in an ORT equilibrium. The second issue arises because of our ignorance about the distribution of political influence in a perfectly competitive democracy, and it applies even if excess burdens are defined without reference to the ORT standard.

Incorporating the Valuation of Public Services

We cannot expect a competitive representative democracy to generate the same marginal choices concerning public goods as a Lindahl bargaining process, yet the valuation of public services remains an integral part in determining the fiscal system's level and structure. Thus, the common practice (Pfahler 1988) of basing the analysis of welfare effects on lump-sum taxation – while failing to take account of the effect of public services on individual choices – will lead to

---

[19] The MEC can be defined as: the marginal loss of consumer surplus from increasing reliance on a particular tax source *less* the additional tax revenue collected (the marginal excess burden of the tax), all divided by the change in tax revenue. If a tax does not generate an excess burden, its MEC is equal to 0. The marginal social cost of funds, another often used measure of the welfare loss due to taxation, is equal to 1 plus the MEC.

[20] Jorgenson and Yun (1991) actually measure the excess burden of each existing tax by calculating an equivalent variation in wealth. They calculate (at prices occurring under the existing tax system) the difference between the wealth required to attain the level of welfare possible with an equal-yield lump-sum tax and the wealth achieved with the existing tax. See also Ballard et al. (1985a) on the efficiency of the U.S tax system.

incorrect measurement of the welfare cost of taxation when people regard public and private goods as substitutes and vote according to their net evaluations of the public policies. If individuals treat government-provided services as complements to taxed commodities, then a true measure of the excess burden (where the effect of public services on the demand for these commodities has been allowed for) must be smaller than an unadjusted one (Atkinson and Stern 1974, Wildasin 1984). Complementarity lowers substitution away from the taxed commodity, thus reducing the distortion or excess burden, while the induced effect on the supply of public goods decreases the need for revenues that must be raised through distortionary taxation.

The argument so far suggests that the rule to equalize MECs will remain valid as a guide to tax reform as long as measures of marginal excess burdens are revised to allow for the substitutability of public and private goods. One should note, however, that such adjustments cannot deal with the possibility that the existing size of government may be too large or too small when compared to an ORT system in which both taxation and the level of public services matter to voters. Because excess burdens, whether unadjusted or adjusted for substitutability, depend on the level of public services (see, e.g. Jorgenson and Yun 1991, p. 496), comprehensive tax reform consistent with an ORT standard of reference will of necessity also require consideration of the proper size of government. Comprehensive reform of this type has not been examined in the literature.

Allowing for Inequalities in Political Influence in an ORT System

A second problem with acting on the rule that MECs should be equalized will arise even if the ORT standard is bypassed in the manner discussed earlier. In a competitive representative democracy in which political influence varies among voters, the equilibrium will exhibit MECs that differ across tax sources even when Pareto efficiency has been achieved. Thus, a proposal to equalize MECs will generally be inconsistent with political equilibrium and may not represent a Pareto improvement.[21] In a perfectly competitive political system where voters care only about their economic welfare, competition will force any party to adopt Pareto-efficient policies. Otherwise, the possibility remains that some other party can propose a Pareto-improving policy platform and thereby increase its electoral support. However, this does not necessarily mean that MECs are equalized, or that unequal MECs indicate the existence of Pareto improvements in taxation that remain to be adopted. Voters differ in

---

[21] An analogous issue that has received some attention in the public finance literature (e.g. Dierker 1986) concerns the application of simple marginal cost pricing in situations where achievement of Pareto efficiency generally requires more sophisticated pricing rules.

their effective political influence on the government even when the franchise is universal. Moreover, *all* methods of redistribution involve full economic costs greater than the costs of the resources transferred, as Gary Becker (1983) and Donald Wittman (1995) remind us. Thus, in seeking to maximize political support by directing resources toward politically sensitive voters, any government will accept an increase in the MEC of a tax source (as usually measured) above that of other taxes, if that is the necessary price for politically desirable redistribution.

It may be helpful to illustrate this last point with a simple model. Assume there are only two tax sources, two proportional tax rates, and one public good. After substitution of the general equilibrium structure, the government budget restraint is given by $G = R_1(t_1, t_2, G) + R_2(t_1, t_2, G)$. The indirect utility function of any voter is $v_h(t_1, t_2, G)$.

In this simplified world, the Nash equilibrium policy outcome can be represented by finding the fiscal system that maximizes $S = \sum_h \theta_h v_h$ subject to the government budget restraint, where θ_h is the sensitivity of voting behavior to a change in welfare. The first-order conditions for the equilibrium tax rates can be written as

$$\frac{\sum_h \theta_h \cdot \partial v_h / \partial t_1}{\partial (R_1 + R_2)/\partial t_1} = \frac{\sum_h \theta_h \cdot \partial v_h / \partial t_2}{\partial (R_1 + R_2)/\partial t_2}. \tag{6.15}$$

If the θs for all voters are equal, (6.15) can be rewritten as

$$\frac{W_1 - \partial (R_1 + R_2)/\partial t_1}{\partial (R_1 + R_2)/\partial t_1} = \frac{W_2 - \partial (R_1 + R_2)/\partial t_2}{\partial (R_1 + R_2)/\partial t_2}, \tag{6.16}$$

where $W_i = \sum_h \partial v_h / \partial t_i$ is the full loss in welfare due to a marginal change in tax rate i (measured, for example, as the sum of equivalent variations in income), the numerator on each side of the equation is the marginal excess burden of the corresponding tax change, and the quotient on each side represents the marginal efficiency cost of each tax source.[22]

Condition (6.16) indicates that, when the θs are equal, the equilibrium tax policy will minimize the total excess burden of the tax system measured by the sum of unweighted welfare losses across individuals. On the other hand, if political influence is distributed unequally as in (6.15), unweighted marginal welfare losses (W_i) for different tax sources may vary significantly even though Pareto efficiency is being achieved.

Policy proposals based on unweighted excess burdens, however measured, may thus be inconsistent with the existing pattern of political influence. Tax

---

[22] To go from (6.15) to (6.16), substitute the definition of W_i, subtract 1 from each side of (6.15), and simplify.

blueprints that are inconsistent in this sense will be of limited interest to party strategists. Parties are not indifferent among points in the Pareto set of policies such as those illustrated in Chapters 2 and 7, since some points involve higher levels of expected political support from the electorate as a whole than do others. Moreover, as we have pointed out earlier, there is no guarantee that proposals based on unweighted excess burdens will lead to Pareto improvements.

If the ORT standard is adopted, it is appropriate to weight marginal excess burdens using influence weights consistent with a perfectly competitive political system. As long as the policy analyst insists that government should be democratic, a perfectly functioning democracy represents an appropriate ideal standard. It would be convenient if equality of effective influence were part of a such a political system, but there is no logical requirement for this to be so. Thus, the problem of the weights remains whether the policy analyst adopts the ORT standard or not.[23]

The problem of the choice of welfare weights has been addressed in the literature on benefit–cost analysis, where an attempt has been made to infer from choices among different projects a set of "distributional" weights that may be used in aggregating individual welfare gains. This literature may contain useful ideas about the appropriate choice or determination of weights. (An alternative method of calibrating the influence weights is presented in Chapter 7.) However, it should be noted that such empirically derived weights reflect more than simply ideas about equity: the public projects used in calculating so-called distributional weights are in fact equilibrium outcomes of democratic politics.

As long as actual influence weights are unknown, it may be sensible for tax policy advisers to proceed on the assumption that the Hicks–Kaldor criterion is appropriate for judging the direction of tax reform. Certainly, advice concerning *strict* Pareto improvements – a stronger requirement than the Hicks–Kaldor criterion, which is satisfied as long as unweighted gains outweigh unweighted losses – will be of interest to parties seeking favor with voters who care about their own economic welfare. However, it is not clear what further advice a policy advisor can provide if a proposal to equalize the MECs of tax sources is rejected, at least not unless he can offer policy makers a more efficient method of achieving their political objectives.[24] Nor can such an advisor argue that politics has corrupted economic choices. This reasoning must also apply to the proposal by Jorgenson and Yun to eliminate mortgage interest deductibility while using the additional revenue to reduce taxes on business capital. (It is

---

[23] Applying ideal weights from an ORT system to aggregate excess burdens defined without recourse to that standard of reference leaves one in between the two approaches to welfare economics. This may be a useful case to explore further.

[24] Work by Kanbur and Myles (1992) and Bergstrom (1993) can been seen as an attempt to develop rules for assessing the efficiency of fiscal systems when proposals must be consistent with political equilibrium.

interesting to note in this regard that some of the recent U.S. flat-tax proposals do not include elimination of the deduction for mortgage interest.)[25]

6.4   RELATION TO OPTIMAL TAXATION

The reader may have noticed certain similarities in the mathematical analysis of this chapter to that found in the optimal tax literature. Since we offer our framework as an alternative to OT, it is reasonable to ask what constitutes the essential difference between the two approaches.

Application of the Representation Theorem involves the maximization of a weighted sum of utilities, but this does not have the same purpose as maximization of a welfare function in optimal taxation. The intent is rather to characterize aspects of a political equilibrium. The form of the political support function is determined *within* the model, as are the weights on the utilities of voters in this function. As a result, the analysis cannot be interpreted "as if" a social planner were designing a blueprint, since such a planner would have to act on exogenously specified goals. Similarity of mathematical technique does not imply similarity in substantive economic analysis in this case. (The reader may want to refer to Chapter 4 for a discussion of this point in a more formal context.)

It is true, of course, that losses of economic welfare matter in both approaches. In OT, their importance derives from the planner's assumed goals. In the proposed approach, welfare losses enter the support function because any political party maximizing expected votes must take such losses into account – as long as individuals base their voting decisions at least in part on the impact of policies on their economic welfare. Note, however, that when choosing policy instruments, the governing party in the probabilistic voting model will weight policy-induced changes in utility by the marginal political sensitivity of individual voters. This differs from what any planner might do when implementing a welfare function that expresses ethical considerations. Such a planner may apply distributional weights to induced welfare changes, but these would have to reflect exogenous value judgments and would differ from the marginal political responses of voters.

As we have tried to show in this chapter, adoption of a framework based on the probabilistic voting model implies a reorientation of thinking and a widening of scope to include political as well as economic markets. The logical structure of OT does not allow for such a broader approach. Researchers attempting to develop a new welfare economics of taxation may find technical guidance in the extensive and often impressive body of work on optimal taxation, but they will not find answers to their most pressing questions in that literature.

---

[25] These proposals are reviewed by Bernstein et al. (1995).

6.5   CONCLUDING REMARKS

The discussion in this chapter indicates that construction of a welfare economics of taxation that includes politics is possible if we combine voting analysis systematically with economic theory. A broader standard of reference that accounts for political as well as economic equilibrium can be defined. Political market failure can be identified, and techniques to analyze its effects on taxation can be developed. No doubt, policy advice about the removal of political market imperfections can be formulated based on such analyses.

Existing measures of unweighted welfare losses due to taxation, adjusted to account for the substitutability of public and private goods, continue to be of use in the broader framework, although advice based on such measures remains tentative in the absence of information on the efficient size of the public sector and the distribution of political influence. Use of welfare measures that are designed only to rank alternative proposals, and which cannot be used to measure deviations from an ideal standard, continue to be of use as well, but also need to be supplemented with information concerning the distribution of political influence so that individual welfare may be appropriately aggregated.

The analysis in the preceding pages has been developed primarily using a probabilistic voting model of a representative democracy. The authors are well aware that other approaches to a normative analysis that includes collective choice have been proposed. The relevant literature includes the writings by Knut Wicksell and Eric Lindahl cited earlier, as well as work of James Buchanan and Gordon Tullock (1962), Geoffrey Brennan and Buchanan (1985), and others who emphasize the normative basis for collective choice at the constitutional level.

The approach we have taken is not meant to preclude pursuit of other approaches to the construction of a new welfare economics of taxation. We find the probabilistic voting framework particularly useful since it offers a well-developed theoretical basis, including work on the existence and stability of equilibrium, while allowing examination of multidimensional policy issues. Moreover, application of the Representation Theorem makes it possible not only to create a direct link to the use of policy instruments through reformulation of the support function, but also to discuss political market failure. Although these aspects appear as distinct advantages, the test of this or any other framework will ultimately be how well it succeeds in implementing the three basic steps underlying all welfare analysis. The authors would feel that they had accomplished their purpose if they succeeded in convincing other researchers to pursue some of the questions raised in the course of this chapter, either with the use of the probabilistic voting model or in some other theoretical framework that allows for welfare analysis in an expanded context.

The broader approach places some new demands on the researcher interested in policy analysis. It is necessary to model tax and other policies as endogenous outcomes of a political system, and to explicitly investigate the effect of changes in political markets on the equilibrium use of tax instruments. Otherwise, it is not possible to distinguish policy changes that are sustainable as equilibria of democratic political systems from those that are not consistent with basic political institutions. A broader framework implies a more inclusive test for judging efficiency: Optimal tax policies in this world (we have referred to them as optimal representative tax policies) must satisfy the requirements both of economic and political markets (Winer and Hettich 1998). Development of such policies seems a most intriguing task.

APPENDIX TO CHAPTER 6: THE PRINCIPAL–AGENT PROBLEM IN A PROBABILISTIC VOTING FRAMEWORK

Let the agent have an indirect utility function that depends on the nature of public policies (as in Breton and Wintrobe 1982, for example), say $v^A = v^A(s)$. To fix ideas we may think of the agent as a representative bureaucrat who is given the tasks of advising the government and actually implementing tax policy. We shall think of the principal as the governing party.

The agent chooses s so as to maximize her own welfare, subject to the constraint that the incumbent (i) must achieve a minimally acceptable level of support from the electorate relative to that for the opposition party (o). (This formulation is suggested by Holtz-Eakin 1992.) Failure to achieve a minimal level of support means that administrators' jobs are at risk. The structure of the economy and the government budget restraint, which we write generally as $F(s) = 0$, provide additional constraints on the agent. In short, the agent's problem is

$$\max_{\{s\}} v^A \tag{6A.1}$$

subject to

$$EV_i \geq \overline{EV}, \tag{6A.2}$$

$$F(s) = 0, \tag{6A.3}$$

where $EV_i = \Sigma_h \pi_{hi} = \Sigma_h f_h[v^h(s_i) - v^h(s_o)]$ is the expected vote for the incumbent.

The first-order conditions for this problem include

$$\left[\frac{\partial v^A}{\partial s_{ik}} + \delta \cdot \sum_h \left(\frac{\partial f_h}{\partial v^h} \cdot \frac{\partial v^h}{\partial s_{ik}}\right)\right] \bigg/ \frac{\partial F}{\partial s_{ik}} = \alpha \quad \text{for} \quad k = 1, 2, \ldots, K, \tag{6A.4}$$

here K is the number of policy instruments, δ is the Lagrange multiplier for the constraint on expected support, and α is the multiplier for the other constraint. These conditions may be replicated by maximizing, subject to $F(s) = 0$, the following weighted sum of the utilities of the agent and of the voters:

$$S^{**} = v^A + \delta \cdot \sum_h \theta_h v^h, \tag{6A.5}$$

where $\theta_h = \partial f_h / \partial v^h$. If the weights in (6A.5) are fixed at their Nash equilibrium values, the maximization of S^{**} can be used to characterize the equilibrium. Thus, the principal–agent problem, as formulated here, leads to the trading off in equilibrium of the welfare of voters with the welfare of the agent. If the agent is also a voter, say person H, the outcome effectively weights the utility of the agent by $1 + \delta\theta_H$ and that of ordinary voters by $\delta\theta_h$.

PART THREE

APPLIED GENERAL EQUILIBRIUM ANALYSIS

CHAPTER 7

Tax Policy in a Computable Model
of Economic and Political Equilibrium
Co-authored with Thomas Rutherford*

As, in spite of the great differences in form between birds and quadrupeds, there is one Fundamental Idea running through all their frames, so the general theory of the equilibrium of demand and supply is a Fundamental Idea running through the frames of all the various parts of the central problem of Distribution and Exchange.

Alfred Marshall (1890, p. vii)

We think the attempt to operationalize a large body of existing theory, developed through the 1950s and 1960s and devoted largely to nonconstructive proofs of the existence of equilibrium, is beneficial in the long run. We also believe that the insights generated on policy issues by using techniques of this kind, if quantified in the appropriate way, can help to raise the level of policy debate. The use of any model of social process is not without problems, but done in an intelligent and focused way and in the context of contemporary debates on policy issues, the rewards can be large.

John Shoven and John Whalley (1992b, p. 280)

We showed in Chapter 4 that, in a world described by the probabilistic voting model, decision makers choose policies that are economically as well as politically efficient. These policies reflect three essential elements: the demands of voters, differences in their political responses and influence, and the operation and constraints of the private economy.

The theoretical results suggest several basic questions to the researcher interested in studying tax policies in democratic countries: Is there any evidence to support the contention that decision makers in such countries choose policies from the set of available efficient alternatives? What impact do voter demands and differences in effective political influence have on actual policies? How does the operation of the private economy affect the set of available alternatives that are efficient from both an economic and a political point of view?

---

* This chapter is based on Rutherford and Winer (1995).

In this chapter, we develop a framework to address these questions. We construct a computational general equilibrium model containing a public and a private sector, a well-defined set of tax policy choices, and three groups of competing voters. We then calibrate this model to data for the United States for the years 1973 and 1983.[1] The analysis allows us to investigate sets of efficient policies, to look at voter demands and voter influence in a quantitative manner, and to show the interdependence of the private and public sectors in an explicit way.

The simple graphic description of probabilistic voting equilibrium presented in Chapter 2 may serve as a generic background for the more complex analysis in this chapter. In both cases, we have three groups of voters, with the policy alternatives consisting of combinations of two proportional tax rates. The diagrams indicate the essential elements in such an analysis: the preferences of voting groups, the most preferred combination of tax rates for each group (the ideal points), and the Pareto set of policies. In addition, they illustrate the choice of rates by the governing party, a choice that does not correspond to any group's ideal point but instead represents some weighted average of most desired rate combinations, with the weights reflecting the perception by parties of how different voters respond to changes in their welfare. (In Chapter 4, these weights are denoted θ_h and appear in the political support functions such as (4.3).)

The diagrams in Chapter 2 are drawn for idealized taste patterns – indifference curves are assumed to be circular – and they present schematic Pareto sets that do not account explicitly for the interaction of public and private choices. When the analysis is implemented in a more realistic context, these assumptions must be dropped. In this chapter, we construct actual Pareto policy sets for combinations of two tax rates, using data for the United States in the two years mentioned. The analysis shows that such regions can be delineated but that their shapes are of a much more complex nature than the diagrams would suggest.

The actual analysis also shows that it is important to distinguish between weighted and unweighted voter demands. Both the changes in what voters most prefer (ideal points) and in the influence weights $\left(\text{the } \theta_h\right)$ used by the governing party to reflect political responses and influence are important for examining tax policy and for understanding how it evolves.

Furthermore, it is of interest to ask hypothetical questions concerning policy choices in situations where relative political influence differs from what is actually observed. We carry out several such experiments in this chapter. By combining influence weights calculated for 1973 with data for 1983, we obtain an understanding of how relative influence on tax policy has changed over

---

[1] The choice of dates is determined by the availability of data, as we shall explain.

time. We also analyze what would have happened to equilibrium tax rates if influence had been distributed more equally among the three groups in both 1973 and 1983.

One may note that the distinction between weighted and unweighted voter demands cannot be made in some other frameworks, such as the median voter model, where one voter is completely decisive. The results in this chapter indicate that ideal points as well as the weights reflecting the relative effective influence of different voters play a role in actual policy, thus supporting the use of a model that can encompass the separate investigation of influence weights.

The message in this chapter, and throughout the book, is that tax policy is part of a general equilibrium that has both political and economic components. We reinforce this point here by building a computational general equilibrium model and applying it to U.S. data. The analysis shows that mistakes are likely if we adopt a less inclusive framework. This is demonstrated with the derivation of Pareto sets that take account explicitly of the general equilibrium effects of taxation and Pareto sets that do not reflect these effects. The two types of Pareto regions turn out to be quite different, indicating that mistakes are likely if we confine ourselves to a partial framework. This message will apply not only to probabilistic voting but also to alternative models, since we can expect the predicted equilibrium to be in or near the Pareto set implied by a particular framework – as Leif Johansen, quoted in Chapter 4, also points out. Ignoring general equilibrium effects may thus result in predictions that relate to a significantly distorted Pareto set.[2]

In implementing the model, we rely on the Representation Theorem introduced in Chapter 4 and briefly restated in Chapter 6. It proves possible to numerically optimize an appropriately chosen political support function subject to the general equilibrium structure of the economy and, by so doing, to replicate the equilibrium values of tax rates, public expenditures, and private prices and quantities actually observed at particular points in time.[3]

The weights in the political support function representing the effective political influence of different groups at a given time are not known. Moreover, changes in these weights cannot be inferred by observing whether average income or welfare for a group has risen or fallen over the period in question. A decline in income or welfare for the members of a group, for example, is consistent with an increase in influence for the group (in which case the fall in welfare is less than would otherwise be observed), as well as with a decline in that influence. However, in the probabilistic spatial voting

---

[2] Drissen and van Winden (1993) make a similar point by comparing the theoretical predictions of their general equilibrium model of fiscal policy, in which policy outcomes are also part of the equilibrium, with those of a partial equilibrium framework.

[3] The model is programmed and solved using GAMS (Brooke, Kendrick, and Meeraus 1988).

framework implemented here, influence weights can be determined in the calibration of the model so that, for each available data set, the model replicates actual values of policy instruments along with observed prices and quantities.[4]

The structure of the private economy in the model that we use for our experiments is provided by the well-known GEMTAP tax model of the United States constructed in 1985 by Charles Ballard, Don Fullerton, John Shoven, and John Whalley; this model has been calibrated to the original data set for 1973 and to a new data set for 1983 constructed by Karl Scholz and augmented by Charles Ballard (see Scholz 1987).[5] We have amended this model to include individual demands for public goods. The GEMTAP model was originally conceived as a way of assessing the consequences of alternative, equal-yield tax blueprints; the level of public services was not an integral part of the equilibrium. The model has had a substantial effect on normative policy analysis, and for a good reason. It represents a substantial intellectual achievement, operationalizing in a revealing manner the general equilibrium view of the economy, thereby permitting the equilibrium consequences of taxation (emphasized originally by Arnold Harberger and others) to be taken fully and numerically into account. However, when studying a democratic political system, it seems essential to us that voters be modeled as individuals who receive at least some public services in return for the taxes they pay.[6]

Modeling political competition in an applied equilibrium setting introduces additional complexity into a situation that is already technically demanding. The model that is implemented therefore contains a highly aggregated version of the U.S. fiscal system and three interest groups distinguished by the level and source of their household incomes. The aggregation of fiscal instruments and of voters into three interest groups allows us to study the behavior of the model using graphical methods, which is of substantial practical importance. In the future it will no doubt be possible to enlarge the dimensionality of the policy space that is represented in the model and to enrich the structure of the interest groups.

---

[4] An analogous calibration technique has been used by several authors to uncover the parameters governing the preference functions of policy makers; see for example Ross (1984) and the references cited therein. It has also been used, by Ahmad and Stern (1984) and others, in a general equilibrium optimal taxation framework to uncover the weights of a social welfare function that, when optimized, results in the tax system actually observed. One should recall, however, that the calibration of our model does not reveal parameters of a policy maker's preferences or of a social welfare objective. Rather, it reveals the precise form of a function whose constrained maximization replicates a competitive political equilibrium.

[5] See also Shoven and Whalley (1992b).

[6] The way in which we have modeled private demands for public services (along with other essential features of the model) is presented in this chapter in schematic or simplified form, without recourse to computer code. A more technical specification of the model structure is found in the appendix to the paper by Rutherford and Winer (1995).

There are some other restrictions placed on the analysis. The basic nature of policy instruments concerning public expenditures and taxation, including the definition of tax bases, is assumed to be given rather than to emerge in equilibrium as the result of optimizing decisions by political agents, as in the models presented in Chapters 3 and 4. The capital stock is endogenized through international capital flows only, following Lawrence Goulder, John Shoven, and John Whalley (1983), and the model is not solved in a dynamic context. The government budget is balanced each period and government debt has no effect on welfare. How the Pareto sets and counterfactual simulations would be affected by relaxation of these features of the model remains to be explored.

7.1 PROBABILISTIC VOTING IN AN APPLIED EQUILIBRIUM CONTEXT

The voting model that serves as a basis for the computable equilibrium model is an extension of the one that was introduced in Chapter 4. Assume that the electorate can be partitioned into N interest groups with n_h identical voters in group h.[7] The utility function U^h of the representative voter in interest group h is assumed to be composed of two parts:

$$U^h = u^h(x_h, G) + \xi_h. \tag{7.1}$$

The first part, u^h, depends directly on private consumption of a vector of goods and factors x_h and the level of a single public good G, and indirectly via economic structure on a vector of tax rates τ. The second part ξ_h represents the evaluation of each political party by the voter on nonpolicy matters such as ideology, personality, or competence.[8] The difference in the nonpolicy evaluations of the incumbent (i) and the opposition (o),

$$b_h = \xi_{hi} - \xi_{ho}, \tag{7.2}$$

represents a utility bias in favor of the incumbent party that is independent of x, G, and τ.

The probability π_{ho} that voter h supports the opposition is assumed to be a function of the utility differential and the nonpolicy bias term:

$$\pi_{ho} = \begin{cases} 1 & \text{if} \quad u_o^h(x_{ho}, G_o) - u_i^h(x_{hi}, G_i) > b_h, \\ 0 & \text{otherwise,} \end{cases} \tag{7.3}$$

[7] The particular model of expected vote maximization presented here has its origins in the work of Fair (1978), Coughlin and Nitzan (1981a), Borooah and Van der Ploeg (1983), Enelow and Hinich (1984), and Coughlin et al. (1990a,b).

[8] For an interesting discussion of the nonpolicy component of utility, see Hinich and Munger (1994).

where $u_k^h(x_{hk}, G_k)$, abbreviated hereafter as u_k^h, is the utility of voter h if the policies of party k are adopted; π_{hi} is similarly defined with the inequality in (7.3) reversed.

Let the nonpolicy bias b_h be a random variable from the perspective of parties, and assume that it has a uniform distribution over the real interval $[m_h^*, m_h^{**}]$ such that $m_h^* < (u^{ho} - u^{hi}) < m_h^{**}$.[9] If the cumulative distribution function for b_h is D, then the probability *as seen by a party* that h votes for the opposition is given by the probability that b_h is less than the utility differential in favor of the opposition:

$$D(u_o^h - u_i^h) = \alpha_h\{(u_o^h - u_i^h) - m_h^*\}, \tag{7.4}$$

where $\alpha_h = 1/(m_h^{**} - m_h^*)$ is the sensitivity of the probability of voting to a change in individual welfare. The probability that h votes for the incumbent is $1 - D$.

The assumption that the utility differential is always contained in the interval on which b_h is defined ensures that, as far as a party can determine, every voter always has a positive probability of voting for it. Consequently, neither party can afford to completely ignore the voters in any interest group when designing its policy platform, though groups whose voting behavior is perceived to be more sensitive to changes in welfare will be given more attention by party strategists. Otherwise, as discussed in Chapter 2, vote cycling rather than an equilibrium may emerge as voters who are treated badly by the government – because the probability they will support the government is zero – seek and receive promises of better treatment from the opposition, leading to a bidding war between the parties.

Each party chooses policies so as to continuously maximize its expected vote. Using (7.4), the incumbent's expected vote can be expressed as:

$$EV_i(\tau, G) = \sum_{h=1}^{h=N} n_h - \sum_{h=1}^{h=N} \theta_h(u_o^h - u_i^h - m_h^*), \tag{7.5}$$

where $\theta_h = n_h\alpha_h$. The θ_h play an important role in what follows, since we may use these weights as a measure of the relative political influence of each *group* of voters.

After the government budget restraint and the constraints placed on political optimization by the structure of the economy are substituted into the objective

---

[9] For further discussion of the admissible types of probability functions, see for example Lindbeck and Weibull (1987), Feldman and Lee (1988), Enelow and Hinich (1989), and Austen-Smith (1991).

function (7.5), and given the policy choices of the opposition, first-order conditions for optimal policy choices are of the form

$$\sum_{h=1}^{h=N} \theta_h \frac{\partial u^h}{\partial \tau_j} = 0 \quad \text{for} \quad j = 1, 2, \ldots, J, \tag{7.6}$$

where we assume that there are J tax instruments in total. Maximization of expected votes requires that all available tax policy instruments be adjusted until their vote productivity across groups is equalized. Analogous conditions for the optimal choice of G and for the policy platform of the opposition also apply. The use of the summation in (7.6) acknowledges that, since the general equilibrium structure of the economy has been substituted into the party's objective, each of the J policy instruments may affect every voter represented in (7.5).

Application of the Representation Theorem introduced in Chapter 4 indicates that the fiscal system that emerges in a Nash equilibrium of the electoral game, in which the platforms chosen by both parties converge, can be characterized by maximizing a political support function $S = \sum_h \theta_h u_h$ subject to the same constraints as faced by each party, where the "influence weights" θ_h are defined as before. The constraints consist of the general equilibrium structure of the private economy and the government's budget constraint. The computable equilibrium model described in this chapter operationalizes this synthetic optimization problem for the United States.

To briefly recap the formal logic of the Representation Theorem, optimization of the political support function S can be used to characterize the equilibrium policy platform because, after the substitution of all constraints into the support function, the first-order conditions for this problem are identical to those for optimal policy choices by each party in the Nash equilibrium given in (7.6). Second-order conditions which ensure that each party is maximizing expected votes at the solution to the problem of optimizing political support are also satisfied, though the fulfillment of these conditions is not simply assumed in this chapter as it was in Chapter 4. Since each expected vote function is linear in indirect utilities – that is, in the u_k^h after substitution of the equilibrium structure of the private economy – satisfaction of second-order conditions for maximization of expected votes depends on the concavity of a weighted sum of these indirect utility functions with respect to policy instruments. It turns out that, at least in the neighborhood of the actual tax policy outcomes in 1973 and 1983, sufficient concavity of the weighted sum does exist for an equilibrium policy platform to be computed.

Before proceeding, we also recall that the form of the support function indicates that, when a group's θ increases, its welfare will be addressed more favorably by the government in the equilibrium.

7.2   AN APPLIED EQUILIBRIUM MODEL WITH A COMPETITIVE POLITICAL SECTOR

Using the Representation Theorem allows us to state the computable model we have actually implemented as a specific nonlinear optimization problem: that of choosing tax rates on capital, τ_K, and labor, τ_L, along with the size of public expenditures, G, to maximize political support S subject to the general equilibrium structure of the economy as represented by an amended version of the GEMTAP model. We write that problem schematically here without substituting the constraints into the objective function as we have done in the previous section, followed immediately by a list of notation and discussion of important aspects of the model formulation.[10] Note that optimization of the political support function in (7.7) is with respect to tax rates only, since the size of government is determined residually by the government budget restraint (7.15). Interest groups – that is, groupings of GEMTAP households (as discussed at length in what follows) – are again indexed by h:

$$\max_{\tau_K, \tau_L} \sum_h \theta_h u^h(d_h, l_h, G) \tag{7.7}$$

subject to the following conditions.

   i. *Market clearance in goods.* Domestic output plus imports equals government demand (to produce G), household demand, and export demand:

$$\sum_j \frac{\partial \Pi_j}{\partial p_i} y_j + \overline{\text{im}}_i \left(\frac{p_i}{e}\right)^{\sigma_{\overline{\text{im}}}} = \frac{\partial C_G}{\partial p_i} G + \sum_h d_{ih} + \overline{\text{ex}}_i \left(\frac{p_i}{e}\right)^{\sigma_{\overline{\text{ex}}}}. \tag{7.8}$$

   ii. *Market clearance in labor.* Sectoral demand equals labor supply (initial endowment less leisure demand):

$$\sum_j -\frac{\partial \Pi_j}{\partial \widetilde{w}} y_j = \sum_h (L_h - l_h) \tag{7.9}$$

  iii. *Market clearance in capital.* Sectoral demand equals net domestic supply:

$$\sum_j -\frac{\partial \Pi_j}{\partial \widetilde{r}} y_j = \left(\sum_h K_h\right)\left(\frac{\rho}{e}\right)^{\sigma_K}. \tag{7.10}$$

---

[10] The formulation presented here captures most of the relevant features of the model. A complete algebraic description of our model is provided in Rutherford and Winer (1995). Further details of the GEMTAP structure are found in Ballard et al. (1985a) and in Shoven and Whalley (1992b).

iv. *Foreign exchange balance.* The value of commodity and net capital imports equals the value of commodity exports:

$$\sum_i p_i \overline{\text{im}}_i \left(\frac{p_i}{e}\right)^{\sigma_{\overline{\text{im}}}} + \rho\left(\sum_h K_h\right)\left[\left(\frac{\rho}{e}\right)^{\sigma_K} - 1\right] = \sum_i p_i \overline{\text{ex}}_i \left(\frac{p_i}{e}\right)^{\sigma_{\overline{\text{ex}}}}.$$

(7.11)

v. *Zero excess profit.* Net-of-tax profit per unit activity is zero in all sectors:

$$\Pi_j(p, w, \rho, \tau_K, \tau_L) = 0.$$

(7.12)

vi. *Utility maximization.* Commodity demand, leisure demand, and notional demand for public output optimize utility subject to a budget constraint defined in terms of real broadly defined income (net of income tax and the valuation of public goods): d_{ih}, l_h, g_h solve

$$\max_{d,l,g} u_h(d_{ih}, l_h, g_h) \quad \text{subject to}$$

$$\sum_i p_i d_{ih} + v_h g_h = \rho K_h + w(L_h - l_h) + v_h G$$

(7.13)

$$- p_N \overline{T}_h - \tau_K t_h^I \left(\rho K_h + w(L_h - l_h) - p_N \overline{T}_h\right).$$

vii. *Notional individual demands for public goods.*[11] Private valuations of public output (v_h) are chosen such that, for all groups h, notional demand for public output equals actual output:

$$g_h = G.$$

(7.14)

viii. *Government budget balance.* The value of government provision equals the value of tax revenue from labor, capital, and personal income:

$$C_G(p)G = \sum_j y_i \left[\tau_L t_j^L \frac{\partial \Pi_j}{\partial \tilde{w}} w + \tau_K t_j^K \frac{\partial \Pi_j}{\partial \tilde{r}} \rho \right]$$

$$+ \sum_h \left[p_N \overline{T}_h + \tau_K t_h^I \left(\rho K_h + w(L_h - l_h) - p_N \overline{T}_h\right) \right].$$

(7.15)

7.2.1 Notation

In the following list of notation, the term "benchmark" refers to the observed 1973 or 1983 values of policy instruments, prices, quantities, and endowments that constitute the data sets to which the model is calibrated so that it replicates, as an equilibrium, those actual data.

---

[11] As will be discussed later, a "notional" demand for the public good is the individual demand for it given the private marginal evaluation of the public good. The term "notional" denotes that the individual demand is not effective since the public good cannot be supplied in different quantities to different people.

Endogenous variables defining an equilibrium include:

τ_K, τ_L average capital-income and labor tax rates, the values of which are determined through the optimization of the political support function;

p_i, w, ρ market prices for output of good i, labor, and capital, the values of which equalize supply and demand;

p_N a numeraire price index;

y_j sectoral output levels, the values of which respond to positive and negative values of net profits;

K_h, L_h endowments of capital and labor of group h;

l_h, d_{ih} demands for leisure and good i by the representative member of group h;

g_h, ν_h notional demand for public output, and the marginal valuation of public output by the representative member of group h in a simulation;

G the aggregate level of public output, which is determined through the government budget restraint.

Variables determined in the calibration so that the equilibrium of the model replicates a benchmark data set include

$\theta_h, \theta_h/n_h$ the political influence weight for group h, and the weight of the representative member of the group, where n_h is the number of people in interest group h.

Functions that characterize preferences and technology include:

$\Pi_j(\cdot)$ unit profit functions (for sectors $j = 1, 2, \ldots,$ 19) that characterize constant-returns-to-scale technologies for producing market goods;

$C_G(p)$ a unit cost function for public goods production (also a constant-returns technology);

$\dfrac{\partial \Pi_j}{\partial p_i}, -\dfrac{\partial \Pi_j}{\partial \tilde{r}}, -\dfrac{\partial \Pi_j}{\partial \tilde{w}}$ commodity output, labor, and capital demand per unit activity in sector j as defined by Shepard's lemma, where $\tilde{w}_j = w(1 + \tau_L t_j^L)$ and $\tilde{r}_j = \rho(1 + \tau_K t_j^K)$ are user costs for labor and capital;

$\dfrac{\partial C_G}{\partial p_i}$ cost-minimizing demand for commodity i per unit output of good G.

Key parameters which characterize international trade possibilities include:

$\overline{im}_i, \overline{ex}_i$ imports and exports of good i in a benchmark;

$\sigma_{\overline{im}}, \sigma_{\overline{ex}}$ import supply and export demand elasticities;

σ_K elasticity of foreign capital flows with respect to the rate of return;

e the real exchange rate (the ratio of a price index of imports to a price index of exports).

Exogenous parameters that characterize the benchmark tax structure include:

t_j^l, t_j^K tax rates on labor and capital inputs in sector j;

t_h^l marginal income tax rates for group h in the benchmark;

$\overline{I}_h, \overline{T}_h$ benchmark factor income (labor and capital) and gross income tax payment (used for the linear approximation of the marginal income tax schedule).

Finally, two variables and a parameter, to be introduced and discussed shortly in order to cardinalize utility are:

$r_h, r_h/n_h$ real broadly defined income of group h (net of taxes and the private valuation of public goods) and real income of the representative member of the group;

σ_r the coefficient of relative risk aversion, assumed to be the same for all individuals.

7.2.2   Discussion of Important Features of the Model

We consider in turn the representation of fiscal structure in the model and other important simplifications of economic structure, the definition of interest groups, the calibration of the influence weights $(\text{the } \theta_h)$, and the manner in which public goods are introduced into the GEMTAP structure. We then turn (in Section 7.3) to the question of how utility is to be cardinalized so that the political support function in (7.7), which combines utilities of different interest groups, is well-defined.

The Stylized Representation of Fiscal Structure and Other Simplifications

Incorporating political competition and endogenous public policies within an applied equilibrium framework introduces additional complexity into a setting that is already computationally and analytically demanding. We therefore implement a model that contains an aggregated version of the fiscal system

Table 7.1. Average tax rates and the size of government in the benchmark data sets, 1973 and 1983

Tax on:	1973	1983
Labor services (τ_L)	.092	.125
Capital services	.492	.468
Personal income	.085	.057
Capital and income (τ_K)	.170	.140
Labor and income	.088	.087
Government relative to private consumption (G/X)	.370	.337

with three endogenous policy instruments: a combined capital-income tax τ_K, a tax on labor supplies τ_L, and one pure public good G. Negative tax rates are permitted and signify subsidies to the corresponding factor. Since one instrument is determined residually by the government budget restraint, equation (7.15), this aggregation enables us to study solutions to the complex nonlinear optimization of the support function using two-dimensional graphs. In defining the combined tax on capital services and personal incomes in simulations, we fix at the appropriate benchmark values (i) the ratios of capital taxes across sectors, (ii) the ratio of capital to income taxes, and (iii) marginal personal income-tax schedules.

The reduction in the dimensionality of the policy space – which, it should be noted, is not sufficient to eliminate voting cycles under deterministic voting – results in a fiscal structure that appears to capture the stylized facts concerning average tax rates over the decade after 1973. Table 7.1 shows that, across the benchmark data sets, τ_L increases by about one third from 0.092 in 1973 to 0.125 in 1983. Over the same period, τ_K decreases by about one sixth from 0.170 to 0.140. The table also shows what would occur if we had aggregated labor and personal income taxes instead of capital and personal income taxes; the increase in the taxation of labor supply and the reduction in personal income taxes over the decade are then completely hidden from view.

The GEMTAP model contains tax parameters that we do not make use of, in the sense that they remain fixed at their benchmark values rather than being determined as part of the electoral equilibrium. Our defense of this simplification is that the model is complicated as it stands and that graphical methods of studying the model's properties are of great benefit. We hope that, in the future, researchers will be able to increase the dimensionality of the policy space substantially and will be able to use nongraphical methods of analyzing the characteristics of the resulting model.

Other important simplifying assumptions concerning the nature of economic structure have also been adopted. As equation (7.10) illustrates, the capital stock is endogenized through international capital flows, following Goulder et al. (1983). Capital flows depend on the real after-tax price of capital services in the United States, $\tilde{r}$, relative to the real exchange rate e, and on the constant elasticity with respect to the relative net of tax price of capital, σ_K. This is an amendment to the original GEMTAP structure that provides an important margin for the response of the capital stock to taxation. We set $\sigma_K = 0.5$ and note that the model calibrates successfully when values of this parameter up to 1.0 in 1973 are assumed; however, it does not calibrate in 1983 when $\sigma_K = 1.0$ or higher.[12]

As in the original GEMTAP model, the government budget is balanced each period and government debt has no effect on welfare. Moreover, we do not solve the model in a dynamic context. Relaxation of these and other features of the model is left for future research.

The Definition of Interest Groups

Although there are many ways to define interest groups, we are restricted by the nature of the GEMTAP benchmark data sets in which individual households are grouped by household personal income. We chose to aggregate the original GEMTAP groupings of households into three interest groups according to a combination of two characteristics: the level of gross household personal income and the share of factor income from ownership of capital. The use of these characteristics is in the general tradition of many models of interest-group politics.

We focus first on the definition of interest groups for 1973. We aggregate all households in the data set for this year into three groups. As recorded in Table 7.2, the lower-income group P consists of a large number (37.5 percent of the population) of low- and moderately low–income taxpayer-voters. The middle-income group M, the largest of the three at 56.8 percent of the population, has substantial amounts of both labor and capital income, though labor income dominates. The upper-income group R is by far the smallest and wealthiest of the groups. Members of the upper-income group derive a substantially higher proportion of their income from capital than do members of the other groups.

---

[12] Further consideration of the sensitivity of the model to this and other parameters is contained in Rutherford and Winer (1995).

Table 7.2.   Definition and characteristics of interest groups, 1973 and 1983

Year	Interest Group	GEMTAP Household Groups* Household Personal Income Range (Average Factor Income)	Share of Capital Income (percent)	Share of Labor Income (percent)	K/L Ratio	Share of Population (percent)
1973						
	Lower Income (P)	H1 - H4 0-$5999 ($2490)	12.7	8.3	0.29	37.5
	Middle Income (M)	H5 - H11 $6000-$24999 ($12800)	48.1	74.3	0.12	56.8
	Upper Income (R)	H12 >$25000 ($38300)	39.2	17.4	0.42	5.7
1983						
	Lower Income (P)	H1 - H7 0-$24999 ($8700)	17.6	21.5	0.17	44.1
	Middle Income (M)	H8 - H11 $25000-$74999 ($22500)	46.2	63.4	0.15	49.4
	Upper Income (R)	H12 - H14 >$75000 ($53700)	36.2	15.1	0.51	6.4

Notes to Table 7.2: Incomes are in current dollars. The household income ranges refer to gross household personal incomes, while the figures in parentheses refer to average factor incomes for the groups. Note that prices approximately doubled between 1973 and 1983.

The grouping of households in 1983 maintains, as far as possible given the original data set, the same distribution across interest groups of income from capital as occurred in 1973. Our desire to have interest groups defined in a consistent fashion across the two selected years – by share of capital income as well as by level of personal income – plays a role in the choice of which households to group together in 1973 and in 1983. The definition of interest groups used for 1973 is one that allows a reasonable low–middle–high grouping of GEMTAP households in that year and, at the same time, permits the grouping of households in 1983 with a similar within-year distribution of income from capital ownership. As can be seen in Table 7.2, this method of defining interest groups results in the lower-income group being somewhat larger and the middle-income group being somewhat smaller in 1983 than in 1973.

Taking the richest GEMTAP subaggregate of households (H7 in the GEM-TAP notation) out of the low-income group in 1983 and adding it to the middle-income interest group reduces the relative size of the lower-income group in 1983 substantially (from about 44 percent in Table 7.2 to about 34 percent, which is similar to the 1973 figure) and increases the size of the middle-income interest group (from 49 percent to 60 percent). However, when this alternative definition of interest groups is used and the counterfactuals discussed later are recomputed, the general nature of our conclusions remains more or less the same. Further work on the definition of interest groups would doubtless be worthwhile, but we shall leave that work for another time.

Calibration of the Influence Weights

The reason for aggregating households into three groups is that unique calibration of the corresponding political influence weights $\left(\text{the } \theta_h\right)$ requires that the number of groups be equal to the number of policy instruments. To see why this is so, we recall first-order conditions (7.6) for maximization of the political support function after the general equilibrium structure has been substituted into it. For convenience, these conditions are restated here in a sightly different form:

$$\sum_{h=1}^{h=N} \left(\frac{\partial u^h}{\partial s_j} \right) \cdot \theta_h = 0 \quad \text{for} \quad = 1, 2, \ldots, J + 1. \tag{7.6'}$$

The s_j in these conditions refers to either a tax rate or the level of public goods, so that there are $J + 1$ first-order conditions in total, and we have reversed the order in which the terms on the left side of (7.6) appear.

One way to calibrate the θs is to compute the partial derivatives in the foregoing conditions at a benchmark equilibrium numerically and then, with the resulting numbers inserted into conditions (7.6'), consider this as a system of linear equations to be solved simultaneously for the unknown weights. (This is the method used by Winer and Rutherford 1993.) Such a solution for the θs will exist and be unique if the number of such equations is equal to the number of unknowns. Thus, if we wish to have three instruments – two tax rates and a public good – so that there are three equations in (7.6'), it is necessary to aggregate households into three groups because the number of such groups determines the number of unknown θs that must be solved for.

The method we actually use to calibrate the weights is analytically equivalent to the one just outlined, but it makes use of a programming trick that we shall relegate to an appendix. Calibration is successful – that is, a benchmark data set can be modeled as a Nash equilibrium in a competitive political economy – if all of the calibrated weights are positive. Nonnegativity of the weights is not sufficient for successful calibration, because if some group were assigned zero weight then the expected vote functions for the parties might not then be continuous in the policy instruments and vote cycling could occur, as we have discussed previously. A negative weight does not have a meaningful interpretation in our framework.

In actual implementation of the calibration procedure, it is necessary to specify the domain of the policy instruments over which the numerical computation (of the partial derivatives in the system of equations (7.6′) and of the quantities in the actual calibration procedure outlined in the Appendix to this chapter) is to be conducted. Since the calibrated weights are a vital part of the definition of an equilibrium, so too is the choice of this domain.

In calibrating the influence weights, we restrict the numerical algorithm we have used to a local neighborhood of the benchmark values of the policy instruments; our reasoning is that, in any single election, candidates are restricted to choosing among limited alternative directions of change from the status quo. This notion of what may be called a "local electoral equilibrium" has also been used by G. H. Kramer and A. Klevorick (1974), Thomas Romer (1977), Alex Cukierman and Allan Meltzer (1991), Peter Coughlin (1992, Chap. 6), and others. We return to the choice of a local versus global domain on which to calibrate the model and define an electoral equilibrium in Section 7.3, where an interesting graphical representation is provided of why the distinction matters in the model of the United States that we have constructed.

The Demand for Public Goods

It does not seem sensible to construct a model of a competitive political system without also incorporating the two most important reasons why those taxes exist: redistribution of income and the provision of public services. The redistributive motive for taxation is implicit in GEMTAP tax structure as we have amended it. This structure even allows for the existence of net subsidies to factors that are modeled as negative tax rates in the version implemented here. Individual demands for public services are not, however, included in the original model.

The approach we take to the incorporation of individual demands for a public good leads to an explicit role in the model for the private valuations of public goods, and it permits us to define a measure of individual real income that includes the valuation of these goods. Assume that a representative household actually solves a problem of the following form, where the h subscript denoting the representative member of each interest group is omitted for convenience:

$$\max_d U(d,G) \quad \text{subject to}$$

$$\sum_i p_i d_i = \sum_i p_i \omega_i - t. \tag{7.16}$$

In (7.16), t is the total tax collected from the representative individual in any interest group, and both t and the level of the single pure public good G that we include in the model are considered to be exogenous from the individual household's perspective when that individual decides what goods to consume and factors to supply.

This problem is an adequate characterization of the private demand for private goods, $d_i(p, G)$. For our purposes, however, it is helpful to construct a private demand function, $d_i(p, \nu)$, and its analog for the public good, $g(p, \nu)$, both of which explicitly incorporate the private valuation ν of the public good. We refer to $g(p, \nu)$ here and in the schematic of the model given earlier as a "notional demand" for the public good, since individuals cannot by themselves adjust the quantity of the public services that they consume.

We proceed by observing that the consumer's problem stated in (7.16) is equivalent to

$$\max_{d,g} U(d, g) \quad \text{subject to}$$

$$\sum_i p_i d_i = \sum_i p_i \omega_i - t, \qquad (7.17)$$

$$g = G.$$

To go from (7.16) to (7.17), we substitute the individual demand for the public good, g, into the utility function and add the constraint that what the individual consumes is equal to what the government supplies, G, because the public good is by definition equally consumed by all voters.

The solution to problem (7.17) includes a Lagrange multiplier λ for the private income constraint and a Lagrange multiplier μ for the public good constraint.[13] We may interpret μ as the agent's marginal utility of the public good, and we may think of the ratio $\nu = \mu/\lambda$ as the amount of money the agent would be willing to pay for an additional unit of the public good. As indicated, this ratio is what we define as the private valuation of the public good.

If ν were given at a level consistent with the solution to (7.17), we could then combine the two constraints in (7.17) and reformulate the household's problem to read

$$\max_{d,g} u(d, g) \quad \text{subject to}$$

$$\sum_i p_i d_i + \nu g = \sum_i p_i \omega_i - t + \nu G. \qquad (7.18)$$

The last transformation leads to a representation of the consumer's optimization problem for a general equilibrium framework with an extended set of

---

[13] Several public goods may be incorporated into the model if desired, in which case there will be one multiplier for each public good included.

prices (p, ν), demands (d, g), and endowments (ω, G). In (7.18), the individual's real broadly defined income – real personal income net of the payment of taxes and the valuation of public services – can be measured on either the "uses" (left) side or the "sources of income" (right) side of the extended constraint in (7.18).[14] We shall make use of this broadly defined income in operationalizing the political support function in a manner discussed in the next section, where the real income of a group is denoted by r_h and the real income of a representative member of the group is denoted by r_h/n_h.

Equation (7.13) in the model schematic implements the problem outlined in (7.18), and it determines the functional form of the notional demand for public services along with that of the demands for private goods. The constraint $g = G$ appears in the schematic of the model as equation (7.14) and ensures that private valuations of the public good are consistent with (7.13) or (7.18) as a representation of individual optimization.

One should note that the valuation of the public good determined in (7.14) is not in general equal to the tax-price paid by the representative household in each interest group. Taxes actually paid by any individual are determined as part of the electoral equilibrium, not by a Lindahl bargaining process. The private valuation ν is a hypothetical price that measures what the individual voter would be willing to pay for another unit of G so that, given the relative prices of private and the public good, the optimum for the voter would involve consuming just the quantity of the public good that he or she is in fact provided with in the equilibrium.

The method just outlined of determining private valuations of the public good comes into play when the full model is either simulated or shocked in some manner, and it determines departures of the private valuations from the values we assign prior to calibration to a benchmark data set. When the model is *calibrated* to a benchmark data set, we must impose valuations of public services in order to completely specify the nature of underlying individual preferences. Since little is known about these marginal valuations, we assume for our base case that they are uniform across all individuals and that their sum is equal to the marginal cost of public goods production.[15] The equality of the sum of the marginal valuations and the marginal cost of public goods production is the well-known Samuelson (1954) condition for Pareto efficiency in the presence of public goods when the excess burden of taxation and the complementarity of public and private goods is ignored. Expenditure shares in utility functions are then calibrated, following John Piggott and John Whalley (1987), so that

---

[14] The concept of the after-fisc or broadly defined income, including the valuation of public services, has been used by many authors – most notably by Irwin Gillespie (1980) in his studies of fiscal incidence.

[15] The marginal cost of another unit of the public good is set to 1 in a benchmark.

– given the valuations of the public good and private goods prices – each household demands just the private–public bundle of goods that they in fact are observed to consume.[16]

It is also necessary to parameterize utility functions with respect to the degree of substitutability between public and private goods. We again follow Piggott and Whalley, assuming a constant elasticity of substitution between public and private goods that is equal to one half. This implies (Shoven and Whalley 1992b, p. 96) an uncompensated elasticity of demand with respect to the private "price" of public services of -0.5 if the public good expenditure shares are small, a figure roughly consistent with some empirical estimates.[17]

7.3   CARDINALIZATION OF UTILITY AND CONCAVITY OF THE SUPPORT FUNCTION

In order for the political support function (7.7) to be numerically optimized, it is necessary to specify how the utility functions are cardinalized so that their weighted sum may be unambiguously defined.[18] The problem could be avoided if it were possible to specify a direct link between tax instruments and the voting behavior of different groups. However, empirical estimates of such popularity functions, recently surveyed by Peter Nannestad and Martin Paldam (1994), are still "a weak and unstable analytical tool" (p. 238).

The approach we take is to redefine the u^h that enters the support function as

$$u^h(r_h/n_h) = \begin{cases} \dfrac{(r_h/n_h)^{1-\sigma_r}}{1-\sigma_r} & \text{if} \quad \sigma_r > 0, \sigma_r \neq 1, \\[2mm] \log(r_h/n_h) & \text{if} \quad \sigma_r = 1, \end{cases} \tag{7.19}$$

where r_h/n_h is the real broadly defined income of the representative member of group h introduced earlier in (7.18), and where σ_r is the coefficient of relative risk aversion, assumed to be equal for all households.[19] This functional form has often been used in the literature; see for example Blanchard and Fischer (1989, p. 44) and Boadway and Bruce (1984, p. 277). In our base case we assume that $\sigma_r = 1$, so that utility is given by the log of real income, and we present a sensitivity analysis of the central results to this assumption.

[16] The sensitivity of the results we discuss later to assumptions about the benchmark valuations of public services is considered by Rutherford and Winer (1995). Experiments reported there suggest that the results are not sensitive to deviations from the Samuelson condition for a sum of private evaluations of public goods between 0.7 and 1.3.

[17] See the work of Bergstrom and Goodman (1973) and Pommerehne and Schneider (1978).

[18] Coleman (1990, Chap. 29) provides an interesting discussion of the cardinalization issue.

[19] The value of σ_r is equal to $\left[-u''(r/n)\right]/u'$.

When $\sigma_r = 1$, the political support function that is optimized takes the log-linear form of the Nash welfare function, though we hasten to recall that the support function is not a social welfare function but is rather a part of the method we use to characterize an electoral equilibrium. In the event that $\sigma_r = 1$, the equilibrium could be said to replicate a Nash bargaining solution, an interpretation suggested by Eric Drissen and Frans van Winden (1993, p. 497). It is also of interest that the log-linear form of the support function emerges from the version of the Representation Theorem that results when the probability of voting for a candidate is described by a binary Luce model rather than by assumption (7.4) (Coughlin 1992, p. 99). The existence of the alternative interpretations of the model that are possible when $\sigma_r = 1$ enhances the interest in results based on this parameter value.

The curvature of the utility function for each voter increases with the assumed value for σ_r. Moreover, when σ_r is increased, the responsiveness of utility to changes in real income of voters with lower incomes grows relative to the sensitivity of utility of better-off voters. The calibrated influence weight for the lower-income group, θ_P, must then decline relative to the weights for other groups in order to explain why a now more politically sensitive group does not receive a more beneficial tax treatment than was observed to occur. The results discussed in section 7.5 illustrate the decline in the calibrated values of θ_P as σ_r is increased.

Existence and uniqueness of a fiscal platform that maximizes political support depends on the concavity of the support function (7.7) as amended by (7.24). It is not clear what the actual effective concavity of the support function will be after substitution of the general equilibrium structure we employ, even though the direct utility functions are concave. However, as indicated earlier, we will see that for the model we have constructed, there is sufficient concavity for a wide range of values of σ_r.

7.4   PARETO SETS AND THE IMPORTANCE OF GENERAL EQUILIBRIUM TO THE STUDY OF POLITICAL ECONOMY

It is convenient to begin an investigation of the behavior of the model by graphing the Pareto sets of tax policies for the United States in 1973 and 1983. These sets are constructed so that, at any point in them, there is no change in tax rates or in the level of the public good that would be unanimously preferred by all interest groups. Given the particular form of the utility function (7.19), the Pareto sets are invariant to alternative assumptions about σ_r.[20]

---

[20] It may be noted that the Pareto set for any year is equivalent to the set of policies for which calibration yields positive θs, since each such calibration to a given policy platform implies that a particular weighted sum of voter utilities is maximized with this choice of policies.

Construction of the Pareto sets does not depend on the probabilistic model of voting behavior, which comes into play in determining the nature of the political equilibrium. The Pareto sets depend only on the nature of preferences and the equilibrium structure of the private economy. These Pareto sets would therefore remain the same even if voting behavior were strictly deterministic.

In the base case ($\sum_h n_h \nu_h = 1$; $\sigma_K = 0.5$; $\sigma_r = 1$), the Pareto set is shown by the enclosed area in Figure 7.1a for 1973 and in Figure 7.1b for 1983, where τ_K is on the vertical axis and τ_L is on the horizontal axis.[21] (Recall that the size of public expenditure is determined residually by the government budget constraint.)

Figures 7.1a and 7.1b are standard diagrams used in the analysis of electoral outcomes (see e.g. Figure 2.2). Here they are numerically constructed – to our knowledge, for the first time – in an applied equilibrium setting with actual data. The outer edge of the Pareto sets represents contract curves between the three income groups. These contract curves are not straight lines as in Chapter 2 and in textbook discussions of the spatial voting model, reflecting the fact that the indirect utility functions do not have indifference curves represented by concentric circles. (An illustration of what the indifference curves look like will be given shortly.) The benchmark or actual outcome is denoted B, and the points P^*, M^*, and R^* are the ideal points for the representative agent of the respective interest groups.

As expected, given the source of factor incomes for each group, lower-income voters want higher taxes on capital and lower taxes on labor, while the opposite is the case for the richest taxpayers. The middle-income group, which has substantial income from both sources, prefers an intermediate outcome. By reference to the dotted line through B showing all pairs of tax rates that yield the same total tax revenue, it can be seen that the lower-income voters want a larger public sector whereas the middle-income group and the richer voters prefer a somewhat smaller one.

The Pareto sets exclude very high tax rates on both labor and capital, as well as outcomes in which both tax parameters are very low. In these cases, it is possible to find alternative policies that improve everyone's welfare and thereby increase political support. For example, in 1973 with very high tax rates above, say, $\tau_L = \tau_K = 0.4$, all groups can be made better off by lowering tax rates and the level of the public good. Only if marginal valuations of the public good were much higher might some groups be prepared to endure the

---

[21] Constructing the Pareto sets is not an easy computational exercise. The nonlinearity of the large number of optimization problems that must be solved (one for each point on the contract curves) often leads to a solution that appears to represent successful calibration but is not, and vice versa. Factor prices and other variables can fall into a region with negative or nonsense values, leading the algorithms of GAMS to fail even when a proper solution exists.

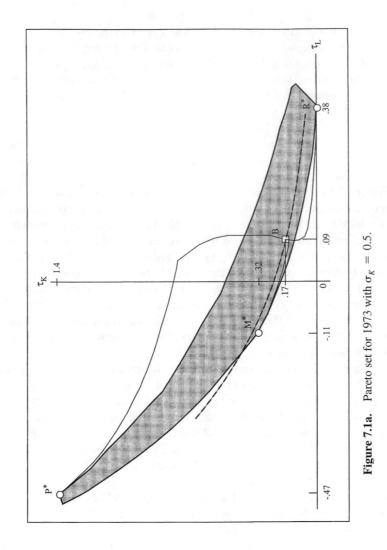

Figure 7.1a. Pareto set for 1973 with $\sigma_K = 0.5$.

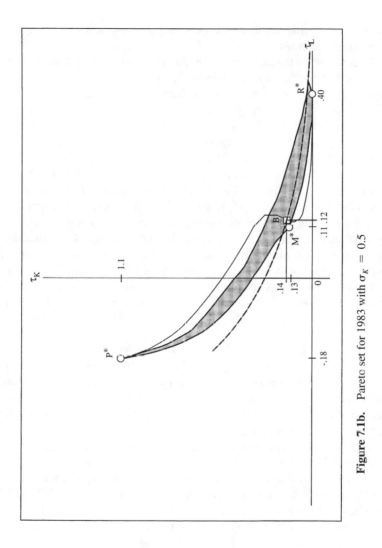

Figure 7.1b. Pareto set for 1983 with $\sigma_K = 0.5$

losses in full income required to support the larger public sector made possible by such high tax rates.

The point M^* is the median in each dimension of the policy space. It differs substantially from the benchmark in 1973, and is similar to it in 1983. This M^* could be a "structure-induced" equilibrium (as discussed in Chapter 2) with strictly deterministic voting, *provided that* voting was effectively restricted to one tax parameter at a time and voters and legislators saw no connection between these two dimensions, even in their minds. Under probabilistic voting, B is the stable equilibrium in spite of the multidimensional issue space.

In Figure 7.1a, the solid line going up from the benchmark B and then left to ideal point P^* – and the solid lines going down through B and then left and right to ideal points M^* and R^*, respectively – show how determination of the point of maximum utility for each group changes as a search over successively larger neighborhoods of B is conducted. The nonlinearity of the lines demonstrates the practical importance of searching for an equilibrium within a small neighborhood of the benchmark. Calibration of weights that allow the benchmark to be replicated by maximizing a political support function depends on the numerical computation of changes in utility with respect to the tax rates, and these changes are evidently different when defined over different domains of the policy space.[22]

Calculated indifference curves for the three groups in the neighborhood of the benchmark are shown in Figures 7.2a and 7.2b, which correspond to Figures 7.1a and 7.1b, respectively. The curves u_R, u_M, and u_P through B are the indifference curves for the R, M, and P groups, respectively. That the curves all intersect at B indicates that this point would not be a stable equilibrium if voting were strictly deterministic.

To get a sense of how important the general equilibrium setting is for political economy, we may compare Pareto sets (with base case parameters) when factor incomes are exogenously fixed at their benchmark or status quo levels with Pareto sets from the full model. It can be seen in Figures 7.3a and 7.3b that when factor incomes are fixed, the Pareto sets are dramatically smaller, and that ideal points are greatly displaced from their true (general equilibrium) positions given in Figures 7.1a and 7.1b. The shrinking of the Pareto sets reflects the inability of each group to benefit from the indirect effects of tax policy on factor incomes when those incomes are exogenously fixed. In our view, a comparison of Figures 7.1 and 7.3 suggests strongly that the general

---

[22] The shape of these lines also hints at the possibility that the equilibrium may be quite sensitive to economic shocks that change the relationship between indirect utilities and policy instruments. In other words, there is a suggestion here (but not more than a suggestion) that what looks like political instability could result from "nonlinearities" that make an equilibrium sensitive to shocks. A great deal has been made of the role of nonlinearities in social systems in recent years. For one interesting discussion in a political economy context, see Cassing and Hillman (1986).

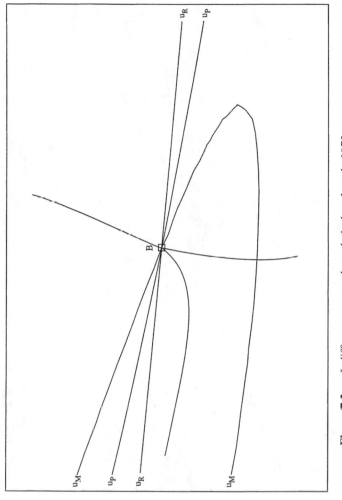

Figure 7.2a. Indifference curves through the benchmark, 1973.

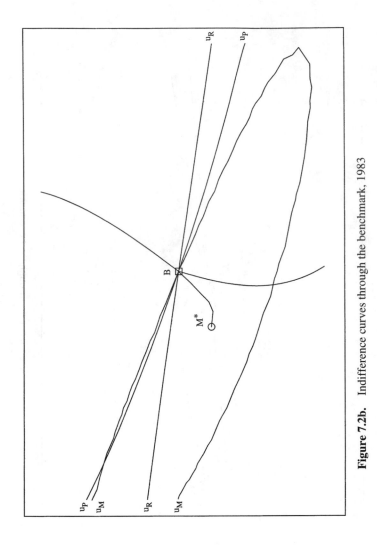

Figure 7.2b. Indifference curves through the benchmark, 1983

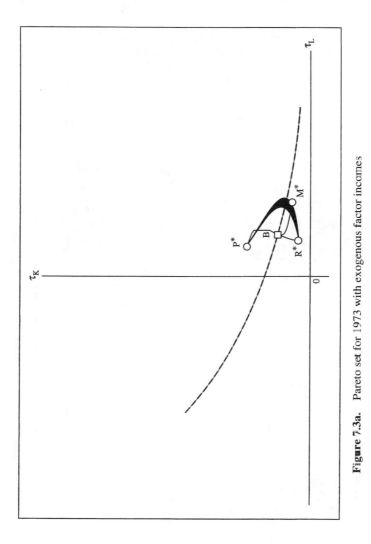

Figure 7.3a. Pareto set for 1973 with exogenous factor incomes

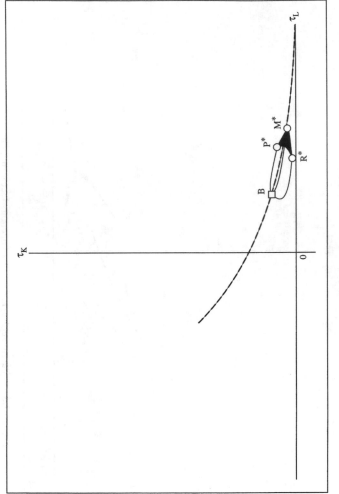

Figure 7.3b. Pareto set for 1983 with exogenous factor incomes

equilibrium consequences of policy should be taken into account in any study of the political economy of the public sector.

7.5   CALIBRATION AS A PRELUDE TO STUDYING THE ECONOMIC AND POLITICAL DETERMINANTS OF U.S. FISCAL HISTORY

In order to use this model to study the economic and political determinants of fiscal history, we must first calibrate the influence weights using the method outlined earlier. Calibrated weights for 1973 and 1983 are presented in Table 7.3 for three different assumed values of σ_r, the coefficient of relative risk aversion. In all cases it is assumed that the sum of marginal evaluations of the public good $\sum_h n_h v_h$ is equal to 1 (the marginal cost of public good provision in a benchmark) and that the elasticity of capital flows σ_K is 0.5. To permit comparisons to be made across groups and years, the weights are reported on a per-capita basis $(= \theta_h/n_h)$ and divided by θ_P/n_P. In the base case with $\sigma_r = 1$, where utility is measured by the log of average real broadly defined income, the calibration results for 1973 indicate that members of the upper-income group are about four times more influential than members of the other two groups on a per-capita basis. This bias in favor of higher-income voters

Table 7.3.   Calibrated per capita weights, 1973 and 1983 $\left(\text{divided by } \theta_P/n_P\right)$

σ_r	Benchmark	θ_P/n_P	θ_M/n_M	θ_R/n_R
	1973			
0		1.000	.432	.695
$(u^h = r_h/n_h)$				
1		1.000	1.140	3.780
$(u^h = \log r_h/n_h)$				
2		1.000	3.004	20.576
	1983			
0		1.000	.508	.620
1		1.000	.812	1.644
2		1.000	1.297	4.361

Notes to Table 7.3: With base-case parameters $(\sum_h n_h v_h = 1; \sigma_K = 0.5)$.
r_h/n_h is average real broadly defined income for group h.

diminishes over time. In 1983, this higher-income group is only about twice as influential as the middle-income group, and just over 1.5 times as influential as lower-income voters. We return to this intriguing pattern later.

The calibration results reported in Table 7.3 confirm our previous argument about how the influence weights vary with the assumed value of σ_r. In each year as σ_r is increased, the per capita influence of the lower-income voters decreases relative to the per-capita influence of the other groups. Recall that this is because a smaller weight must be assigned to a now more influential (i.e., politically more sensitive) group of lower-income voters. Otherwise, it would not be possible to explain why the fiscal system remains as in the given benchmark data to which the model is (still) calibrated.

7.6 COUNTERFACTUAL SIMULATIONS WITH POLITICAL INFLUENCE HELD AT 1973 LEVELS

A computable equilibrium model comes into its own when it is used to construct counterfactual scenarios. Given calibrated influence weights for 1973, we can use the model to show what equilibrium tax rates in 1983 would have been if political influence had remained unchanged over the decade. This permits an explicit decomposition of changes in fiscal policy into two parts: one that is due to changes in ideal points that represent what different voters would like to see happen, possibly due to changes in the structure of the economy or to economic shocks; and one that is due to changes in the relative effective influence of the different interest groups, as revealed by changes in the calibrated influence weights. It turns out that both parts are important for a full understanding of fiscal history.

The decomposition of changes in tax policy is realized by maximizing political support (7.7) subject to the 1983 economy when the influence weights θ_h in the support function take on their 1973 calibrated values. Differences between tax rates in this counterfactual and the benchmark tax rates in 1973 or 1983 reflect only changes in economic structure or economic shocks, while the difference between the counterfactual tax system with unchanged weights and the new benchmark tax system in 1983 reflects the consequences of changes in relative political influence.

For selected values of σ_r, counterfactual simulations showing what would have happened in 1983 had political influence remained unchanged are shown in Figure 7.4 by "plus" signs. In the case where $\sigma_r = 1$, it can be seen in the figure that the evolution of economic structure alone would have led to even lower capital taxes $(\tau_K = 0.08)$ and to even higher labor taxes $(\tau_L = 0.19)$ than actually occurred by the end of the decade. The counterfactual τ_K is about 43 percent less than in the 1983 benchmark; the counterfactual τ_L is about 58

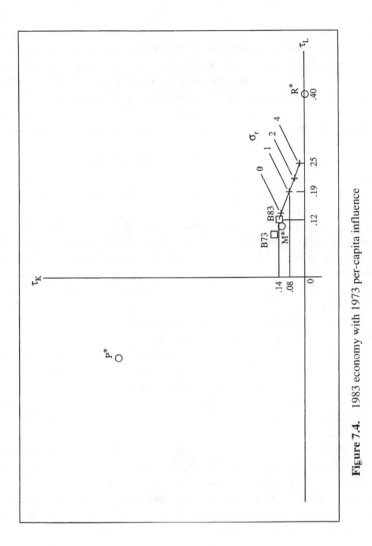

Figure 7.4. 1983 economy with 1973 per-capita influence

percent higher. These deviations from the 1983 benchmark are larger than the corresponding differences between 1973 and 1983 benchmark tax rates.

It is reasonable to suspect that increasing openness of the economy is a key factor explaining the results obtained by combining the 1973 calibrated weights with the 1983 economy, for two reasons. First, in the model with 1983 data, capital flows are more sensitive in equilibrium to a given change in taxation than in the model for 1973. An exogenous 10 percent increase in τ_K in 1983 leads to capital outflows that are 40 percent greater in equilibrium than when the same tax increase is introduced in 1973.[23] To moderate the consequences for factor incomes of the increased equilibrium sensitivity of capital flows to taxation, it is politically advantageous (in the model) to shift the burden of taxation toward labor.

Second, trade flows are larger relative to aggregate income in the 1983 model. Increasing openness in this sense dampens the responsiveness of the exchange rate to a given tax-induced increase in capital outflows. As a result, the effect on economic well-being of capital taxes will not be offset to the same extent by depreciation of the exchange rate, and political competition will tend to drive taxes on capital and high incomes down and those on labor up. To confirm this reasoning we may consider what happens in the model with 1973 weights and 1983 data when exports and imports are exogenously cut by, say, 90 percent. Closing the model in this way should result in a new equilibrium that is closer to the 1983 benchmark than are the counterfactuals in Figure 7.4. Assuming $\sigma_r = 1$, we find in fact that τ_K in Figure 7.4 rises by 25 percent (from 0.08 to 0.1) and τ_L falls by about 20 percent (from 0.19 to 0.15);[24] that is, average tax rates move a considerable distance back toward their 1983 benchmark values.

Some further information about the role of the foreign sector in determining the results in Figure 7.4 can be gained by comparing the 1983 economy in Figure 7.1b with a simulation of what that economy would look like if it were completely closed off to trade; this is shown in Figure 7.5.[25] The comparison reveals that, when the economy is closed, the ideal point for the middle-income group is displaced upward and to the left while the other ideal points remain more or less unaffected. This suggests that it was the effect on middle-income

---

[23] The sensitivity of capital flows referred to here depends on the equilibrium structure of the economy and not just on the elasticity parameter σ_K in equation (7.12), which is the same in both years.

[24] In this simulation, exports and imports are exogenously reduced by the same proportion and then added to the government sector.

[25] "Closing" the economy means: net exports and capital flows are fixed as in the 1983 benchmark, and changes in the value of net exports relative to the benchmark in the simulation are absorbed by the government in the form of a change in general revenue.

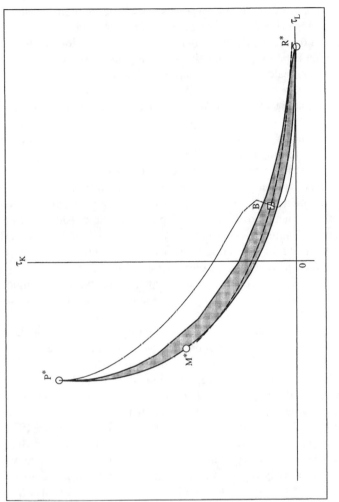

Figure 7.5. Pareto set for 1983 – no external trade

voters of increased international exposure of the economy that made the observed trends in tax rates over the decade politically profitable.

In view of the results discussed here, the obvious question that now presents itself is: What kept taxes on capital from falling and those on labor from rising to the extent revealed by the counterfactuals in Figure 7.4? The answer the model provides, which is implicit in the pattern of the calibrated weights in Table 7.3, is that the effective relative political influence of lower-income voters *increased* over the decade. (Equivalently, one could say that the result is due to a decline in the influence of higher-income voters.) If one accepts a value for σ_r of 1 or higher, simulations based on using 1973 weights with 1983 benchmark data indicate that an increase in the per-capita influence of lower-income voters over the decade kept the tax on capital from being driven down even further and that on labor from rising even more than actually occurred.

How might such a novel result be explained? One possibility is suggested by the work of Thomas Husted and Larry Kenny (1997) on the fiscal effects of the U.S. extension of the voting franchise in the 1960s and 1970s. The evidence they present suggests that elimination of poll taxes and literacy tests in the 1960s, especially in southern states, led to an increase in the number of voters with relatively low incomes and to an increase in social welfare spending. Leonard Dudley has suggested that a rapid decline in the cost of communication in the 1970s reduced the costs of organizing and coordinating large interest groups, including those that represent lower-income people.[26]

In interpreting the result concerning the evolution of the influence weights, two additional points should be kept in mind. The first is that the counterfactuals likely reflect developments that occurred in the 1970s. The trend in the relative size of the influence weights recorded in Table 7.3 may not continue into the 1980s. (Unfortunately, benchmark data sets for years after 1983 do not exist, so we cannot calibrate influence weights for later years.) Second, the lower-income group is large and heterogeneous, and the influence weight for this group is properly regarded as an average over heterogeneous members. The influence of lower-income voters at the lower boundary may have fallen while the average for the group as a whole increased.

It should also be noted that the simulations in Figure 7.4 are not invariant with respect to the value of σ_r. A lower value, such as zero, implies a relatively higher calibrated weight for the lower-income voters in 1973 (see again Table 7.3) and thus a smaller decline in τ_K relative to its 1983 benchmark value when that larger weight is combined with the 1983 data. A somewhat weaker (but still interesting) conclusion can be reached that encompasses the counterfactual with $\sigma_r = 0$ as well as those with $\sigma_r \geq 1$: As a whole, the results indicate that the decline in the capital income–tax rate between 1973 and 1983 was

---

[26] Private communication – but see also Dudley (1991).

not due to a shift in the balance of political power away from lower-income voters.[27]

7.7   THE CONSEQUENCES OF EQUALITY OF POLITICAL INFLUENCE

Another interesting experiment that can be conducted using the model yields an answer to the following question: What would happen to tax rates if equality of political influence on a per-capita basis were (somehow) introduced? The contrast between actual outcomes and this counterfactual provides interesting information about the role played by inequalities in relative influence at a given point in time.

To discover what might occur if there were equality of effective influence among and within interest groups, we replace the calibrated values of the θ_h in the support function (7.7) by weights equal to n_h, where n_h is the size of group h. The altered, hypothetical support function is then optimized subject to the equilibrium structure of the private economy.

The results of such experiments for 1973 and 1983 are shown in Figures 7.6a and 7.6b, respectively. The hypothetical equilibrium under equality of influence for $\sigma_r = 1$ is given in both diagrams at point E. Not surprisingly, in 1973 the outcome under equality involves the subsidization of labor and a much higher tax on capital than actually occurred. Because the calibrated weights for 1973 with $\sigma_r = 1$ imply that the per-capita influence for richer voters is about four times that of lower-income voters, the introduction of equality of influence leads to an outcome that is more favorable to the latter. Assuming a higher (lower) value for σ_r magnifies (diminishes) the difference between the original and the postequality equilibria, as shown in the figure, because a higher (lower) value of this parameter leads to more (less) inequality in the initial situation for the reason discussed earlier.

For 1983 data, the introduction of equality does not lead to an equilibrium that departs as substantially from what actually happened, regardless of the assumed value for σ_r. With $\sigma_r = 1$, for example, the postequality equilibrium (at point E) is quite close to the 1983 benchmark. This similarity of actual and counterfactual outcomes is to be expected in the light of the greater equality in the calibrated weights in 1983 than in 1973. The increased openness of the economy may also play a role in reducing the differences between actual and

---

[27] Rutherford and Winer (1995) also show the effect of using the 1983 calibrated weights with the benchmark data for 1973. Here, in the more closed economy of the early 1970s, capital taxes are higher and labor taxes are lower than in the 1973 benchmark, and the question that arises is: Why didn't taxes take on these values in 1973? The answer the model provides to this question is, by construction, consistent with the answer to the previous question concerning the simulations in Figure 7.4: lower-income voters were not as influential in 1973 as they were in 1983.

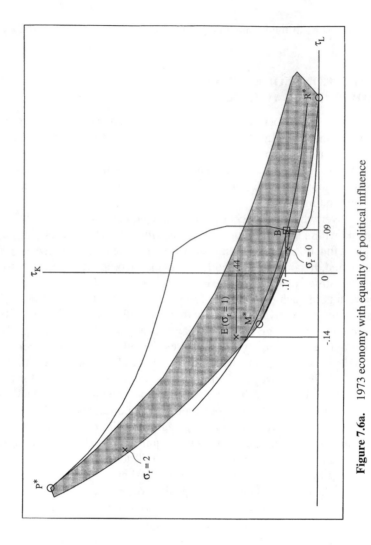

Figure 7.6a. 1973 economy with equality of political influence

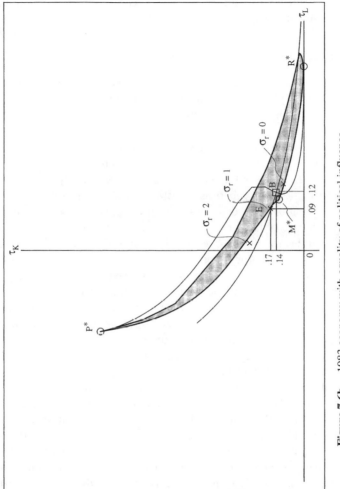

Figure 7.6b. 1983 economy with equality of political influence

postequality outcomes by increasing the full cost of redistribution in the more open economy of 1983.

7.8   CONCLUSIONS

The computable model of economic and political competition presented in this chapter allows explicit study of the broader equilibrium in which fiscal policy is determined along with private prices and quantities. The model permits the computation of the basic elements of the spatial voting framework for the United States as a whole, including ideal points, indirect indifference curves, contract curves, and the Pareto set of tax policies for representative members of three interest groups defined by level and source of incomes.

Implementation of probabilistic voting theory using the Representation Theorem also allows the determination of weights representing the relative political influence of the three groups in equilibrium. The weights in the support function that measure the relative influence of interest groups in equilibrium are not known, but it is possible to calibrate them so that the solution to the synthetic optimization problem yields observed values of tax rates and public expenditures. The calibrated values of the influence weights are, by construction, consistent with the view that public policy in a democratic society reflects the balancing of opposing interests, some of which are more effectively represented in equilibrium than others.

We have used the calibrated influence weights to study the economic and political determinants of changes in U.S. tax policy over the decade after 1973, a period during which taxes on both capital and high personal income fell while those on labor income rose substantially. Counterfactual simulations using weights for 1973 with benchmark data for 1983 eliminate changes in political influence as a source of tax policy developments, thereby isolating the consequences for fiscal policy of changes in economic structure. In these simulations, taxes on capital are generally much lower and taxes on labor much higher than in the 1983 benchmark data. In other words, these counterfactuals indicate that if political influence had not changed over the decade, capital taxes would have fallen substantially more and labor taxes would have risen to a much greater extent than actually occurred. Investigations with the model suggest that increased international exposure of the U.S. economy was an important factor in explaining these results.

The question that then arises is not "why did taxes on capital fall between 1973 and 1983?" but rather "why did capital income taxes not fall further?" The answer the model provides is that an increase in the relative influence of lower-income voters kept taxes on capital and high incomes from falling and taxes on labor from rising even further than was observed to occur. The reasons for this increase in the relative influence of lower-income voters over the

1970s remain to be explored. Since the influence weights are calibrated, the model does not provide one. We have tentatively suggested that the increase in the relative influence of lower-income voters – or, equivalently, the decline in the influence of higher-income groups – may reflect changes in the nature of electoral participation by lower-income voters that began in the 1960s; it may also be due to declines in the cost of organizing large groups of people that were not previously politically active.

In a second set of experiments, we compared actual tax policy outcomes with what would have happened had political influence been equally distributed across all American citizens. It turns out that in 1973, the introduction of complete equality on a per-capita basis would have led to much higher taxes on capital and to the subsidization of labor incomes. For 1983, however, the hypothetical imposition of equality of influence has a more muted effect. Indeed, with $\sigma_r = 1$, the actual and postequality outcomes are quite close together. This result reflects the greater equality of calibrated weights in 1983 as compared to 1973. It may also be due, at least in part, to the increased openness of the economy and the consequent rise in the full cost of using the tax system to redistribute income.

Most importantly, in our view, the results as a whole illustrate the importance of the broader equilibrium setting to the study of fiscal history. Pareto sets constructed in ignorance of the general equilibrium structure are much smaller, and ideal points are greatly distorted from their true (general equilibrium) positions. The general lesson to be learned here is that spatial voting models that are not cognizant of the general equilibrium consequences of policy platforms are likely to be misleading. By integrating advances in probabilistic voting theory with applied general equilibrium modeling, we have shown in this chapter how an applied equilibrium framework encompassing both economic and political competition may be constructed and used to gain a fuller understanding of the factors responsible for the course of public affairs.

APPENDIX TO CHAPTER 7: CALIBRATION OF THE INFLUENCE WEIGHTS

The influence weights (the θ_h) for each group can be conveniently calculated by solving the following synthetic programming problem:

$$\max_{r_h} \sum_{h=1}^{h=3} r_h \quad \text{subject to}$$

$$F\big(r_1, r_2, r_3, \tau_L, \tau_K, G, X\big) = 0, \quad r_h \geq \bar{r}_h, \tag{7A.1}$$

where r_h/n_h is the level of real, broadly defined income (net of taxes and the private valuation of public services), of the representative member of group h

as in (7.18), $\bar{r}_h$ is an arbitrary lower bound on r_h in a benchmark, and $F(\cdot)$ represents the general equilibrium structure of the private economy.

The θ_h can be calculated from the Lagrange multipliers for the lower bounds on the r_h. To see this, write the Lagrangian for the preceding problem as

$$\mathcal{L} = \sum_h r_h - \lambda F + \sum_h \alpha_h (r_h - \bar{r}_h). \tag{7A.2}$$

The first-order conditions associated with the r_h are

$$1 - \lambda \cdot \partial F / \partial r_h + \alpha_h = 0 \quad \text{for} \quad h = 1, \ldots, 3. \tag{7A.3}$$

Now consider the original problem of choosing the r_h to maximize support S in (7.7) with $u^h = r_h / n_h$, subject to the general equilibrium structure F. If $\bar{\theta}_h$ is a benchmark political weight, the first-order conditions for the r_h are

$$\bar{\theta}_h / n_h - \lambda \cdot \partial F / \partial r_h = 0 \quad \text{for} \quad h = 1, \ldots, 3. \tag{7A.4}$$

Comparison of the two sets of first-order conditions indicates that the benchmark per-capita weight for each h is equal to $1 + \alpha_h$. The weights are normalized to sum to unity by setting

$$\frac{\bar{\theta}_h}{n_h} = \frac{1 + \alpha_h}{H + \sum_j \alpha_j}, \tag{7A.5}$$

where H represents the number of groups. The correspondence of the political weights and Lagrange multipliers in an appropriately specified maximization problem has also been discussed by Ben van Velthoven (1989).

With the more general definition of u^h in (7.19), the left side of (7A.5) becomes $\theta_h / n_h \cdot (r_h / n_h)^{-\sigma_r}$.

PART FOUR

STATISTICAL ANALYSIS
OF TAX STRUCTURE

CHAPTER 8

Introduction to Statistical Research

> The analytical models introduced in earlier chapters of this book
> are skeletons, as all useful analytical models must be. They are
> designed to isolate important relationships in any theory.... Such a
> theory must be supplemented with the data of experience before
> any genuine understanding of fiscal processes can be achieved.
>
> James Buchanan (1968, p. 151)

Explaining observed differences in the use of taxation and in the structure of
fiscal systems is an important task for political economy. Taxation lies at the
heart of political power and is crucial to the operation of the public sector, thus
providing a test case for judging the relevance of collective decision models.
At the same time, empirical research is facilitated by the existence of excellent
quantitative information on government revenues, including data of both a
cross-sectional and a historical nature.

In the preceding chapter we showed how applied equilibrium modeling
could be used to gain a better empirical understanding of fiscal history. This
chapter sets the stage for statistical modeling. We derive a general set of estimating equations that are consistent with the framework we have developed,
and we use it for a discussion of the issues that arise when making the transition from theory to statistical work. The specific nature of the research presented in the following two chapters is introduced, and previous empirical
work on the political economy of tax structure is reviewed.

Before turning to the derivation of estimating equations, it will be helpful to
have an overview of the framework developed in the preceding chapters. We
argued that tax systems can be understood as sets of related policy instruments
that are being shaped and used deliberately in the course of the struggle for
power. Political parties balance two competing aims in choosing a revenue system. On the one hand, they prefer to differentiate among heterogeneous taxpayers, with the aim of raising revenue with as little loss of electoral support as
possible. On the other hand, they must consider the transaction and enforcement costs caused by giving special treatment to different taxpayers, since
these costs divert resources that can be used to provide services that are
demanded by the electorate. The resulting compromise is a tax skeleton containing all the essential elements of revenue systems observed in the real

world: multiple tax bases, separate rate structures, and a variety of special provisions. Actual revenue systems must therefore be interpreted as the outcome of simultaneous choices across all three of these policy dimensions.

In making fiscal choices, political parties take into account economic, political, and administrative factors that determine the nature of electoral support associated with alternative ways of taxing. All of the usual economic factors that determine the consequences of taxation for economic welfare are relevant, since voting behavior depends in part on how individual welfare is affected by tax policy. The choice of a policy platform is also affected by the responsiveness of voting behavior to changes in economic welfare and hence by anything that determines the nature of such responses, including interest-group membership. Administration costs vary with the structure and level of taxation and must be taken into account as long as there are alternative uses of these resources that generate political support. Because there is no respite from political competition, the government is forced continually to readjust tax structure in response to changes in these economic, political, and administrative determinants.

To complete this overview of the theory, it is important to note that fiscal policy making is subject in the first instance to the general equilibrium structure of the economy and, in a more subtle manner, to the constraints imposed on political competition by existing political institutions.

8.1 A GENERAL SET OF ESTIMATING EQUATIONS

Going from the general theoretical framework to a specific set of estimating equations is a challenging exercise. As a first step in the derivation of estimating equations, we consider the following version of the probabilistic voting model introduced in previous chapters. Interest groups, fiscal relations between governments in a federation, and government debt – features that were not included in the model of Chapters 3 and 4 – are introduced in a simple manner here in order to accommodate the particular empirical applications that we are interested in.

We begin as usual by assuming that competition for office forces each party to propose a tax structure $s = \{s_1, s_2, \ldots, s_K\}$ and the level of a public good G so as to continually maximize expected votes. The vector s of tax instruments is defined so as to contain only nonnegative elements, and it includes all aspects of revenue structure such as the various components of tax bases, tax rates, and special provisions.

The expected vote for the governing party, $EV = \sum_h n_h f_h$, is defined over N groups of voters, each of which contains an exogenously determined number

n_h of relatively homogeneous members; f_h is the probability that the representative taxpayer in group h will vote for the incumbent.[1]

The probability that any representative taxpayer votes for the government depends on the way in which that taxpayer's indirect utility v^h is affected (i) by fiscal structure, (ii) by a vector z of variables that reflect aspects of intergovernmental fiscal relations (of particular importance in the application developed in the next chapter),[2] and (iii) by a vector x of exogenous variables that will be specified later.

The choice of a policy platform is constrained by the budget restraint, $R = G + A$, where R is total revenues from all sources and A is total administration costs. The levels of R and A may depend on fiscal structure as well as on z and x. Political optimization by each party is also subject to the general equilibrium structure of the private economy and to fiscal relationships with other governments, which we write schematically as $F(s, G, z, x) = 0$. In this formulation, F does not include the government budget restraint.

The model can be interpreted in a manner that allows for an intertemporal dimension to political competition. (This interpretation will be particularly relevant to the application of the model in Chapter 10.) Individual utility v^h now represents the *present value* of expected utilities over a horizon that political parties think is relevant for voter h.[3] In this formulation, each tax instrument appearing in the vector of policy instruments is time-dated, including values for the stocks of public debt of different maturities and tax rates for each tax base in future years. Finally, the government budget restraint stated earlier may be thought of as a set of restraints, one applying to each time period, with revenues R in every period defined to include the net issue of debt of different maturities less interest payments in that period.

In the intertemporal version of the model, political parties care about the future only because (and to the extent that) voters do. Each party continues to maximize expected support at every point in time by announcing both current and future values of fiscal instruments. Party platforms contain both current and future levels of fiscal instruments because current political support for any

---

[1] The appearance of interest groups in this formulation is suggested by Coughlin et al. (1990a,b).

[2] Suppose that we are modeling the choice of tax structure by a province or state in a federal system. Then the vector z will include the tax-price of public goods provided by the central government. As a result of the relationship between the tax systems of the two levels of government, this tax-price may be affected by the revenue structure chosen by the provincial or state government, making it an endogenous variable in a model of provincial or state tax structure. See for example Feldstein and Metcalf (1987).

[3] The discount rate to be used in computing the present value of utility for voter h is the one that the parties *think* would be employed by this voter in making the same calculation.

party depends to some extent on voters' views about how public policy will affect them in the future.

Application of the Representation Theorem to the model just described (with or without the intertemporal dimension) allows us once again to characterize the equilibrium by maximizing an appropriately defined political support function subject to the government budget restraint and the general equilibrium structure. Given *individual* vote sensitivities $\theta_h = \partial f_h / \partial v^h$ and allowing explicitly for the existence of different groups of relatively homogeneous voters, this problem may be stated as:

$$\max_{\{s,G\}} S = \sum_h n_h \theta_h v^h(s, G, z, x) \tag{8.1}$$

subject to

$$G = R(s, z, x) - A(s, z, x), \tag{8.1a}$$

$$F(s, G, z, x) = 0, \tag{8.1b}$$

$$s_k \geq 0 \quad \text{for} \quad k = 1, 2, \dots, K, \tag{8.1c}$$

$$G > 0. \tag{8.1d}$$

The first-order conditions for the synthetic optimization problem include

$$-\frac{\partial}{\partial s_k}(S - \mu F) \Big/ \left\{ \frac{\partial}{\partial s_k}(R - A) \right\} \geq \lambda \quad \text{for} \quad k = 1, 2, \dots, K, \tag{8.2a}$$

$$\frac{\partial}{\partial G}(S - \mu F) = \lambda, \tag{8.2b}$$

where λ is the Lagrange multiplier associated with the budget constraint and μ is the multiplier associated with the general equilibrium structure. These conditions indicate that, in the equilibrium, fiscal instruments are adjusted until the marginal effect on political support per dollar of net revenue (net of administration costs) is equalized across all fiscal instruments in use. The inequalities in (8.2a) acknowledge that, because of the nature of political opposition or for other reasons, some fiscal instruments may not actually be used at all times. For example, if s_k is a tax rate that is set at zero (or not used) in the equilibrium, then (8.2a) indicates that the marginal political cost per dollar of revenue associated with a small increase in s_k, given by the left side of (8.2a), is greater than the marginal political benefit of another dollar of public services, λ. The fact that some instruments may not be used in the equilibrium complicates empirical applications of the framework.

One way of representing a solution to the first-order conditions, assuming that one exists, is by a set of simultaneous semireduced-form equations of the following kind: For $k = 1, 2, \ldots, K$,

$$s_k = s_k\big(s_1, s_2, \ldots, s_{k-1}, s_{k+1}, \ldots, s_K, G, n_1, \ldots, n_N, z, x\big), \quad s_k \geq 0; \tag{8.3a}$$

$$G = G\big(s_1, s_2, \ldots, s_K, n_1, \ldots, n_N, z, x\big), \quad G > 0. \tag{8.3b}$$

Although the system of equations represented by (8.3a) and (8.3b) must be simplified before empirical work can be conducted, it is by no means the most general statement of an equilibrium fiscal system that is consistent with our theoretical framework. The structure of expenditures has been suppressed in order to focus on revenue structure. In addition, no account is taken here (or in the statistical work reported in the following chapters) of the fact that fiscal instruments representing such features as the definition of a particular tax base are themselves the result of optimizing decisions by elected officials – officials who continually adjust the precise specification of each policy instrument to accommodate changes in administration costs, the structure of the economy, and the composition of the electorate.

The problems of doing empirical research with systems of equations like (8.3a) and (8.3b) resemble the difficulties associated with empirical work in any general equilibrium context. Indeed, the problems are more acute here than is usually the case since the equilibrium framework has been made broader than the one typically relied upon by including the interaction between the private economy and political optimization. In such a setting, the empirical researcher must be willing to justify why some particular part of the larger revenue system is deserving of special attention, or must decide how to simplify the system further if he or she wishes to model a complete revenue system.

8.2   IMPOSING ADDITIONAL STRUCTURE

Equations (8.3) are implemented in different ways in the next two chapters in order to emphasize different aspects of the theoretical framework and to permit investigation of specific features of actual tax systems in the United States and Canada.

In Chapter 9 we will first estimate a single equation representing a part of the larger system in order to investigate in some detail the factors responsible for variations in the mid-1980s in the reliance by U.S. states upon a major revenue source, the income tax.[4] Only one revenue source is explicitly treated, but the estimating equation is designed to take into account the fact that the income tax is part of a larger revenue system.

---

[4] The single-equation model is an updated version of earlier work (Hettich and Winer 1984).

The dependent variable in the equation we estimate is the ratio of income tax collections to personal income, which is a useful and appropriately normalized measure of a states's reliance on this tax source. As an interesting way of choosing explanatory variables, several hypotheses about the relationship between an equilibrium tax structure and political opposition to taxation are proposed and tested.[5]

This single-equation model is then supplemented with an additional equation explaining the decision by state governments to create a specific special provision in the income-tax base – namely, a credit for the payment of local property tax. The two-equation–simultaneous system allows us to study the interdependence of different parts of the tax skeleton, albeit in a particular context. This is in marked contrast to most previous statistical work on tax systems, which does not acknowledge the integrated nature of the components of any tax structure.

Not all U.S. states actually make use of the income tax, and some that levy such a tax do not offer a property tax credit or rebate. Hence, the simultaneous system we estimate in Chapter 9 has limited dependent variables on both sides of each equation, as well as endogenous variables on the right side of each equation that arise because we are studying two parts of a larger equilibrium fiscal system. Estimation of these equations is not straightforward.

Economic factors determining the political payoff from alternative fiscal choices are given prominence in Chapter 9. In Chapter 10 we take a more balanced view of the roles of economic, political, and administrative factors in a study of an entire tax system viewed as an equilibrium policy outcome. We investigate the factors behind the evolution of the revenue system of the Government of Canada from 1867 to 1913, when public revenues consisted primarily of tariffs, excises, and the issue of debt. In order to model a complete revenue system, it is necessary to give less attention to the interdependence of various structural elements than in the investigation of U.S. state income taxation.

As in the models of debt surveyed in Chapter 2, we simplify further here by assuming that only public debt has an explicit intertemporal character, even though the promised levels of all policy instruments, including tariff and excise rates, are, in principle, important to voters who care about the future. Thus, fiscal platforms consist of current taxation – that is, tariffs and excises – and deficit financing. On the other hand, and in contrast to most empirical research on taxation, we explicitly allow for the fact that the government is concerned with the effects of all of its policy choices on the future welfare of voters, and thereby on its current political support, by modeling the manner in

---

[5] These hypotheses are different from, but complementary to, those advanced by Gillespie (1991), who generally takes a similar approach to taxation in his nonstatistical study of Canadian fiscal history.

which it forecasts the future levels of variables used in formulating its current policy platform.

The work in Chapter 10 makes use of Irwin Gillespie's (1991) historical revision of the public accounts of Canada. Gillespie's own study of Canadian fiscal history using these data focuses on the birth and death of tax sources since the origins of the modern state, and it relies upon budget speeches and political debates. Our complementary investigation employs statistical modeling and emphasizes the factors responsible for the changing balance between revenue sources during a period when the list of major revenue sources remained the same.

8.3   AN OVERVIEW OF EXISTING STATISTICAL WORK ON THE POLITICAL ECONOMY OF TAX STRUCTURE

There is a substantial body of statistical work dealing with the explanation of tax systems. We review selected aspects of this literature in this and the next section as a way of inquiring into additional issues and problems that confront researchers wishing to model actual tax systems, while at the same time placing our own contribution into perspective with respect to the literature as a whole. A brief overview of literature in this section is followed in the next by a more detailed discussion of how estimating equations are derived in two studies that we have found to be generally helpful in our own work, though the focus of concern in these studies differs from ours in various ways. Throughout the discussion, references to the literature are intended to be illustrative rather than comprehensive.

The different branches of the existing empirical literature can be distinguished by the underlying theoretical model adopted. Although there is not yet much empirical work on tax structure that is based directly on a probabilistic spatial voting model, a substantial body of work exists that is consistent with this approach. "Consistency" here means that tax structure is modeled as an equilibrium outcome of competition between political parties for electoral support, and that the choice of tax and other policies made by the government reflects a balancing of opposing interests in the electorate.[6]

In addition to work consistent with the probabilistic voting model, there is empirical work relying on the median voter model, the Leviathan model, and

---

[6] We may include in this category empirical work based on van Winden's (1983) interest function, which is a weighted sum of voter utilities with weights reflecting effective political influence. Van Winden suggests that bargaining (between groups) as in Nash (1950) may serve as a justification for such a model.

the structure-induced equilibrium tradition. Finally, there is a body of statistical work that does not use collective choice models but instead views tax structure as something chosen to maximize the welfare of a representative citizen, or to minimize the aggregate welfare cost of taxation. It is useful to include this work in our review along with the political economy models.

Existing empirical research on tax structure in the probabilistic voting tradition, or research that is consistent with this approach, can be surveyed according to how the estimating equations (8.3) have been operationalized. Some studies in this tradition have analyzed particular parts of this revenue system in substantial detail. As we noted, our study of the structure of U.S. state fiscal systems presented in Chapter 9 is of this type. Other examples include Pamela Moomau and Rebecca Morton (1992) on property taxation, as well as Lawrence Kenny and Mark Toma (1997), who examine the choice between income taxation and the inflation tax in the United States. We may also include here work on the political economy of tariffs by authors such as Richard Caves (1976), Gerald Helleiner (1977), Robert Baldwin (1986), and Stephen Magee, William Brock, and Leslie Young (1989). The work on tariffs is marked by attempts to explicitly investigate the role of interest groups.

A few authors have estimated a set of equations representing the entire revenue system, where the dependent variables are different revenue sources or the corresponding revenue shares. This includes the work of Friedrich Schneider and Werner Pommerehne (1980), who examine the revenue structure of Australian national governments in a paper we discuss at greater length in the next section; Robert Inman's (1989) model of fiscal structure in U.S. cities; and the analyses by Howard Chernick (1992) and William Hunter and Michael Nelson (1989) of U.S. state revenues. The model of revenue composition in nineteenth-century Canada that we present in Chapter 10 is a study of the factors responsible for the evolution of a revenue system as a whole.

Finally, there are some recent papers that have attempted to estimate the political costs or consequences for electoral support associated with alternative tax policies. These include Peter Nannestad and Martin Paldam (1996), John Ashworth and Bruno Heyndels (1997), and Stuart Landon and David Ryan (1997).[7] Landon and Ryan, for example, calculate the effect on the incumbent's percentage of the vote of a $1 increase in taxation from each of several sources using pooled data for Canadian provinces. They find that provincial sales taxation has a lower marginal political cost in this sense than do direct taxes on persons. Also, both of these tax sources are found to have

---

[7] Empirical research on the political consequences of alternative tax sources is complemented by a body of work in a political science tradition that deals in part with how governments choose or manipulate the characteristics of tax and other policy instruments for political profit. See for example Rose (1985) and Peters (1991).

higher political costs at the margin than do natural resource royalties, user fees, and corporate income taxes. It remains to be seen whether the observed inequality of marginal political costs reflects disequilibrium in the political system, the failure or inability of political parties to optimize fully, or statistical bias from aggregation across political jurisdictions where politically optimal tax mixes differ substantially.

Empirical research departing from the median voter framework results in estimating equations that are quite similar to those found in studies that assume that governments maximize expected votes or some similar objective (Sjoquist 1981, Gade and Adkins 1990, Goodspeed 1992). This should not be surprising because the model has the same basic structure as equations (8.3), except that the electoral objective is replaced by the utility function of the median or decisive voter. The same holds for representative agent models not based on a collective choice mechanism, where the objective function is replaced by the utility function of a representative citizen. Much of this work (Feldstein and Metcalf 1987, Metcalf 1993) investigates tax structure of U.S. states. Finally, the similarity extends to estimating equations reflecting the view that governments minimize the aggregate welfare cost of taxation. Research based on this assumption includes Robert Barro's (1979, 1986) investigations of debt and tax smoothing, as well as papers by Gregory Mankiw (1987), James Poterba and Julio Rotemberg (1990), and Bharat Trehan and Carl Walsh (1990) on the choice between "seigniorage" and current taxation.

However, models based on probabilistic voting, median voters, and representative agents are not observationally equivalent when differences among voters are acknowledged. Heterogeneity plays a significant role only in the probabilistic voting approach. Distinguishing between models thus hinges on consideration of how differences in preferences or political influence among voters affect tax structure.

One way of investigating the importance of heterogeneity in political influence is to include as regressors the size (n_h) of various interest groups and/or proxies for the gains or losses from the policy process that these groups expect.[8] This is the route we have taken in the model presented in Chapter 10. Econometric studies also adopting this approach include Paul Renaud and Frans van Winden (1987) and Inman (1993). Such work, including our own, is only partially successful because results concerning the role of interest groups tend not to be robust.

The problem may be partly attributable to the difficulties of appropriately representing interest groups in an estimating equation. Interest-group size,

---

[8] Van Winden (1997) surveys theoretical work on the role of interest groups in political economy models.

which appears in the stylized model, may not be an adequate proxy for interest-group influence insofar as effective influence depends on additional factors such as wealth. Measures of the potential gains or losses of various groups are not necessarily closely related to effective influence either, and are often difficult to use because of correlation with aggregate economic factors that also appear as regressors.

Qualitative and historical (as opposed to econometric) evidence concerning the role of special interest groups appears to be more definitive. Studies by John Witte (1985), Dennis Mueller (1990), Cathie Martin (1991), and Glenn Fisher (1996) on the evolution of various aspects of tax structure in the United States, by Gillespie (1991) on the evolution of Canadian taxation, and by Carolyn Webber and Aaron Wildavsky (1986) on world tax history all suggest that some groups are more influential than others. It is a matter of concern for both sides when applied econometricians have a hard time capturing what astute students of tax history regard as obvious.

The role of interest groups aside, investigations using the probabilistic voting and representative agent frameworks have identified four types of variables that appear to play a statistically significant role in the determination of revenue composition in democratic states; we shall see this reflected in both of the statistical studies we present. First, revenue composition in any political jurisdiction depends on the relative size of alternative potential tax bases, with relatively larger or faster growing bases being relied upon more extensively. This sort of tax spreading is consistent with the view that increasing reliance on relatively faster-growing or larger bases keeps tax rates and excess burdens to a minimum. It may also be consistent with the view that spreading the tax over a large base minimizes political opposition to taxation by reducing the burden any single taxpayer bears relative to the costs of organizing opposition.

Second, revenue composition depends on the extent to which tax burdens can be shifted to other jurisdictions, with sources of revenue that permit shifting being favored. Shifting can be accomplished through the taxation of interjurisdictional trade or by strategically adjusting revenue structure to make use of interjurisdictional fiscal arrangements. For example, deductibility of state income taxes against federal tax liabilities leads U.S. states to rely more heavily on income taxation, a fact that shows through clearly in the results presented in Chapter 9.

A third significant factor in the determination of tax structure is interjurisdictional tax competition, though results here are more contentious. A debate is emerging over the modeling of such competition since it is not clear how to identify the jurisdictions that any state may compete with (Case, Hines, and Rosen 1993). There is also a dispute over whether the data indicate that competition forces tax rates of competitor states to move together, or whether (and to what extent) interstate variation in tax systems can persist. Some authors conclude that a state's geographic neighbors follow suit when it raises its tax rates (Case 1993, Besley and Case 1995a). Others (Chernick 1991, 1997) argue that there may be tax-haven effects in the face of interstate commuting, with residential states maintaining lower rates and adjacent states, where employment is centered, having higher ones.[9] We contribute to this debate in Chapter 9, but we do not resolve it.

Finally, the scale of the public sector seems to be of some importance in the determination of the composition of revenue sources, though this result is less clearly established than the others.

The number of empirical papers that are based either on a Leviathan or structure-induced equilibrium model is still quite limited. A Leviathan would impose a multidimensional tax structure similar to that used by a democratic regime in order to maximize tax revenues, although with higher average tax rates. It is, therefore, not surprising that empirical research – based on the assumption that governments maximize the size of the budget – by James Kau and Paul Rubin (1981) or Charles Breeden and William Hunter (1985) utilizes estimating equations that are also consistent with vote maximization.[10] Other relevant work includes Randall Holcombe and Jeffrey Mills (1991), who argue that growth of government in the countries of the European Union is closely associated with the introduction of broad-based value-added taxes.

Figure 8.1 illustrates the difficulty of distinguishing between the two models. The figure shows that as the rate–revenue relationship (or Laffer curve) for any particular taxable activity shifts outward owing to economic growth or other factors, the change in tax structure under Leviathan (who tries to be at the point of inflection of the relevant curve) will be highly correlated with the evolution of tax structure in a competitive democratic regime.

One way to distinguish between Leviathan and a democratic regime is by investigating the role of democratic institutions in the evolution of tax structure. Such institutions do not appear in the stylized model behind equations (8.3) because the probabilistic voting framework usually treats them as implicit constraints on political optimization. However, if they could be represented in estimating equations and shown to be significant determinants of tax structure, the Leviathan model would be contradicted since democratic institutions would be established as binding constraints on political agents. Similarly, evidence that interest-group pressures had significantly influenced tax structure

---

[9] The two views are not necessarily inconsistent. Low-tax jurisdictions may be able to coexist simultaneously with high-tax jurisdictions as long as interstate tax differentials stay within a certain band.

[10] Although the model of Kau and Rubin (1981) focuses mainly on the size of government, it is a seminal contribution to the empirical Leviathan literature that contains many interesting suggestions concerning the relationship between tax structure and the size of government.

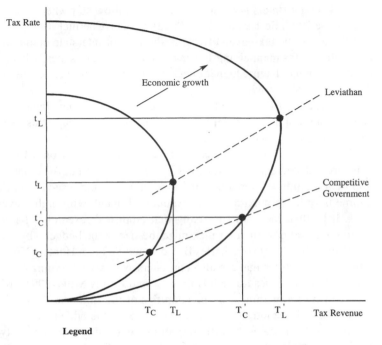

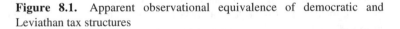

Legend

T_C, t_C = Tax revenue and tax rate in a competitive political system

T_L, t_L = Tax revenue and tax rate under Leviathan

Figure 8.1. Apparent observational equivalence of democratic and Leviathan tax structures

would refute the assumption of the Leviathan model that the government cares only about economic factors and is oblivious to interest-group politics.

Schneider and Pommerehne (1983) provide evidence on the effect of electoral constraints on tax structure in Australia. Holcombe and Mills (1992) show that the probability of the reelection of incumbents is positively associated with the size of the U.S. government deficit, and Francis Berry and William Berry (1990) argue that adoption of lotteries by U.S. states is related to electoral considerations. Timothy Besley and Anne Case (1995b) relate tax structure to term limits for U.S. state governors. Poterba (1994) studies the effect of budgetary institutions on fiscal choices by U.S. states.

Further statistical evidence on political factors is presented in Chapter 10. As yet, however, much of the evidence is qualitative and historical, including work by Sven Steinmo (1989) on international differences in tax systems and their connection to differences in basic political institutions, by Albert Breton (1996) (as well as in Chapter 11 of this book) on fiscal policy processes in parliamentary and congressional political systems, and by Susan Hansen (1983) on the relationship between institutional features of U.S. state politics and tax structure. Work of this sort also includes that by Charles Stewart (1991) and Mathew McCubbins (1991), who explore the role of a divided Congress in explanations of U.S. tax reform in the mid-1980s.

Formal integration of institutional factors is theoretically most advanced in the structure-induced equilibrium approach, although empirical work with respect to tax structure in this tradition is just beginning. For example, the empirical results of Inman and Michael Fitts (1990), who examine a long time period in the United States, suggest that such institutional features as the decline of centralized authority in the House of Representatives (following reforms of Congress in the mid-1970s) have had a significant effect in increasing total expenditures, but they appear to have left tax policy – as measured by the aggregate size of tax expenditures – unaffected.[11] Their explanation for differing results on the two sides of the budget relies on the unchanged power of the House Ways and Means Committee over the tax-reform agenda and on the power of strong, independent presidents to block tax changes. We discuss the type of estimating equation used by Inman and Fitts in the following section.

To complete our overview of the empirical literature, we note that estimating equations (8.3a) and (8.3b) imply that tax structure and the level of public expenditure are simultaneously determined, and that this implication of the model may be subjected to empirical testing. Investigations concerning the direction of causality between tax structure and public spending include the work of Holcombe and Mills referred to earlier, J.A. Stockfish (1985), George von Furstenburg, Jeffrey Green and Jin-Ho Jeong (1986), Kevin Hoover and Steven Sheffrin (1992), and Sheffrin (1996).[12] The results of these investigations are mixed, and it does not seem possible at this time to reach any general conclusions about the causality issue. In Chapter 9 we allow for the possibility that tax structure and the aggregate level of public spending are simultaneously determined. In Chapter 10, it proves useful to proceed on the assumptions that tax structure depends on a forecast of the size of the budget and that this forecast is predetermined with respect to current tax policy choices.

8.4   A MORE DETAILED LOOK AT SOME ESTIMATING EQUATIONS IN THE LITERATURE

As a complement to the preceding review, it is useful to consider the nature of the estimating equations in more detail for two of the papers cited earlier. Since the equations used in Chapters 9 and 10 differ in various ways from those

[11] We have argued in Chapters 3 and 5 that the concept of the "tax expenditure" is seriously flawed. What role such criticism plays in the interpretation of these results remains to be seen.

[12] The paper by Sheffrin (1996) includes a useful summary of empirical work on the causality question.

adopted by the authors of these papers, the discussion provides another way of setting our own work in perspective. We proceed informally, confining to footnotes the discussion of the algebraic equations used in the two papers.

It should be noted that, although we do consider the two papers discussed to be seminal contributions, our primary purpose here is to provide further introduction to the empirical literature on the political economy of taxation, rather than to single out particular authors for praise or criticism.

In an early contribution to empirical political economy, Friedrich Schneider and Werner Pommerehne (1980) present a model of Australian tax and expenditure structure along with a model of government popularity. Schneider and Pommerehne estimate one equation for each policy instrument and include instruments from both sides of the budget in their framework. In each equation, there are three types of explanatory variables, reflecting administrative and economic constraints on policy choices, reelection constraints, and ideological influences.[13] By way of contrast, only the first type of variable appears in equations (8.3), and there are variables representing the size and influence of interest groups that are not included in the Schneider–Pommerehne equations. Moreover, the vectors z and x in (8.3) include variables that reflect the nature of opposition to taxation by different voters, as distinct from the constraints under which governments act when addressing such opposition. It should also

---

[13] In schematic form, the systematic part of the equation for the level of each policy instrument can be written as follows:

$$\text{INST}_{ti} = a_i + b_i \cdot \text{INST}_{t-4} + \sum_j c_{j,i} \cdot X_{j,t-2} + d_i \cdot \text{DYR}_{t-2} \cdot \left(\text{LEAD}_{t-2} - \text{LEAD*}\right)$$
$$+ e_i \cdot \text{DYR}_{t-2} \cdot \text{TSLE}_{t-2}$$
$$+ f_i \cdot \left(1\text{-DYR}_{t-2}\right) \cdot \left(\text{LEAD}_{t-2} - \text{LEAD*}\right) \cdot \text{ID}(\text{conservative})$$
$$+ g_i \cdot \left(1\text{-DYR}_{t-2}\right) \cdot \left(\text{LEAD}_{t-2} - \text{LEAD*}\right) \cdot \text{ID}(\text{social democrat}).$$

Here INST represents different government instruments, such as the levels of various types of government expenditures or taxes, with the subscripts t and i referring to quarter and type of instrument. The X_j stand for explanatory variables that appear because of administrative and economic constraints, including changes in the balance of payments, the budget deficit, and the rate of growth of real wages. Each of these variables enters the equation with a particular lag that varies from two to four periods (or quarters).

The coefficients d and e reflect the effects of reelection constraints. Among the variables representing such constraints is the dummy variable DYR that assumes a value of 1 when the difference between the popularity of the government and that of the opposition before an election (LEAD) falls below some critical level (LEAD*, assumed to be 0 percent) and a value of 0 otherwise. The variable DYR interacts with the popularity deficit LEAD $-$ LEAD*, as well as with TSLE, a simple step function that indicates the time since the last election.

Ideological influences, the third type of variable in the equation, are represented by: the interaction of $(1 - \text{DYR})$, reflecting political leeway available to cater to ideological tastes; the popularity deficit (LEAD $-$ LEAD*); and a dummy variable ID(k), which is equal to 1 when both a party of type k is in power and (LEAD $-$ LEAD*) $\geq$ 0 and is equal to 0 otherwise. A more detailed definition of variables is given in Appendix I of the 1980 paper.

be pointed out that the precise nature of the variables that represent administrative and economic constraints in the following two chapters and in the Schneider–Pommerehne paper is not the same, reflecting the unique orientation of each study.

Schneider and Pommerehne do not assume that election constraints are always completely binding. This also stands in contrast to the model outlined previously, where parties are forced to continually maximize expected electoral support. The reelection constraint variables in the Schneider–Pommerehne model reflect the view that electoral considerations are more pressing and lead to a different policy mix when an election approaches, or when the party in power is doing poorly in the polls.

The implied lack of perfect political competition enables the incumbent party to cater to the ideological tastes of party members, hence the presence in their equations of a variable standing for such tastes. In principle, ideological preferences also influence the mix of policy instruments. Right-wing governments, for example, are hypothesized to desire a smaller public sector, greater price stability, balanced foreign trade, and so on, leading to the increased reliance by such governments, ceteris paribus, on policies that contribute to these goals.[14]

The equations for the use of policy instruments are complemented by a separate equation explaining the popularity of the government in power.[15] In turn, as we have noted, the popularity of the government appears along with other variables reflecting reelection constraints in the equation for each policy instrument. The system is not explicitly simultaneous, however, as the dependent variable in the popularity equation is not used directly on the right side of the equations explaining instrument use. (See notes 13 and 15 for further details.)

It is interesting that the estimating equations of Schneider and Pommerehne may be derived in a probabilistic voting setting by using the extended framework presented in the Appendix to Chapter 6. There, politicians are assumed to maximize their own welfare subject to a reelection constraint and the structure

---

[14] There is a large body of empirical work dealing with the extent to which ideological slack or principal–agent problems may exist in the public sector. For some references to the literature, see Holsey and Borcherding (1997, pp. 587–8).

[15] Ignoring the error term, a typical popularity equation is

$$\text{POPG}_t = a \cdot \text{POPG}_{t-1} + \Sigma_j b_j \cdot Y_{j, t-1} + c \cdot \text{PL}_{kt} + d \cdot \text{PD}_{kt},$$

where POPG is the current popularity of the *government* as measured by the percentage of citizens expressing a willingness to vote for the government at the next election; the Y_j represent economic variables including the rates of inflation and unemployment, real growth of income, and the change in the balance of payments; PL_k is a dummy variable intended to reflect the popularity level of government party k, equal to 1 when party k is in power and 0 otherwise; and PD_k is a step function representing the inevitable "depreciation" over time of the popularity of government party k, set equal to 1 when that party is in power and 0 otherwise.

of the economy. If we allow the reelection constraint to be determined endogenously by the state of the government's popularity (in the Appendix to Chapter 6, the minimum acceptable level of electoral support for the incumbent is fixed exogenously for expositional convenience), a system of equations similar to those used by Schneider and Pommerehne will emerge as a representation of the model in semireduced form.

In one of the first empirical applications of the structure-induced equilibrium approach, Robert Inman and Michael Fitts (1990) construct a model of decision making under the norm of universalism in a system with single-member constituencies. They develop separate estimating equations for the aggregate size of the budget and the structure of taxation, with the latter being proxied by an estimate of the aggregate value of tax expenditures. Unlike (8.1), these equations are not derived by optimizing a political support function defined over the electorate as a whole. Rather, the relationships explaining the size of the budget and of tax expenditures are determined by aggregating equations for fiscal policies that are politically optimal for separate constituencies.

Inman and Fitts argue that individual legislators do not take into account the full social cost of the programs delivered on behalf of their own constituents when deciding upon the demands they will make in the national legislature, since the voters in their district pay only a part of the costs of any national program. As a result of the tendency for legislative bargains at the national level to embody a norm of universalism – that is, an attitude of "You scratch my back and I'll scratch yours" – the overall federal budget is too large, as are the number and size of tax deductions, exemptions, and credits. Furthermore, there may be a tendency to place too much reliance on deficit financing.

The estimating equation that emerges from these considerations includes explanatory variables that reflect voter demands for government policies. This type of variable also appears in equations (8.3), although the set of variables that we actually use differs from those employed by Inman and Fitts, as well as from those used by Schneider and Pommerehne, reflecting the somewhat different purpose of our own investigation. In addition, the relationship estimated by Inman and Fitts contains a proxy for the strength of the President and for the percentage of seats in the House of Representatives controlled by the majority party.[16] They hypothesize that strong presidents and big majorities reduce

---

[16] Leaving aside the error term, a stylized version of the type of equation used by Inman and Fitts can be written as follows:

$$G_t(\text{or } E_t) = a + b \cdot (M/N)_t^2 + c \cdot (M/N)_t + d \cdot \text{SPres}_t + e \cdot C_t + \Sigma_j f_j \cdot X_{jt}.$$

In this equation, G is federal real per-capita spending excluding defense, social security, and debt interest; E is real per-capita tax expenditures; M/N is the percentage of House congressional districts controlled by the majority party; SPres is a dummy variable that has the value 1 when a president is judged to be independent and "strong" and 0 otherwise; C is a measure of the full economic cost per dollar of federal taxation; and the X_j are variables determining the

aggregate spending and the granting of tax favors by forcing legislators from each constituency to internalize more fully the national costs of public programs for their districts.

In Chapters 9 and 10, we emphasize aspects of the larger picture that differ from those chosen by the authors of the two papers just discussed. In contrast to Schneider and Pommerehne, we do not consider principal–agent problems and ideological slack, nor do we include proxies for the structure of the national legislature in our estimating equations, as do Inman and Fitts. Instead, the statistical relationships in Chapter 9 are designed to highlight the links between different parts of the tax skeleton, while those in Chapter 10 are suitable for studying the evolution of a revenue system as a whole. Like all empirical researchers who wish to understand equilibrium outcomes, we must decide on what features of the larger revenue system to emphasize and on how best to simplify in the pursuit of tractable estimating equations that allow investigation of those aspects of the fiscal system that are of special interest to us.

8.5 CONCLUDING REMARKS

The preceding overview of the empirical literature illustrates the diversity of research that has been conducted by scholars who are trying to enlarge the scope of empirical political economy to include the modeling of fiscal systems. Much of this work does not fully reflect the broader equilibrium approach to political economy taken in this book, yet the approaches, issues, and problems reviewed in the course of our survey provide a useful background for the statistical modeling to be presented in the following chapters.

---

demand for government policies. They include (without specification of lags or interactions between variables) real per-capita GNP, deviation of the actual from the expected rate of unemployment, ratio of public debt to GNP, percentage of employment in manufacturing, percentage of the population living in urban areas, percentage of the population less than 15 years of age, and nonfederal public sector wages per capita. More detailed definitions are provided in an appendix to the 1990 paper.

Because E is not actually observed for the long period studied, the identity $R = \alpha + \tau Y - E$ is used to derive an estimating equation for R, where R is defined as real per-capita federal revenues excluding payroll taxes for social insurance, τ is an average marginal tax rate, and Y is real per capita GNP. Inman and Fitts expect estimates of the coefficients d and e to be negative in the equation for G and positive in that for R (so that, given the foregoing identity, they are negative in the derived equation for E). A possible hypothesis is that coefficients b and c will be negative in the equation for G and positive in the one for R. This means that, as M/N increases, G will fall and R will rise (so that E will decline). An alternative hypothesis states that b and c take on values that imply G grows and R declines with M/N, but that this effect diminishes at the margin as M/N increases.

CHAPTER 9

Income Taxation and Special Provisions
Evidence from U.S. States

> We cannot, therefore, too carefully endeavor to verify our the-
> ory ... with the most trustworthy accounts of those which have been
> actually realized.
>
> John Stuart Mill (1836)

In this chapter we adapt our theoretical framework to explain observed differences among U.S. states in their reliance on income taxation and in their
related use of selected special provisions. Data are for the mid-1980s. In the
course of this investigation, hypotheses about the general nature of political
opposition to taxation are proposed and tested, and the importance of modeling
the interdependence of different parts of a tax structure is considered.

The income tax represents one of two revenue sources that predominate at
the state level (the other major source is general sales taxation). Yet we
observe considerable variation among states in the relative reliance on this
base, making it a significant subject for study in the present context. We initially estimate the following equation in order to investigate the factors lying
behind such variation:

$$\text{YRATE*} = \alpha_0 + \alpha_1 z + \alpha_2 x + \alpha_3 G + \varepsilon; \tag{9.1}$$

$$\text{YRATE} = \begin{cases} \text{YRATE*} & \text{if} \quad \text{YRATE*} > 0, \\ 0 & \text{if} \quad \text{YRATE*} \le 0. \end{cases}$$

Here z is an endogenous, continuous variable and x represents a vector of
exogenous variables, all of which are discussed at length in the chapter; G is
the size of government; and ε is an error term. Subscripts denoting state and
time are omitted for convenience.[1]

The dependent variable in this Tobit estimating equation, YRATE*, represents unobserved political opposition to reliance on personal income as a tax
base. Such opposition may exist even when income taxation is not part of the

---

[1] The estimating equation (9.1) differs from that used in our earlier work on state income taxation
(Hettich and Winer 1984) in two important ways: the dependent variable is the average rate of
tax instead of the share of income taxation in total revenues; and endogenous variables (z) appear
on the right-hand side of the equation. The estimation results for equation (9.1) are consistent
with the results using the equation for the income-tax share in the earlier paper.

equilibrium tax structure in a state. YRATE, which may be zero, is the actual reliance on the income-tax base as measured by the ratio of personal income tax revenue to personal income in the state. The dichotomous nature of YRATE acknowledges that, owing both to the particular characteristics of voters in a state and to fixed administration costs or other constraints on the design and implementation of tax instruments, an income tax may not be in use in all states.[2]

We do not estimate an equation for the size of public expenditures corresponding to equation (8.3b), although we allow for the endogeneity of the size of the public sector in the estimation procedure. In addition to an equation for the size of government, a complete explanation of state tax systems would include the determination of federal and local fiscal systems which are connected to the state system through tax deductions and credits granted by one level of government for taxes paid to other levels as well as via intergovernmental grants. Moreover, a full model would also include strategic competition over tax bases between levels of government. In such a situation, it is necessary to simplify by focusing on aspects of the revenue system that seem particularly relevant, and by looking at selected parts of the larger system, while being aware of the general equilibrium nature of the fiscal system in the country as a whole.

9.1   CHOOSING EXPLANATORY VARIABLES

The effect on expected votes associated with changes in different components of the revenue system cannot be observed directly, so the analyst must adopt an indirect approach. Empirical research can proceed by identifying factors that vary among political units and that may explain different equilibrium choices for fiscal instruments. To help the reader follow along with the discussion of explanatory variables chosen for inclusion in equation (9.1), a list of variables is provided in Table 9.1. (We ignore for the moment the variables listed in the table that relate to the equation explaining the CREDIT for the payment of property tax.) All variables in the table have been defined independently of state size or have been normalized, where appropriate, by state income or population in order to minimize problems due to heteroscedasticity in cross-section samples.

Before proceeding with the discussion of explanatory variables, we note that even though this chapter extends empirical research falling into the

---

[2] It should be noted that the unobserved (starred) value of the dependent variable, not its observed (unstarred) counterpart, appears in equation (9.1). Thus there are no "unique solvability" or "consistency" requirements to be met by the estimated coefficients. See Schmidt (1981) for further discussion.

Table 9.1.   Explanatory variables*

YRATE Equation		Predicted Sign	Definition
Endogenous:	CREDIT	+	1 if credit or rebate for the payment of local property tax
	TAXPRICE	-	1 - (proportion of itemizers times average federal marginal tax rate of itemizers)
	GN	?	total expenditures per capita
Exogenous:	TRAVEL	-	travel-generated business receipts per dollar of personal income
	RBY	-	mineral production per dollar of personal income (the resource tax base relative to the income-tax base)
	SBY	-	retail trade per dollar of personal income (the sales-tax base relative to the income-tax base)
	BONDLIMIT	+	1 if either nominal dollar or percentage (of state funds, tax revenue or state or taxable property) limitation on issue of debt
	STD	-	standard deviation of percent year-over-year change in real personal income, 1970-1986
	POOR/RICH	+	ratio of number of taxpayers with less than $25,000 adjusted gross income to number with more than $50,000
	REGION	+	average of YRATEs in geographically neighboring states
	NATIONWIDE	+	YRATE in state with most similar value of POOR/RICH
CREDIT Equation			
Endogenous:	YRATE	+	average personal income-tax rate (ratio of personal income-tax revenue to personal income)
Exogenous:	HOUSEPRICE	+	percent change in house prices, 1970-80
	OWNERSHIP	+	percent of housing that is owner-occupied
	OVER 65	+	percent of population over age 65
	LOCAL	+	ratio of local government expenditures to state expenditures
	BONDLIMIT	-	as above

* All variables are defined on a state by state basis

probabilistic voting tradition, it also has a relation to work on state finance based on other approaches, some of which we have referenced in Chapter 8. There is an extensive literature dealing with selected aspects of state fiscal systems, such as interstate tax competition and the federal tax deduction for state income taxes, that does not model political behavior in formulating estimating equations. Because the same factors play a role in our analysis, we shall refer to this literature whenever appropriate.

9.1.1   Hypotheses about Opposition to Taxation

In deciding what variables to use in (9.1), it is helpful and interesting to proceed by considering hypotheses about the nature of opposition to taxation and about the constraints under which political competition proceeds. To begin, we propose that:

H1. Opposition to the use of a tax depends on effective (rather than nominal) tax prices. The government will use available opportunities to lower the effective tax-prices of those voters most likely to offer political opposition.

Exemptions, deductions, credits, and variations in the definition of the taxable base can be employed so as to lower the impact of particular taxes on groups of voters most likely to offer effective opposition.[3] In addition, rate schedules can be adjusted or redrawn to achieve the same purpose. Another method of lowering the effective tax-price of public services is to shift the burden of taxation to other jurisdictions. Taxes can be passed on to higher levels of government that have offset provisions or deductions for taxes paid to lower levels of government in their revenue systems. In addition, geographic shifting may be accomplished through taxation of goods or factors that are traded across jurisdictional boundaries.[4]

In the context of an explanation for reliance on income taxation at the state level, the discussion of hypothesis H1 suggests use of the variables TAXPRICE and TRAVEL. TAXPRICE and TRAVEL represent factors that reduce opposition by lowering effective tax rates for state taxpayers at the expense of those who live elsewhere. The existence of a federal tax deduction for income taxes paid to state governments lowers the cost of state tax liabilities for those who itemize on their federal returns. This aspect of fiscal policy has received much attention in the literature on state finance in recent years (see e.g. Feldstein and Metcalf 1987, Holtz-Eakin and Rosen 1988, Lindsay 1988, Chernick 1991, Metcalf 1993, and Pollock 1991.) We use the variable TAXPRICE to measure the effect of the deductibility of state income taxes on the after–federal tax burden implied by a state's nominal income-tax structure. The lower is TAXPRICE, the smaller is the after–federal tax burden of state income taxes and the weaker will be opposition to reliance on the state income tax. Hence we expect TAXPRICE to have a negative coefficient.

---

[3] This view of structural features of particular taxes is suggested by the discussion in Buchanan and Pauly (1970), Lindsay (1972), and Buchanan (1976), as well as by our theoretical framework.

[4] See for example McLure (1967), Hogan and Shelton (1973), or Sjoquist (1981).

TAXPRICE is defined as $(1 - p \cdot m)$, where p is the proportion of itemizers in a state and m is the average federal marginal tax rate of itemizers (Feldstein and Metcalf 1987, p. 712). Because the decision by a state to rely more heavily on the personal income tax will influence the individual taxpayer's decision on whether or not to itemize, and because it will also influence the federal marginal tax rate faced by itemizers (since that marginal rate depends on the magnitude of deductible state income taxes), TAXPRICE is an endogenous variable in the equation for YRATE* and is represented by z in equations (8.3). In the estimation of this equation by two-stage least squares and the other instrumental variables methods described in this chapter, we follow Feldstein and Metcalf in employing as an instrument a synthetic tax-price constructed by using the TAXSIM model of the National Bureau of Economic Research. This synthetic variable is highly correlated with TAXPRICE but is uncorrelated with the error term in the YRATE equation.[5]

Taxing visitors (and interstate commerce in general; see McLure 1967) represents a second way in which fiscal burden may be moved to nonresidents. To indicate a state's potential for such shifting, we include TRAVEL, defined as domestic travel-generated business receipts per dollar of state personal income. A negative sign is predicted.[6]

A second general hypothesis concerning opposition to taxation leads to another important set of variables that are appropriately included in the equation explaining reliance on income taxation. We propose:

H2. The more revenue that is raised per dollar of potential tax base with a particular tax, the more political opposition (in total and at the margin) there will be to that tax.

The term "potential tax base" denotes the base gross of exemptions and deductions – for example, total expenditure on consumption in the case of a general sales tax. Increases in revenue collection per dollar of potential base imply a

---

[5] The synthetic tax-price is computed for the calendar year preceding the fiscal year covered by the dependent variable. One may note that these tax-prices are referred to in the literature as "average-dollar" tax-prices, since average marginal tax rates are used in their definition. We also used the "first-dollar" synthetic tax-price with similar results. The exact definition of this alternative variable is given in Feldstein and Metcalf (1987, p. 722). We are indebted to Gilbert Metcalf for constructing these variables using the TAXSIM model of the National Bureau of Economic Research.

[6] As in Gade and Adkins (1990) and in Hettich and Winer (1984), we also constructed an updated version of the variable first suggested by McLure (1967) to reflect the potential for exporting of state taxes through interstate commerce; the value added in manufacturing for national markets as a proportion of total value added in the state. Though Gade and Adkins found this variable useful in estimating their own model, it was not significant in initial estimation of the model considered here and is not included in the tables of results.

larger effective burden (including the excess burden) for those who bear the tax increases. As the loss in full income rises, it becomes rational for taxpayers to use resources in organizing opposition and in trying to shift some of the burden to other groups.[7] Because of fixed costs of organization, opposition both in total and at the margin is likely to be small at low rates of taxation but to become a growing concern to the government as a particular base is relied upon more heavily. For these reasons, the marginal political cost curves in Figure 3.1 were drawn with positive slopes.

Hypothesis H2 has an interesting implication for the composition of revenues. Holding other things constant, the relative importance of a particular tax in total revenue will depend on the size of alternative potential bases available to the government. In terms of Figure 3.1, considered as applying to the choice between two tax bases, an exogenous increase in the size of tax base 1 would shift the corresponding marginal political cost curve downward, resulting in an increase in R_1/R and a decrease in R_2/R at the new equilibrium. This will occur because exogenous increases in a base allow the government to collect the same revenue from the now larger base with a lower rate, thus reducing the opposition associated with increased reliance on that base. Since the marginal political cost of increasing the rate on the growing base is now lower, political competition forces the government to rely more heavily on that base.

As in Hettich and Winer (1984) and in several subsequent papers by other authors, we represent potential alternative tax bases by RBY, the ratio of the state's resource-tax base to personal income (the base for the income tax) and by SBY, the state's sales-tax base relative to personal income. In both cases, negative signs are expected. In addition, we introduce a variable related to the state's ability to raise revenues through debt, since borrowing is a policy instrument that can substitute for taxation. It is represented by BONDLIMIT and has been based on recent work by Jurgen von Hagen (1991), who provides a classification of constitutional and other restrictions applying to state debt. Since the variable assumes a value of 1 if the state is subject to nominal debt limits or percentage limits (and is 0 otherwise), we expect a positive sign.[8]

The variability of income as a tax base also plays a role in determining reliance on income taxation. Consider the following general hypothesis about opposition to taxation:

---

[7] It may also be rational to adjust economic behavior in such a way that the size of potential bases is changed. The example most often discussed concerns the influence of taxation on the choice between work and leisure.

[8] If one thinks of debt as a tax on future economic activity, the relative size of the potential 'base' on which debt is levied should be included in the equation. However, it is very difficult to define and measure the appropriate potential base in this case (we say more about proxying the base for debt in the next chapter).

H3. Other things being equal, tax sources more subject to fluctuations generate greater political opposition (in total and at the margin).

Governments will try to reduce uncertainty about the yield of the revenue structure. Taxpayers and public decision makers will both prefer tax systems yielding stable revenue streams to those giving fluctuating receipts, in order to avoid the continuing costs of adjustment associated with fluctuating revenues.[9] Thus, governments will attempt to limit revenue fluctuations for a given rate structure by relying more heavily, ceteris paribus, on tax bases with lower variability, a point initially made in the context of state tax systems by Robert Vogel and Robert Trost (1979). This may be particularly true for those governments who lack the power to create money and must finance deficits by borrowing or tax increases.[10] A similar argument also applies to any given tax base, with states that have a more stable experience with a particular tax base placing greater reliance on it. In equation (9.1) we represent base variability for the income tax with STD, the standard deviation of (the year-over-year percentage change in) real personal income for the period from 1970 to 1986. A negative sign is predicted.

Taxpayers may organize opposition to taxation, but they can also react in a quite different way: by leaving the jurisdiction. Following Albert Hirschman (1970), the two alternatives have been characterized in the literature as "voice" and "exit." The possibility that exit affects fiscal actions by the government leads to the next hypothesis:

H4. The tax pattern in competing political units serves as a constraint on fiscal structure.

Governments know that various human resources and other factors of production may be lost to competing political units. A net loss of factors has a depressing effect on the local economy and may create strong criticism by

---

[9] As Barro (1979) has noted, governments can lower the overall burden of taxation by using debt to smooth total revenues when tax revenues fluctuate. But they may also try to adjust tax structure in order to reduce reliance on tax sources that are relatively unstable.

[10] Vogel and Trost (1979) have shown that there is a relationship between the variability of state income and the choice of tax structure; they found that states with high variability of their income tax base adopt policies to make tax receipts less responsive to economic fluctuations. This result is consistent with our argument that the variability of a tax base is a determinant of political costs.

political opponents and dissatisfaction among affected groups of voters.[11] The
literature on state and local taxation contains many references to tax competition among governmental units at the same level (see e.g. Gold 1991, Tannenwald 1991). Because such competition can assume many different forms, it is
difficult to formulate variables that fully capture the influence of competitive
forces of this nature. Interstate competition may involve many aspects of the
fiscal system and not just the tax instruments represented by the dependent
variables in our equations. Nonetheless, we investigate competition with
respect to the use of the personal income tax.

Since interstate competition is likely to be more intense in situations where
labor mobility is less costly, it seems reasonable to use a variable that reflects
the use of the income tax in neighboring states to indicate the nature of regional
tax competition. We use REGION, the average YRATE in such states, as an
indicator of geographical tax competition. If a state's neighbors raise their tax
rates then it will also be possible for this state to increase rates, and thus tax
revenues,[12] without precipitating politically damaging migration.[13] A positive
sign on REGION is expected.

Taxpayers (and firms) who are considering a move to anywhere in the country may face fixed costs that are greater than those associated with moves to
nearby locations, especially when interstate commuting is feasible.[14] But once

---

[11] Hypothesis H4 is related to the so-called Tiebout literature, a body of work concerned with the
effects of spatial mobility on the provision of local public services. It should be noted, however,
that our approach differs in an essential respect from that generally adopted in the Tiebout literature. Whereas we emphasize the effect of exit on government action in an explicit model of
political decision making, the Tiebout tradition does not specify a mechanism of political choice.
We should also note that we are aware of the difficulty of distinguishing between exit and voice
as forms of political opposition. In an open economy such as a state, competition may be stimu-
lated by comparisons between "domestic" and "foreign" policy actions without migration actually occurring (Salmon 1991, Besley and Case, 1995).

[12] As argued in Chapter 3, it is not rational for governments to levy tax rates that place themselves on
the backward (or downward) sloping part of any Laffer curve, since they can then increase
revenue and political support by cutting tax rates. Therefore, tax rates and total tax revenues in
such a model will always be positively correlated.

[13] California is used as the neighbor for Hawaii, and an average of YRATE in Washington and
Oregon is used as the value of REGION for Alaska. Although REGION is treated as an exogenous variable in Table 9.1, the possibility exists that neighboring states will be subject to common omitted shocks, the most likely of which are those related to regional variations in the level
of aggregate economic activity. Such shocks may be captured by variables already included in
the equation, such as RBY, SBY, or TRAVEL, but it is difficult to know what instruments to use
in allowing for REGION to be correlated with the error term. We shall return to the question of
whether REGION should be considered an endogenous variable.

[14] For example, the psychological and traveling costs of commuting to a neighboring state to work
may be low compared to the corresponding costs of changing both one's place of work and residence in order to move to a more distant location.

the decision to move has been taken, the marginal costs associated with changing the distance moved may be quite low. In this case, as argued in Hettich and Winer (1984), states may also be forced to compete with all other states regardless of the distances involved. To reflect national competition for taxpayers who are highly mobile, we use NATIONWIDE, the YRATE in the state with the most similar social conditions. To construct NATIONWIDE, states are classified according to the variable POOR/RICH, defined as the ratio of the number of taxpayers with less than $25,000 in adjusted gross income to the number whose adjusted gross income exceeds $50,000. As in the case of REGION, a positive coefficient is expected on NATIONWIDE.

Work by Robert Inman (1989) and Howard Chernick (1992) raises the possibility that distributional considerations may enter fiscal choices directly. Because income taxation is a favored tool for carrying out distributive policies, greater pressure for adoption of such policies may result in greater reliance on personal income as a tax base. We test for this effect by including POOR/RICH as a separate variable in equation (9.4a), since it can also be looked at as a rough measure of income disparity in each state.[15] Higher values of POOR/RICH are likely to be associated with greater pressure for reliance on income taxation and thus with higher income-tax rates.[16]

The nature of costs faced by voters in organizing opposition to taxation helps to explain a further aspect of opposition to taxation and leads to another explanatory variable. Because excess burdens grow with tax rates at an increasing rate, and because there are economies of scale in voter organization and in the dissemination of information, we expect the incentive for and effectiveness of opposition to grow with effective tax rates at an increasing rate. As a result:

H5. Opposition or political costs to the government grow at an increasing rate as revenue collection per dollar of potential base is raised.

---

[15] These ratios are based on data from TAXSIM supplied by Gilbert Metcalf. Another possible basis for identifying competitor states might involve looking at a broad indicator of industrial structure, such as value added for national markets, as in Hettich and Winer (1984). We tried this variable in place of POOR/RICH without success. Other ways of judging the identity of a state's most important competitors could involve the use of racial composition or per-capita income (as in Case et al. 1993). In all cases, a clear theoretical argument for choosing a particular variable is absent.

[16] Of course, it is possible to increase the progressivity of the marginal rate structure without changing the average rate. If pressure for redistribution is mainly reflected in choice of marginal rate structures at a given average tax rate, we will not observe a relationship between POOR/RICH and YRATE. YRATE remains the appropriate dependent variable in the present context, however, since our focus in the YRATE equation is on the decision about reliance on personal income as a source of revenue. In a study focusing on the redistributive content of the fiscal system, one may wish to use measures of the progressivity of the tax system as dependent variables, as in Chernick (1991, 1997), or public expenditures which are closely associated with aid for poorer people, as in Kristov, Lindert, and McClelland (1992).

It is because of H5 that the marginal cost curves in Figure 3.1 become steeper as revenue from any source (and hence as revenue per dollar of a given potential base) increases. Note that marginal political costs for various tax sources may grow at differing rates, implying that, ceteris paribus, the composition of revenues will depend upon the scale of the public sector.[17] Accordingly, total state expenditures per capita, GN, is included in our estimating equation to reflect possible scale effects that may operate in fiscal choices across states. Since it is a policy instrument chosen by the state along with tax structure, GN is regarded as an endogenous variable.

9.2   DATA AND ESTIMATION RESULTS FOR THE INCOME-TAX EQUATION

The data consist of observations on the 50 states for the years 1985 and 1986. These years precede the Tax Reform Act of 1986 and follow adjustments to the severe recession of 1980–82, thus representing a period of relative stability in the tax systems of the states (Gold 1991, p. 206).

Table 9.2 summarizes selected aspects of state reliance on the personal income tax for the fiscal year 1985. (Also included in the table are data relating to the credit for property taxes paid, which we ignore for the moment.) As a proportion of total revenues (including borrowing), income tax revenues in 1985 vary widely across states, ranging from zero to 64 percent. Six states do not tax any component of income, while Alaska raises a very small residual amount from a recently discontinued income tax. The corresponding average tax rates (YRATE) assume values from zero to 3.86 percent of personal income in Oregon. Although these rates also vary somewhat across the two years of the sample, the main source of variation derives from the cross-section component of the data.

Since equation (9.1) contains the continuous endogenous variables TAXPRICE and GN, and since only six of the observations for YRATE are censored, we estimate this equation by two-stage least squares. (The instruments used are described in the notes to the table.) Results of the estimation are given in Table 9.3. The signs and significance of coefficients reported in Table 9.3 accord with the predictions in Table 9.1 with the following exceptions. The reliance on income as a base does not appear to be significantly related to the existence of bond limits (BONDLIMIT), the relative number of poor taxpayers (POOR/RICH), nor to the size of the state's public sector (GN). Most notably, the coefficient on REGION, the variable representing competition for mobile factors within a region of contiguous states, is both significant and of opposite sign to that predicted in Table 9.1. Contrary to our hypothesis, higher tax rates

---

[17] This last point is also relevant in the context of discussing the introduction of new taxes.

Table 9.2.   Aspects of state personal income-tax structure, fiscal year 1985

STATE	YTR	YRATE(%)	CREDIT	STATE	YTR	YRATE(%)	CREDIT
Alabama	0.22	1.65	0	Montana	0.26	1.99	1
Alaska(1)	0.00	0.01	0	Nebraska	0.22	1.53	0
Arizona	0.20	1.49	1	Nevada(4)	0.00	0.00	1
Arkansas	0.25	1.90	1	New Hampshire(2)	0.04	0.16	0
California	0.34	2.55	1	New Jersey	0.20	1.45	0
Colorado	0.36	1.91	1	New Mexico	0.05	0.52	1
Connecticut(2)	0.07	0.50	1	New York	0.44	3.71	1
Delaware	0.44	4.02	0	North Carolina	0.37	2.77	0
Florida	0.00	0.00	0	North Dakota	0.09	0.93	1
Georgia	0.35	2.28	0	Ohio	0.27	1.96	1
Hawaii	0.28	2.94	1	Oklahoma	0.21	1.81	1
Idaho	0.33	2.38	1	Oregon	0.64	3.86	1
Illinois	0.25	1.53	1	Pennsylvania	0.24	1.61	1
Indiana	0.29	1.88	0	Rhode Island	0.20	2.12	1
Iowa	0.27	2.28	1	South Carolina	0.29	2.38	0
Kansas	0.32	1.78	1	South Dakota(4)	0.00	0.00	1
Kentucky	0.24	1.94	0	Tennessee(3)	0.02	0.12	1
Louisiana	0.10	1.04	0	Texas	0.00	0.00	0
Maine	0.29	2.15	1	Utah	0.30	2.46	1
Maryland	0.38	2.52	1	Vermont	0.27	2.19	1
Massachusetts	0.40	3.33	0	Virginia	0.40	2.36	0
Michigan	0.33	2.40	1	Washington	0.00	0.00	0
Minnesota	0.42	3.77	1	West Virginia	0.27	2.58	1
Mississippi	0.14	1.07	0	Wisconsin	0.34	3.19	1
Missouri	0.27	1.58	1	Wyoming(5)	0.00	0.00	0

Notes to Table 9.2: YTR = relative reliance on personal income taxation (personal income tax revenue ÷ total state revenue including the issue of debt); YRATE = reliance on income tax base as measured by the average personal income tax rate (personal income tax revenue ÷ personal income, in percent); CREDIT = 1 if there exists a property tax relief program (a tax credit or a direct payment to qualified individuals), = 0 otherwise.

(1) The actual figure for YTR = .0006, representing residual collections on repealed tax.

(2) Income tax applies to interest and dividend income only.

(3) Income tax on certain interest or dividends only.

(4) Property tax credit takes the form of a rebate given to selected homeowners.

(5) Rebate is for sales as well as property tax payed.

Sources: see "Variables and Data Sources" at the end of the chapter.

Table 9.3. Reliance on income taxation, U.S. states, fiscal years 1985 and 1986. Two-stage least-squares estimation

Dependent variable is average personal income tax (YRATE)

	(1)	(2)	(3)	(4)	(5)
TAX-PRICE	-265.31 (-1.55)	-277.31 (-1.64)	-253.96 (-3.40)	-281.07 (-4.38)	-281.29 (-4.39)
TRAVEL	-15.70 (-1.14)	-16.17 (-1.18)	-16.47 (-1.21)	-16.58 (-1.21)	-17.21 (-1.31)
RBY	-25.40 (-2.62)	-25.41 (-2.62)	26.42 (-3.70)	-22.91 (-4.53)	-22.93 (-4.54)
SBY	-2.43 (-0.53)				
BOND-LIMIT	0.25 (0.13)	0.23 (0.13)	0.28 (0.15)	0.30 (0.17)	
STD	-1.06 (-1.80)	-1.04 (-1.78)	-1.04 (-1.77)	-0.87 (-1.62)	-0.85 (-1.63)
POOR/RICH	0.07 (0.14)	0.07 (0.15)			
REGION	-0.61 (3.73)	-0.60 (-3.72)	-0.62 (-4.22)	-0.60 (-4.15)	-0.61 (-4.28)
NATION-WIDE	0.18 (2.42)	0.18 (2.42)	0.19 (2.50)	0.18 (2.42)	0.18 (2.45)
GN	0.001 (0.59)	0.001 (0.56)	0.001 (0.69)		
R^2	0.46	0.46	0.46	0.46	0.47
S	7.69	7.68	7.72	7.76	7.76

Notes to Table 9.3: Estimation using SHAZAM (White et al., 1990). The constant term is not reported. "t" statistics are in brackets. R^2 is adjusted. S is the standard error of the estimate. Instruments used in addition to exogenous variables in Table 5.1 (see the list of variables at the end of the chapter for definitions): FIRST, P25, P50, P100, PMAR, POP, POPNW, SMSA, POVERTY, MCAP, as well as the average dollar tax-price discussed in the footnotes.

in a state's geographic neighbors appear to lead to a *lower* rate in that state. On the other hand, NATIONWIDE, which represents competition within the country as a whole, has the expected positive, significant sign.

We shall postpone further discussion of the results for the income-tax equation, including the unexpected sign on the coefficient of REGION, until after the presentation of estimation results for the two-equation system that includes both an equation for YRATE and an equation explaining the income-tax credit for the payment of property tax.

9.3   THE INTERACTION BETWEEN RELIANCE ON A BASE AND THE STRUCTURE OF THE BASE

It is not surprising that existing empirical research based on a general equilibrium approach to political economy does not reflect the full simultaneity of policy choices implied by formal reasoning: theoretical complexity, data limitations, and difficulties related to econometric procedure all prevent implementation of a fully comprehensive approach. As we have argued earlier, in designing empirical work one is thus faced with the necessity of limiting the investigation to a particular aspect of the larger system. So far, most statistical studies dealing with fiscal systems at the state level, including our own work (Hettich and Winer 1984), have focused on what determines the pattern of revenues. Special provisions, although an important element in practice, have not as yet been integrated separately into the analysis. To emphasize the view that such structural features of a tax system are integrated components of a policy platform, we investigate the joint use of two tax instruments by U.S. state governments: reliance on the personal income-tax base and the introduction of a special provision linked to the income tax.

Of the many special provisions available to state governments, we analyze the granting of tax relief for the payment of local property taxes. Property-tax relief is a sensitive political issue, and while many states have granted such relief by effectively altering the structure of the income tax, many others have chosen not to do so. It should be noted that we do not focus on property-tax relief as a separate issue or attempt to explain the general nature of property taxation across states.[18] Our concern is with examining this aspect of the tax system as a representative structural element.

The model we estimate consists of equation (9.1a) for the income tax – which is just equation (9.1) with the addition of CREDIT* on the right-hand side, representing pressure on public decision makers for adoption of a property-tax credit or rebate – and a new equation explaining CREDIT* in which YRATE* appears as an explanatory variable:

---

[18] For a useful discussion of the structure of the property-tax credit, see Fisher and Rasche (1984).

$$YRATE^* = \beta_0 + \beta_1 CREDIT^* + \beta_2 z + \beta_3 x_1 + \beta_4 G + \varepsilon_1, \quad (9.1a)$$

$$YRATE = \begin{cases} YRATE^* & \text{if} \quad YRATE^* > 0, \\ 0 & \text{if} \quad YRATE^* \leq 0. \end{cases}$$

$$CREDIT^* = \gamma_0 + \gamma_1 YRATE^* + \gamma_2 x_2 + \varepsilon_2, \quad (9.2)$$

$$CREDIT = \begin{cases} 1 & \text{if} \quad CREDIT^* > 0, \\ 0 & \text{if} \quad CREDIT^* \leq 0. \end{cases}$$

CREDIT* represents *unobserved* political pressure to grant local property-tax relief in the form of a credit or rebate against the payment of state taxes, and CREDIT is a dichotomous variable that takes the value 1 if property-tax relief is actually given and 0 if it is not provided. CREDIT* appears in the equation for YRATE* because opposition to reliance on the income tax may be reduced by the creation of a special provision that reduces the income-tax liability of a selected group of taxpayers (in this case, homeowners). YRATE* is included in the equation explaining CREDIT* because greater pressure for a state to rely on income taxation as a revenue source will increase the pressure to create special provisions in the income-tax base, making it more likely that special provisions such as property-tax credits or rebates will be instituted. We expect that the estimated coefficient on CREDIT in equation (9.2) and the coefficient on YRATE in equation (9.1a) will both be positive.

The choice of explanatory variables for equation (9.1a) in addition to YRATE* stems primarily from consideration of hypotheses H1 and H2, discussed earlier. Since pressure to introduce a special provision granting property-tax relief emanates from a particular group of taxpayers, namely homeowners, explanatory variables must relate primarily to the characteristics of that group. The first one in this category, HOUSEPRICE, defined as the percentage change of average house prices in the state from 1970 to 1980, reflects recent growth in the property-tax base.[19] We expect a positive sign since such growth tends to cause higher property-tax bills, thus creating increased pressure for relief.

The variable OWNERSHIP, defined as the proportion of a state's housing that is owner-occupied, represents the relative size of the target group. Again, a positive relationship is expected. A similar argument applies to the third variable, OVER65, standing for the percentage of the state's population over 65 years of age. Taxpayers in this age group frequently are homeowners and are also politically active. Many will be on fixed incomes, so they may react more strongly to increases in property tax bills than the general population, constituting a vocal subgroup of those interested in property-tax relief. A positive sign for the coefficient of over 65 is predicted.

---

[19] The dates are determined by the availability of data.

The equation also includes an explanatory variable of a more general nature: LOCAL represents the ratio of local public expenditures to total expenditures by governments at both the state and local levels. It stands for the relative size of the local sector and is assumed to be largely independent of tax structure choices at the state level. We expect higher values to result in greater pressure for tax relief, since a larger local share generally implies higher property-tax rates. A positive coefficient is expected.

In a completely general model, one would allow for a relationship between the relative size of the various levels of government and the income-tax structure chosen by each level. One may also want to endogenize the size of alternative tax bases as well, such as resources or retail sales, in such a complete model. Our choice of what variables to treat as exogenous reflects a judgment made on the basis of availability of instruments, degrees of freedom, and our intuition about which interdependencies that are not formally modeled are likely to be important to the process determining the structure of the state income tax.

As a final variable we include BONDLIMIT, which also appears in the first equation, in order to represent the possible influence of such restrictions on the structure of the income-tax base. In the past, the effects of bond limitations have been investigated in order to analyze the ability of states to avoid them by engaging in off-budget activities (Bennett and DiLorenzo 1983). Attempts have also been made to determine whether per-capita debt figures, or debt-to-income ratios, are lower where bond limitations are more severe (von Hagen 1991, Poterba 1994). When we are concerned with revenue structure, we must expect a more pervasive effect since the various components of the revenue system are interrelated. In consequence, we test for the possibility that constraints on the ability to issue debt will make it less likely for a state to yield to pressure for property-tax relief. A negative sign is expected on the coefficient of BONDLIMIT in the CREDIT* equation.

9.3.1   Estimation of the Two-Equation System

As Table 9.2 records, 31 states have a credit or rebate (CREDIT) for the payment of local property tax in 1985.[20] The value of CREDIT for each state is the same for both years of the sample. Note that Nevada and South Dakota have a rebate but no income tax. This is not a problem from the perspective of

---

[20] Of the 31 states with a value of CREDIT = 1, 15 states have a rebate only; the rest have a tax credit or both a credit and a rebate (ACIR 1986, Table 71). The value of credit for Wyoming is set to zero because the rebate is for sales and property tax, and we could not discover which aspect of the rebate was dominant. This one observation is not likely to affect our conclusions.

the model, since opposition to state income taxes may exist and be influenced by the structure of special provisions even though no income tax is actually collected.

Estimation of (9.1a) and (9.2) is complicated by the censored and dichotomous nature of the dependent variables and by the presence of additional endogenous variables on the right side of (9.4).[21] As G. S. Maddala (1983, p. 246) points out, devising consistent estimators of the coefficients in the two-equation system along with appropriate standard errors is a demanding task. The presence of endogenous variables TAXPRICE and GN on the right side of (9.1a), in addition to CREDIT, creates a particularly difficult situation. The problem arises since the set of equations being considered forms part of a larger system that is not completely specified. As a result, it is not possible to know the conditional distribution of the errors that arise in estimating a set of equations with limited dependent variables by the two-step methods discussed in the literature.[22] Accordingly, we use two quite different estimation procedures. The simpler method, the results of which are given in Table 9.4, consists initially of estimating a reduced-form Tobit equation for YRATE and a reduced-form Probit equation for CREDIT. Then the actual values of the dependent variables on the right side of the system (9.1a)–(9.2) are replaced by the predicted values of these variables from the reduced-form estimation. Equation (9.2) is then estimated by the Probit method.[23] No account is taken here of possible cross-equation correlation of errors.[24]

The second method, reported in Table 9.5, employs an instrumental variables, method-of-moments estimator in the Hotztran statistical program (Avery and Hotz 1985). This includes a further allowance for heteroscedasticity in addition to the normalization of variables by income or population noted earlier. To ensure convergence of the nonlinear optimization algorithm that minimizes the weighted sum of orthogonality conditions, most variables that are insignificant in

---

[21] Again we note that, since the model is formulated using the unobserved values of dependent variables on the right side of the equations, there are no "unique solvability" requirements to be met by the estimated coefficients. If the actual values of YRATE and CREDIT had been used instead, the system of qualitative variables would have to be recursive, with either YRATE or CREDIT absent from the right side of the system. The results in Tables 9.3 and 9.4 do suggest that the model could be reformulated without CREDIT in the YRATE* equation, and with YRATE instead of YRATE* on the right side of the CREDIT* equation. The formulation we have presented seems more natural to us, however.

[22] As a consequence, the estimation methods discussed by Newey (1987) or Rivers and Vuong (1988) cannot be used, since these endogenous variables are not present in the simultaneous equation systems they consider.

[23] This method would produce consistent estimators if there were no endogenous variables on the right side of (9.1a) besides CREDIT*.

[24] Fixed effects for each state are not included in the equations.

Table 9.4. Income-tax structure, U.S. states, fiscal years 1985 and 1986. Two-step estimation

Dependent variable is average personal income tax (YRATE) — Two-stage least squares

	(1)	(1a)	(1b)	(2)	(3)	(3a)	(4)	(4a)
CREDIT	-0.32 (0.11)	-0.01		0.09 (0.03)	0.01 (0.00)	4.11 (1.41)	-0.15 (-0.05)	3.40 (1.18)
TAX-PRICE	-288.30 (-1.70)	-0.40	-265.31 (-1.55)	-260.07 (-3.48)	-260.44 (-3.49)	-229.99 (-3.18)	-282.30 (-4.39)	-288.41 (-4.59)
TRAVEL	-15.22 (-1.09)	-0.09	-15.70 (-1.14)	-16.57 (-1.20)	-17.09 (-1.27)	-21.46 (-1.61)	-17.04 (-1.26)	-21.00 (-1.57)
RBY	-24.26 (-2.53)	-0.37	-25.40 (-2.62)	-25.66 (-3.51)	25.75 (-3.53)	-26.97 (-3.82)	-23.07 (-4.12)	-19.99 (-3.56)
SBY	-2.50 (-0.53)	-0.04	-2.43 (-0.53)					
BOND-LIMIT	0.18 (0.10)	0.01	0.25 (0.13)	0.30 (0.16)				
STD	-1.00 (-1.61)	-0.15	-1.06 (-1.80)	-1.01 (-1.62)	-0.98 (-1.64)	-1.43 (-2.40)	-0.84 (-1.54)	-1.02 (-1.89)
POOR/RICH	0.11 (0.25)	0.05	0.07 (0.14)					
REGION	-0.60 (-3.69)	-0.34	-0.61 (-3.73)	-0.61 (-4.18)	-0.62 (-4.33)	-0.63 (-4.45)	-0.61 (-4.27)	-0.60 (-4.29)
NATION-WIDE	0.18 (2.37)	0.18	0.18 (2.42)	0.19 (2.48)	0.18 (2.51)	0.19 (2.66)	0.18 (2.44)	0.17 (2.46)
GN	0.001 (0.42)	0.06	0.001 (0.59)	0.001 (0.57)	0.001 (0.57)	0.002 (1.61)		
R^2	0.45		0.46	0.46	0.46	0.48	0.46	0.48
S	7.69		7.69	7.72	7.72	7.61	7.77	7.64

Credit or rebate for local property tax (CREDIT) — Probit estimation

	(5)	(5a)	(6)	(7)
YRATE	0.05 (2.31)	0.46	0.05 (2.38)	0.04 (2.21)
HOUSE-PRICE	0.02 (3.49)	1.91	0.02 (3.49)	0.01 (3.22)
OWNER-SHIP	-0.01 (-0.45)	-0.51		
OVER65	21.18 (2.82)	1.45	20.55 (2.76)	21.33 (2.89)
LOCAL	2.46 (1.57)	0.54	2.51 (1.60)	2.66 (1.62)
BOND-LIMIT	-0.51 (-1.60)	-0.18	-0.55 (-1.76)	
χ^2	22.35 (6df)		22.14 (5df)	18.97 (4df)
R^2cu	0.27		0.27	0.24
PREDICT	0.76		0.74	0.65

Notes to Table 9.4: Estimation using SHAZAM (White et al., 1990). The constant term is not reported. "t" statistics are in brackets. R^2 is adjusted. S is the standard error of the estimate. X^2 is the likelihood ratio test statistic ("df" denotes degrees of freedom). R^2cu is the Cragg-Uhler R-square.

PREDICT is the percent of correct predictions (using 0.5 as the critical probability). Columns (1), (2), (3) and (4) are based on two-stage least

squares with the predicted value from a reduced-form probit equation for CREDIT used as one of the instruments. Column (1a) reports

standardized (beta) coefficients corresponding to column (1). Column (1b) repeats column 1 of Table 9.3. Columns (3a) and (4a), corresponding to

columns (3) and (4), report two-stage least-squares estimates based on use of the set of variables {HOUSEPRICE, OWNERSHIP, OVER65,

LOCAL} as instruments in place of the predicted value from the reduced-form probit for CREDIT. Otherwise these equations are the same as in

the corresponding columns. Other instruments used in columns (1) to (4a) are given below. Columns (5) and (6) are based on probit estimation

with predicted values from a reduced-form Tobit equation for YRATE used as an explanatory variable instead of YRATE. Column (5a) reports the

elasticity of the index at the means of the right-side variables. Instruments used in addition to exogenous variables in Table 1 (see the list of

variables at the end of the chapter for definitions): FIRST, P25, P50, P100, PMAR, POP, POPNW, SMSA, POVERTY, MCAP, as well as the

average dollar tax-price discussed in the footnotes.

Table 9.4 in the YRATE equation are omitted in the estimation recorded in Table 9.5. In this estimation we have used the predicted values of CREDIT and YRATE from reduced-form Probit and Tobit estimation (respectively) as instruments for these variables, and we have used the synthetic tax-price discussed previously as an instrument for TAXPRICE. The results are similar to those based on the first estimation procedure.

The signs of coefficients in Tables 9.4 and 9.5 generally correspond to the predicted signs in Table 9.1, and several of the results are of particular interest. Moreover, the results of estimation of equation (9.1a) with CREDIT included are very similar to those in Table 9.3 where CREDIT and equation (9.2) are not part of the model. To help the reader compare the results of estimation of (9.1) alone with the results for the two-equation system, the first column in Table 9.3 is included in Table 9.4. Because the signs and significance of coefficients are quite similar across estimation methods, the following discussion of the results refers to both Table 9.4 and Table 9.5 unless otherwise noted.

The results indicate that reliance on personal income, as measured by YRATE, has a significant and positive effect on the decision to give a CREDIT for the payment of the local property tax. This indicates that there is a significant connection between the reliance on income as a revenue source and structural features of the income tax. Although there is some indication of the effect of a credit in reducing opposition to the income tax, this effect is not statistically significant in equations (3a) and (4a) of Table 9.4.

One should note that income-related property-tax credits are just one of many special features of state income-tax structures, and that such credits may not have a detectable influence by themselves on opposition to the income tax. The increased reliance on the income tax leads to opposition from many sources. The coefficient on CREDIT in the income-tax equation captures just one of the ways in which the government addresses that opposition. The granting of a credit to a few specific groups of taxpayers (e.g., poorer or older homeowners) will presumably reduce opposition to the income tax, but this effect may be difficult to detect if the taxpayers involved are not large in number or if the credit is small in magnitude. This may explain why the results do not confirm causality in both directions.

Judging by the standardized coefficients in column (1a) of Table 9.4, the factors most influential in the decision about reliance on the income-tax base are the price (TAXPRICE) of federal public services facing state taxpayers, a result that emphasizes the importance of acknowledging links between fiscal systems at different levels in a federation; the size of the natural resource tax base relative to personal income (RBY);[25] and competition with neighboring

---

[25] When Alaska is omitted from the sample, the coefficient on RBY is somewhat less important but still significant.

Table 9.5. Income-tax structure, U.S. states, fiscal years 1985 and 1986. Instrumental variables, orthogonality condition estimation

Dependent variable is income tax rate (YRATE) Tobit estimation		
	(1)	(2)
CREDIT	-0.72 (-0.29)	-0.72 (-0.28)
TAXPRICE	-377.71 (-2.57)	-330.40 (-4.57)
TRAVEL	-32.30 (-1.89)	-33.40 (-1.94)
RBY	-26.12 (-3.41)	-27.89 (-4.69)
STD	-0.83 (-1.60)	-0.77 (-1.52)
POOR/RICH	0.17 (0.34)	
REGION	-0.66 (-3.03)	-0.70 (-3.86)
NATIONWIDE	0.18 (2.44)	0.18 (2.43)
R^2(LATENT)	0.50	0.49
Log L	-526.44	-527.47

Dependent variable is credit for local property tax (CREDIT) Probit estimation			
	(3)	(4)	(5)
YRATE	0.05 (2.53)	0.05 (2.58)	0.04 (2.30)
HOUSEPRICE	0.02 (4.03)	0.02 (4.15)	0.01 (3.45)
OWNERSHIP	-0.01 (-0.48)		
OVER65	22.68 (2.47)	22.14 (2.48)	22.63 (2.73)
LOCAL	2.65 (1.81)	2.71 (1.82)	2.77 (1.82)
BONDLIMIT	-0.49 (-1.52)	-0.52 (-1.67)	
R^2(LOG-LIKE)	0.24	0.24	0.20
Log L	-53.15	-53.27	-54.69

Notes to Table 9.5: Estimation using HOTZTRAN (Avery and Hotz 1985). The estimates reported are based on use of optimal weighting of orthogonality conditions (OPTWT = 0 in HOTZTRAN). "t" statistics are in brackets. R^2(LATENT) is the latent R^2 reported by HOTZTRAN. R^2(LOG-LIKE) is the log-like R^2 reported by HOTZTRAN. Log L is the log-likelihood. The instrument for CREDIT (YRATE) is the predicted value from the reduced form Probit (Tobit) equation. The instrument for TAXPRICE is the synthetic taxprice discussed in the text.

states (REGION). Tax competition with other states in the country as a whole (NATIONWIDE) and the variability of the income-tax base (STD) are of somewhat lesser importance.

The results given in Tables 9.3–9.5 are all based on the assumption that REGION is an exogenous variable. It is possible, however, that tax rates of geographically neighboring states are correlated because of the existence of economic shocks that affect several neighboring states at the same time, or because of strategic interaction between the tax policies of neighboring states (Besley and Case 1995a). In either case, REGION will be correlated with the error term in the equation for YRATE and should be considered an endogenous variable. To allow for this possibility, REGION was added to the list of endogenous right-side variables in equation (9.4a) and predicted values of tax rates from a corresponding reduced-form Tobit equation were used in the two-step estimation procedure just described. Results of this procedure are essentially the same as reported in columns (3a) and (4a) of Table 9.4 and so are not given here. It appears that the sign of the coefficient on REGION does not depend on whether this variable is treated as exogenous or endogenous.[26] We also note that a comparison of the results in Table 9.3 with those in Table 9.4 indicates that the sign on REGION does not depend on whether or not CREDIT is included in the equation explaining reliance on income taxation.

The results with respect to both geographic neighbors and competition within the country as a whole are similar to those obtained by Howard Chernick (1991, 1997), who suggests that the negative sign on (his version of) REGION may be the consequence of a tax-haven effect. If income is taxed at the location of employment and if there is interstate commuting, an incentive could exist for states with the most employment to keep rates high and for residential states to keep them low. Examples (Chernick 1991, p. 27) may be New Hampshire with a YRATE of 0.16 percent and Massachusetts with a rate of 3.33 percent in 1985. Other low–high pairings include Connecticut (YRATE = 0.50 in 1985) and New York (3.71) as well as Washington (no tax) and Oregon (3.86). If confirmed by other studies, such a pattern of results could serve as the starting point of further theoretical work on interstate tax

---

[26] Using time-series data, Besley and Case (1995) find that increases over time in individual tax liabilities in a given state are *positively* associated with increases in tax liabilities in neighboring states, a result they attribute to "yard-stick" competition, in which voters in any state look at neighboring states' tax systems when deciding how to cast their ballots. Such a result is not inconsistent with the negative coefficient on REGION in the cross-section study reported here. (We use two years of data, but most of the variation in the data comes from the cross-section component.) Taking the results of both investigations at face value suggests that an equilibrium tax rate (or tax liability differential) between competing neighboring states exists and is maintained over time. When one state deviates "too far" from this equilibrium differential, it seems that the reaction of voters forces the state to bring its tax structure back into line.

competition. As yet, it remains unclear what theoretical model could produce this type of tax competition.[27]

The equation explaining the decision to grant property-tax relief also works well. Only the variable representing house ownership (OWNERSHIP) is clearly insignificant. Coefficients on other variables have the expected signs, including BONDLIMIT, which is significant at 10 percent in some equations. Although the results in Tables 9.4 and 9.5 constitute only a first step in integrating structural features of the tax system into empirical research, they indicate that it is possible to model jointly the structure of a tax base and the extent of reliance on that base.

As a final comment on the results, we note that state property tax relief may have a substantial influence on the structure of local tax systems, whereas the decision to grant a CREDIT for local property taxes does not appear to influence the overall pattern of state revenue sources. This relationship between fiscal systems in a federation may deserve further investigation.

9.4   CONCLUDING REMARKS

In this chapter we have studied the revenue system as a set of related instruments, including tax bases, rate structures, and special provisions. The use of these instruments depends on political objectives and is constrained by competition between political parties, existing political institutions, and the general equilibrium structure of the economy. Because they are a mix of policy instruments, fiscal systems cannot be described adequately by a unique parameter. Understanding a tax system requires the study of at least two instruments as well as explicit allowance for their interdependence.

The approach to the modeling of fiscal systems that incorporates political decision making within an equilibrium context is being applied by a growing number of researchers. We have formulated two models in this tradition. The first model focuses on the extent of reliance by U.S states on one important revenue source, the income tax, taking into account that this revenue source is

---

[27] Bucovetsky (1991) has investigated tax competition between states of unequal population in a paper that may be relevant to the present context. In his model, the smaller state levies the lower rate under certain conditions. The same sort of result appears in work by Kanbur and Keen (1993). It should also be noted that Ladd (1992) has found that competition between counties in large metropolitan areas (which are assumed not to compete with central cities) operates in the "usual" manner, with higher tax burdens in each county being positively associated with higher burdens in neighboring counties. Whether this contradicts the results for REGION found here – or, rather, indicates that competition between suburban counties that do not compete with central cities operates differently than interstate competition – is not clear.

part of an integrated revenue structure. The second model is designed to investigate the simultaneous choice of a tax share and a special revenue provision. This model deals with the decision by U.S. states on how heavily to rely on income as a tax base relative to other revenue sources, and the related decision on whether to introduce a credit or refund for the payment of local property taxes. The construction and analysis of both models acknowledges the possibility of links among different state revenue systems arising from tax competition. In addition, allowance has been made for connections between state fiscal systems and those of federal and local governments, connections that may result from specific structural features present at each level.

Considering the results for both models as a whole, four types of results stand out concerning state tax systems. First, the relative size of tax bases (and, beneath this, the structure of economic activity) is an important factor in determining the relative reliance on different bases. Second, the explicit allowance at the federal level for taxes paid at other levels of government has a substantial effect on state fiscal systems by changing the burden of state taxes. Third, tax competition between neighboring states seems to proceed in a quite different manner than interstate competition within the country as a whole. This last finding may be related to the fact that migration between neighboring states is subject to different fixed and marginal costs than migration within the country as a whole, as well as to the asymmetry in size between many neighboring states. And finally, the extent to which a revenue source is used is a significant factor in decisions concerning the structure of that base.

The empirical results presented in this chapter indicate that applied research on the joint use of fiscal instruments is feasible and can yield significant conclusions. However, our investigation also points to some unresolved difficulties. As indicated in earlier discussion, probabilistic voting provides the theoretical background for research based on the political economy view of taxation that is implemented empirically here. As yet, there have been few attempts to link this more general approach to the functioning of institutions for which a detailed decision structure has been spelled out.[28] Even though estimating equations used in most empirical work informed by this new view are based on broad principles consistent with the underlying theory, they do not represent the unique product of a decision framework reflecting actual institutional detail. We attempt to forge a more direct link between institutional arrangements and actual fiscal policy outcomes in Chapter 11.

Finally, the focus on policy instruments as part of a larger equilibrium system raises two related difficulties for research. The first is of a statistical nature. Since a particular instrument may not be used by all decision makers in

---

[28] Exceptions include Inman's (1989) statistical study of local tax systems in the United States, where a complex and rather specialized governing structure is specified.

the sample, dependent variables may be censored or dichotomous. As illustrated in our empirical analysis, this can lead to systems of simultaneous equations where both these types of dependent variables are present, requiring the use of special estimation techniques.

The second problem is of a more conceptual nature. In a world in which fiscal structure is an equilibrium outcome of political and economic competition, it is necessary to study the nature of links empirically in order to find those that are most important. For states, this requires studying interdependencies between instruments at the same level of government as well as between levels of government. The basic techniques are similar to those used in other investigations of equilibrium systems: one can analyze the effects on the system as a whole of changing exogenous factors that have an impact on particular parts of the system; and one can consider the strength of interdependencies by estimating structural or semireduced-form relationships. Additional work that would guide empirical researchers in choosing relevant parts of the system for study and in their selection of estimating equations would be of great help in advancing research in this area.

9.5   VARIABLES AND DATA SOURCES

All data are on a state-by-state basis for calendar years 1985 and 1986 unless otherwise indicated.

Variable	Definition	Sources
BONDLIMIT	1 if either nominal dollar or percentage (of state funds, tax revenue or state or taxable property) limitation on issue of debt	(2)
CREDIT	1 if credit or rebate for the payment of local property tax; 0 otherwise	(1)
FIRST	Synthetic "first dollar" federal tax-price (Feldstein and Metcalf 1987, pp. 721–2) constructed using the NBER'S TAXSIM model for 1984 and 1985	(8)
GN	Total state expenditures (fiscal-year basis) per capita	(3)/(4)
HOUSEPRICE	Percent change in house prices, 1970–80	(5)
LOCAL	Ratio of local government expenditures to state expenditures (fiscal-year basis)	(6)
MCAP	State highway miles per capita, 1985	(7)/(4)
NATIONWIDE	YRATE in state with most similar value of POOR/RICH as for YRATE (fiscal-year basis)	
OVER65	Percent of population over age 65	(6)/(4)

OWNERSHIP	Percent of housing that is owner-occupied	(5)
PMAR	Fraction married	(8)
POOR/RICH	Ratio of number of taxpayers with less than $25,000 adjusted gross income to number with more than $50,000	(8)
POP	Population	(4)
POPNW	Population nonwhite in 1988	(9)
POVERTY	Percent of population below poverty level	(5)
P25; P50; P100	Fraction of federal income tax returns with adjusted gross income between $25,000 and $50,000; between $50,000 and $100,00; over $100,000	(8)
RBY	Mineral production per dollar of personal income	(6)
REGION	Average of YRATEs in geographically neighboring states	(11)/(6)
SBY	Retail trade per dollar of personal income	(6)
SMSA	Percent of population in SMSA	(6)
STD	Standard deviation of percentage year-over-year change in real personal income, 1970–86	(6)
TAXPRICE	$1 -$ (proportion of itemizers times average federal marginal tax rate of itemizers)	(8)
TRAVEL	Travel-generated business receipts per dollar of personal income income	(10)/(6)
YRATE	Average personal income tax rate = ratio of personal income tax revenue to personal income (fiscal-year basis)	(11)/(6)

Sources of Data (U.S. government publications unless otherwise noted)

1. Advisory Commission on Intergovernmental Relations (ACIR), *Significant Features of Fiscal Federalism* 1985, Tables 70 and 71;
2. Von Hagen (1991), Table 1;
3. *State Government Finances*, 1985 and 1986, Table 9;
4. ACIR, *Significant Features of Fiscal Federalism*, 1989, vol. 2, Table 2;
5. *State and Metropolitan Area Data Book*, 1986;
6. *Statistical Abstract of the United States*, 1987, 1988 and 1989;
7. *Federal Highway Administration Statistics*, 1985;
8. Data supplied by Gilbert Metcalf using the NBER's TAXSIM model, calendar years 1984 and 1985;
9. *Current Population Report* 1988, P-25, Tables 1 and 2;
10. *The Impact of Travel on State Economies*, 1985 and 1986, Table 5;
11. *State Government Tax Collections*, 1985 and 1986, Table 3.

CHAPTER 10

Debt and Tariffs

The Evolution of the Canadian Revenue System

> The spirit of a people, its cultural level, its social structure, the
> deeds its policy may prepare – all this and more is written in its fis-
> cal history, stripped of all phrases.
>
> Joseph Schumpeter (1918, p. 101)

> Writing history is constructing a coherent story of some facet of the
> human condition through time. Such a construction exists only in
> the human mind. We do not recreate the past; we construct stories
> about the past. But to be good history, the story must give a consis-
> tent, logical account and be constrained by the available evidence
> and the available theory.
>
> Douglass North (1990, p. 131)

More than eight decades ago, Joseph Schumpeter (1918) published an outstanding essay on the fiscal state. He argued that the ability to tax lies at the
very heart of political power and that the rise of the modern political state was
shaped by fiscal evolution in medieval and postmedieval times. Although he
was primarily interested in the influence of fiscal power on political power, he
also raised a related set of questions about what forces shape fiscal structure
itself. He clearly recognized that revenue systems consist of a number of
related components chosen in the light of three types of influences: economic,
political, and administrative. But he did not provide a framework of how these
factors interact to shape evolving revenue systems, perhaps because he had not
yet formed an economic theory of political action.

Schumpeter's essay was published in German and had no influence on the
study of public finance in English-speaking countries. It was not until the
1960s that American scholars became interested in the development of revenue
systems. Initial work was primarily an outgrowth of the attention devoted to
developing countries. Studies by Harley Hinrichs (1966) and Richard Musgrave (1969) fall into this category. Hinrichs was mainly interested in linking
stages of economic and fiscal development, whereas Musgrave emphasized the
roles of changing opportunities to tax and of administration costs (so-called tax
handles) in the evolution of tax structure. Although these authors were certainly aware of the role of political factors as well as administrative and

economic ones in shaping tax systems, it was not until the 1970s that all three types of influences were explicitly included in some empirical studies of taxation and in the analysis of public policy in general. Even then, as the review of the literature in Chapter 8 indicates, most studies of taxation have been concerned with particular parts or aspects of the broader equilibrium.

In this chapter we return to the broader vision implicit in Schumpeter's essay. We consider a revenue system as an integrated package of components and argue that all three basic influences – economic, political, and administrative – must be taken into account in understanding the evolution of the system as a whole. In support of this view we investigate the role these three types of factors have played in the development of the revenue structure of the central government in Canada from 1871 to 1913, a period when major revenue sources consisted of the tariff, debt, and excises.

The model we use for this purpose is a particular version of the general reduced-form system introduced in Chapter 8. The empirical analysis distinguishes between government plans and ex post observations of public revenues and emphasizes the derivation of hypotheses linking economic, political, and administrative variables to revenue structure.

10.1   A MODEL OF EVOLVING REVENUE STRUCTURE

As a first step in the historical investigation, let revenue structure at time t be represented by revenues raised from different sources including debt, $R_{1t}, R_{2t}, \ldots, R_{Jt}$. This treatment abstracts from the role of special provisions in the tax system, which were a focus of the empirical work presented in the previous chapter. Data limitations as well as the complexity of special provisions make it impossible to employ a more comprehensive definition in a historical study of the present kind.

We shall think of revenue structure as being chosen *after* a forecast of total revenue requirements, G_F, has been made, thus abstracting from the simultaneous determination of the tax and expenditure sides of the budget. In a more detailed version of the model, expenditure structure would be represented more fully – for example, by distinguishing between public expenditures for current consumption and expenditures on capital projects.

Next, we adopt a particular form for the political support function in the Representation Theorem, the maximization of which subject to the government budget restraint can be used to replicate the equilibrium in a competitive political system. (Other constraints imposed by the structure of the private economy are assumed to have been substituted into the support function and the budget restraint.) We assume that the support function is of the Cobb–Douglas type:

$$S = \prod_{j=1}^{j=J} \left(R_{jt} \right)^{\delta_{jt}} \quad \text{for} \quad t = 1, 2, \ldots, T, \tag{10.1}$$

where the δ_{jt}, which reflect the loss in support from raising revenue from source j and take into account the general equilibrium structure of the private economy, are defined by

$$\delta_{jt} = \exp(\alpha_j \cdot X_{jt}). \tag{10.2}$$

The X_{jt} include all economic, political, and administrative factors that determine the net effect on support of raising revenue from each source and spending on public services what remains after administrative expenses. The precise specification of these factors will be dealt with at length later. To allow for the possibility that the marginal loss in support from relying on each revenue source may change with the size of the public sector, each vector X_{jt} also includes G_F.[1]

To specify the government budget restraint that links the choice of revenue sources directly, let administration costs associated with tax source j at time t be $A(a_{jt})$, where a_{jt} is a vector of exogenous factors that is also included in X_{jt}.[2] Then the government budget restraint relevant to the determination of revenue structure is given by

$$G_{Ft} = \sum_{j=1}^{J} R_{jt} - \sum_{j=1}^{J} A(a_{jt}) \quad \text{for} \quad t = 1, 2, \dots, T. \tag{10.3}$$

Maximization of (10.1) subject to (10.3) leads to the following first-order conditions for two revenue sources j and k:

$$\ln(R_{jt}/R_{kt}) = \beta_{jk} \cdot X_{jkt} \quad \text{for} \quad j \neq k, \quad t = 1, 2, \dots, T, \tag{10.4}$$

where $\beta_{jk} = (\alpha_j, -\alpha_k)$ and $X_{jkt} = (X_{jt}, X_{kt})'$.

Equation (10.4), which is not yet in a form that can be estimated, has the convenient property that the ratio of any two revenue sources depends only on factors affecting the political costs of raising revenue from these two sources. It also has the desirable characteristic that the dependent variable consists of the ratio of two revenue sources, a ratio that – unlike the revenue sources themselves – does not exhibit obvious time trends.[3]

---

[1] Beggs and Strong (1982) include an additive error term inside the brackets in (10.2) to reflect imperfect understanding of deterministic forces. This source of error can be included in the error term in the final estimating equation (10.5).

[2] It should be noted that administration costs are assumed not to depend on the extent to which any tax source is used. (This condition was mistakenly omitted from Winer and Hettich 1991a.)

[3] As a check on the results, other functional forms will be used as a basis for alternative estimating equations.

In order to complete the derivation of an estimating equation, it is necessary to deal with the difference between planned and actual or observed revenues. This is a long-standing problem in the empirical study of government behavior, although it is not often confronted directly (and we did not do so in Chapter 9). Observed revenue structure reflects two types of influences. It has a planned component, representing deliberate choices by government officials based on information available to them. In addition, it reflects unanticipated events. Actual tariff revenues, to take an example that will prove to be useful, are the result of a tariff structure chosen by public officials, given their anticipation of the size of imports and of other factors such as interest-group pressure, which determined the relative emphasis that they wanted to place on this source. However, actual collections also reflect the effects of unanticipated fluctuations in international trade and in variables, such as domestic income, that influence the demand for imports.

We shall conceive of actual tax revenue from any source R_j^a as consisting of two parts: planned revenues R_j^p, which depend on decisions by government based on available information; and an unanticipated component R_j^u, which depends on errors made by the government in forecasting variables such as the size of tax bases. Since the model is properly viewed as providing an explanation of government decisions based on available information, the left side of (10.4) must then be reinterpreted as $\ln(R_{jt}^p/R_{kt}^p)$. Taking this reinterpretation into account, along with the fact that it is possible to collect data only on actual revenue structure, suggests the following estimating equation:

$$\ln(R_{jt}^a/R_{kt}^a) = \beta_{jk} \cdot X_{jkt} + \mu_{jkt} \quad \text{for} \quad j \neq k, \quad t = 1, 2, \ldots, T, \qquad (10.5)$$

where

$$\mu_{jkt} = \ln(R_{jt}^a/R_{kt}^a) - \ln(R_{jt}^p/R_{kt}^p),$$

and where the vector X_{jk} must now be interpreted as information, including forecasts, upon which the government bases its revenue plans. The error term μ_{jkt} represents the influence of unanticipated developments occurring between the time a revenue plan is made and the time actual revenues are realized.[4]

In order to estimate (10.5), it is necessary to approximate the information X_{jk} used by the government in making its fiscal plans – and to do so in such a manner that μ_{jk} has zero mean, is serially uncorrelated, and is uncorrelated

---

[4] If we allow for imperfect understanding of deterministic forces in the manner indicated in a previous footnote, the error term will reflect this source of error as well as random developments after a revenue plan has been implemented. Such an error structure has been discussed by Lovell (1986, p. 121).

with X_{jk}. We shall employ a two-pronged approach. In some cases (to be discussed more fully), it is both possible and desirable to construct forecasts of key variables underlying fiscal plans using auxiliary regressions and then to use these forecasts as explanatory variables. In other cases, we shall simply use values of variables lagged by one period to reflect the basic information available to the government.

Because the equations will be used to explain the issue of debt as well as the choice of current taxation, it is important to be specific about the intertemporal nature of the model before we discuss the choice of explanatory variables. As noted in Chapter 8, we employ a simple intertemporal structure. We assume that political parties care about the future only because they think that voters do. Thus, each party is concerned with how voters' evaluations of future taxes needed to finance interest payments on the public debt affect its *current* level of political support. Similarly, each party is concerned with the effects of current taxation (tariffs and excises) and the current level of public services on the future welfare of voters.

We do not impose the constraint that the government budget be in balance in present-value terms over the sample period as a whole. The government simply responds from period to period to the intertemporal (and other) concerns of citizens and interest groups. The attention that the incumbent party pays to the future effects of its policies is reflected in estimating equation (10.5), where the government's forecasts of certain variables are included as part of the model explaining the tax structure of the current period.

We stated earlier that the evolution of revenue systems is influenced by three broad classes of exogenous factors – economic, political, and administrative factors – all of which are included in the X_{jk}. To make the model a useful framework for empirical study of the evolution of revenue systems, it is necessary to construct time series representing these factors and to predict their impact on the government's choice of revenue structure. This task will be accomplished in the next section.

10.2   TESTING THE MODEL

10.2.1   Choice of Country and Period: Canada, 1871–1913

Work on tax structure by Hinrichs and Musgrave suggests that the development of revenue systems is linked to broad trends in economic development and that revenue systems pass through several phases. This chapter applies the model to Canada during an early stage of its growth, encompassing the time from the establishment of modern central government to the beginning of the First World War. During this time, no major new revenue sources were intro-

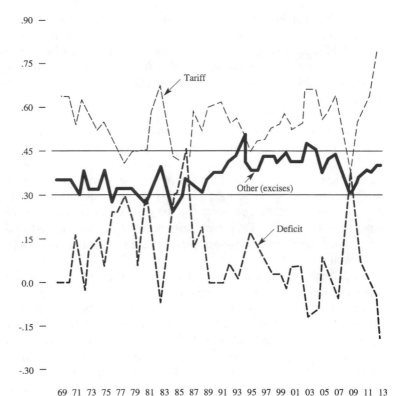

Figure 10.1. Major revenue sources as a proportion of total financial requirements, government of Canada, 1868–1913

duced at the federal level. The period includes intervals of rapid and sustained growth as well as of prolonged recession.[5]

The evolution of the Canadian federal revenue system from Confederation to the First World War is shown in Figure 10.1, where annual revenues from different sources are plotted as a percentage of the total. As the figure indicates, there were three major revenue sources: customs duties, borrowing (i.e., the deficit), and excises. Other miscellaneous revenues constituted a minor share of the total. Unlike modern governments, the Canadian authorities during

---

[5] Statistical data on Canada's early revenue system are relatively good. A major source is Perry's work (1955) on the history of the Canadian tax system. Other important sources are new series on federal tax revenues by Gillespie (1991) as well as estimates of national income statistics for the nineteenth century by Urquhart (1986) and the well-known *Historical Statistics of Canada* (1983). An appendix on data sources follows the text as Section 10.5.

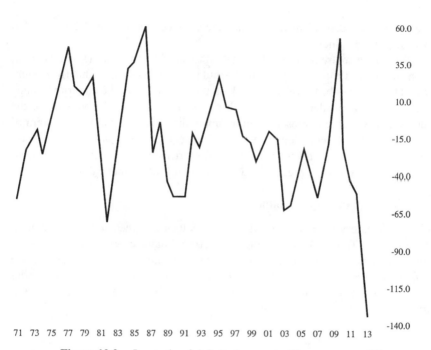

60.0

35.0

10.0

-15.0

-40,0

-65.0

-90.0

-115.0

-140.0

71 73 75 77 79 81 83 85 87 89 91 93 95 97 99 01 03 05 07 09 11 13

Figure 10.2.   Log ratio of deficit plus non-tariff revenue to tariff revenues, 1871–1913 (data scaled by 100)

this period did not have a central bank and did not use money creation as a significant source of revenue.[6] One may note that excises, which were imposed almost exclusively on alcohol and tobacco, accounted for a relatively constant proportion of total revenues. An explanation of evolving revenue structure in nineteenth-century Canada must therefore focus primarily on borrowing and the tariff.

Estimating equation (10.5) requires that the dependent variable be expressed as the log of the ratio of revenues from two different sources. In this case, the ratio of obvious interest is the deficit divided by customs duties. However, this ratio assumes negative values when the deficit turns into a surplus (see Figure 10.1), so that the logarithm cannot be defined for all time periods. We therefore use the log of the ratio of the deficit plus all other nontariff revenues to tariff revenues as the dependent variable, a choice that seems justified in view of the relative constancy of revenues from other sources. The plot of this variable is presented in Figure 10.2. One should note the considerable

---

[6] For further discussion of the issue of uncovered Dominion of Canada notes, see Rich (1988).

variation in the dependent variable and the absence of any trend that is revealed by the plotted values.

We shall also use the ratio of the deficit to tariff revenues as a second dependent variable. Although this second formulation deviates somewhat from equation (10.5), it will be useful as a check on the robustness of the empirical results because this dependent variable excludes excises. A third formulation of the dependent variable is presented in an appendix, where a complete system of two revenue share equations is estimated instead of one equation for the ratio of revenues. The two revenue shares are for tariffs and for the deficit plus non-tariff revenues, both expressed as a proportion of total financial requirements.

10.2.2   Explanatory Variables

The explanatory variables considered for inclusion in the estimating equation are listed in Table 10.1 according to the three major categories – economic, political, and administrative – and by major revenue source. Also shown are the predicted signs.[7] A fourth category of variables is also considered in order to allow for the possibility that the composition of expenditures and the size of the public sector may influence tax structure.

Economic Factors

We start by discussing economic variables for the tariff and borrowing. The focus of the discussion is on three issues. We decide upon the precise nature of the variables to be included in the estimating equation; we deal with the issue of forecasting raised earlier; and we discuss some characteristics of debt that suggest inclusion of two additional variables. In choosing variables to represent economic factors, we make use of the analysis in the previous chapter.

As argued in Chapter 9, the size of bases is central in explaining changes in revenue shares (recall hypothesis H2). In equilibrium, political costs of raising an extra dollar must be the same across all revenue sources. When a base grows, the political costs of raising an extra dollar from that base decline. This is because the marginal dollar can now be raised using a lower tax rate, implying a smaller welfare loss and thus less political opposition than before. As a result, the government will reestablish equilibrium in tax structure by increasing total revenue collected from the expanded base while raising less elsewhere (assuming the overall size of the public sector remains constant).

In making revenue choices the government must estimate the size of tax bases, including the base upon which debt is levied. Since the tariff was a major source of revenue for the Canadian federal government (see Figure 10.1), we think it reasonable to assume that considerable effort was devoted to

---

[7] Table 10.1 gives a particular formulation for each variable. In some cases alternative formulations were also tried. Results of these experiments are reviewed in subsequent footnotes.

Table 10.1.   Explanatory variables considered for inclusion in initial estimating equation and predicted signs

		Predicted Sign	Definition
Economic			
Tariff			
	IMF	-	Forecast imports based on entire sample
	IMF1, IMR1	-	Forecast and errors based on moving regressions
Borrowing			
	POP-	+	Population
	FPD/N-	-	Federal and provincial debt per capita
	FAL/Y-	+	Liabilities of commercial failures per $GNP
Political			
Tariff			
	MFG/N-	?	Manufacturing output per capital
	COOP-	?	Membership in farm cooperatives
	UNION-	?	No. of union locals
	EXEMPT	?	Effective protection
	OPP	?	Opposition to tariff
	USC/N-	-	U.S. customs per capita
	USTRF	-	U.S. tariff policy
Borrowing			
	USD/N-	+	U.S. debt per capita
Administrative			
Tariff			
	ADVSE	-	Ad valorem versus specific rates
	HV/IM-	I	Proportion of high value imports
Borrowing			
	YLDF	-	Forecast bond yield based on entire sample
	YLDF1, YLDR1	-	Forecast and errors based on moving regressions
Other			
	RAIL	+	Extraordinary public capital expenditures
	RF	?	Public sector size forecast

Variables with names ending in a minus sign are lagged by one year.

making satisfactory forecasts of annual imports. We model the government's efforts in this regard in two ways, which correspond to different assumptions concerning the government's knowledge of economic structure. In the first we regress imports for the entire period 1871–1913 on two lags of imports, per-capita income and a time trend. The predicted values from this regression, IMF, are then used as forecasts of the tariff revenue base. This approach is appropriate if it is assumed that underlying economic structure is unchanged over the period and that the government forms its expectations rationally. Such an interpretation of rational forecasting implies that the residual from the forecasting equation has zero mean and is uncorrelated with IMF. Even though the errors made by the government in forecasting imports will to some extent influence the difference between planned and actual revenues, such errors are not systematic. Hence this model of government forecasting implies that μ in equation (10.5) will have zero mean and be uncorrelated with IMF. The sign on IMF is expected to be negative, since the dependent variable is expressed as the log of the ratio of the deficit plus other taxes to tariff revenue.[8]

In view of the substantial volatility of imports of the nineteenth century, it may be appropriate to assume more limited knowledge of long-run economic structure on the part of the government. To model the government's behavior in the face of greater uncertainty about long-run trends, we use one-step-ahead-forecasts based on moving regressions. The regressions are constructed as a second-order autoregression using five observations. The resulting time series of forecasts is denoted by IMF1 in Table 10.1; the time series of forecast errors is called IMR1. Unlike the residual from a regression over the entire sample period, IMR1 will not be uncorrelated with IMF1 over the sample period as a whole. In this case, we include IMR1 as an additional explanatory variable in the estimating equation to ensure that the error term in the equation will continue to be uncorrelated with the explanatory variables.[9]

The base for the second major revenue source, borrowing, is more difficult to specify. Deficits create tax liabilities in the future, so we can think of the present value of expected future national income as the relevant base. Unfortunately, there is no directly observable measure of this concept that could be forecast in order to construct the analog to IMF or IMF1 for debt. However, economic history of the period suggests that population growth, primarily through immigration, was perceived as an indicator of future growth and prosperity in nineteenth-century Canada, where labor was scarce in relation to other economic resources. We shall use population lagged one period (POP−)

---

[8] The dependent variable also includes excises in the numerator. They were levied primarily on the consumption of tobacco and alcohol, and as shown in Figure 10.1, they constitute a relatively stable share of total revenues. Since the fluctuations in the dependent variable are weakly associated with developments in excise taxation, we have not emphasized the determinants of revenues from excises. Moreover, it is difficult to find a proxy for the base of excise taxation that is not highly correlated with other explanatory variables. A possible candidate is per-capita income, since the consumption of alcohol and tobacco appears to be closely related to income. But per capita income is highly correlated with the forecast of imports, which is already included in the equation.

[9] The coefficient on IMR1 will reflect only passive adjustment of tariff revenue to unanticipated fluctuations in imports (and the appropriate adjustment of the deficit required by the budget restraint). It does not reflect discretionary adjustment of revenue structure in response to anticipated changes in imports.

to represent the information underlying forecasts of the base for borrowing. A positive sign on POP− is expected.

Since we wish to think of debt as a tax on future income, we must include the existing stock of government debt in the estimating equation. Outstanding debt represents the extent to which public claims have already been created against future income. Because voters will be concerned with expected tax rates resulting from total liabilities against such income, an additional dollar of public borrowing will imply higher future tax rates − and hence a higher welfare loss − if it occurs in the face of a larger existing stock of public debt. (One may note that this is true whether or not the Ricardian equivalence theorem holds.) Furthermore, provincial governments may also have borrowed in the past against the same expected income stream. The relevant variable is therefore combined federal and provincial debt per capita (FPD/N−), with a negative predicted sign.[10]

There was considerable fluctuation in economic activity during the period under investigation, especially in the years from 1870 to 1895 (see e.g. Skelton 1913, Chap. 4). When private individuals are faced with sharp fluctuations in income, they even out their consumption streams with the help of borrowing from private sources. In addition, they may demand that the government adopt policies to cut tax rates and to issue public debt in order to help them maintain more stable disposable incomes, especially if they suffer from liquidity constraints. (This conclusion is consistent with hypothesis H3 in Chapter 9). Thus, if people put a positive value on greater stability in their consumption streams, the political costs of borrowing will be less during times with more pronounced cyclical downturns in economic activity. We use total liabilities of commercial failures per dollar of GNP (FAL/Y−), an indicator of the state of the business cycle, to represent the demand for consumption smoothing through the public sector. A positive coefficient is predicted.[11]

---

[10] Like all other variables, debt is measured in current dollars. One should note, however, that the future burden of present debt will be related to price-level changes occurring in the future. Deflation will raise the real burden of a given nominal debt. If it were possible to formulate an appropriate expectations variable concerning *long-term* price-level changes, then it could be included in the estimating equation. We see no plausible way of formulating such a variable.

[11] It may be useful to note here that the type of smoothing reflected in the coefficient on FAL/Y− differs from that discussed by Barro (1979). He argues that the government will issue debt to maintain revenues in the face of short-term fluctuations in the tax base. Adjusting rates instead would create higher deadweight losses since the excess burden of any tax tends to increase with the square of the tax rate. In the present context, the government would make use of debt to smooth tariff rates if it expected the change in imports to be temporary. However, any such government action would be reflected in the coefficient on expected imports IMF or IMF1 rather than in the coefficient on FAL/Y−, since the latter is estimated holding expected imports constant.

Political Factors

The second major category of explanatory variables represents political forces. Constructing proxies for political factors that influence government decisions in a time-series context is a particularly challenging task, one that was not directly addressed in the previous chapter. We distinguish between two types of such factors, those related to the activities of domestic interest groups and those reflecting the impact of U.S. action on Canadian policy. In developing proxies for the effect of interest-group activity, we focus on the tariff because political debates in nineteenth-century Canada paid primary attention to this revenue source. We also raise a measurement problem not considered in connection with economic variables – namely, whether continuous or discontinuous proxies represent a more appropriate way of modeling the influence of political forces. Although they are the best available, the variables to be introduced here only indirectly represent information underlying the formulation of revenue plans, and we do not attempt to generate explicit forecasts of them.

Table 10.1 shows three continuous variables standing for the influence of the three most important domestic interest groups (manufacturing output per capita, number of union locals, membership in farm cooperatives). Although each one is a somewhat imperfect proxy, they represent reasonable measures of the changing size of these groups given the limited statistical data available for the period. In interpreting the variables, it is important to recall that the tariff serves a double function: it is a revenue source, but it also provides a means of granting protection to domestic industry. We expect manufacturing interests and unions to have a demand for tariff protection and farm groups to oppose the use of customs duties.

Table 10.1 predicts no signs for MFG/N−, UNION−, and COOP−. In the model, the government would set tax rates below the revenue-maximizing point if it were dealing with a tax used only for the raising of revenues.[12] However, additional demands for the use of the policy instrument, such as exist for the tariff, may result in rates placing us on the backward-bending portion of the rate–revenue relationship.[13] Predicted signs for the variables representing demand for protection will differ depending on whether we are on the upward- or the backward-sloping segments of the curve. The same is true for variables

---

[12] This argument incorporates the elasticity of imports with respect to tariff rates.

[13] In Chapter 3, taxation was considered primarily as a means of raising revenue. If taxation is used to achieve other objectives, including protection for some industries from foreign competition, points located on the backward-bending parts of a Laffer curve may be consistent with political equilibrium.

standing for the influence of forces opposing the tariff. As a result, no hypotheses about signs can be formed.[14]

Use of the three continuous variables, to the extent that they properly measure the size of the relevant interest groups, implies that the government annually readjusts revenue structure in accordance with the changing relative size of these groups. It is possible, however, that interest groups exercise influence on government fiscal behavior in a different, discontinuous manner, since the dynamics of group formation may result in political pressures that fluctuate and change abruptly (Oliver, Maxwell, and Teixeira 1985, Cassing and Hillman 1986). Unfortunately, it is not clear what data could be used to represent such fluctuating political pressures. We include two dummy variables, EXEMPT and OPP, with steps in the years when large discontinuous changes occurred in the tariff that can be related to major interest groups, in order to proxy discontinuous political influence on tariff policy. EXEMPT and OPP can be seen respectively as representing the culmination of pressures from manufacturing interests for special protection and from consumers and farmers for a lowering of tariff rates. It should be noted that, although these variables reflect the result of pressure rather than the pressure itself, their influence on revenue structure can be properly interpreted only within the context of our theory.

During the period studied, Canada and the United States were competing for both immigrants and capital resources, and outmigration to the United States was a concern to the Canadian government. We may regard U.S. tariff structure as imposing limits on Canadian ability to use customs duties as a policy instrument without precipitating politically damaging trade and factor flows. We proxy the influence of U.S. fiscal development on the Canadian

---

[14] To check whether other continuous variables would work better than MFG/N−, we tried MFG/Y , manufacturing output divided by GNP, and NM/N−, the ratio of employment in manufacturing to total employment. Neither of these variables was significant or altered other results substantially. We also tried, without success, using the year-over-year increase and rate of change in the number of union locals rather than the level. It is not clear which of these formulations best represents the political strength of organized labor (or of other interest groups). The lagged level of union locals appears to work best. For discussion of the demand for protection by business interest in eighteenth- and nineteenth-century Canada, see Porritt (1908), McDiarmid (1946), Dales (1966), and Forster (1986). On unionism in the same periods, see Logan (1928) and Forsey (1982). Note that only time series on union locals are available, since data on individual membership are generally unavailable on a continuous basis. We also tried levels, first differences, and rates of change in membership in western farm co-ops and in the Grange, a central Canadian farm movement of the 1870s and 1880s. None of these variables proved successful in the estimating equation. In addition, we considered time series on the number of homesteads instead of membership in western farm co-ops, since newly arrived settlers can be expected to face substantial risks and hence will be interested in compensatory government action. This proved unsuccessful. For discussion of farm movements, see Wood (1924) and Stiles (1972).

tariff in two ways. Because Canadian political debates often include comparisons of particular revenue sources in the two countries, we use U.S. customs collections per capita (USC/N−). A negative sign is expected for this variable, based on the assumption that a higher U.S. tariff would lower political costs to the Canadian government of relying on this revenue source. It may be, of course, that the influence of U.S. policy operates discontinuously. We introduce the dummy variable USTRF with steps in 1890 and 1897, two years during which the United States created substantial new tariff barriers affecting Canada. This is to test for the possibility that certain identifiable U.S. actions led to a strong, abrupt Canadian reaction. Since U.S. actions in 1890 and 1897 should lead to greater reliance on the tariff in Canada, USTRF should have a negative coefficient.[15]

The government's use of the second major revenue source, borrowing, may also be influenced by political pressures. We have not formulated proxy variables for interest-group activity in this case, since the political debates of the time reveal no clear links between the use of debt and the activities of particular representative groups. We include U.S. debt per capita (USD/N−) to reflect the possible impact of policy in the United States, because the indebtedness of Canada's neighbor was used as a standard of comparison in debates surrounding Canadian federal borrowing. Since the deficit enters the numerator of the dependent variable, the expected sign of USD/N− is positive.

Administrative Factors

The third group of explanatory variables in Table 10.1 relates to administrative costs. During the period under study, the federal government changed the basis of many tariffs from ad valorem rates to specific per-unit excises in the face of declining prices. We represent this switch in policy with a dummy variable having a step in the relevant year (ADVSE). Because frequent adjustments of tariff rates are costly to implement, ADVSE can be given an administrative interpretation. It will be cheaper to maintain revenues in times of falling prices

---

[15] If the increase in the U.S. tariff leads to a substantial devaluation of the Canadian dollar, and if tariff revenues rise at unchanged tariff rates because (in percentage terms) import prices denominated in Canadian dollars increase by more than the reduction in quantities imported (the J-curve effect), then a negative coefficient would be observed even though the Canadian government may not have taken any discretionary action. However, the estimating equation controls for this relationship between USTRF and tariff revenues since the Canadian dollar value of imports appears as a separate explanatory variable. The coefficient on USTRF therefore reflects the government's discretionary response to a change in U.S. policy at a given level of imports. One should note that no distinction is made in the formulation of the estimating equation between short-run and long-run responses to changes represented by USTRF or other explanatory variables. The nature of the data does not allow the degrees of freedom necessary for a thorough investigation of the lag structure in policy formation.

with specific excises than with repeated changes in advalorem rates. A negative sign is expected.

A second administrative variable relates to the costs of enforcing the tariff. We take the proportion of high value imports in total imports (HV/IM−) to serve as an indicator of such costs, since valuable, low-bulk items are easier to smuggle. An increase in this proportion requires greater enforcement, making the tariff a more costly revenue source and thus suggesting a positive coefficient for the variable.[16]

The final variable in this category relates to the bond yield. We view the bond yield as an administrative cost of borrowing, since a higher interest rate for new government debt implies that fewer public services can be provided for a given amount of borrowing. Political discussions of the period suggest that government officials had considerable specialized knowledge of the London financial markets where most borrowing took place. We simulate their forecast of the bond yield using a regression including time and two lags of YLD and covering the whole period (YLDF), as well as with one-step-ahead forecasts based on moving regressions (YLDF1). In the latter case, the residual YLDR1 is included in the estimating equation for the same reasons as IMR1.

Other Determinants

The remaining two explanatory variables in Table 10.1 relate to expenditure structure and the scale of the public sector. We pointed out in the discussion of the model that one useful way of expanding the description of the expenditure side would be to distinguish between public expenditures on current consumption and on capital goods. Voters may evaluate borrowing by the government differently depending on whether borrowed funds are spent on long-lasting capital assets or on short-term public consumption. One may expect that political opposition to public borrowing will be lower when capital projects that yield benefits over long periods are being financed. The data do not permit a consistent empirical distinction between current and capital outlays to be made over the whole sample period. It is possible, however, to account for capital expenditures on transcontinental railroad construction by using a dummy variable RAIL, with steps in the two years when such expenditures were clearly of extraordinary magnitude. A positive sign for the coefficient of RAIL is expected.

Finally, we include the forecast of total financial requirements RF (equal to public expenditures including administration costs) as a proxy for public sector

---

[16] We may also regard HV/IM− as one indicator of the elasticity of the base on which the tariff is levied; an increase in any tariff rate is more likely to result in reduction in the taxable base (legal imports) if imports can be easily smuggled instead of declared. If this is so, then an increase in HV/IM− will increase the deadweight costs associated with the tariff. Thus, we have another reason why we should expect a positive sign for HV/IM−.

size.[17] We use RF rather than G_F, which appears in the government budget restraint (10.3), since we do not have a measure of total administration costs that can be subtracted from total revenues to yield a measure of expenditures exclusive of such costs. RF is the prediction from a regression using time and two lags of total financial requirements over the 1871 to 1913 period. Since the size of government exhibits limited volatility, we judged it appropriate to use a forecasting equation based on the entire sample. The forecast of total financial requirements is assumed to be predetermined with respect to current tax structure.[18] No sign is predicted for the coefficient of RF, since no clear hypothesis can be formed on how public sector size influences tax structure.

10.3   ESTIMATION AND RESULTS

All equations were estimated for the period from 1871 to 1913 using ordinary least squares. Estimation of (10.5) explicitly enforces the government's budget restraint. Note that, since we deal with only two revenue sources, the variance–covariance structure of μ in (10.5) that results from imposing the budget restraint reduces to the simple homoscedastic case (Beggs and Strong 1982).

Preliminary estimation suggests eliminating several variables because of low statistical significance or for other reasons. The U.S. debt variable USD/N− reveals a strong downward trend following the U.S. Civil War and as a result is collinear with other variables exhibiting a trend such as POP−. Collinearity also explains why USD/N− is insignificant. United States customs (USC/N−) has very low significance, indicating that Canadian revenue structure is not influenced on a year-by-year basis by U.S. tariff structure. (Deflating U.S. customs revenue by U.S. income instead of by U.S. population does not change results.) It may be that overall tax burdens rather than specific taxes are the basis for international tax competition and, if so, we should not expect variables such as USC/N− to be significant (Hettich and Winer 1984). However, it is difficult to formulate variables reflecting competition that works in this broader manner. Finally, there is the further possibility that the influence of U.S. actions on Canadian policy is intermittent and thus not captured well by a continuous variable.

One can readily see why neither the forecast bond yield (YLDF or YLDF1) nor errors in such forecasts (YLDR1) are significant. The bond rate fluctuated

---

[17] Financial requirements or total expenditures, as in Gillespie (1991), consist of interest payments, purchases of goods and services (including administration), plus subsidies to the provinces and railroads. Financial requirements are equal to the sum of all tax revenue plus the deficit.

[18] An estimating equation that includes RF can also be interpreted as the second stage of an instrumental variables approach in which the size of government is treated as endogenous and is replaced by the instrument RF. (The t-statistics reported in the tables are not based on two-stage least-squares estimation, however.)

very moderately over the sample period, with the year-to-year change always remaining below one-half percentage point. Thus, the implications of changes in the bond yield for administrative costs were not likely to be of great interest to the government. MFG/N , the variable representing the demand for protection by manufacturers, also has very low significance.[19] We shall return to this result later.

We also dropped COOP−, representing western farm cooperatives, from the equation. In some equations this variable has a coefficient significant at 10 percent, but with the wrong (i.e., a negative) sign. The problem here is that COOP grows at a high rate after 1900, when western settlement, tariff revenue, and imports were all increasing quite rapidly. These strong trends after 1900 unfortunately make it impossible to separate the effects of the tariff base and of western farm co-ops on revenue structure. Finally, the size of government, RF, was dropped because its coefficient is not generally significant. This suggests that government size and revenue structure may have been determined independently in the nineteenth century.[20]

Four versions of the model with the remaining explanatory variables are presented in Table 10.2.[21] The difference between versions lies in the definition of the dependent variable and in the variables used to proxy anticipated imports. Additional results are provided in an appendix, which reports on an approach using revenue shares as dependent variables in a two-equation system.

Table 10.2 shows estimated standardized (beta-) coefficients and t-values for the various equations. The adjusted values of the R^2 vary from 0.76 to 0.82, while the Durbin–Watson and adjusted Box–Pierce statistics generally indicate the absence of serial correlation of the residual. Tests for heteroscedasticity based on the Breusch–Pagan chi-squared statistic indicate that no problem exists in this regard, and use of White's (1980) heteroscedasticity-consistent estimator yields essentially the same results as those reported in the table. Table 10.2 and the Appendix to this chapter demonstrate that the choice of dependent variable does not substantially affect the results except for variables representing the role of administration costs.[22]

---

[19] One should recall our discussion (in a previous footnote) of several alternatives to these variables that also proved unsuccessful in the estimating equation.

[20] RF was significant in only one equation (column 2 of Table 10.2). Using per-capita income YN and population POP- in the forecast of total revenue requirements does not substantially alter the results concerning RF or other variables.

[21] Gillespie's data on revenue structure used for the dependent variables are on a fiscal-year basis. We believe use of fiscal-year data to be more appropriate since we have no information on the pattern of revenues and expenditures within fiscal years. Because the data for explanatory variables are on a calendar-year basis, a lag in the response by government of approximately six months is built into the estimating equations.

[22] Treating IMR1, FAL/Y−, and HV/IM− as jointly endogenous variables using two-stage least squares does not alter the results either.

Table 10.2. Revenue structure, Government of Canada, 1871–1913

	Dependent variable is ln(R-CUS)/CUS		Dependent variable is DS/CUS	
	B-STD	B-STD	B-STD	B-STD
IMF	-1.65		-0.66	
	(-4.77)		(-2.17)	
IMF1		-1.40		-0.57
		(-4.52)		(-2.12)
IMR1		-0.44		-0.21
		(-3.67)		(-2.00)
POP-	2.19	2.35	1.48	1.58
	(3.23)	(3.24)	(2.49)	(2.51)
FPD/N-	-1.27	-1.35	-1.14	-1.17
	(-3.04)	(-3.08)	(-3.11)	(-3.09)
FAL/Y-	0.62	0.58	0.57	0.55
	(5.70)	(5.12)	(5.94)	(5.55)
UNION-	-0.59	-0.85	-0.40	-0.54
	(-1.36)	(-1.86)	(-1.04)	(-1.36)
EXEMPT	0.60	0.55	0.67	0.64
	(3.18)	(2.82)	(4.04)	(3.81)
OPP	0.67	0.69	0.57	0.58
	(2.59)	(2.59)	(2.53)	(2.52)
USTRF	-0.33	-0.34	-0.62	-0.62
	(-1.17)	(-1.16)	(-2.49)	(-2.45)
ADVSE	-0.03	-0.01	-0.18	-0.20
	(-0.11)	(-0.01)	(-0.88)	(-0.89)
HV/IM-	0.01	0.14	0.24	0.30
	(0.07)	(0.79)	(1.62)	(2.02)
RAIL	0.25	0.27	0.50	0.52
	(2.63)	(2.47)	(5.92)	(5.48)
R^2	.77	.76	.82	.82
D.W.	1.83	1.86	2.20	2.17
B.P. (10)	10.92	14.77	10.35	10.83
B-P	14.46	13.50	13.04	15.55

Notes to Table 10.2: Estimation using SHAZAM (White et al., 1990). B-STD = standardized regression coefficient. The constant term is not reported. "t" - statistics are in brackets. R^2 is adjusted. D.W. = Durbin-Watson statistic. B.P. (10) = adjusted Box-Pierce statistic for lag-length of 10. B-P = Breusch-Pagan heteroscedasticity test chi-squared (11 or 12 d.f.) A minus sign following a variable indicates a one-period lag.

The signs of coefficients in Table 10.2 are generally as expected. The economic variables work particularly well. The standardized regression coefficients indicate that the variables representing revenue bases (IMF or IMF1 and POP−) and the extent to which debt has been relied upon in the past (FPD/N−) have a predominant influence on revenue structure and that forecasts of revenue bases are important determinants of fiscal choices. (The choice of method used to forecast imports does affect these results.) The results for POP− and FPD/N− indicate that the government was concerned with the future excess burden of current deficits, as well as with the excess burden of current taxation, a conclusion made more forceful by the fact that POP− and FPD/N− are highly significant despite their low variance relative to that of the dependent variable.

Political factors also play a role, although they do not perform as well as the economic variables. Continuous variables representing political factors are not significant, with the exception for some equations of the variable representing the influence of labor on the tariff. UNION− in the equations using IMF1 has a t-statistic that reaches −1.86 in column two of Table 10.2 and −1.98 in the Appendix. The poor performance of continuous political variables raises the question of how to formulate appropriate measures representing the influence of political coalitions. Dennis Mueller and Peter Murrell (1985, p. 24) have argued that the most obvious indicators of interest-group strength may not be adequate proxies in many instances. In our case, for example, the size of the manufacturing sector (MFG/N−) may not reflect the political influence of manufacturers, since such influence may depend on the nature and size of political contributions. Unfortunately, data on such payments are not available. On the other hand, the power of unions may be related fairly closely to the size of their membership (proxied by UNION−) as long as union members are active voters.

As we have argued before, political influence may exercise a discontinuous impact on government decision making. The variables representing the intermittent influence of two preeminent groups who clearly tried to influence tariff policy in the sample period – manufacturers and farmers – are indeed significant.[23] The influence of U.S. tariff policy also appears to work in a discontinuous manner. Substantial changes in external constraints (USTRF) affect Canadian revenue structure in the expected direction.

---

[23] We also explored the effect of the introduction in 1879 of the system of protective tariffs called the "National Policy" because of the great deal of attention devoted to this event in Canadian economic history. As expected, the sign on a dummy variable with a step in this year (NATPOL) is negative, although NATPOL is not significant at 10 percent in any of the equations. Results for other variables do not change in a material fashion when NATPOL is added to the equation. The insignificance of NATPOL suggests that the National Policy may have been exclusively directed at tariff structure rather than also being concerned with the raising of revenue. We also considered a dummy variable representing the party in power (Liberal or Conservative), but this variable was not significant.

The third category of variables, consisting of those measuring administration costs, does not perform as well as the other two. In this case, as noted earlier, results depend on the choice of the dependent variable. The t-values are substantially larger and the coefficients have the predicted sign for both HV/IM− and ADVSE when DS/CUS is used as the dependent variable. The weak performance of these variables may reflect the difficulty of formulating proxies that accurately capture the influence of administration costs over time in a developing economy such as nineteenth century Canada. Finally, we note that in the fourth category of variables, RAIL is highly significant, indicating a possible relation between revenue and expenditure structure at least in the case where extraordinary capital expenditures did occur.

The focus of this chapter is on the implementation of a model based on expected vote maximization. While we do not systematically consider the explanation of the data by other possible approaches, one can use the results to comment on the performance of the current model in relation to other frameworks of analysis.

A simple model of government behavior that does not contain any formal link to an electoral process and that is sometimes used to explain fiscal history assumes that the government passively adjusts to variations in tax bases so as to maintain a predetermined level of public expenditures. The variation in the composition of revenues is then determined mainly by fluctuations in the major tax base, represented in our study by imports. Analysis of our results shows clearly that such a model is dominated by the one that we use. The equations containing both IMF1 and IMR1 include the entire base for the tariff since total actual imports equal the sum of these two variables. Though both variables are significant, they are not the only important or significant determinants and, when used by themselves as explanatory variables, produce an adjusted R^2 of no greater than 0.25 regardless of the choice of dependent variable.

There are alternative models in the literature that integrate economic and political behavior. However, as we argued in Chapter 2, most are not suitable for an analysis of tax structure. The median voter model, for example, has a stable equilibrium only in situations where the issue space is unidimensional; it cannot be used to analyze multidimensional choices. The one framework presenting a possible alternative to expected vote maximization is the Leviathan model (Brennan and Buchanan 1980, Kau and Rubin 1981), where the government maximizes revenues and is not constrained by any electoral process. If government acts in this manner, only economic factors matter; political factors will not affect the evolution of tax structure. Although the effects of economic variables predominate in the estimating equations, our results show that the Canadian government was also influenced by political forces. A Lagrange multiplier test for the joint significance of the variables EXEMPT, OPP,

UNION−, and USTRF yields a chi-squared statistic with four degrees of freedom (equal to the sample size times the R^2 from the auxiliary regression) of 12.9, which is clearly significant at the 95 percent level.[24]

10.4   CONCLUSION

As economists such as Schumpeter and Musgrave have long recognized, explaining the evolution of revenue systems must be a major task of positive economics. The chapter contributes to this task by demonstrating that a model explaining the pattern of revenue sources based on the probabilistic spatial voting model can be used successfully to explain the evolution over time of a complete revenue system.

There is evidence that economic, political, and administrative factors all play a role in shaping revenue structure. Economic variables reflecting factors underlying the excess burden of current and future taxation (i.e., debt) work best, perhaps because they are easiest to measure. The conclusions for the political and administrative variables are somewhat more tentative both because there are difficult data problems to overcome for the period studied and, in the case of political factors, because we still lack a full understanding of the way in which the influence on government policy occurs.

Our findings support the view that the revenue system is an integrated whole and that one must model all major revenue sources, including debt, or at least allow formally for interdependence among them. In the case of the tariff, there has been a tendency to study it apart from the revenue system as a whole, mainly because the analysis of import duties has been part of international trade rather than of public finance. In nineteenth-century Canada, borrowing and the tariff were clearly competing sources of revenue and were used jointly as fiscal instruments by the government.

The framework proposed in this paper provides a broader perspective than is usually adopted in studying fiscal institutions. The empirical investigation appears to give reasonable support to this broader view. Although the data are confined to Canada, the approach has general application and can be used to

---

[24] This test is described in Ramanathan (1995). See also Engle (1982). For purposes of comparison with the results in the second column of Table 10.2, we note that estimation without the political variables gives the following (t-statistics are given in parentheses):

$$\ln\{(R - \text{CUS})/\text{CUS}\} = -1.3 \text{ IMFI} - 0.4 \text{ IMRI} + 1.6 \text{ POP}- - 0.5 \text{ FPD/N}-$$
$$(-4.1) \qquad (-3.4) \qquad (3.5) \qquad (-1.2)$$

$$+ 0.5 \text{ FAL/Y}- + 0.2 \text{ HV/IM}- - 0.2 \text{ ADVSE}- + 0.4 \text{ RAIL.}$$
$$(4.1) \qquad (0.8) \qquad (-0.8) \qquad (3.2)$$

Adjusted $R^2 = .67$; DW $= 1.39$.

examine the evolution of fiscal systems in other democratic societies and in nations at all stages of economic development.

10.5   VARIABLES AND DATA SOURCES

Variable	*Definition*	*Sources*
ADVSE	Dummy variable with positive step in 1886 (switch to specific tariff rates)	(3)
COOP	Membership in western farm coops	(11),(12)
CUS	Tariff revenue of Govt. of Canada	(1)
DS	Deficit of Govt. of Canada (negative if a surplus)	(1)
EXEMPT	Dummy variable with positive step in 1883 (tariff exemption granted for many raw materials)	(3)
FAL/Y	Total liabilities of commercial failures per dollar of GNP	(4) p. 194, and Y
FPD/N	Total federal and provincial debt outstanding (cumulated values of DS and provincial deficits) per capita	(6) 1932/1933, p. 736 and DS, POP
HV/IM	High-value, low-volume imports (spirits and wine, fancy goods and silks, satins and laces) as proportion of total imports	(3) pp. 628–29
IM	Total imports	(2) series G384
IMF	Forecast of IM based on regression using a constant, time, two lags of IM, and two lags of YN	
IMF1	One-step-ahead forecast of IM based on moving regression using a constant and two lags of IM (with five observations)	
IMR1	Residual from preceding forecast	
MFG/N	GNP originating in manufacturing per capita	(7) Table 1, and POP
MN/N	Total employees in manufacturing industries per capita, census data interpolated linearly	(2) series R21, and POP
NATPOL	Dummy variable with positive step in 1879 (introduction of National Policy)	
OPP	Dummy variable with positive steps in 1894 (tariff reductions on wide class of consumer goods and agricultural implements) and in 1898 (British Preferential Tariff of 33-1/3 percent)	(3)

POP	Total population	(5) pp. 240–1
R	Total financial requirements, Govt. of Canada, consisting of net interest payments, purchases of goods and services including administration, plus subsidies to provinces and railways	(7)
RAIL	Dummy variable = 1 in 1886 and 1909, = 0 clsc	
RF	Forecast of R based on regression using a constant, time, and two lags of R, 1870–1913	
UNION	Number of union locals	(10)
USC/N	U.S. tariff revenue per capita	(8) Series Y260, Series A7
USD/N	Debt of U.S. federal government per capita	(8) Series Y494
USTRF	Dummy variable with positive steps in 1890 (McKinnlcy tariff) and 1897 (Dingley tariff)	
Y	GNP at market prices	(7) Table 1
YLD	Average yield on Dominion Government Bonds	(9)
YLDF	Forecast of YLD based on regression using a constant, time, and two lags of YLD, 1870–1913	
YLDF1	One-step-ahead forecast of YLD based on moving regression using a constant and two lags of YLD (with five observations)	
YLDF1	Residual from preceding forecast	
YN	GNP per capita	Y and POP

Sources of Data

1. Gillespie (1991) (c)
2. *Historical Statistics of Canada* (Leacy 1983)
3. Perry (1955, vol. 2)
4. Skelton (1913)
5. Firestone (1958)
6. Canada Year Book (various years)
7. Urquhart (1986)
8. *Historical Statistics of the United States* (1975)
9. Rich (1988)
10. *Labor Gazette* 1902–03, 1910–11; *Labor Organizations in Canada* (Department of Labor) (1955); Forsey (1982); Logan (1928)

11. Stiles (1972)
12. Wood (1924)

Notes

a. Figures for 1871 set to 1872 value, and figures for 1912 and 1913 are set to 1911 value.
b. Figures for 1902 are average of Forsey and Logan figures, with analogous adjustment for 1903–10. We have taken the Logan and Forsey figures as correct when there is a conflict with data from the *Labor Gazette*.
c. Data on fiscal-year basis.

APPENDIX TO CHAPTER 10: TWO-EQUATION SYSTEM ESTIMATION

The estimating equation developed in the chapter uses as the dependent variable the log of the ratio of all revenue less the tariff to tariff revenue. However, another approach to estimation of the model is to estimate two separate equations, one explaining the share of all revenue except the tariff in total financial requirements, $(R - \text{CUS})/R$, and one explaining the share of the tariff in total requirements, CUS/R:

$$(R - \text{CUS})/R = \beta_1^0 + \beta_1 X + \varepsilon_1, \qquad (10\text{A}.1)$$

$$\text{CUS}/R = \beta_2^0 + \beta_2 X + \varepsilon_2, \qquad (10\text{A}.2)$$

subject to $(R - \text{CUS})/R + (\text{CUS}/R) = 1$, where β_i^0 is a constant term, β_i is a row vector of coefficients for the column vector of explanatory variables X, ε_i is an error term, and time subscripts have been omitted for convenience.

It should be noted that the constraint on the sum of the values of the dependent variables implies $\beta_1^0 + \beta_2^0 = 1$ and $\beta_1 + \beta_2 = 0$, where the latter sum is across the coefficients for a given element of X at each point in time, and that $\varepsilon_1 + \varepsilon_2 = 0$ in each period. The two equations must therefore be estimated under the constraint that the two revenue shares sum to unity in each period, and this can be accomplished by using exactly the same set of explanatory variables in each equation (see e.g. Bodkin 1974).

The results for the two-equation system are presented in Table 10A.1 using the same explanatory variables as in Table 10.2. If a variable such as IMF has a negative coefficient in Table 10.2, then it has a negative coefficient in the equation for $(R\text{-CUS})/R$ and a positive coefficient in the equation for CUS/R. The opposite is true for variables, such as POP−, that have positive coefficients in Table 10.2. The pattern of significance of variables as well as the relative

Table 10A.1. Estimation of two-equation system explaining revenue structure of Government of Canada, 1871–1913

	Dependent variable is (R-CUS)/R		Dependent variable is CUS/R	
	B-STD	B-STD	B-STD ·	B-STD
IMF	-1.56 (-4.57)		1.56 (4.57)	
IMF1		-1.30 (-4.24)		1.30 (4.24)
IMR1		-0.41 (-3.46)		0.40 (3.46)
POP-	2.21 (3.30)	2.32 (3.22)	-2.21 (-3.30)	-2.32 (-3.22)
FPD/N-	-1.27 (-3.11)	-1.34 (-3.08)	1.27 (3.11)	1.34 (3.08)
FAL/Y-	0.65 (6.03)	0.60 (5.41)	-0.65 (-6.03)	-0.60 (-5.41)
UNION-	-0.59 (-1.39)	-0.90 (-1.98)	0.59 (1.39)	0.90 (1.98)
EXEMPT	0.61 (3.29)	0.56 (2.92)	-0.61 (-3.29)	-0.56 (-2.92)
OPP	0.69 (2.70)	0.70 (2.67)	-0.69 (-2.70)	-0.70 (-2.67)
USTRF	-0.34 (-1.22)	-0.34 (-1.18)	0.34 (1.22)	0.34 (1.18)
ADVSE	-0.04 (-0.17)	-0.03 (-0.13)	0.04 (0.17)	0.03 (0.13)
HV/IM-	0.03 (0.15)	0.15 (0.85)	-0.03 (-0.15)	-0.15 (-0.85)
RAIL	0.27 (2.83)	0.29 (2.66)	-0.27 (-2.83)	-0.29 (-2.66)
R^2	.78	.76	.78	.76
D.W.	1.84	1.87	1.84	1.87
B.P. (10)	12.60	15.99	12.60	15.99
B-P	13.33	13.49	13.33	13.49

See notes to Table 10.2.

size of beta coefficients is essentially the same as in Table 10.2. Thus, estimation of the two-equation system of revenue shares indicates that the results in Table 10.2 are quite robust.

PART FIVE

POLITICAL INSTITUTIONS AND TAXATION

CHAPTER 11

Tax Systems in Congressional and Parliamentary Countries

> Institutions are the rules of the game in a society or, more formally,
> are the humanly devised constraints that shape human interaction.
> In consequence they structure incentives in human exchange,
> whether political, social, or economic.
>
> Douglass North (1990, p. 3)

Institutions do not appear explicitly in the voting model that serves as the framework for the preceding chapters. Nonetheless, the institutions of democracy are essential to the meaning of the model. It makes sense to use voting analysis as a basis for the study of fiscal systems in situations where political competition for public office is a well-established tradition. Democratic institutions are therefore an essential aspect of any such investigation, even if they are not formally part of the mathematical formulation.

In this chapter we investigate the role that certain institutional arrangements in democratic states may play in the determination of tax structure. In particular, we consider the nature of intragovernmental or structural competition in the congressional system of the United States and the parliamentary system of Canada, and we investigate the importance of differences in such competition for the determination of tax structure in the two countries.

Structural competition is an aspect of political systems that differs from competitive behavior related to political parties. The essence of such competition is best captured by the expression "checks and balances." Following Albert Breton (1996), we may say that it exists in any situation where there are competing centers of power within a governing structure. Checks and balances may arise from a written constitution, or they may result from less formal institutional arrangements creating countervailing forces within a government, or between governments in a federal system.

This chapter shows that intragovernmental competition has important consequences for policy outcomes. We compare two countries where checks and balances operate in significantly different ways. The United States has a formal division of political powers involving the president, Congress, and the courts. In contrast, Canada employs a parliamentary system where the division between the executive and legislative branches is much less pronounced and where the courts, at least until recently, have played a more restricted role.

Although structural competition is singled out for emphasis, it cannot be separated entirely from other elements of the political process. Tax systems are also affected by federal competition and by international pressures arising from the mobility of capital and human resources across national boundaries. Since these factors operate quite differently or with different force in the two countries, they must be taken into account in any comparison of tax structures. In principle, allowance should also be made for possible differences in the operation of electoral and bureaucratic competition in the United States and Canada. We would contend, however, that such differences are of lesser importance for the present investigation, since we shall focus on very broad features of the two tax systems.

We begin the analysis with a description of checks and balances and of the policy process relating to tax matters operating at the federal level in the two countries. Next we recall how tax structure can be considered an endogenous outcome of the political process. The influence of economic factors and international pressures is dealt with in a subsequent section. This sets the stage for several hypotheses on how observed features of structural competition in the two countries will result in differences in the two tax systems.[1] We then evaluate these hypotheses in the light of available evidence. The chapter ends with a short set of concluding remarks on the success and limitations of this type of investigation.

11.1 STRUCTURAL COMPETITION AND THE TAX POLICY PROCESS

A review of the nature and functioning of U.S. institutions shows that the formal separation of powers between the executive and the legislature has a determining influence on how tax policy is made. The division of Congress into two houses that are elected according to different rules also has a significant impact. (The courts, though essential for the functioning of the whole system, do not play a direct role in the making of tax policy.)

Major tax proposals generally originate with the president, who sends them to the House of Representatives, where they are referred to the Ways and Means Committee.[2] Here they undergo a thorough process of review and rewriting, with formal and often lengthy public hearings a part of the process.

---

[1] Breton (1996, Chap. 4) also investigates the effects of differences between congressional and Parliamentary systems. However, he concentrates on the opposite side of the budget and on the balancing of aggregate spending and total revenues, and he is primarily concerned with differences in policy processes. Our focus is on the implications of political systems for tax policy outcomes.

[2] The description of the tax policy process in the United States relies primarily on Pechman (1987, Chap. 3).

Eventually a bill is sent to the floor of the House, where it is voted on under a rule restricting the ability of House members to offer amendments. Once a bill has been passed, it goes to the Senate.

The relevant committee in the Senate is the Finance Committee, which now begins its own process of redrafting and hearings. The result may be a bill differing significantly from the House version. Debate in the full Senate is less restricted than in the House, with amendments of a substantive nature being offered from the floor. After passage, the Senate bill, together with the House version, goes to a conference committee where a compromise is fashioned. The result must be approved by both houses, whereupon the bill is sent to the president, who must sign it into law or veto it within a prescribed period. (A veto can be overridden by a two-thirds majority in Congress.)

Congress generally responds to proposals made by the president, but it can also act on its own. Initiatives may be taken in either house. Although the Constitution states that revenue bills must originate in the House of Representatives, the Senate can take the lead by attaching major provisions or new tax legislation to minor bills that are sent over to the House. The tax policy process is further complicated by so-called technical bills, miscellaneous bills, and special-interest legislation containing tax provisions, which are inserted into the congressional agenda by members as feasible. Both the legislative and the executive branches have their own extensive bureaucracies for dealing with the analysis and preparation of tax bills. The president relies primarily on the Treasury, although the Council of Economic Advisors and the Office of Management and Budget also play a role in tax policy. Congress has the Joint Committee on Taxation, a standing committee with a permanent staff that serves primarily a research function. In addition, there is the Congressional Budget Office, available to both houses, and tax committees also have their own permanent staffs.

The tax policy process in Canada differs radically from the process just described for the United States.[3] In the parliamentary system, the executive and legislative branches are linked closely, with the prime minister and his cabinet serving as elected members of Parliament. Since defeat of a major tax bill (or even part of it) would result in the government's fall and in a new election, tax bills are in almost all cases passed by Parliament without substantive changes.[4] As head of the majority party, the prime minister knows that he has the required number of votes for passage (strict party discipline is observed in all such votes).

---

[3] The tax policy process in Canada is described in Good (1980) and Hartle (1982).

[4] Only two budgets (1974 and 1979) have been defeated since 1867 (see Table 11.2). The defeat of the Turner budget in 1974 may have been engineered by the government. A third budget, in 1981, faced extraordinary opposition and was partly withdrawn by the government.

The most important phase of the tax policy process in Canada occurs within the federal bureaucracy. Until recently, the fashioning of federal tax bills has been the almost exclusive domain of the Department of Finance. The main players are a group of selected officials in the department, especially those appointed to the Budget Committee, and the minister of finance. Ministers heading other departments and even the prime minister have exercised only a minor influence, although it must be remembered that those preparing major revenue bills would try to anticipate (and avoid) major objections from other parts of the government.[5]

To a Canadian official in the Department of Finance, the U.S. tax policy process must appear cumbersome and unwieldy. Indeed, the length of the process is one of the major differences between the two countries. In Canada, "it usually takes six weeks to prepare a budget."[6] (As in the United States, tax matters are studied on an ongoing basis, and background research is therefore available at the start of this period.) Budget debate in parliament lasts up to six days. The remaining steps are usually also quite brief and do not, in any case, involve substantive changes. After assured passage by the Senate, the bill receives royal assent, thus becoming law.[7] In the United States, a lengthy period will generally intervene between the president's message to Congress and final enactment. Bills are occasionally passed into law within a month, but longer delays are the general rule. In the postwar period, delays have lasted as long as 44 months, with 6 to 11 months being most common.[8] It must also be noted that some proposed tax bills die in Congress, thus never reaching enactment.

Length is but one aspect of the process. A more basic difference lies in the number of participants who have a political base of their own. Tax legislation in the United States requires extensive negotiations among such players, a costly process that occasionally results in failure to reach any agreement. As one observer comments: "practically every major presidential tax proposal is

---

[5] On the role of the prime minister, see Hartle (1982, pp. 27–30) and Breton (1996, Chap. 4). It appears that prime ministers mainly influenced the budget stance, but that they did not get involved in specifics. According to Hartle: "The impression that most [interviewees] gave was that while they recognized the Prime Minister's right to demand change in a budget, the [Finance] Department would have been both surprised and annoyed if he had actually done so." The power of Finance is indicated by the following comment by a former Minister of Finance: "When Jack Austin, the Prime Minister's principal secretary at the time, attempted to create a semi-formal and permanent advisory group from outside, I was Minister. I gave [the] Prime Minister the choice between the group and my resignation" (p. 29).

[6] Hartle (1982, p. 24).

[7] The government can introduce a Ways and Means motion allowing it to implement tax changes while waiting for tax bills to pass through the full process.

[8] Table 3-1 in Pechman (1987, p. 40) gives a summary of legislative history for major tax bills enacted between 1948 and 1982.

thoroughly revised by Congress, and not a few are either ignored or rejected outright."[9]

Because it involves a greater number of participants and is carried out at least in part in the open, the U.S. process generates a large amount of public information relating to the tax system. This contrasts with the famous secrecy provisions in Canada, which ensure that no information on particular provisions becomes public before the budget speech is read in Parliament. Since subsequent debate is usually brief and of a different nature than in the U.S. Congress, the Canadian policy process yields a decidedly smaller flow of public information concerning tax matters.[10]

11.2   TAX STRUCTURE AS AN EQUILIBRIUM IN A COMPETITIVE POLITICAL SYSTEM

Actual tax systems are the outcome of many past policy choices. Legal tax codes are lengthy and complex documents, often running to thousands of pages. As Pechman points out with regard to the U.S. tax code: "Few people have mastered its technicalities and nuances."[11]

We have argued throughout the book that tax structures can be understood as an equilibrium outcome of the political process. If governments maximize the probability of reelection, they take account of how voters evaluate public goods and services and how they respond to the loss in full income created by taxation. At the same time, governments are constrained by the ability of taxpayers to adjust economic behavior in order to escape the full impact of taxation.

Because taxpayers vary in economic characteristics and political responses, it would be to the government's advantage to treat each taxpayer-voter differently. However, complete differentiation would create large administrative costs. Since resources spent on administration reduce the government's ability to provide public goods, which are valued positively by voters, political decision makers will balance the gains from differentiated treatment against the loss resulting from a lower level of public output. As argued in Chapters 3 and 4, this process leads to the creation of all the basic elements of tax structure. Economic activities are combined into tax bases, taxpayers are grouped into rate brackets across bases, and special provisions are used to create desired subgroupings. There will be a unique politically optimal tax structure at any point in time. As exogenous forces change, the government will attempt to

---

[9] Pechman (1987, p. 37).

[10] Although our concern here is with the tax policy process, one may note that differences between the expenditure budgetary processes in the United States and Canada, as described in Breton (1996, Chap. 4), are analogous.

[11] Pechman (1987, p. 38).

establish a new equilibrium conforming to the new situation. Thus, tax systems undergo continual change over time.

The model of tax structure presented in Part I of this book serves as a theoretical background for the present inquiry. Although it does not contain detailed political institutions, it implies that different political constraints on optimization by governments will result in observable differences in tax structure. At the same time, it makes clear that economic responses also enter in a systematic way and must be considered along with political factors.

11.3   DOMESTIC AND INTERNATIONAL ECONOMIC INFLUENCES ON TAX SYSTEMS

Given the major differences in institutions and in the process of policy formation, one may expect tax systems in the United States and Canada to look quite different. However, policy makers respond not only to the exigencies of politics but also to pressures reflecting national and international economic forces. Indeed, economic pressures may override political factors in many cases.

Domestic economic influences on tax structure are much alike in the two countries, with both having a similar industrial structure and organization of agriculture. Since individuals have much the same types and sources of income on both sides of the border, and since other relevant factors (e.g., income levels, patterns of consumption, business practices, and attitudes toward self-reporting) are quite similar, we would expect the sorting or grouping process referred to in the previous section to yield comparable fiscal institutions.

In Canada's case, international economic pressures are probably even more important than domestic factors. Canada has strong incentives to make the tax treatment of income from capital and, to a lesser extent, of income from wages and salaries similar to such treatment in the United States because of the international mobility of capital and skilled human resources. Since the Canadian economy relies heavily on foreign investment, primarily from the United States, it must offer after-tax rates of return similar to rates available in competing markets.[12]

Although the same yields to private investment can be achieved under different fiscal institutions, similarity in tax structures facilitates international comparisons and is an advantage to firms operating on both sides of the border. Over the years, Canada has chosen to adapt its tax system to its U.S. counterpart. There are many instances where substantial changes in Canadian taxation followed such changes in the United States, with the reform of 1988 being a

---

[12] Although there are tax credits available to U.S. companies operating in Canada, such offsets in the United States to tax liabilities incurred in Canada are not unlimited.

good example. Like the U.S. Tax Reform Act of 1986, the Canadian tax measures of 1988 lower and simplify marginal rates under the personal income tax, expand the tax base of the personal and corporate income taxes, and adjust corporate tax rates downward – all to maintain alignment of tax treatment.[13]

Forces toward conformity are strong, but there is room for significant differences in fiscal institutions, particularly with respect to the taxation of human capital, real property, natural resources, and consumption, where international mobility is a less important constraint. Economic influences do not preclude the importance of political factors or the significance of the policy process for tax structure.

11.4 SOME HYPOTHESES

Starting from the description of the policy process in Section 11.1, we propose several hypotheses on how differences in structural competition affect tax systems in the two countries.

The existence of checks and balances increases the cost of reaching and enforcing agreements. As indicated, this can result in large delays and even in the eventual abandonment of proposals. We may therefore expect participants in the policy process to look for ways to economize on agreements and political enforcement costs.[14] One way to achieve such economies is to remove particularly contentious issues from the regular process so that the same issues do not have to be reexamined on a repeated basis. This line of reasoning leads to the following hypothesis:

H1. The United States will make more extensive use of earmarking and trust funds in structuring its tax system.

The length of the tax policy process in the United States also makes it more difficult to use discretionary tax changes as a tool of economic policy. This suggests a difference in the use of policy instruments for stabilization and other purposes in the two countries. Hence:

H2. Canada will make more extensive use of discretionary tax policy, and rely less heavily on automatic fiscal responses, than the United States.

---

[13] For a discussion of changes in U.S. and Canadian tax legislation in the 1980s, see Musgrave (1987), Ort (1988), and the various comparisons in Shoven and Whalley (1992a).

[14] Political bargains or vote trades necessary to reach agreements must be enforced if political markets are to function effectively. Some research (Liebowitz and Tollison 1980, Weingast and Marshall 1988) shows that the committee system performs this role in the U.S. Congress. Breton (1996) argues that, in parliamentary systems, such trades are enforced by senior bureaucrats who have legitimate access to cabinet documents. This may be why it is necessary in parliamentary systems to have a permanent and nonpartisan civil service.

Another consequence of the length of the policy process relates to the government's ability to readjust tax structure. Exogenous shocks may lead more rapidly to public debate in the United States because of the greater openness of the congressional system. However, resolution of the issue will occur more quickly in a parliamentary system, where the government can take more rapid action. Indeed, many issues are acted upon in Canada without public or parliamentary debate. Thus we have a third hypothesis:

H3. Canada will respond more promptly to exogenous economic shocks by restructuring taxation.

Separation of powers between the legislature and executive creates problems of agent control between branches. Congress writes laws, but it must rely on the executive branch for their administration. But the president is elected independently and so has his own political constituency and interests, which will not necessarily coincide with those of Congress. No similar agent problem exists in a parliamentary system. (Political decision makers in both systems face problems of delegation with regard to the bureaucracy.)[15] This argument is summarized as follows:

H4. Tax laws in the United States will be more complex and have more special provisions, reflecting legislative attempts to control the executive.

The more open process of policy formation in the United States creates more public information on planned changes and on the impact of existing taxes. Together with the fact that decision makers involved in the process represent constituencies covering different geographical areas, this leads to a demand for policy compromises that are perceived publicly as equitable and as regionally fair. In Canada, where federal tax policy is formed mainly within

---

[15] It might be argued that competition among bureaus in Canada substitutes to some extent for competition among branches of government in the United States. However, bureaus in the United States have more entry points – they can make themselves heard in Congress as well as within the executive budgeting process. Bureaucratic competition operates therefore in both countries as an additional factor, and it is not clear where it has a more important influence. As far as Canada is concerned, one should note that cabinet solidarity limits the scope of other ministers to undo tax policies by the Minister of Finance through subsidies or regulation in their own policy areas (Breton 1996, Chap. 4).

the Department of Finance, public perception of particular tax instruments plays a less important role. We therefore have a fifth hypothesis:

H5. The United States will place greater emphasis on tax bases that have wide public support and are perceived to have a fair regional distribution.

A final point relates to the interaction of checks and balances with federalism. Under a parliamentary system, the central executive can engage in direct negotiations with units at the lower level of government with the expectation that agreements reached in this manner will be ratified by Parliament. (Similarly, heads of provincial governments can expect passage by their legislatures.) In the Canadian case, direct negotiations between levels of government are further facilitated by the relatively small number of provinces. The United States faces a quite different situation. The formal division of powers at the national and state levels, together with the larger number of states, prevents any directly negotiated agreements. This suggests a sixth hypothesis:

H6. Federal–provincial relations are a direct influence on Canadian tax structure, whereas fiscal systems at the two levels are largely independent in the United States.

11.5   TESTING THE HYPOTHESES

We shall use descriptive and qualitative data consistent with the proposed hypotheses to support our main thesis: Structural political competition matters for policy outcomes. Some of the data we rely upon are for 1985 or for a short interval close to that date. Other data cover the decade between 1970 and 1980 or refer to a longer time period that ends in 1985. Exact dates are provided in the tables and in the footnotes, and all data refer to the central governments in both countries. Given available sources in the two countries, these choices result in a reasonably consistent body of data with which to "test" the various hypotheses. Some further comments on methodology will be found in the concluding section of the chapter.

We started by proposing in hypothesis H1 that political decision makers in the United States would make more extensive use of earmarking and trust funds in order to remove contentious issues from the regular decision process and to economize on agreement and political enforcement costs. The most important observation bearing on this hypothesis concerns the treatment of income security, an issue that is politically very sensitive.

Income security has two components: (i) public pensions linked in some manner to contributions made during the recipients' earning lives, and (ii) various types of public assistance related to some measure of present need. Both countries make use of special funds financed by payroll taxes for the pension component, with the needs component coming out of general revenues. However, in the United States, the pension component represents a much larger proportion of total resources devoted to income security – about 63 percent in contrast to about 32 percent in Canada for 1986–87.[16] This difference in approach is also reflected in the relative importance of payroll taxes in the two countries, as shown in Table 11.1. In the United States in 1985, payroll taxes of the central government earmarked for social security make up 28 percent of its total revenues, while in Canada the corresponding figure amounts to only about 10 percent.[17] Moreover, as Table 11.1 indicates, the greater emphasis on payroll taxes at the federal level in the United States has persisted for a considerable period of time. The United States has thus provided a significantly larger proportion of payments for income security through a separate trust fund financed with earmarked taxes. One may also note that the heavier emphasis on earnings-related payments in the United States may represent a further attempt to lessen potential political controversy surrounding issues of income maintenance.

The special status of social security as a policy issue in the United States is confirmed by an episode that has no counterpart in the Canadian experience. In the late 1970s and the early 1980s, widespread concern arose over the future solvency of the social security fund. In his first term of office, President Reagan appointed a special bipartisan commission to study the present and future conditions of the social security system. The system is financed by payroll taxes on a pay-as-you-go basis, so judgments concerning future solvency depend crucially on projections of economic and demographic variables, an area where there is considerable latitude for debate and disagreement. In this instance, both the president and Congress were intent on avoiding controversy. Recommendations made by the commission in 1983 were proposed by the

---

[16] Figures are for fiscal year 1986–87. For the United States, see the *Economic Report of the President*, 1987, Table B-74. The information for Canada is taken from *The National Finances, 1986–87*, Chapter 8. Health and unemployment insurance expenditures are excluded, and the Canadian figure includes the Quebec Pension Plan (Cansim D11231 for calendar year 1986) in addition to the Canada Pension Plan.

[17] The figures for Canada include unemployment insurance as well as contributions to the Canada and Quebec pension plans. Despite this, the U.S. reliance on employment taxes for the financing of social security is still more than twice that found in Canada in 1985.

Table 11.1. Composition of major revenue sources, federal Governments of Canada and the United States, selected years 1929 to 1985 (cash flow basis, as percent of total financial requirements)

Year(a)	Persona(b)		Employment(c)		Corporation		Sales & Excises		Customs		Other(d)		Deficit(d,e)	
	Can.	U.S.	Can.	U.S.	Can.	U.S.	Can.	U.S.	Can.	U.S.	Can.	U.S.	Can.	U.S.
1929	6.8	40.0	--	--	9.5	42.8	31.9	18.6	51.5	20.0(f)	8.5	9.6	-23.1	31.0
1955	28.4	43.2	3.4	11.5	22.8	26.1	23.8	13.2	8.5	0.9	7.7	0.6	5.4	4.4
1985	26.3	36.0	10.3	28.0	8.4	6.4	9.2	3.8	3.4	1.3	8.1	2.1	34.3	22.4

Notes to Table 11.1:

a) Fiscal year ending in year named.

b) Includes estate and gift taxes (U.S.), and succession duties (Can.).

c) Includes payroll taxes (U.S.), unemployment insurance contributions (Can.), and contributions to Canada Pension Plan. Also includes employee contributions for federal retirement and supplementary medical insurance (U.S.).

d) Includes earnings of Federal Reserve Banks (U.S.), special energy taxes and charges (Can.), and investment income of Canada Pension Plan. Excludes other return on investments (Can.) and foreign exchange transactions (Can.).

e) " - " indicates surplus

f) Estimate

Sources: Canada 1929 and 1955 from Gillespie (1991) and calculations by authors; Canada 1985 from *The National Finances 1986-87*, Tables 5.5, 6.3. United States 1929 from *Historical Statistics of the U.S.* (1975), Tables Y339 - 373 and Y567 - 589; United States 1955 from Pechman (1987), Tables D-1, D-4; United States 1985 from *Economic Report of the President 1987*, Table B-74.

president as legislation and enacted promptly by Congress without significant change or lengthy debate – a substantial departure from normal budgetary processes. Special financing arrangements removing social security from the regular budgetary process were joined by a special political course of action removing the issue even farther from the usual decision-making process.

Debate over the solvency of the Canada Pension Plan has of course occurred in Canada from time to time as the population has aged. However, in contrast to the American experience, such debate has not lead to substantial departures from the normal budgetary process.

According to H2 we expect Canada to make more extensive use of discretionary tax policy. Evidence concerning this hypothesis is presented in Tables 11.2–11.4. Table 11.2 lists major discretionary tax changes undertaken by the central governments in both countries over the period 1970–80. Because the Canadian economy is highly integrated with that of the United States, it is unlikely that differences in the history of discretionary tax policy over this period would have been due to substantial differences in macroeconomic experience and in the demand for stabilization.[18] Indeed, one may suspect that the greater reserves of oil and natural gas in Canada relative to domestic consumption reduced the need for macroeconomic policy responses in Canada to the oil shocks of 1973 and 1979. Yet Table 11.2 shows that there were about twice as many large, discretionary tax changes in Canada as in the United States.

The evidence in Table 11.2 is reinforced by calculations of the OECD (Organization for Economic Cooperation and Development) presented in Table 11.3, concerning the source of changes in personal income tax liabilities from 1975 to 1982, a period which includes the second oil shock of 1979 and the 1981–82 recession. After allowing for the effects on tax liabilities of changes in the number of tax units, in average income, in distribution, and in fiscal drag due to growth in real income and inflation, the OECD finds that the change in tax liabilities due to discretionary policy and formal indexation is about 1.6 times as great in Canada as in the United States over a similar period. (The U.S. data extend to 1983.) Most of the change in tax liabilities in Canada *not* accounted for by automatic responses to economic conditions are attributed to the effects of formal indexation, which might appear to represent automatic rather than discretionary tax policy. However, although indexation of the personal income tax was introduced by the federal government in Canada in 1974, Table 11.4 indicates that the nature of indexation has been altered sub-

---

[18] Because Canada is a small open economy, the source of macroeconomic shocks is different there than in the United States. Nonetheless, integration of the two economies produces a macroeconomic history in Canada similar to that in the United States.

Table 11.2. Major tax changes, United States and Canada, 1970–1980

United States		Canada	
Title	Revenue impact (billions, U.S.)	Title	Revenue impact (billions, Can.)
Revenue Act, 1971	- 8.0	Tax Reform Proposals, 1971/72 (inclusion in income of 1/2 capital gains)	- 0.32
		Budget, June 1971 (removal of 3% surtax on personal and corporate income)	- 0.39
		Program, Oct. 1971 (temporary personal and corporate tax cuts)	- 0.40
		Budget, May 1972 (corporate tax reduction; increased depreciation allowances)	- 0.61
		Budget, Feb. 1973 (indexing of personal income tax, 1974 and personal tax cuts)	- 2.72
		Budget, May 1974 (tax increase for oil & mining corps.; home ownership plan; $1,000 interest income deduction)	- 0.49
Tax Reduction Act, 1975	- 22.8	Budget, Nov. 1974 (long list of changes; budget defeated)	- 2.17 (74&75)
		Budget, June 1975 (oil related excises)	+ 0.43
Tax Reform Act, 1976	+ 1.6		
Tax Reduction and Simplification Act, 1977	- 8.6	Budget, March 1977 (increased investment tax credits; long list of tax cuts)	-1.53
		Budget, April 1978 (sales tax cut; child tax credit introduced)	- 0.84
Revenue Act, 1978	- 18.9	Budget, November 1978 (sales tax reduction)	- 1.53
		Budget, December 1979 (increase in excises on fuels; energy tax credit; other substantial changes; budget defeated)	+2.70
Crude Oil Windfall Profits Tax Act, 1980	+12.2	Financial Statement, April 1980 (new energy taxes, corporate surtax)	+0.49

Notes to Table 11.2: U.S. Sources - Pechman (1987, Table 3-1). Canadian Sources - Gillespie (1978, Table A-1) and Doman (1980, Appendix 1). The U.S. list is based on Pechman's personal judgement of what is a "major" tax change. The Canadian list involves revenue changes at least 1/10 as great as the Tax Reform Act of 1976, as well as a "substantial" change in tax structure.

Omitted Canadian budgets (and revenue impact) are Budget December 1970 (+ 0.17) and Budget May 1976 (+0.19). The defeat of budgets (and therefore the government) in 1974 and 1979 are unique in Canadian fiscal history. No other budgets have been defeated in the period from 1867 to 1998.

Table 11.3. Overall breakdown of the change in income tax liabilities into six explanatory components as percentage of tax liabilities in the base year

	base year	compari-son year	tax liabilities in base year	change in no. of tax units	change in average income	distribu-tional effect	real fiscal drag	nominal fiscal drag	effects of indexation and changes in legislation	tax liabilities in compari-son year
			(1)	(2)	(3)	(4)	(5)	(6)	(7)	(8)
Canada	1975	1982	100	18.4	113.0	1.3	4.5	102.3	-106.6 (-99.0)	233.0
United States	1975	1982	100	16.7	89.2	7.1	3.9	69.7	-64.8	221.7

Notes to Table 11.3: The effect of formal indexation provisions is shown in parentheses in column (7).

Source: OECD, *Personal Income Tax Systems Under Changing Economic Conditions*, Paris, 1986, Table 4.2

Table 11.4.   History of indexation of the personal income tax in Canada

Date	Measure
1974	Brackets and exemptions fully indexed.
1983/84	Indexing limited to 6% in 1983 and 5% in 1984 as anti-inflation measure.
1984	Exemption for dependents de-indexed.
1985	Full indexing of brackets resumed.
1986	Indexing limited to inflation rate less 3%.

Compound effect on tax brackets and exemptions since 1973 = + 161%.

Notes to Table 11.4: Source - *The National Finances, 1986-87*, p. 7:5. The U.S. personal income tax system was partially indexed beginning in 1986. See Pechman (1987, p. 114).

stantially four times since its inception. In Canada, indexation appears to be another instrument of discretionary policy, no less subject to legislated change than most other aspects of tax structure. On the other hand, we suspect that the indexation of federal personal income taxes introduced in the United States in 1986 will not be subject to congressional manipulation to the extent that it has been in Canada.

Hypothesis H3 concerns the speed of policy response in the two countries to the same sort of information. We do not know of any studies that have attempted to measure systematically the policy lag between recognition of a need for legislation and the passage of legislation by type of exogenous shock to a political equilibrium, and we cannot suggest any rough measures that would provide a quick test of the hypothesis. The tax policy lags in the two countries (discussed in Section 11.1) are suggestive of a longer lag in the United States, but this is an average over all types of legislative responses; the timing and nature of shocks is not controlled.

The next hypothesis (H4) concerns the complexity of tax systems. No direct measures of complexity for the United States and Canada are available, but such complexity should be reflected in tax forms and formal legislation. As a first attempt at testing H4, one may count the number of pages in the personal income-tax forms of each country. Excluding explanatory text, the U.S. federal form has 18 pages; the Canadian form has only 14, including 1 page related to the federal collection of provincial income-tax revenue. In the United States, unlike in Canada, state income tax is not collected by the federal government, a situation we shall return to in the context of H6. If we compare federal and state forms in the United States with the Canadian system of joint federal–provincial collection, we find that the U.S. system requires 22 pages.[19] The U.S. system thus appears, by this simple measure, to be substantially more complicated.

A similar analysis of the relevant personal and corporate income tax acts in both countries reinforces the impression given by the comparison of tax forms. A complete *Income Tax Act* for Canada was published in 1970. The English version of this act has 212 one-column pages. The United States *Internal Revenue Code*, title 26, has the equivalent of 2,234 one-column pages (1,117 two-column pages). The print size in both acts is approximately the same. This indicates a much greater degree of complexity in the U.S. system.

The passage of time does not appear to have altered this conclusion. By 1982, the U.S. Code had grown to the equivalent of 4,104 one-column pages (2,052 two-column pages in two volumes). The Canadian code is not available in a codified form for this date, but a standard *annotated* version (Stikeman 1983) required 1,446 pages, approximately equivalent to 2,170 of the standard one-column pages.

It might be argued that the much larger population of the United States requires a much more complex tax system. The United States has more than ten times the population of Canada, yet there is no reason to believe that the tax system would be ten times as complex. In the equilibrium model of tax structure developed in Part I, complexity of tax structure depends on the nature of the economic and political heterogeneity that the government must address in its search for electoral success, as well as on the administrative cost of doing so. The United States and Canada are broadly similar with respect to complexity of industrial organization, the degree of cultural and regional diversity, and the degree of political diversity. Furthermore, there is no reason to believe that the technology of administering taxes and administration costs differ markedly between the two countries.

Hypothesis H5 states that the United States will rely more heavily on taxes that have wide support and are perceived as regionally fair. The suggestion is supported by data on revenue composition in Table 11.1. Figures for 1929, 1955, and 1985 show that the United States has consistently placed a greater emphasis on the personal income tax, the source of revenues best fitting the description of a preferred tax given in the hypothesis. Although the gap between the two countries has narrowed since 1929, when the United States raised 40 percent of total revenues through personal income taxation (compared to 6.8 percent for Canada), it still remained considerable in 1985 (36.0 percent for the Unites States versus 26.3 percent for Canada). One may also want to note that, in the data shown in Table 11.1, Canada makes more exten-

---

[19] We have used 1987 tax forms and the tax forms for the state of California in this comparison.

sive use of sales taxation at the federal level, with the manufacturer sales tax being the primary source of revenue in this category. This tax, which played a major (though diminishing) role from 1929 until its replacement by the Goods and Services Tax in 1991, can hardly have claimed acceptance as regionally fair because it was often perceived as falling more heavily on consumers and producers in the industrialized provinces. It is questionable whether a tax of this nature could have passed the wider scrutiny of the U.S. political process.

The difference in public information generated by the tax policy process may also account for the difference in treatment of an important component of the personal income tax base. In contrast to the United States, Canada did not tax capital gains until 1972, when one half of such gains were added to the base as part of the major tax reform initiated by the report of the Royal Commission on Taxation, thus making the treatment of capital gains comparable to U.S. practice. In 1982, the Conservative government again abolished the taxation of capital gains for most taxpayers by instituting a lifetime exemption of $500,000 for such gains. This exemption was later reduced to $100,000, but capital gains treatment still contrasts sharply with the United States, where such gains were included fully in the regular income-tax base as part of the 1986 tax reform.

The final hypothesis (H6) concerns the impact of federal–provincial arrangements on tax structure in the two countries. In Canada, explicit agreements between the federal government and the provinces on sharing the bases for the personal and corporate income taxes have a long history, going back at least to World War II. For the majority of provinces, income taxes are collected by the federal government on their behalf.[20] This gives the federal government control over the definition of income-tax bases while greatly reducing taxpayer compliance costs, since the same annual tax return is used for both federal and provincial taxes. It also makes the two levels of government more sensitive to each other's tax policies, since they are both setting rates on the same tax base. In the United States, any interdependence between tax systems at the two levels of government is much less direct. The only feature of the U.S. federal tax system that represents a direct link to state systems is the provision allowing deduction of state and local tax payments from the federal tax base. However, this provision is not the result of joint negotiations between levels of government but instead represents a unilateral federal choice. Indeed, the provision was altered in the 1986 federal tax reform, when state and local *sales* taxes were excluded from the list of allowable deductions. The political system in the United States does not permit the negotiated accommodations that are such a distinguishing feature of Canadian federalism. (Explicit fiscal interdependence in Canada extends beyond taxation to the joint determination of federal

---

[20] In Canada, only the province of Quebec collects its own personal income tax. Alberta, Ontario, and Quebec collect their own corporate income taxes.

grants, which represent a more significant component of the Canadian federal budget than of its U.S. counterpart.)[21]

11.6   CONCLUSION

In this chapter, we ask how differences in political institutions affect policy processes and outcomes. In particular, we consider how differences in checks and balances between the United States and Canada, viewed as differing constraints on the competitive political process in the two countries, influence tax policy processes and tax policy outcomes. We find that differences in checks and balances do matter, even after allowance is made for domestic economic pressures and the international mobility of capital and labor.

We have presented evidence concerning the effect of structural competition on tax systems using qualitative and suggestive data. Although we have not carried out formal tests, the evidence presented indicates that there is reasonable empirical support for most of the hypotheses and that further econometric testing would be worthwhile. It would be feasible, for example, to expand the number of observations by including more countries for each type of political system. However, any such extension would require a measure indicating the strength or degree of structural competition; there is considerable variation among countries with parliamentary systems, and among countries with congressional systems in addition to the variation between the two groups. We have not developed such a measure but suspect that it would focus primarily on the relation between the executive and the legislative branches of government. Quantitative indicators could reflect the time it takes for the legislature to act on proposals by the executive, the number of substantive changes made by the legislative branch in proposals submitted by the executive, and the number of instances where the legislature initiated policies on its own without a request from the executive. It may be best to interpret any such indicators with regard to a particular policy area. If we take taxation as the area studied, structural differences in tax systems can then be explained as a function of such quantitative measures and of other relevant variables, such as those representing economic forces.

A second way of expanding empirical work is to use time-series data for two or more countries. This is an attractive possibility for testing hypotheses concerning frequently repeated policy choices such as those relating to economic stabilization or responses to exogenous shocks (H2 and H3). One may

---

[21] In 1985, grants constituted 19.4 percent of outlays in Canada but only 10.1 percent of outlays in the United States (see *The National Finances* and the *Economic Report of the President*). Even though Canadian budget cuts in the 1990s have led to a reduced presence for the federal government in provincial finances, that role is still substantial, and federal–provincial negotiations in health care and other important areas remain a feature of the fiscal policy process.

note in this connection that structural or intragovernmental competition has not yet been systematically studied in the macroeconomic literature. To take just one example, the debate concerning rules versus discretion has been conducted without reference to the effect of political institutions. This chapter suggests that answers to this debate should differ for countries with congressional and with parliamentary systems.

The research reported here also has implications for the debate on tax constitutions. In the recent literature on the role of government, there has been much emphasis on constraining the government's ability to tax through constitutional provisions (see, most notably, Brennan and Buchanan 1980). This literature is essentially normative and lacks an empirical foundation. Studying the effects of existing constitutional arrangements on policy outcomes provides a way of investigating the problem empirically. Choice between constitutional provisions requires a knowledge of benefits and costs attached to available and feasible alternatives. Empirical work on the relationship between existing institutional arrangements and policy outcomes is a useful step toward understanding such benefits and costs.

CHAPTER 12

Conclusion

> If you start out with a story, you must think it to its conclusion.
>
> Friedrich Dürrenmatt (1962, p. 95)

> There is much more that should be said, but certainly not on this occasion. When I started this, I knew, from experience, that I'd never finish it. Life seems to consist of "unfinished business."
>
> Frank Knight (1950, p. 281)

Doing research in economics, as in other social sciences, differs from the writing of a good story or play. Successful work in both fields starts with an initial premise, but the economist, unlike the playwright, will rarely reach a final cathartic conclusion. To use Frank Knight's phrase, there is simply too much "unfinished business." In fact, one may want to go farther than Knight and claim that good research, like life, consists of unfinished business.

12.1 WHAT HAS BEEN ACHIEVED

Like other large research undertakings, this book presents new insights and also leaves significant areas to be explored. In order to provide an overall perspective, it is useful to describe briefly what, in our view, has been achieved in the preceding chapters. The book presents a new approach to the study of taxation that integrates collective choice with economic analysis and views fiscal policies as equilibrium outcomes. The resulting framework allows us to treat a wide range of issues in a unified manner. Moreover, the analysis is based on a collective choice model that allows exploration of multidimensional issues in an equilibrium setting.

Some of the new insights relate to the nature of economic policies. The analysis shows how tax instruments can be seen to arise endogenously as a consequence of the sorting of taxpayers into rate bands, and of taxable activities into tax bases, and how special provisions are introduced into the tax system for similar reasons. Our theoretical treatment integrates heterogeneous taxpayers, administration costs, and self-selection into a consistent framework and develops the conditions under which an equilibrium tax structure will satisfy the criterion of Pareto efficiency, a result we refer to as the Representation

284

Theorem. It is an implication of our analysis that the mix of tax instruments is an endogenous outcome of the interaction of voters, parties, and economic decision makers pursuing their self-interest.

The book also evaluates existing normative approaches to taxation from a collective choice perspective, giving a critical assessment of major theories from this point of view. We examine the nature of normative analysis implied by our approach and suggest what steps are necessary to create an efficiency analysis of taxation consistent with our framework. A new normative standard based on probabilistic voting (the optimal representative tax system) is proposed and contrasted as a viable alternative to Lindahl equilibrium.

Although playwrights and economists use different standards and criteria, both have methods to make appropriate "reality checks" of their work. Economists use a variety of empirical approaches to test their conclusions against what is observed in actual situations. Several of these are represented in the book. We start by using our framework in the context of a computational general equilibrium model, employing it to analyze several significant aspects of recent U.S. fiscal history. A different approach is represented by econometric research on variations in the use of tax instruments among U.S. states, and on the historical evolution of fiscal structure in Canada. We link this work to the research and results of others who have also examined the use of tax instruments empirically, often from quite different theoretical perspectives. Finally, we employ a more informal methodology based on descriptive statistics to investigate the influence of congressional and parliamentary political institutions on tax structure.

We believe that the book serves an important purpose by bridging different areas relevant to the study of the public sector. The analysis links general voting theory to the examination of specific economic policies. It systematically connects public finance with collective choice. Furthermore, theoretical modeling, computational general equilibrium analysis, and statistical research are all used to examine a similar range of fiscal policies. The book also provides a link between positive and normative analysis through the Representation Theorem, thus offering the possibility of examining fiscal policies in a public choice context from both these starting points.

12.2   A NEW BALANCE IN PUBLIC SECTOR ANALYSIS

We started the research program resulting in this book in part because we became aware of a curious imbalance in public sector economics. Collective choice analysis has gained increasing acceptance in the profession and has found its way into most textbooks on public finance, but it is still viewed primarily as a way to explain voting choices concerning the output of public goods given previously determined cost- or tax-sharing arrangements.

The imbalance is reflected in most available textbooks, including those that we have used in our own teaching of public sector economics over the years, and from which we have learned much ourselves. Most of these books devote a separate chapter to public choice in which voting models are introduced and linked to the determination of budget size in a simple framework with one or more public goods. The material is usually placed near the beginning of the book, and is presented as part of the discussion on public expenditures.

When matters of taxation are introduced in the second half of the text, public choice no longer plays an explicit role. There is little or no analysis of how tax systems emerge from voting choices or of how the differences in tax structure among similar jurisdictions (at the local, provincial, and state levels) are related to democratic choice. Students who were introduced to the notion of a political equilibrium with regard to public expenditures are given little guidance in applying the same ideas to the revenue side of the budget.[1]

Because textbooks are written to reflect the state of research rather than to expand the literature, it would be unfair to blame their authors for this imbalance. Although there is a growing literature on the relation between voting and taxation, much of it reviewed in this book, we nevertheless feel that researchers who work in the collective choice tradition have paid insufficient attention to taxation in the past. This may be due to the emphasis on the median voter model, which has permeated the literature, and to its limitations in the face of the multidimensional nature of fiscal choices.

It would be presumptuous to claim that one book can redress an imbalance of this nature. Yet we believe that the questions asked and the work reported in the previous chapters clearly point the way toward a more integrated treatment of taxation in public sector analysis. Our focus on the tax side of the budget is deliberate and should be seen in this light. Although the approach we have adopted could no doubt be expanded to include a more detailed treatment of the expenditure side, we believe that taxation is most in need of attention at this time.

12.3   DIMENSIONS OF GENERALITY

We argue for a broader view than is commonly adopted in research on taxation, believing that it is both useful and necessary to see tax polices in the context of a wider system and to acknowledge the importance of linkages among

---

[1] Three examples of textbooks following this approach (and that we have used over the years) are Robin Boadway and David Wildasin (1984), Richard and Peggy Musgrave (1989), and David Hyman (1996). A similar treatment is also found in Joseph Stiglitz (1988) and Harvey Rosen (1992).

various parts or elements of the overall structure. This is reflected in the models presented in various parts of the book. We do not advocate generality for its own sake, however, and recognize that analytical design must be adapted to the question at hand.

Anyone familiar with general equilibrium analysis in economics will recognize that there are degrees of generality, and that different models that are all accepted as "general" representations of the economy can vary widely in their structural elements and in the details that are included. Successful research, even if more inclusive in nature, requires abstraction and simplification. As Martin Shubik (quoted at the beginning of Chapter 2) put it so well: "The suitability of a model depends as much on what is left out as on what is put in."

Differences in generality also mark the analysis in this book. There are three basic components or building blocks for the arguments pursued in the previous chapters: a collective choice mechanism, a depiction of the private sector, and a representation of the tax system. While all three elements play a role throughout the book, they are elaborated to different degrees depending on the application and the specific purpose of the analysis. The reader may gain a better understanding of the interplay of the various elements and of the possibilities for further analytical development by considering how assumptions are varied across different applications.

Table 12.1 presents a summary of key assumptions in different parts of the book. The framework in Chapter 2 contains the least detail in the development of the three modeling elements. Assumptions were chosen to make possible a graphic comparison of different collective choice models and to contrast their predictions concerning tax rates and budget size. The restrictive nature of some of the surveyed models suggests a very simple tax structure (two given bases with one proportional rate on each base) and a rather limited interaction between public and private sectors.

Chapter 3 puts the focus on the creation of tax structure, presenting the most general treatment in the book of tax bases, rate structures, and special provisions, which are shown to arise endogenously as a result of economic and political choices in the face of transaction costs. The discussion starts with a characterization of the government's strategy and provides for an explicit link with the private sector. In Chapter 4, the political process is modeled in more detail and self-selection by taxpayers is added to the description of private behavior. However, the greater generality in the treatment of these elements makes it necessary to restrict the nature and character of tax instruments available to policy makers.

The private economy receives its most detailed treatment in Chapter 7. Where the supply side has previously been suppressed, it is now represented as part of a general equilibrium model of the private sector that is integrated with

Table 12.1. Key assumptions in alternative models

	Modelling Elements		
Chapter	Collective Choice	Private Sector	Elements of Tax Structure
2	4 different collective choice models, each with 3 (groups of) taxpayers	Size of aggregate tax base varies with tax rate	Two given bases with one proportional rate on each base applying to all voters (benefit and lump-sum taxation excluded)
3	Government strategy that maximizes expected votes	Size of taxable activities and individual welfare losses vary with tax rates	Endogenous determination of all elements of tax structure including rate structures, tax bases, and special provisions
4	Equilibrium in a competitive political contest between parties	As in ch 3. Self-selection behavior also allowed for. Supply side of economy suppressed	Effective tax rates and rate structures endogenous. Only one taxable base for all voters (labor income)
7	As in ch 4	Full general equilibrium model of private economy. Selectivity behavior not allowed for	Two effective proportional tax rates on two given bases (labor services and a hybrid of capital services and personal income)
9/10	Same analysis as in ch 4 implied	Same analysis as in ch 7 implied, but self-selection allowed for implicitly by coefficients of estimating equations	Stylized representation of elements of tax structure in each model, depending on application

public sector behavior. Some simplifications are needed elsewhere, however. Tax structure is restricted to two proportional tax rates and two bases, and self-selection behavior is no longer allowed for.

The theoretical discussion presents the background for the statistical analysis in Chapters 9 and 10. Since the focus in this part of the book is on statistical estimation, the theoretical structure is implied rather than developed in detail. The elements of tax structure are represented in stylized form, depending on the particular application, with difficulties in statistical modeling preventing a fully general treatment of the type given in Chapter 3.

Although most economic studies with a strong theoretical component have an underlying "conceptual architecture," it is often difficult for the reader to perceive the relevant outline. Yet, it is essential to understand how the major building blocks fit together. A fuller appreciation of how the analysis is supported and limited by different underlying assumptions helps one to see more clearly what has been accomplished, as well as what remains to be done.

12.4   FURTHER RESEARCH

Of course, there remains plenty of unfinished business. Since the reader has been alerted to shortcomings and possible extensions of the analysis throughout the preceding chapters, we will only touch on the most important issues here. The most readily apparent extension concerns the treatment of the expenditure side of public budgets. Though the level of expenditures is determined endogenously (together with tax structure) in the theoretical framework, the division of expenditures among different uses is not analyzed, and the possible connection between specific taxes and expenditures is discussed only informally. On the tax side, the analysis could benefit from a more detailed treatment of debt as a policy instrument, although it should be noted that debt is included in the theoretical and some of the empirical work. Finally, it should be pointed out that other policy instruments, such as regulation, may serve as substitutes for taxation and should be studied in conjunction with tax policies.

Further work is also needed on normative issues. Areas that require attention include the identification and modeling of imperfections in political markets, the linking of the functioning of political markets to the use of specific policy instruments, and the measurement of welfare effects of policies in a broader context that includes collective choice mechanisms.

In empirical work, there remains room for improvement by making a more specific connection between the theoretical model and the estimating equations. A possible route to achieving this may lie in more specifically integrating institutions – which are now represented only in a very generalized version in probabilistic voting – into the theoretical and empirical framework.

Even though the book presents theoretical arguments for preferring the probabilistic voting model over alternative approaches, it does not reject research based on other frameworks. Chapter 8 reviews such work and points out that it is often difficult to distinguish empirically between the predictions of alternative collective choice models. Further econometric work of a comparative nature would advance our understanding of how most effectively to model political processes affecting taxation.

The emphasis on the general equilibrium nature of policy outcomes also raises difficult questions for econometric work. The systematic examination of how to choose limited aspects of general systems for statistical research on tax structure remains in its infancy. Appropriate choices of this nature become even harder to make when other policy instruments that may be partially sub-stitutable for taxation are included in the analysis, and when the impact of out-side shocks on policy equilibrium is examined in this broader context.

12.5   TAXES, TARIFFS, AND FISCAL HISTORY

A major focus of the book is to develop a positive theory grounded in collec-tive choice that explains the nature and characteristics of tax systems presently observed in democratic countries. However, the message is much broader; it goes beyond such specific policy choices as special tax provisions, the share of the income tax in total revenues, and the trade-off between income and sales taxation. The general equilibrium view suggests the interdependence of all fis-cal instruments, including instruments (such as the tariff and debt) that have been studied extensively in the economic literature in isolation from the rest of public budgets. And if this broader view applies to choices in the present, it must also have relevance for explaining the past.

Seen in historical perspective, revenue structure as a whole is a reflection of broad economic and political developments in society. As pointed out by Schumpeter (1918), it is a visible and exceptionally well-documented record of these developments, making it a subject of particular interest for economic research. Fiscal policies are not imposed on us by unconstrained politicians, arbitrarily and in isolation of other developments in society, as is often claimed in public debates. Political competition, economic growth, the chang-ing composition of output, trends in international trade, cyclical patterns, and the growth of interest groups all have an influence on revenue structure and should play a role in estimating equations that seek to explain major fiscal changes over time.

A broader view of public policy as emerging from a collective choice process – operating against the background of a heterogeneous population and a changing economic and political structure – has direct implications for the examination of specific fiscal instruments. For example, if one wants to under-stand the role of the tariff during a period when it was a significant revenue source, one must acknowledge that this tax is affected by the availability of alternative revenue sources and that its use is influenced by large shocks any-where in the social system, including changes in views about the future, in liq-uidity constraints, and in political developments altering the relative influence of different interest groups. One may object that it is easy to proclaim a gen-eral equilibrium message of this nature but much harder to identify the statis-tically important developments responsible for equilibrium trends in public policy. We believe that the empirical work reported in this book makes a use-ful start toward such identification, and hope that it will serve as a stimulus for further broadly based research on fiscal history in the United States, Canada, and other countries.

There are a number of conceptual issues in the study of political economy that need to be resolved in any future work, whether done by historians or by students of contemporary public policy. To develop more robust conclusions about the history or origins of public policy, researchers must deal more effectively with the problems of measuring the political influence of different groups in society, and they must find ways of linking any resulting indices to commonly used economic statistics. In addition, they must face up to the difficulty of relating discontinuous political events to a background of more gradual and consistent change in economic factors, as well as find ways to reflect the influence of institutions on measured changes in economic variables.

12.6   FOUR POLICY CONCEPTS

As economic theory changes and develops, policy issues are seen in a new light and from new perspectives. To maintain its intellectual underpinning, economic policy analysis must retain its essential link to theoretical research.

A new theoretical framework leads to a reevaluation of major concepts used in policy analysis. We can illustrate this with four such concepts: special tax provisions; tax "reform"; tax complexity; and measurement of the impact of taxes on economic efficiency. All four concepts have been central to the economic analysis of fiscal policy, and they are likely to remain at the core of public debates for years to come.

The discussion in earlier chapters shows that integrating collective choice into policy analysis has significant implications for all four concepts and the issues related to them. The fact that these implications are not as yet widely acknowledged in much of the literature may reflect two causes: economic theory is not unified in its attitude toward, and treatment of, collective choice; and policy analysis may assume an impetus of its own and at times lose its direct connection to mainstream economic theory.

The discussion in Chapter 3 demonstrates that special tax provisions and changes or "reforms" in the tax system can be seen from a positive analytical perspective. Such an analysis suggests that competitive democratic regimes will create tax systems with many special provisions and will adopt frequent significant tax changes or "reforms" as part of their strategy to stay in office. The understanding that these features of fiscal systems represent equilibrium outcomes conflicts with the conclusions reached in the well-known literature on tax expenditures, and in many other types of writings on tax reform.

The conflict can be seen most clearly in discussions that link special provisions and reform to reductions in tax complexity. Proposals for flat taxes are perhaps the best-known instance of this. They are designed to replace existing tax structures with much simpler schemes that eliminate most (or all) special provisions and that provide for a single tax rate (or a very limited number of rates) on a streamlined tax base.

The formal analysis in Chapters 3 and 4 suggests that tax complexity is a logical outcome of a political process in which politicians attempt to maximize expected votes in order to obtain power or to stay in power. When taxpayers are grouped into rate bands and taxable activities are combined into bases in response to administration costs and self-selection behavior, the resulting tax structure remains complex. Although the theoretical discussion does not rule out equilibrium tax systems that are as simple as those suggested in some recent flat-tax proposals, it suggests that such schemes, or any broadly based tax without special provisions, are not compatible with vigorous political competition and do not represent lasting equilibrium outcomes of democratic societies.

In addition to considering special provisions and reforms from a positive point of view, we can also analyze them in a normative context. Though much of the policy-oriented literature interprets the concepts in this manner, it often uses normative analysis that has been largely abandoned by current economic theorists. This is most apparent in the work on tax expenditures, which has its economic basis in the writings of Henry Simons and others dealing with a comprehensive income tax. More recent approaches to normative analysis generally reject the premises of this earlier literature. This is true for approaches that include collective choice as an integral part, such as the Leviathan model and the normative interpretation of probabilistic voting. It also holds for optimal taxation, the most influential normative approach that disregards the influence of collective choice. Writings on tax expenditures appear untouched by such changes in perspective and seem to have lost their connection to current developments in economic theory.

The final policy concept – measurement of the welfare effects of taxation – derives from welfare economics, a part of the discipline that has a distinguished past but that does not account for collective choice in specifying the standard of reference against which changes are measured. As outlined in Chapter 6, redefinition of the baseline requires a new approach to the measurement of welfare losses.

Since economics does not provide a unified normative approach, the policy analyst must choose his or her own point of departure. We argue strongly that such a starting point should include collective choice as an integral part, and that there are theoretical frameworks available to provide a basis for such a more inclusive analysis.

The book provides a central message concerning policy analysis – namely that political equilibrium must count along with economic equilibrium. This implies that special provisions or reforms must either be seen in a positive context as the outcome of the political system or be evaluated in relation to a standard of reference that accounts for collective choice. Similarly, welfare losses from taxation must be measured in relation to a more inclusive frame of reference.

12.7   AN EVOLVING TRADITION

Although it provides a new perspective, the work reported in this book falls into a long tradition. The authors were not aware of the close connection between their work and that of Scandinavian economists, who can be seen as the founders of collective choice analysis for the public sector, until they read the late writings of Eric Lindahl (also quoted in Chapter 4), who said in an article published in 1959:

> That the taxation forced on the minority is also influenced to some extent by the benefit and ability principles can most readily be explained on the basis of the concept of "political cost". ... The resistance of the minority to taxation which it considers unjust can be assumed to be less if the minority can discover a certain measure of justice in the injustice. ... In other words, the amount of taxation which the majority can force upon a minority is greater, given the political cost, the greater is the attention which the majority pays to the interests of the minority. (p. 22)

Readers of Chapter 3 (and related parts of the book) will recall the central role played by the concept of political costs in our theoretical framework, and they will readily recognize that Lindahl's view of the accommodation of minority interests in the fiscal process is mirrored in the operation of probabilistic voting.

In retrospect, the contributions by Wicksell and Lindahl, first published at the end of the last and at the beginning of the present century, look prophetic. Their importance seems even greater now than nearly forty years ago, when Richard Musgrave (1959) introduced them to a larger audience of English-speaking economists in his *Theory of Public Finance*. While the specific mechanisms suggested by the two Scandinavian scholars may have been amended or reformulated, and the historical context within which they discussed some of the proposed solutions may have passed, the questions that they raised remain as vital today as when they were first suggested.

The analysis and discussion in the book has been developed primarily with the use of the probabilistic voting model of representative democracy. We find this framework particularly useful because it can draw on a well-developed theoretical basis, including work on the existence and stability of equilibrium, while allowing the examination of multidimensional issues. Moreover, application of the Representation Theorem makes it possible to establish a link between positive and normative analysis. We also believe that the framework best reflects the balancing of interests, widely observed in democratic fiscal politics, that Lindahl seems to have had in mind in the passage just quoted.

The emphasis on probabilistic voting is not meant, however, to preclude work based on other approaches that also addresses the essential questions raised by Wicksell and Lindahl. The authors feel that this book will have achieved its purpose if it stimulates others to expand the collective choice analysis of fiscal policy and to explore some of these questions in greater depth, regardless of the specific approaches that may be used.

Bibliography

Advisory Commission on Intergovernmental Relations [ACIR] (various years). *Significant Features of Fiscal Federalism.* Washington, DC.

Ahmad, Ehtisham, and Nicholas Stern (1984). "The Theory of Reform and Indian Indirect Taxes," *Journal of Public Economics* 25: 259–98.

(1991). *The Theory and Practice of Tax Reform in Developing Countries.* Cambridge: Cambridge University Press.

Alesina, Alberto (1988). "Credibility and Policy Convergence in a Two–Party System with Rational Voters," *American Economic Review* 78: 796–805.

Alesina, Alberto, and Allan Drazen (1991). "Why Are Stabilizations Delayed?" *American Economic Review* 81: 1170–88.

Alesina, Alberto, and Howard Rosenthal (1995). *Partisan Politics, Divided Government and the Economy.* Cambridge: Cambridge University Press.

Alesina, Alberto, and Guido Tabellini (1992). "Positive and Normative Theories of Public Debt and Inflation in Historical Perspective," *European Economic Review* 36: 337–44.

Anderson, G. M., D. T. Martin, and R. D. Tollison (1987). "Do Loopholes Decrease or Increase Revenue?" *Economia delle scelte publiche* 2: 83–95.

Anderson, Simon P., Amos Katz, and Jacques–Francois Thisse (1994). "Probabilistic Voting and Platform Selection in Multi–Party Elections," *Social Choice and Welfare* 11: 305–22.

Aranson, Peter H., Melvin J. Hinich, and Peter C. Ordeshook (1974). "Election Goals and Strategies: Equivalent and Nonequivalent Candidate Objectives," *American Political Science Review* 68: 135–52.

Ashworth, John, and Bruno Heyndels (1997). "Politicians' Preferences on Local Tax Rates: An Empirical Analysis," *European Journal of Political Economy* 13: 479–502.

Atkinson, Anthony B. (1995). *Public Economics in Action: The Basic Income Flat Tax Proposal.* Oxford: Clarendon Press.

Atkinson, Anthony B., and Nicholas H. Stern (1974). "Pigou, Taxation and Public Goods," *Review of Economic Studies* 41: 119–28.

Atkinson, Anthony B., and Joseph E. Stiglitz (1980). *Lectures on Public Economics.* New York: McGraw-Hill.

Aumann, R. J., and M. Kurz (1977). "Power and Taxes," *Econometrica* 45: 1137–61.

Austen–Smith, David (1987). "Interest Groups, Campaign Contributions and Probabilistic Voting," *Public Choice* 54: 123–39.

(1991). "Rational Consumers and Irrational Voters: A Review Essay on *Blackhole Tariffs and Endogenous Policy Theory* by Stephen Magee, William Brock, and Leslie Young," *Economics and Politics* 3: 73–92.

Avery, Robert B., and V. Joseph Hotz (1985). *Hotztran User's Manual, Version 2.0.* Old Greenwich, CT: CERA Economic Consultants Inc. (Computer code, dated 1988.)

Balcer, Y., and E. Sadka (1983)."Horizontal Equity in Models of Self–Selection with Applications to Income Tax and Signalling Cases," in E. Helpman, A. Razin, and E. Sadka (Eds.), *Social Policy Evaluation.* New York: Academic Press, pp. 235–45.

Baldwin, Robert E. (1986). *The Political Economy of U.S. Import Policy.* Cambridge, MA: MIT Press.

Ballard, Charles L., and Don Fullerton (1992). "Distortionary Taxes and the Provision of Public Goods," *Journal of Economic Perspectives* 6: 117–32.

Ballard, Charles L., Don Fullerton, John B. Shoven, and John Whalley (1985a). *A General Equilibrium Model for Tax Policy Evaluation.* Chicago: University of Chicago Press.

Ballard, Charles L., John B. Shoven, and John Whalley (1985b). "General Equilibrium Computations of the Marginal Welfare Costs of Taxes in the United States," *American Economic Review* 75: 128–38.

Baron, David P. (1994). "Electoral Competition with Informed and Uninformed Voters," *American Journal of Political Science* 88: 33–47.

Barro, Robert J. (1979). "On the Determination of the Public Debt," *Journal of Political Economy* 87: 940–71.

(1986). "U.S. Deficits Since World War I," *Scandinavian Journal of Economics* 88: 195–222.

Becker, Gary (1983). "A Theory of Competition Among Pressure Groups for Political Influence," *Quarterly Journal of Economics* 98: 371–400.

Beggs, J., and S. Strong (1982). "Cake Slicing and Revealed Government Preference," *Bell Journal of Economics* 13: 534–40.

Bennett, James T., and Thomas J. DiLorenzo (1983). *Underground Government: The Off–Budget Public Sector.* Washington DC: Cato Institute.

Bergstrom, Theodore C. (1993). "Benefit–Cost Analysis and Distortionary Taxes: A Public Choice Approach," working paper, University of Michigan, Ann Arbor (July).

Bergstrom, Theodore C., and Robert P. Goodman (1973). "Private Demands for Public Goods," *American Economic Review* 63: 280–96.

Berliant, Marcus, and Miguel Gouveia (1992). "On the Political Economy of Income Taxation," working paper, University of Rochester, New York (April).

(1993). "Equal Sacrifice and Incentive Compatible Taxation," *Journal of Public Economics* 51: 219–40.

Bernstein, Rachelle B., Andre P. Fogarasi, and Richard A. Gordon (1995), "Tax Reform 1995: Looking at Two Options," *Tax Notes*, July, pp. 327–33.

Berry, Francis Stokes, and William D. Berry (1990). "State Lottery Adoptions as Policy Innovations: An Event History Analysis," *American Political Science Review* 84: 395–415.

Besley, Timothy, and Anne C. Case (1995a). "Incumbent Behavior: Vote Seeking, Tax Setting and Yardstick Competition,"*American Economic Review* 85: 25–45.

(1995b)."Does Electoral Accountability Affect Economic Policy Choices: Evidence from Gubernatorial Term Limits?" *Quarterly Journal of Economics* 110: 769–98.

Bhagwati, Jagdish N., Richard Brecher, and T. N. Srinivasan (1984). "DUP Activities and Economic Theory," *European Economic Review* 24: 291–307.

Bird, Richard (1970). "The Tax Kaleidoscope: Perspectives on Tax Reform in Canada," *Canadian Tax Foundation*, 18: 444–73.
  (1991). "Tax Administration and Tax Reform: Reflections and Experience," in Javad Khalilzadeh–Shirazi and Anwar Shaw (Eds.), *Tax Policy in Developing Countries.* Washington, D.C: World Bank, pp. 38–56.
  (1992). *Tax Policy and Economic Development.* Baltimore: Johns Hopkins University Press.
Black, Duncan (1958). *The Theory of Committees and Elections.* Cambridge: Cambridge University Press.
Blackley, Paul R., and Larry DeBoer (1987). "Tax Base Choice by Local Governments," *Land Economics* 63: 227–36.
Blanchard, Olivier Jean, and Stanley Fischer (1989). *Lectures on Macroeconomics.* Cambridge, MA: MIT Press.
Blaug, Marc (1980). *The Methodology of Economics.* Cambridge: Cambridge University Press.
Blondel, Jean, and Jean–Louis Thibeault (1988). "The Study of Western European Cabinets," *European Journal of Political Research*, 16: 115–23.
Boadway, Robin W. (1997). "The Role of Second Best Theory in Public Economics," in B. Curtis Eaton and Richard G. Harris (Eds.), *Trade, Technology and Economics: Essays in Honor of Richard G. Lipsey.* Cheltenham, UK: Edward Elgar.
Boadway, Robin W., and Neil Bruce (1984). *Welfare Economics.* Oxford: Basil Balckwell.
Boadway, Robin W., and Michael Keen (1993). "Public Goods, Self-Selection and Optimal Income Taxation," *International Economic Review* 34: 463–79.
Boadway, Robin W., and Harry M. Kitchen (1984). *Canadian Tax Policy*, 2nd ed. (Canadian Tax Paper, no. 76), Toronto: Canadian Tax Foundation.
Boadway, Robin W., and David E. Wildasin (1984) *Public Sector Economics*, 2nd ed. Boston: Little, Brown.
Bodkin, Ronald G. (1974) "Additively Consistent Relationship for Personal Savings and the Categories of Consumption Expenditures, U.S.A., 1949–1963," Cowles Foundation paper no. 403, Yale University, New Haven, CT.
Borcherding, Thomas E., and Robert T. Deacon (1972). "The Demand for the Services of Non–federal Governments," *American Economic Review* 62: 891–901.
Borooah, Vani K., and Frederick Van der Ploeg (1983). *Political Aspects of the Economy.* Cambridge: Cambridge University Press.
Boyer, Marcel, and Jean-Jaques Lafont (1988). "Expanding the Informativeness of the Price System with Law," Industrial Organization working paper, Carleton University, Ottawa (July).
Bradford, David F. (1977). "Discussion of Stiglitz-Boskin Paper," *American Economic Review*, 67(1) (February): 314–15.
  (1982). "The Possibilities for an Expenditure Tax," *National Tax Journal* 35: 243–51.
Break, George F. (1984). "Avenues to Tax Reform: Perils and Possibilities," *National Tax Journal*, March; pp. 1–8.
Break, George F., and Joseph A. Pechman (1975). *Federal Tax Reform: The Impossible Dream?* Washington DC: Brookings Institution.
Breeden, Charles, and William J. Hunter (1985). "Tax Revenue and Tax Structure," *Public Finance Quarterly* 13: 216–24.

Brennan, Geoffrey (1981). "Tax Limits and the Logic of Constitutional Restriction," in
    H. Ladd and T. N. Tideman (Eds.), *Tax and Expenditure Limitations* (COUPE
    Paper on Public Economics). Washington DC Urban Institute, pp. 121–38.
    (1988). "The Public Choice Approach to Tax Reform," *Government and Policy* 6: 41–52.
Brennan, Geoffrey, Cecil Bohanon, and Richard Carter (1984). "Public Finance and
    Public Prices: Towards a Reconstruction of Tax Theory," *Public Finance* 39:
    157–79.
Brennan, Geoffrey, and James Buchanan (1980). *The Power to Tax: Analytical Foun-
    dations of a Fiscal Constitution.* Cambridge: Cambridge University Press.
    (1985). *The Reason of Rules.* Cambridge: Cambridge University Press.
Brennan, Geoffrey, and Loren E. Lomasky (1993). *Democracy and Decision: The Pure
    Theory of Electoral Preference.* Cambridge: Cambridge University Press.
Breton, Albert (1974). *The Economic Theory of Representative Government.* Chicago:
    Aldine.
    (1991). "The Organization of Competition in Congressional and Parliamentary Gov-
    ernments," in A. Breton, G. Galeotti, P. Salmon, and R. Wintrobe (Eds.), *The
    Competitive State.* Dordrecht: Kluwer, pp. 13–38.
    (1996). *Competitive Governments: An Economic Theory of Politics and Public
    Finance.* Cambridge: Cambridge University Press.
Breton, Albert, and Anthony Scott (1978). *The Economic Constitution of Federal
    States.* Toronto: University of Toronto Press.
Breton, Albert, and Ronald Wintrobe (1982). *The Logic of Bureaucratic Conduct.* Cam-
    bridge: Cambridge University Press.
Brooke, Anthony, David Kendrick, and Alexander Meeraus (1988). *GAMS: A User's
    Guide.* Redwood City, CA: Scientific Press.
Brosio, Giorgio, and Carla Marchese (1993). "Voting Rights and the Demand for Pub-
    lic Expenditure: An Analysis of the Redistributive Impact of Universal Suffrage,"
    in A. Breton, G. Galeotti, P. Salmon, and W. Wintrobe (Eds.), *Preferences and
    Democracy.* Dordrecht: Kluwer, pp. 329–50.
Brown, R. D. (1984). "Canada–U.S. Tax Treaty, Unitary Taxation, and the Future,"
    Canadian Tax Journal 32: 547–71.
Buchanan, James M. (1964). "Fiscal Institutions and Efficiency in Collective Outlay,"
    American Economic Review 54: 227–35.
    (1968). *The Demand and Supply of Public Goods.* Chicago: Rand McNally.
    (1975). *The Limits of Liberty: Between Anarchy and Leviathan.* Chicago: University
    of Chicago Press.
    (1976). "Taxation in Fiscal Exchange," *Journal of Public Economics* 6: 17–29.
Buchanan, James M., and Dwight R. Lee (1982). "Politics, Time and the Laffer Curve,"
    Journal of Political Economy 90: 816–19.
Buchanan, James M., and Mark V. Pauly (1970). "On the Incidence of Tax Deductibil-
    ity," *National Tax Journal* 23: 157–67.
Buchanan, James M., and Jenifer Roback (1987). "The Incidence and Effects of Public
    Debt in the Absence of Fiscal Illusion," *Public Finance Quarterly* 15: 5–25.
Buchanan, James M., and Gordon Tullock (1962). *The Calculus of Consent.* Ann
    Arbor, MI: University of Michigan Press.
Buchanan, James M., and Richard E. Wagner (1977). *Democracy in Deficit: The Polit-
    ical Legacy of Lord Keynes.* New York: Academic Press.

Bucovetsky, Sam (1991). "Asymmetric Tax Competition," *Journal of Urban Economics* 30: 167–81.

Calvert, Randall (1986). *Models of Imperfect Information in Politics.* New York: Harwood.

Canadian Tax Foundation (various years). *The National Finances.* Toronto: Canadian Tax Foundation.

Case, Anne C. (1993), "Interstate Tax Competition After TRA86," *Journal of Policy Analysis and Management* 12: 136–48.

Case, Anne C., James R. Hines, and Harvey S. Rosen (1993). "Budget Spillovers and Fiscal Policy Interdependence," *Journal of Public Economics* 52: 285–307.

Cassing, James H., and Arye L. Hillman (1986). "Shifting Comparative Advantage and Senescent Industry Collapse," *American Economic Review* 76: 516–23.

Caves, Richard E. (1976). "Economic Models of Political Choice: Canada's Tariff Structure," *Canadian Journal of Economics* 9: 278–300.

Cebula, R. J. (1980). "Voting with One's Feet: A Critique of the Evidence," *Regional Science and Urban Economics* 10: 91–167.

Chen, Yan (1994). "Electoral Systems, Legislative Process and Income Taxation," unpublished working paper, Department of Economics, University of Michigan, Ann Arbor (August).

Chernick, Howard (1991). "The Effect of Distributional Constraints and Interstate Tax Competition on State Decisions to Tax: An Econometric Model," paper presented to the NBER Summer Institute on State and Local Finance (Cambridge, MA).

   (1992). "A Model of the Distributional Incidence of State Taxes," *Public Finance Quarterly* 20: 572–85.

   (1997). "The Choice of Tax Base and Government Behavior: On the Determinants of Tax-Progressivity in Subnational Jurisdictions." Paper at the International Seminar in Public Economics, Oxford, UK, December.

Cicero, Marcus Tullius. Quoted in Jeffrey L. Yablon, "As Certain as Death – Quotations about Taxes," *Tax Notes*, November 14, 1994.

Coase, Ronald H. (1960). "The Problem of Social Cost" *Journal of Law and Economics* 3: 1–44.

Coleman, James S. (1990). *Foundations of Social Theory.* Cambridge, MA: Harvard University Press.

Cooper, Russell (1984). "On Allocative Distortions in Problems of Self Selection," *Rand Journal of Economics* 15: 568–77.

Coughlin, Peter J. (1986). "Elections and Income Redistribution," *Public Choice* 50: 27–91.

   (1990a). "Majority Rule and Election Models," *Journal of Economic Surveys* 4: 157–88.

   (1990b). "Candidate Uncertainty and Electoral Equilibria," in J. Enelow and M. Hinich (Eds.), *Advances in the Spatial Theory of Voting.* Cambridge: Cambridge University Press, pp. 145–66.

   (1992). *Probabilistic Voting Theory.* Cambridge: Cambridge University Press.

Coughlin, Peter J., Dennis C. Mueller, and Peter Murrell (1990a). "Electoral Politics, Interest Groups and the Size of Government," *Economic Inquiry* 28: 682–705.

   (1990b). "A Model of Electoral Competition with Interest Groups," *Economic Letters* 32: 307–11.

Coughlin, Peter J., and Shmuel Nitzan (1981a). "Electoral Outcomes with Probabilistic Voting and Nash Social Welfare Maxima," *Journal of Public Economics* 15: 113–22.

(1981b). "Directional and Local Equilibria with Probabilistic Voting," *Journal of Economic Theory* 24: 226–40.

Courant, Paul N., and Edward M. Gramlich (1990). "The Impact of the Tax Reform Act of 1986 on State and Local Fiscal Behavior," in Joel Slemrod (Ed.), *Do Taxes Matter?: The Impact of the Tax Reform Act of 1986.* Cambridge, MA: MIT Press, pp. 243–75.

Cowell, Frank A. (1990). *Cheating the Government: The Economics of Evasion.* Cambridge, MA: MIT Press.

Cukierman, Alex, and Allan H. Meltzer (1989). "A Political Theory of Government Debt and Deficits in a Neo–Ricardian Framework," *American Economic Review.* 79: 713–32.

(1991). "A Political Theory of Progressive Income Taxation," in A. Meltzer, A. Cukierman, and S. Richard (Eds.), *Political Economy.* Oxford University Press, pp. 76–108.

Dahl, Robert A. (1989). *Democracy and Its Critics.* New Haven, CT: Yale University Press.

Dales, J. H. (1966). *The Protective Tariff in Canada's Development.* Toronto: University of Toronto Press.

Darby, Michael, and Edi Karni (1973). "Free Competition and the Optimal Degree of Fraud," *Journal of Law and Economics* 16: 67–88.

Denzau, Arthur T., and Michael C. Munger (1986). "Legislators and Interest Groups: How Unorganized Interests Get Represented," *American Political Science Review* 80: 89–106.

Diamond, P. A. and J. A. Mirrlees (1971). "Optimal Taxation and Public Production I–II," *American Economic Review* 61: 8–27, 261–78.

Dierker, Egbert (1986). "When Does Marginal Cost Pricing Lead to Pareto–Efficiency?" *Journal of Economics Zeitschrift fur Nationalokonomie*, Suppl. (5), pp. 41–66.

Dixit, Avinash, Gene M. Grossman, and Elhanan Helpman (1996). "Common Agency and Coordination: General Theory and Application to Tax Policy," working paper no. 11–96, Foerder Institute for Economic Research, Tel Aviv University (April).

Doman, Andrew (1980). "The Effects of Federal Budgetary Policies 1978–80 on the Distribution of Income in Canada," *Canadian Taxation*, Summer, pp. 112–22.

Downs, Anthony (1957). *An Economic Theory of Democracy.* New York: Harper and Row.

Driessen, Patrick (1987). "A Qualification Concerning the Efficiency of Tax Expenditures," *Journal of Public Economics* 33: 125–31.

Drissen, Eric, and Frans A. A. M. van Winden (1993). "A General Equilibrium Model with Endogenous Government Behaviour," in W. Barnett, M. Hinich and N. Schofield (Eds.), *Political Economy: Institutions, Competition, and Representation.* Cambridge: Cambridge University Press, pp. 487–522.

Dudley, Leonard M. (1991). *The Word and the Sword.* Oxford: Basil Blackwell.

Dudley, Leonard M., and Claude Montmarquette (1987). "Bureaucratic Corruption as a Constraint on Voter Choice," *Public Choice* 55: 127–60.

Dürrenmatt, Friedrich (1962). *The Physicists.* New York: Grove Press (1964). Original German version, "Die Arche," copyright 1962 by Peter Schifferli, Verlags AG (Zurich).

Enelow, James M., James W. Endersby, and Michael Munger (1993). "A Revised Probabilistic Spatial Voting Model of Elections: Theory and Evidence," in Bernard

Groffman (Ed.), *Information, Participation and Choice*. Ann Arbor: University of Michigan Press, pp. 125–40.

Enelow, James M., and Melvin J. Hinich (1984). *The Spatial Theory of Voting*. Cambridge: Cambridge University Press.

(1989). "A General Probabilistic Spatial Theory of Elections, " *Public Choice* 61: 101–13.

(1990). *Advances in the Spatial Theory of Voting*. Cambridge: Cambridge University Press.

Engle, R. F. (1982). "A Generalized Approach to Lagrangian Multiplier Diagnostics," *Annals of Econometrics* 20: 83–104.

Epple, Dennis, and Allan Zelenitz (1981). "The Implications of Competition among Jurisdictions: Does Tiebout Need Politics?" *Journal of Political Economy* 89: 1197–1217.

Escarraz, Donald Ray (1967). "Wicksell and Lindahl: Theories of Public Expenditures and Tax Justice Reconsidered," *National Tax Journal*, 20: 137–48.

Fair, Ray (1978). "The Effect of Economic Events on Votes for President," *Review of Economics and Statistics*, 60: 159–73.

Feldman, Alan, and K. Lee (1988). "Existence of Electoral Equilibria with Probabilistic Voting," *Journal of Public Economics* 35: 205–27.

Feldstein, Martin S. (1976a). "Compensation in Tax Reform," *National Tax Journal* 29: 123–30.

(1976b). "On the Theory of Tax Reform," *Journal of Public Economics* 6: 77–104.

(1980). "A Contribution to the Theory of Tax Expenditures: The Case of Charitable Giving," in Henry Aaron and Michael Boskin (Eds.), *The Economics of Taxation*. Washington DC: Brookings Institution, pp. 99–122.

(1985). "Debt and Taxes in the Theory of Public Finance," *Journal of Public Economics* 28: 233–45.

(1987). "The Efficiency of Tax Expenditures: A Reply," *Journal of Public Economics* 33: 132–5.

Feldstein, Martin S., and Gilbert E. Metcalf (1987). "The Effect of Federal Tax Deductibility on State and Local Taxes and Spending," *Journal of Political Economy* 95: 710–36.

Firestone, O. J. (1958). *Canada's Economic Development 1867–1953*. London: Bowes & Bowes.

Fischer, Stanley (1980). "Dynamic Inconsistency, Cooperation, and the Benevolent Dissembling Government," *Journal of Economic Dynamics and Control* 2: 93–107.

Fisher, Glenn W. (1996). *The Worst Tax? A History of the Property Tax in America*. Lawrence: University of Kansas Press.

Fisher, Ronald C. (1982). "Income and Grant Effects on Local Expenditure: The Flypaper Effect and Other Difficulties," *Journal of Urban Economics* 12: 324–45.

Fisher, Ronald C., and Robert H. Rasche (1984). "The Incidence and Incentive Effects of Property Tax Credits: Evidence from Michigan," *Public Finance Quarterly* 12: 291–320.

Fitts, Michael, and Robert P. Inman (1992). "Controlling Congress: Presidential Influence in Domestic Fiscal Policy," *Georgetown Law Journal* 80: 1737–85.

Foley, Duncan K. (1967). "Resource Allocation and the Public Sector," *Yale Economic Essays* 7: 45–98.

Forsey, Eugene (1982). *Trade Unions in Canada, 1812–1902.* Toronto: University of Toronto Press.

Forster, Ben (1986). *A Conjunction of Interests: Business, Politics and Tariffs, 1825–1870.* Toronto: University of Toronto Press.

Frey, Bruno S. (1979). "Economic Policy by Constitutional Contract," *Kyklos* 32: 307–19.
    (1983). *Democratic Economic Policy: A Theoretical Introduction.* Oxford: Martin Robertson.

Friedman, Milton (1953). "Choice, Chance, and the Personal Distribution of Income," *Journal of Political Economy* 61: 277–90.

Frohlich, Norman, and Joe A. Oppenheimer (1988). "Experiments on Taxation, Participation, Stability, and Productivity," paper presented at Public Choice meetings (February, San Francisco).

Fudenberg, Drew, and Jean Tirole (1991). *Game Theory.* Cambridge, MA: MIT Press.

Fullerton, Don (1982). "On the Possibility of an Inverse Relationship between Tax Rates and Government Revenues," *Journal of Public Economics* 19: 3–22.

Gade, Mary N., and Lee C. Adkins (1990). "Tax Exporting and State Revenue Structures," *National Tax Journal* 43: 39–52.

Gale, William G. (1995). "Building a Better Tax System: Can a Consumption Tax Deliver the Goods?" *Tax Notes*, November 6, pp. 781–785.

Gardner, Roy (1981). "Wealth and Power in a Collegial Polity," *Journal of Economic Theory*, 25: 353–66.

Genser, Berndt (1992). "Tax Competition and Harmonization in Federal Economies," in Hans–Jurgen Vosgerau (Ed.), *European Integration in the World Economy.* New York: Springer-Verlag, pp. 200–37.

Gillespie, W. Irwin (1978). *In Search of Robin Hood.* Toronto: C. D. Howe Research Institute and Canadian Economic Policy Committee.
    (1980). *The Redistribution of Income in Canada* (Carleton Library, no. 124). Ottawa: Gage Publishing Co. and the Institute of Canadian Studies.
    (1982). "Tax Reform: The Battlefield, The Strategies, The Spoils," *Canadian Public Administration* 261: 182–202.
    (1991). *Tax, Borrow and Spend: Financing Federal Spending in Canada, 1867–1990.* Ottawa, Ontario: Carleton University Press.

Gold, Steven D. (1991). "Interstate Competition and State Personal Income Tax Policy in the 1980's," in Daphne Kenyon and John Kincaid (Eds.), *Competition among State and Local Governments.* Washington, DC: Urban Institute Press, pp. 205–17.

Goldscheid, Rudolph (1925). "A Sociological Approach to the Problems of Public Finance," in Richard A. Musgrave and Alan T. Peacock (Eds.), *Classics in Public Finance.* London: Macmillan (1967).

Good, David A. (1980). *The Politics of Anticipation: Making Canadian Tax Policy.* Ottawa: Carleton University. School of Public Administration.

Goodspeed, Timothy J. (1992). "Redistribution and the Structure of Local Government Finance," unpublished manuscript, Florida International University (January).
    (1997). "Redistributive Tax Structure in Open Federal Economies: Theory and Evidence from Local Governments in OECD Countries," working paper, Department of Economics, Hunter College, New York (April).

Goulder, Lawrence H., John B. Shoven, and John Whalley (1983). "Domestic Tax Policy and the Foreign Sector: The Importance of Alternative Foreign Sector Formulations to Results from a General Equilibrium Tax Analysis Model," in Martin Feldstein (Ed.), *Behavioral Simulation Methods in Tax Policy Analysis*. Chicago: University of Chicago Press, pp. 333–68.

Government of Canada, Department of Finance (1978). *The Tax Systems of Canada and the United States. A Study Comparing the Levels of Taxation on Individuals and Business in the Two Countries*. Ottawa (November).

Government of Ireland (1982). *First Report of the Commission on Taxation, Direct Taxation*. Dublin: Government Publications Sales Office.

Gramlich, Edward M. (1977). "Intergovernmental Grants: A Review of the Empirical Literature," in Wallace E. Oates (Ed.), *The Political Economy of Fiscal Federalism*. Lexington, MA: Lexington, pp. 219–39.

(1982). "An Economic Examination of the New Federalism," *Brookings Papers on Economic Activity* 2: 327–60.

Greene, Kenneth V. (1986). "The Public Choice of Differing Degrees of Tax Progressivity," *Public Choice* 49: 265–82.

Groenewegen, P. D. (1988). "Tax Reform in Australia and New Zealand," *Government and Policy* 6: 93–114.

Grossman, Gene M., and Elhanan Helpman (1994). "Protection for Sale," *American Economic Review* 84: 833–50.

Hamlin, Alan P. (1984). "Constitutional Control of Processes and Their Outcomes," *Public Choice* 42: 133–45.

Hansen, Susan B. (1983). *The Politics of Taxation: Revenue without Representation*. New York: Praeger.

Harberger, Arnold C. (1962). "The Incidence of the Corporation Income Tax," *Journal of Political Economy* 70: 215–40.

(1990). "The Uniform Tax Controversy," in Vito Tanzi (Ed.), *Public Finance, Trade and Development*. Detroit: Wayne State University Press, pp. 3–18.

Harrison, Glenn, and E. E. Rutstom (1990). "Trade Wars, Trade Negotiations and Applied Game Theory," *The Economic Journal* 101: 420–35.

Hartle, Douglas G. (1982). *The Revenue Budget Process of the Government of Canada: Description, Appraisal and Proposals* (Canadian Tax Paper no. 67). Toronto: Canadian Tax Foundation.

Head, John (1974). *Public Goods and Public Welfare*. Durham, NC: Duke University Press.

Helleiner, G. K. (1977). "The Political Economy of Canada's Tariff Structure: An Alternative Model," *Canadian Journal of Economics* 10: 318–25.

Heller, W. P., and Karl Shell (1974). "On Optimal Taxation with Costly Administration," *American Economic Review, Papers and Proceedings* 64: 338–45.

Hennipman, P. (1982). "Wicksell and Pareto: Their Relationship in the Theory of Public Finance," *History of Political Economy* 14: 37–64.

Hettich, Walter(1979a). "Henry Simons on Taxation and the Economic System," *National Tax Journal* 32: 1–9.

(1979b). "A Theory of Partial Tax Reform," *Canadian Journal of Economics* 12: 692–712.

(1983). "Reforms of the Tax Base and Horizontal Equity," *National Tax Journal* 36: 417–27.

Hettich, Walter, and Stanley L. Winer (1984), "A Positive Model of Tax Structure," *Journal of Public Economics* 24: 67–87. Reprinted in Wallace E. Oates (Ed.), *The Economics of Fiscal Federalism and Local Finance* (International Library of Critical Writings in Economics). Cheltenham UK: Edward Elgar (1998).

(1985). "Blueprints and Pathways: The Shifting Foundations of Tax Reform," *National Tax Journal*, 38: 423–45. Reprinted in Patricia White (Ed.), *Tax Law: Volume II* (International Library of Essays in Law and Legal Theory). Aldershot UK: Dartmouth Publishing Company (1995), pp. 1–25.

(1987). "Federalism, Special Interests and the Exchange of Policies for Political Resources," *European Journal of Political Economy* 3, Special Issue, pp. 33–54.

(1988). "Economic and Political Foundations of Tax Structure," *American Economic Review* 78: 701–12.

(1990). "Basic Issues in the Positive Political Economy of Income Taxation," in Sijbren Cnossen and Richard Bird (Eds.), *The Personal Income Tax – Phoenix from the Ashes?*, Amsterdam: North-Holland, pp. 265–89.

(1993). "Economic Efficiency, Political Institutions and Policy Analysis," *Kyklos* 46: 3–25.

(1995). "Decision Externalities, Economic Efficiency and Institutional Response," *Canadian Public Policy* September, pp. 344–61.

(1997). "The Political Economy of Taxation," in Dennis Mueller (Ed.), *Perspectives on Public Choice*. Cambridge: Cambridge University Press, pp. 481–505.

Hillman, Arye L. (1989). *The Political Economy of Protection*. Chur, Switzerland: Harwood.

Hinich, Melvin (1977). "Equilibrium in Spatial Voting: The Median Voter Result Is an Artifact," *Journal of Economic Theory* 16: 208–19.

Hinich, Melvin, John Leyard, and Peter Ordeshook (1972). "Nonvoting and the Existence of Equilibrium under Majority Rule," *Journal of Economic Theory* 4: 144–53.

(1973). "A Theory of Electoral Equilibrium: A Spatial Analysis Based on the Theory of Games," *Journal of Politics* 35: 154–93.

Hinich, Melvin, and Michael Munger (1994). *Ideology and the Theory of Political Choice*. Ann Arbor: University of Michigan Press.

Hinrichs, Harley H. (1966). *A General Theory of Tax Structure Change During Economic Development*. Cambridge, MA: Harvard University Law School.

Hirschman, A. O. (1970). *Exit, Voice and Loyalty*. Cambridge, MA: Harvard University Press.

Hochman, Harold M., and James D. Rogers (1969). "Pareto-Optimal Redistribution," *American Economic Review* 59: 542–77.

Hogan, Timothy D., and Robert B. Shelton (1973). "Interstate Tax Exportation and States' Fiscal Structure," *National Tax Journal* 26: 553–64.

Holcombe, Randall G., and Jeffrey A. Mills (1991). "The Government Budget Constraint," working paper no. 91–10–3, Florida State University, Tallahassee.

(1992). "Politics and Deficit Finance," working paper no. 92–03–1, Florida State University, Tallahassee.

Holsey, Cheryl M., and Thomas E. Borcherding (1997). "Why Does Government's Share of National Income Grow? An Assessment of the Recent Literature on the U.S. Experience," in D. Mueller (Ed.), *Perspectives on Public Choice: A Handbook*. Cambridge: Cambridge University Press, pp. 562–89.

Holtz–Eakin, Douglas (1992). "Elections and Aggregation: Interpreting Econometric Analyses of Local Governments," *Public Choice* 74: 17–42.

Holtz–Eakin, Douglas, and Harvey S. Rosen (1988). "Tax Deductibility and Municipal Budget Structure," in Harvey S. Rosen (Ed.), *Fiscal Federalism: Quantitative Studies*. Chicago: University of Chicago Press, pp. 107–26.

Hoover, Kevin D., and Steven M. Sheffrin (1992). "Causation, Spending, and Taxes: Sand in the Sandbox or Tax Collector for the Welfare State?" *American Economic Review* 82: 225–48.

Howitt, Peter (1990). "Candidate Preferences versus Uncertainty in Models of Probabilistic Voting," unpublished manuscript, University of Western Ontario.

Hunter, William J., and Michael A. Nelson (1989). "Interest Group Demand for Taxation," *Public Choice* 62: 41–61.

Husted, Thomas A., and Lawrence W. Kenny (1997). "The Effect of the Expansion of the Voting Franchise on the Size of Government," *Journal of Political Economy* 105: 54–82.

Hyman, David N. (1996). *Public Finance. A Contemporary Application of Theory to Policy*, 5th ed., Chicago: The Dryden Press.

Ingberman, Daniel, and Robert P. Inman (1988). "The Political Economy of Fiscal Policy," in Paul G. Hare (Ed.), *Surveys in Public Sector Economics* Oxford: Basil Blackwell, pp. 105–60.

Inman, Robert P. (1987). "Markets, Governments and the 'New' Political Economy," in A. Auerbach and M. Feldstein (Eds.), *Handbook of Public Economics*, vol. 2. Amsterdam: North-Holland, pp. 647–778.

(1989). "The Local Decision to Tax: Evidence from Large U.S. Cities," *Regional Science and Urban Economics* 19: 455–91.

(1993). "Local Interests, Central Leadership, and the Passage of TRA86," *Journal of Policy Analysis and Management* 12: 156–80.

Inman, Robert P., and Michael A. Fitts (1990). "Political Institutions and Fiscal Policy: Evidence from the U.S. Historical Record," *Journal of Law, Economics and Organization* 6, Special Issue, pp. 79–132.

Innis, Harold (1972). "A Defense of the Tariff," in R. Neill (1972), *A New Theory of Value: The Canadian Economics of H. A. Innis*. Toronto: University of Toronto Press, pp. 149–59.

Institute for Fiscal Studies [IFS] (1978). *The Structure and Reform of Direct Taxation* (Report of a Committee Chaired by Professor J. E. Meade). London: Allen & Unwin.

Jacobsen, G. C. (1985). "Money and Votes Reconsidered: Congressional Elections 1972–1982," *Public Choice* 47: 7–62.

Johansen, Leif (1963). "Some Notes on the Lindahl Theory of Determination of Public Expenditures," *International Economic Review* 4: 346–58.

(1965). *Public Economics.* Amsterdam: North-Holland.

(1977). "The Theory of Public Goods: Misplaced Emphasis?" *Journal of Public Economics* 7: 147–52.

Jorgenson, Dale W., and Kun-Young Yun (1990). "Tax Reform and U.S Economic Growth," *Journal of Political Economy* 98(5), part 2, pp. S151–S193.

(1991). "The Excess Burden of Taxation in the United States," *Journal of Accounting, Auditing and Finance* 6: 487–508.

Jorgenson, Dale W., and Ralph Landau (Eds.) (1993). *Tax Reform and the Cost of Capital: An International Comparison.* Washington, DC: Brookings Institution.

Kanbur, S. M. R., and Michael Keen (1993). "Jeux Sans Frontieres: Tax Competition and Tax Coordination When Countries Differ in Size," *American Economic Review*, 83: 877–93.

Kanbur, S. M. R., and G. D. Myles (1992). "Policy Choice and Political Constraints," *European Journal of Political Economy* 8: 1–29.

Kaplow, Louis (1989). "Horizontal Equity: Measures in Search of a Principle," *National Tax Journal* 42: 139–54.

(1995). "A Model of the Optimal Complexity of Legal Rules," *Journal of Law, Economics, and Organization* 11: 150–63.

Kau, James B., and Paul H. Rubin (1981). "The Size of Government," *Public Choice* 37: 261–74.

Kaufman, George G., and Kenneth T. Rosen (1981). *The Property Tax Revolt: The Case of Proposition 13.* Cambridge, MA: Ballinger.

Kenny, Lawrence W., and Mark Toma (1997). "The Role of Tax Bases and Collection Costs in the Determination of Income Tax Rates, Seigniorage and Inflation," *Public Choice* 92: 75–90.

Kenyon, Daphne A., and John Kincaid (Eds.) (1991). *Competition among States and Local Governments: Efficiency and Equity in American Federalism.* Washington, DC: Urban Institute.

Kiesling, H. J. (1990). "Economic and Political Foundations of Tax Structure: Comment," *American Economic Review*, 80: 931–4.

Kirchgassner, Gebhard (1997). "Probabilistic Voting and Equilibrium: An Impossibility Result," paper presented at the European Public Choice Meetings (April, Prague).

Knight, Frank H. (1950). "The Role of Principles in Economics and Politics," reprinted in *On the History and Method of Economics: Selected Essays.* Chicago: University of Chicago Press (1964).

Kolm, Serge-Christophe (1987). "Public Economics," in J. Eatwell, M. Milgate and P. Newman (Eds.), *The New Palgrave: A Dictionary of Economics.* London: Macmillan.

Kramer, G. H. (1977). "A Dynamical Model of Political Equilibrium," *Journal of Economic Theory* 15: 310–34.

Kramer, G. H., and A. Klevorick (1974). "Existence of a 'Local' Cooperative Equilibrium in a Class of Voting Games," *Review of Economic Studies* 41: 539–47.

Kristov, Lorenzo, Peter Lindert, and Robert McClelland (1992). "Pressure Groups and Redistribution," *Journal of Public Economics* 48: 135–63.

Kydland, Finn E., and Edward C. Prescott (1977). "Rules Rather Than Discretion: The Inconsistency of Optimal Plans," *Journal of Political Economy* 85: 473–91.

(1980). "Dynamic Optimal Taxation, Rational Expectations and Optimal Control," *Journal of Economic Dynamics and Control* 2: 79–91.

Ladd, Helen F. (1992). "Mimicking of Local Tax Burdens among Neighbouring Counties," *Public Finance Quarterly* 20: 450–67.

(1993). "State Responses to the TRA86 Revenue Windfalls: A New Test of the Flypaper Effect," *Journal of Policy Analysis and Management* 12: 82–103.

Lafay, Jean-Dominique (1993). "The Silent Revolution of Probabilistic Voting," in A. Breton, G. Galeotti, P. Salmon, and W. Wintrobe (Eds.), *Preferences and Democracy*. Dordrecht: Kluwer, pp. 159–92.

Laffer, Arthur B. (1981). "Government Extractions and Revenue Deficiencies," *Cato Journal* 1: 1–23.

Landon, Stuart, and David L. Ryan (1997). "The Political Costs of Taxes and Government Spending." *Canadian Journal of Economics* 30: 85–111.

Leacy, F. H. (Ed.) (1983). *Historical Statistics of Canada.* 2nd ed. Ottawa: Statistics Canada.

Ledyard, John O. (1984). "The Pure Theory of Large Two-Candidate Elections," in Allan Meltzer, Thomas Romer, and Howard Rosenthal (Eds.), *Public Choice* 44: 7–41.

Lee, Lung–Fei (1981). "Simultaneous Equations Models with Discrete and Censored Dependent Variables," in Charles F. Manski and Daniel McFadden (Eds.), *Structural Analysis of Discrete Data with Econometric Applications*. Cambridge, MA: MIT Press, pp. 346–64.

Levi, Margaret (1988). *Of Rule and Revenue*. Berkeley: University of California Press.

Liebowitz, Arleen, and Robert Tollison (1980). "A Theory of Legislative Organization: Making the Most of Your Majority," *Quarterly Journal of Economics* 94: 261–77.

Lindahl, Eric (1919). *Die Gerechtigkeit der Besteuerung*. Reprinted in part as "Just Taxation: A Positive Solution" (translation by Elizabeth Henderson) in R. A. Musgrave and A. T. Peacock (eds.), *Classics in the Theory of Public Finance*. London: Macmillan (1958).

(1959). "Om Skatteprinciper och Skattepolitik," in *Ekonomi Politik Samhalle*, Festkrift till Bertil Ohlins 60-arsdag, Stockholm 1959: 151–71. Translated by T. L. Johnston as "Tax Principles and Tax Policy," in A. Peacock, R. Turvey, W. Stolper, and H. Liesner (Eds.), *International Economic Papers*, No. 10. London: Macmillan, pp. 7–23.

Lindbeck, Assar (1985). "Redistribution Policy and the Expansion of the Public Sector," *Journal of Public Economics* 29: 309–28.

Lindbeck, Assar, and Jorgen W. Weibull (1987). "Balanced–Budget Redistribution as the Outcome of Political Competition," *Public Choice* 52: 273–97.

Lindblom, Charles E. (1969). *The Policy-Making Process*. Englewood Cliffs, NJ: Prentice Hall.

Lindert, Peter (1989). "Modern Fiscal Redistribution: A Preliminary Essay," working paper no. 55, Agricultural History Center, University of California, Davis (June).

Lindsay, C. B. (1972). "Two Theories of Tax Deductibility," *National Tax Journal* 25: 43–52.

Lindsay, Lawrence B. (1988). "Federal Deductibility of State and Local Taxes: A Test of Public Choice by Representative Government," in Harvey S. Rosen

(Ed.), *Fiscal Federalism: Quantitative Studies*. Chicago: University of Chicago Press, pp. 137–75.

Lodin, Sven–Olof (1978). *Progressive Expenditure Tax – An Alternative?* (Report of the 1972 Government Commission on Taxation). Stockholm: Liber Forlag.

Logan, Harold A. (1928). *The History of Trade-Union Organization in Canada.* Chicago: University of Chicago Press.

Logan, Robert R. (1986). "Fiscal Illusion and the Grantor Government," *Journal of Political Economy* 94: 1304–18.

Lovell, Michael C. (1986). "Tests of the Rational Expectations Hypothesis," *American Economic Review* 76: 110–24.

Lucas, Robert, and Nancy Stokey (1983). "Optimal Fiscal and Monetary Policy in an Economy without Capital," *Journal of Monetary Economics* 12: 55–94.

Luckenbach, Helga (1986). *Theoretische Grundlagen der Wirtschaftspolitik.* Munich: Vahlen.

Maddala, G. S. (1983). *Limited-Dependent and Qualitative Variables in Econometrics.* Cambridge: Cambridge University Press.

Magee, Stephen P., William A. Brock, and Leslie Young (1989). *Black Hole Tariffs and Endogenous Policy Theory.* Cambridge: Cambridge University Press.

Mankiw, N. Gregory (1987). "The Optimal Collection of Seigniorage: Theory and Evidence," *Journal of Monetary Economics* 20: 327–41.

Markusen, James, and Randy Wigle (1989). "Nash Equilibrium Tariffs for the United States and Canada: The Roles of Country Size, Scale Economies and Capital Mobility," *Journal of Political Economy* 97: 368–86.

Marshall, Alfred (1890). *Principles of Economics.* London: Macmillan (1966).

Martin, Cathie J. (1991). *Shifting the Burden: The Struggle Over Growth and Corporate Taxation.* Chicago: University of Chicago Press.

Maslove, Allan M. (1989). *Tax Reform in Canada: The Process and Impact.* Ottawa: Institute for Research on Public Policy.

Mayer, Wolfgang (1984). "Endogenous Tariff Formation," *American Economic Review* 74: 970–85.

Mayer, Wolfgang, and Jun Li (1994). "Interest Groups, Electoral Competition, and Probabilistic Voting for Trade Policies," *Economics and Politics* 6: 59–78.

Mayer, Wolfgang, and Raymond Riezman (1989). "Tariff Formation in a Multidimensional Voting Model," *Economics and Politics* 1: 61–79.

Mayhew, David R. (1974). *Congress: The Electoral Connection.* New Haven, CT: Yale University Press.

Mayshar, Joram (1991). "Taxation with Costly Administration," *Scandinavian Journal of Economics* 93: 75–88.

McCubbins, Mathew D. (1991). "Party Politics, Divided Government, and Budget Deficits," in Samuel Kernell (Ed.), *Parallel Politics: Economic Policy Making in the United States and Japan.* Washington DC: Brookings Institution, pp. 83–118.

McDaniel, Paul R., and Stanley S. Surrey (1985). *International Aspects of Tax Expenditures: A Comparative Analysis.* Deventer, The Netherlands: Kluwer Law and Taxation.

McDiarmid, O. J. (1946). *Commercial Policy in the Canadian Economy*. Cambridge, MA: Harvard University Press.

McKelvey, Richard D. (1976). "Intransitivities in Multidimensional Voting Models and Some Implications for Agenda Control," *Journal of Economic Theory* 12: 472–82.

McLure, Charles E. (1967). "The Interstate Exporting of State and Local Taxes: Estimates of 1962," *National Tax Journal* 20: 49–77.

  (1984). "The Evolution of Tax Advice and the Taxation of Capital Income in the U.S.A.," *Government and Policy* 2.

McLure, Charles E., and George R. Zodrow (1996). "A Hybrid Approach to the Direct Taxation of Consumption," in Michael J. Boskin (Ed.), *Frontiers of Tax Reform*. Palo Alto, CA: Hoover Institution Press.

McNollgast [M. McCubbins, R. Noll, B. Weingast] (1990). "Slack, Public Interest, and Structure-Induced Policy," *Journal of Law, Economics and Organization* 6, Special Issue, pp. 203–12.

Meltsner, Arnold (1972). "Political Feasibility and Policy Analysis," *Public Administration Review* 32: 859–67.

Meltzer, Allan H., and Scott F. Richard (1981). "A Rational Theory of the Size of Government," *Journal of Political Economy* 89: 914–27.

  (1983). "Tests of a Rational Theory of the Size of Government," *Public Choice* 41: 403–18.

  (1985), "A Positive Theory of In-Kind Transfers and the Negative Income Tax," *Public Choice* 47: 231–65.

Metcalf, Gilbert E. (1993). "Tax Exporting, Federal Deductibility and State Tax Structure," *Journal of Policy Analysis and Management* 12: 109–26.

Migué, Jean-Luc (1977). "Controls versus Subsidies in the Economic Theory of Regulation," *Journal of Law and Economics* 20: 213–21.

Mill, J. S. (1817). *Principles of Political Economy* (edited by W. J. Ashly). London: Longmans Green (1921).

  (1836). *On the Definition of Political Economy*. Quoted in Marc Blaug, *The Methodology of Economics*. Cambridge: Cambridge University Press, p. 65 (1980).

Mirrlees, J. A. (1971). "An Exploration in the Theory of Optimum Income Taxation," *Review of Economic Studies* 38: 175–208.

Moomau, Pamela H., and Rebecca B. Morton (1992). "Revealed Preferences for Property Taxes: An Empirical Study of Perceived Tax Incidence," *Review of Economics and Statistics* 74: 176–9.

Mueller, Dennis C. (1989). *Public Choice II*. Cambridge: Cambridge University Press.

  (1990). "Public Choice and the Consumption Tax," in Manfred Rose (Ed.), *Heidelberg Conference on Taxing Consumption*. Heildelberg: Springer-Verlag, pp. 227–40.

  (1997). *Perspectives on Public Choice: A Handbook*. Cambridge: Cambridge University Press.

Mueller, Dennis C., and Peter Murrell (1985). "Interest Groups and the Political Economy of Government Size," in F. Forte and A. Peacock (Eds.), *Public Expenditure and Government Growth*. Oxford: Basil Blackwell, pp. 13–36.

Musgrave, Richard A. (1959). *The Theory of Public Finance*. New York: McGraw-Hill.

  (1969). *Fiscal Systems*. New Haven, CT: Yale University Press.

(1976). "ET, OT and SBT," *Journal of Public Economics* 6: 3–16.

(1980). "An Essay on Fiscal Sociology," in H. Aaron and M. Boskin (Eds.), *The Economics of Taxation*. Washington, DC: Brookings Institution, pp. 361–90.

(1981). "Fiscal Functions: Order and Politics," Acceptance Paper delivered on receiving the Frank E. Seidman Distinguished Award in Political Economy. Memphis, TN: P. K. Seidman Foundation (November).

(1983). "The Nature of Horizontal Equity and the Principle of Broad–Based Taxation: A Friendly Critique," in John G. Head (Ed.), *Taxation Issues of the 1980's*. Sydney: Australian Tax Research Foundation, pp. 21–33.

(1987). "Short of Euphoria," *Journal of Economic Perspectives* 1: 59–72.

Musgrave, Richard A., and Peggy B. Musgrave (1989). *Public Finance in Theory and Practice*. 5th ed. New York: McGraw-Hill.

Musgrave, Richard A., and Alan T. Peacock (1967). *Classics in the Theory of Public Finance*. London: Macmillan.

Myles, Gareth D. (1995). *Public Economics*. Cambridge: Cambridge University Press.

Nannestad, Peter, and Martin Paldam (1994). "The VP–function: A Survey of the Literature on Vote and Popularity Functions After 25 Years," *Public Choice* 79: 213–45.

(1996). "Government's Free Lunch: A Study of Danish Mass-Level Reactions to Possible Tax Cuts," paper presented at the European Public Choice Meetings, (Tiberias, Israel).

Nash, John (1950). "The Bargaining Problem," *Econometrica* 18: 155–62.

(1951). "Non-cooperative Games," *Annals of Mathematics* 54: 286–95.

(1953). "Two Person Cooperative Games," *Econometrica* 21: 128–40.

Nechyba, Thomas (1993). "Fiscal Federalism and Local Public Finance: A Computable General Equilibrium (CGE) Framework," *International Tax and Public Finance* 3: 215–31.

Nelson, Michael A. (1986). "An Empirical Analysis of State and Local Tax Structure in the Context of the Leviathan Model of Government," *Public Choice* 49: 283–94.

Nelson, Phillip (1976). "Political Information," *Journal of Political Economy* 19: 315–36.

Nelson, Robert H. (1987). "The Economics Profession and the Making of Public Policy," *Journal of Economic Literature* 25: 49–51.

Newey, Whitney K. (1987). "Efficient Estimation of Limited Dependent Variable Models with Endogenous Explanatory Variables," *Journal of Econometrics* 36: 231–50.

North, Douglass C. (1990). *Institutions, Institutional Change and Economic Performance*. Cambridge: Cambridge University Press.

North, Douglass C., and Barry R. Weingast (1989). "Constitutions and Commitment: The Evolution of Institutions Governing Public Choice in Seventeenth–Century England," *Journal of Economic History* 49: 803–32.

Oates, Wallace E. (1985). "Searching for Leviathan: An Empirical Study," *American Economic Review* 75: 748–57.

(1991). "On the Nature and Measurement of Fiscal Illusion: A Survey," in W. Oates, *Studies in Fiscal Federalism*. Cheltenham, UK: Edward Elgar, pp. 431–48.

Oliver, P., G. Maxwell, and R. Teixeira (1985). "Interdependence, Group Heterogeneity and the Production of Collective Action: A Theory of the Mass," paper presented at Public Choice meetings (February, New Orleans).

Olson, Mancur (1965). *The Logic of Collective Action.* Cambridge, MA: Harvard University Press.

   (1982a). *The Rise and Decline of Nations.* New Haven, CT: Yale University Press.

   (1982b). "A Political Theory of Regulation with Some Observations on Railway Abandonments: A Comment," in H. Meltzer, P. Ordeshook, and T. Romer (Eds.), *Public Choice* 39: 107–11.

Ordeshook, Peter C. (1986). *Game Theory and Political Theory: An Introduction.* Cambridge: Cambridge University Press.

   (1992). *A Political Theory Primer.* New York: Routledge.

Ordover, Janusz A., and Andrew Schotter (1981). "On the Political Sustainability of Taxes," *American Economic Review Papers and Proceedings* 71: 278–82.

Organization for Economic Cooperation and Development [OECD] (1981). *Long–Term Trends in Tax Revenues of O.E.C.D. Member Countries, 1955–1980.* Paris: OECD.

   (1986). *Personal Income Tax Systems under Changing Economic Conditions.* Paris: OECD.

Ort, Deborah (1988). *Tax Reform 1987: The White Paper Proposals, the Report of the House and Senate Committees, and the Notice of Ways and Means.* (Tax Memo no. 73). Toronto: Canadian Tax Foundation (February).

Osborne, M. J. (1981). "On Explaining the Tax System: Why Do Some Goods Bear Higher Taxes Than Others?" Discussion Paper Series, no. 100, Columbia University, New York.

O'Sullivan, Arthur, Terri A. Sexton, and Steven M. Sheffrin (Eds.) (1995). *Property Taxes and Tax Revolts; The Legacy of Proposition 13.* Cambridge: Cambridge University Press.

Owen, Guillermo (1995). *Game Theory.* 3rd ed. San Diego: Academic Press.

Palda, Filip (1989). "Electoral Spending," Ph.D. dissertation, University of Chicago.

Palda, Kristian S. (1975). "The Effect of Expenditure on Political Success," *Journal of Law and Economics* 18: 745–71.

Pechman, Joseph A. (1985). *Who Paid the Taxes, 1966–85.* Washington, DC: Brookings Institution.

   (1987). *Federal Tax Policy,* 5th Ed. Washington DC: Brookings Institution.

Peck, Richard M. (1986). "Power and Linear Income Taxes: An Example," *Econometrica* 54: 87–94.

Peltzman, Sam (1976). "Toward a More General Theory of Regulation," *Journal of Law and Economics* 19: 219–40.

   (1980). "The Growth of Government," *Journal of Law and Economics* 23: 209–87.

Perry, J. Harvey (1955). *Taxes, Tariffs, and Subsidies,* vol. I and II. Toronto: University of Toronto Press.

Persson, Torsten, and Lars E. O. Svenson (1989). "Why a Stubborn Conservative Would Run a Deficit: Policy with Time-Inconsistent Preferences," *Quarterly Journal of Economics* 104: 325–45.

Persson, Torsten, and Guido Tabellini (1990). *Macroeconomic Policy, Credibility and Politics.* Chur, Switzerland: Harwood.

Peters, B.G. (1991). *The Politics of Taxation.* Cambridge: Basil Blackwell.

Pfahler, Wilhelm (1988). "On Measuring the Welfare Cost of Public Expenditure: A Simple General Equilibrium Approach," in D. Bos, M. Rose, and C. Seidl (Eds.), *Welfare and Efficiency in Public Economics*. New York: Springer-Verlag, pp. 317–37.

Phares, Donald (1980). *Who Pays State and Local Taxes?* Cambridge, MA: Oelgeschlager, Gunn and Nain.

Phelps, E. S. (1977). "Rational Taxation," *Social Research* 44: 657–67.

Phillips, Kevin (1990). *The Politics of Rich and Poor*. New York: Random House.

Piggott, John, and John Whalley (1987). "Interpreting Net Fiscal Incidence Calculations," *Review of Economics and Statistics* 69: 685–94.

Plotnick, Robert (1982). "The Concept and Measurement of Horizontal Equity," *Journal of Public Economics* 17: 373–91.

Plott, Charles (1967). "A Notion of Equilibrium and Its Possibility under Majority Rule," *American Economic Review* 57: 787–806.

(1976). "Axiomatic Social Choice Theory: An Overview and Interpretation," *American Journal of Political Science* 20: 511–96.

Plumb, J. H. (1969). "The Growth of the Electorate in England from 1600 to 1715," *Past and Present* 45: 90–116.

Pollock, Stephen H. (1991). "Mechanisms for Exporting the State Sales Tax Burden in the Absence of Federal Deductibility," *National Tax Journal* 44: 297–310.

Pommerehne, Werner M. (1978). "Institutional Approaches to Public Expenditure," *Journal of Public Economics* 9: 255–80.

(1980). "Public Choice Approaches to Explain Fiscal Redistribution," in Karl W. Roskamp (Ed.), *Public Choice and Public Finance*. Paris: Cujas, pp. 169–90.

Pommerehne, Werner M., and Friedrich Schneider (1978). "Fiscal Illusion, Political Institutions and Local Public Spending," *Kyklos* 31: 381–408.

(1983). "Does Government in a Representative Democracy Follow a Majority of Voters' Preferences? An Empirical Examination," in Horst Hanusch (Ed.), *Anatomy of Government Deficiencies*. New York: Springer-Verlag, pp. 61–84.

Pommerehne, Werner M., and Hannelore Weck-Hannemann (1997). "Tax Rates, Tax Administration and Income Tax Evasion in Switzerland," *Public Choice* 88: 161–70.

Popper, Karl (1962). *The Open Society and Its Enemies*. 4th ed. New York: Routledge and Kegan Paul.

(1988). "The Open Society and Its Critics Revisited," *The Economist* 23: 19–22.

Porritt, E. (1908). *Sixty Years of Protection in Canada, 1846–1907*. London: Macmillan.

Poterba, James M. (1994). "State Responses to Fiscal Crises: The Effects of Budgetary Institutions and Politics," *Journal of Political Economy* 102: 799–821.

Poterba, James M., and Julio J. Rotemberg (1990). "Inflation and Taxation with Optimizing Governments," *Journal of Money, Credit and Banking* 22: 1–18.

Progressive Conservative Party of Canada (1984). *Task Force on Revenue Canada* (April).

Quirk, James, and Saposnik, Rubin (1968). *Introduction to General Equilibrium Theory and Welfare Economics*. New York: McGraw-Hill.

Ramanathan, R. (1995). *Introductory Econometrics with Applications*. Chicago and Orlando: The Dryden Press–Harcourt Brace.

Ramsey, Frank P. (1927). "A Contribution to the Theory of Taxation," *Economic Journal* 37: 47–61.

Rauch, Jonathan (1991). "The Regulatory President," *National Journal*, November 30, pp. 2902–6.

Rawls, J. (1971). *A Theory of Justice*. Cambridge, MA: Harvard University Press.

Renaud, Paul S. A., and Frans Λ. Λ. M. van Winden (1987). "Tax Rate and Government Expenditure," *Kyklos* 40: 349–67.

Rich, Georg (1988). *The Cross of Gold: Money and the Canadian Business Cycle*. Ottawa: Carleton University Press.

Riker, William H. (1986). *The Art of Political Manipulation*. New Haven, CT: Yale University Press.

Rivers, Douglas, and Quang H. Vuong (1988). "Limited Information Estimators and Exogeneity Tests for Simultaneous Probit Models," *Journal of Econometrics* 39: 347–66.

Roberts, K. W. S. (1977). "Voting over Income Tax Schedules," *Journal of Public Economics* 8: 329–40.

Rodrik, Dani (1992). "Political Economy and Development Policy," *European Economic Review* 36: 329–36.

Rogers, Carol Ann (1987). "Expenditure Taxes, Income Taxes, and Time-Inconsistency," *Journal of Public Economics* 32: 215–30.

Romer, Thomas (1975). "Individual Welfare, Majority Voting and the Properties of a Linear Income Tax," *Journal of Public Economics* 4: 163–85.

(1977). "Majority Voting on Tax Parameters – Some Further Results," *Journal of Public Economics* 7: 127–33.

Romer, Thomas, and Howard Rosenthal (1978). "Political Resource Allocation, Controlled Agendas and the Status Quo," *Public Choice* 33: 27–43.

(1979a). "The Elusive Median Voter," *Journal of Public Economics* 12: 143–70.

(1979b). "Bureaucrats versus Voters: On the Political Economy of Resource Allocation by Direct Democracy," *Quarterly Journal of Economics* 93: 563–87.

(1982). "Median Voters or Budget Maximizers: Evidence from School Expenditure Referenda," *Economic Inquiry* 20: 556–78.

(1984). "Voting Models and Empirical Evidence," *American Scientist*, September–October, pp. 465–73.

Rose, Manfred (Ed.) (1990). *Heidelberg Congress on Taxing Consumption*. Heidelberg: Springer-Verlag.

Rose, R. (1985). "Maximizing Tax Revenue While Minimizing Political Costs," *Journal of Public Policy* 5: 289–320.

Rosen, Harvey S. (Ed.) (1988). *Fiscal Federalism: Quantitative Studies*. Chicago: University of Chicago Press.

(1992). *Public Finance*. 3rd ed. Homewood, IL: Irwin.

Rosenthal, Howard (1990). "The Setter Model," in James M. Enelow and Melvin Hinich (Eds.), *Advances in the Spatial Theory of Voting*. Cambridge: Cambridge University Press, pp. 199–234.

Ross, Tom W. (1984). "Uncovering Regulators' Social Welfare Weights," *Rand Journal of Economics*, 15: 152–5.

Roubini, Nuriel, and Jeffrey Sachs (1989). "Political and Economic Determinants of Budget Deficits in the Industrial Democracies," *European Economic Review* 33: 903–38.

Royal Commission on Taxation (1966) (Chaired by Kenneth LeM. Carter). *Report.* Ottawa: Queen's Printer.

Rutherford, Thomas (1987). "Applied General Equilibrium Modelling," Ph.D. thesis, Stanford University.

(1988). "General Equilibrium Modelling with MPS/GE", Department of Economics, University of Western Ontario.

Rutherford, Thomas, and Stanley L. Winer (1990). "Endogenous Policy in a Computational General Equilibrium Framework," working paper no. 9107, Department of Economics, University of Western Ontario (February, revised May).

(1995). "Endogenous Tax Policy in a Computable Economic and Political Equilibrium: With Application to the United States 1973–1983," working paper, School of Public Administration Carleton University, Ottawa Revised (January).

Sadka, E. (1976). "Income Distribution, Incentive Effects and Optimal Income Taxation," *Review of Economic Studies* 43: 261–8.

Salmon, Pierre (1981). "The Logic of Pressure Groups and the Structure of the Public Sector," *European Journal of Political Economy* 3: 55–86.

(1991). "Checks and Balances and International Openness," in A. Breton, G. Galeotti, P. Salmon, and R. Wintrobe (Eds.), *The Competitive State*. Dordrecht: Kluwer, pp. 169–84.

Samuelson, Paul A. (1954). "The Pure Theory of Public Expenditure," *Review of Economics and Statistics* 36: 387–9.

Sandler, Todd (1992). *Collective Action: Theory and Applications.* Cambridge: Cambridge University Press.

Sandmo, Agnar (1984). "Some Insights from the New Theory of Public Finance," *Empirica* 2: 111–24.

Schmidt, Peter (1981). "Constraints on Parameters in Simultaneous Tobit and Probit Models," in Charles F. Manski and Daniel McFadden (Eds.), *Structural Analysis of Discrete Data with Econometric Applications*. Cambridge, MA: MIT Press, pp. 346–64.

Schneider, Friedrich, and Werner M. Pommerehne (1980). "Politico–Economic Interactions in Australia: Some Empirical Evidence," *Economic Record* 56: 113–31.

Schofield, Norman (1978). "Instability of Simple Dynamic Games," *Review of Economic Studies* 45: 575–94.

(1983). "Generic Instability of Majority Rule," *Review of Economic Studies* 50: 695–705.

Scholz, John Karl (1995). "Documentation for 1983 General Equilibrium Data," *Model User Group News* 3(1), University of Waterloo.

Schumpeter, Joseph A. (1918). "The Crisis of the Tax State," translated in A. Peacock, R. Turvey, W. Stolper, and H. Liesner (Eds.), *International Economic Papers*, No. 4. London: Macmillan (1954). Reprinted in Richard Swedberg (Ed.), *Joseph A. Schumpeter: The Economics and Sociology of Capitalism*. Princeton, NJ: Princeton University Press (1991).

(1950). *Capitalism, Socialism and Democracy.* New York: Harper & Row (reprinted 1975).

(1954). *History of Economic Analysis.* Oxford University Press.

Schwadron, Terry, and Paul Richter (1984). *California and the American Tax Revolt: Proposition 13 Five Years Later.* Berkeley and Los Angeles: University of California Press.

Schwartz, Thomas (1994). "Representation as Agency and the Pork Barrel Paradox," *Public Choice* 78: 3–22.

Scitovsky, Tibor (1951). *Welfare and Competition.* Homewood, IL: Irwin.

Seade, Jesus (1977). "On the Shape of Optimal Tax Schedules," *Journal of Public Economics* 7: 203–35.

(1982). "On the Sign of the Optimum Marginal Income Tax," *Review of Economic Studies* 49: 637–43.

Shapley, Lloyd S. (1953). "A Value for n-Person Games," in H. Kuhn and A. W. Tucker (Eds.), *Contributions to the Theory of Games*, vol. II (Annals of Mathematics Studies, no. 28). Princeton, NJ: University Press, pp. 307–17.

Sheffrin, S. M. (1983). *Rational Expectations.* Cambridge: Cambridge University Press.

(1996), "Tax Reforms and the Growth of Government," unpublished paper, International Institute of Public Finance 52nd Congress (August, Tel Aviv).

Shepsle, Kenneth A. (1979). "Institutional Arrangements and Equilibrium in Multi-dimensional Voting Models," *American Journal of Political Science* 23: 27–59.

(1991). *Models of Multiparty Competition.* New York: Harwood.

Shepsle, Kenneth. A., and Barry R. Weingast (1981). "Structure-Induced Equilibrium and Legislative Choice" *Public Choice* 37: 503–19.

(1984). "Uncovered Sets and Sophisticated Voting Outcomes with Implications for Agenda Institutions," *American Journal of Political Science* 28: 49–74.

Shoven, John B. (1983). "Applied General-Equilibrium Tax Modelling," *International Monetary Fund, Staff Papers* 30: 394–420.

Shoven, John B., and John Whalley (1973). "General Equilibrium with Taxes: A Computational Procedure and an Existence Proof," *Review of Economic Studies* 60: 475–90.

(1977). "Equal Yield Tax Alternatives: General Equilibrium Computational Techniques," *Journal of Public Economics* 8: 211–24.

(1984). "Applied General Equilibrium Models of Taxation and International Trade: An Introduction and Survey," *Journal of Economic Literature* 22: 1007–51.

(Eds.) (1992a). *Canada–U.S. Tax Comparisons.* Chicago: University of Chicago Press.

(1992b). *Applying General Equilibrium.* New York: Cambridge University Press.

Shubik, Martin (1982). *Game Theory in the Social Sciences. Concepts and Solutions.* Cambridge, MA: MIT Press.

(1984). *A Game-Theoretic Approach to Political Economy.* Cambridge, MA: MIT Press.

Simon, Herbert A. (1981). *The Sciences of the Artificial,* 2nd ed. Cambridge, MA: MIT Press.

Simons, Henry C. (1938). *Personal Income Taxation: The Definition of Income as a Problem of Fiscal Policy.* Chicago: University of Chicago Press.

(1950). *Federal Tax Reform.* Chicago: University of Chicago Press.

Sjoquist, D. (1981). "A Median Voter Analysis of Variations in the Use of Property Taxes Among Local Governments," *Public Choice* 36: 273–85.

Skelton, Oscar D. (1913). *General Economic History of the Dominion 1867–1912.* Toronto: Publisher's Association of Canada.

Slemrod, Joel (1983). "Do We Know How Progressive the Income Tax System Should Be?" *National Tax Journal* 36: 361–9.

(1990a). "Optimal Taxation and Optimal Tax Systems," *Journal of Economic Perspectives* 4: 157–78.

(Ed.) (1990b). *Do Taxes Matter? The Impact of the Tax Reform Act of 1986*. Cambridge, MA: MIT Press.

Slemrod, Joel, and Shlomo Yitzhaki (1996). "The Cost of Taxation and the Marginal Efficiency Cost of Funds," *International Monetary Fund Staff Papers* 43: 172–98.

Slutsky, Steven (1975). "Abstentions and Majority Equilibrium," *Journal of Economic Theory* 11: 292–304.

Snyder, James M., and Gerald H. Kramer (1988). "Fairness, Self-Interest and the Politics of the Progressive Income Tax," *Journal of Public Economics* 36: 197–230.

Staaf, Robert J. (1978). "Homo Politicus and Homo Economicus: Advertising and Information," in D. Tuerck (Ed.), *The Political Economy of Advertising*. Washington, DC: American Enterprise Institute, pp. 135–57.

Steinmo, Sven (1989). "Political Institutions and Tax Policy in the United States, Sweden and Britain," *World Politics* 41: 500–35.

(1993). *Taxation and Democracy: Swedish, British and American Approaches to Financing the Modern State*. New Haven, CT: Yale University Press.

Stern, Nicholas (1987). "The Theory of Optimal Commodity and Income Taxation," in David Newbery and Nicholas Stern (Eds.), *The Theory of Taxation for Developing Countries*. Oxford University Press, pp. 22–59.

(1990). "Uniformity versus Selectivity in Indirect Taxation," *Economics and Politics* 2: 83–108.

Stewart, Charles H. (1991). "The Politics of Tax Reform in the 1980s," in Alberto Alesina and Geoffrey Carliner (Eds.), *Politics and Economics in the Eighties*. Chicago: University of Chicago Press.

Stigler, George J. (1970). "Director's Law of Public Income Redistribution," *Journal of Law and Economics* 13: 1–10.

(1971). "The Theory of Economic Regulation," *Bell Journal of Economic and Management Science* 2: 3–21.

(1972). "Economic Competition and Political Competition," *Public Choice* 8: 91–106.

Stiglitz, Joseph E. (1982). "Self-Selection and Pareto Efficient Taxation," *Journal of Public Economics* 17: 213–40.

(1987). "Pareto Efficient and Optimal Taxation and the New Welfare Economics," in Alan Auerbach and Martin Feldstein (Eds.), *Handbook of Public Economics 2* Amsterdam: North-Holland, pp. 991–1042.

(1988). *Economics of the Public Sector*. 2nd ed. New York: Norton.

Stiglitz, Joseph E., and Michael J. Boskin (1977). "Some Lessons from the New Public Finance," *American Economic Review, Papers and Proceedings* 67: 295–301.

Stikeman, Harry H. (1983). *Income Tax Act Annotated*, 12th ed. Toronto: Best Publishing.

Stiles, Nancy (1972). "Organizational Change: Emergence and Growth of the Western Farmers' Cooperative," Department of Economics, Queen's University, Kingston, Ontario.

Stockfish, J. A. (1985). "Value Added Taxes and the Size of Government: Some Evidence," *National Tax Journal* 38: 542–7.

Strom, Gerald S. (1990). *The Logic of Lawmaking: A Spatial Theory Approach*. Baltimore: Johns Hopkins University Press.

Stuart, C. (1984). "Welfare Costs per Dollar of Additional Tax Revenue in the United States," *American Economic Review* 74: 352–62.

Surrey, Stanley S. (1973). *Pathways to Tax Reform: The Concept of Tax Expenditures.* Cambridge, MA: Harvard University Press.

Surrey, Stanley S., and Paul R. McDaniel (1985). *Tax Expenditures.* Cambridge: Cambridge University Press.

Tabellini, Guido (1991). "The Politics of Intergenerational Redistribution," *Journal of Political Economy* 99: 335–57.

Tabellini, Guido, and Alberto Alesina (1990). "Voting on the Budget Deficit," *American Economic Review* 80: 37–49.

Tannenwald, Robert (1991). "The U.S. Tax Reform Act of 1986 and State Tax Competitiveness," in Daphne Kenyon and John Kincaid (Eds.), *Competition Among State and Local Governments.* Washington, DC: Urban Institute Press, pp. 177–204.

Tiebout, C. M. (1956). "A Pure Theory of Local Expenditures," *Journal of Political Economy* 64: 416–24.

Tinbergen, Jan (1954). *Centralization and Decentralization in Economic Policy.* Amsterdam: North–Holland.

Trebilcock, Michael J., Douglas H. Hartle, J. Robert Prichard, and Donald N. Dewees (1982). *The Choice of Governing Instrument.* Ottawa: Supply and Services Canada for the Economic Council of Canada.

Trehan, Bharat, and Carl E. Walsh (1990). "Seigniorage and Tax Smoothing in the United States 1914–1986," *Journal of Monetary Economics* 25: 97–112.

Tresch, Richard W. (1981). *Public Finance: A Normative Theory.* Plano, TX: Business Publications and Irwin-Dorsey.

Tullock, Gordon (1967). "The Welfare Costs of Tariffs, Monopolies and Theft," *Western Economic Journal* 5: 224–32.

  (1971). "The Charity of the Uncharitable," *Western Economic Journal* 9: 379–92.

  (1990). "The Cost of Special Privilege," in James Alt and Kenneth Shepsle (Eds.), *Perspectives on Positive Political Economy.* Cambridge: Cambridge University Press, pp. 195–211.

U.S. Department of Commerce, Bureau of the Census (various years). *State Government Tax Collections.*

  (1975). *Historical Statistics of the United States, 1790–1970.*

U.S. Department of the Treasury (1977). *Blueprints for Basic Tax Reform.* Washington, DC: U.S. Government Printing Office.

  (1984). *Tax Reform for Fairness, Simplicity and Economic Growth 3.* Washington, DC: U.S. Government Printing Office.

U.S. Government (1985). *The President's Tax Proposal.* Washington, DC: U.S. Government Printing Office.

U.S. President, Council of Economic Advisors (various years). *Economic Report of the President.* Washington, DC: U.S. Government Printing Office.

Urquhart, M. C. (1986). "New Estimates of Gross National Product, Canada, 1870 to 1926: Some Implications for Canadian Development," in S. Engerman and R. Gallman (Eds.), *Long-Term Factors in American Economic Growth.* Chicago: University of Chicago Press, pp. 9–94.

Usher, Dan (1991), "The Hidden Costs of Public Expenditure," in Richard M. Bird (Ed.), *More Taxing Than Taxes?* San Francisco: ICS Press, pp. 11–65.

(1992). *The Welfare Economics of Markets, Voting and Predation.* Ann Arbor: University of Michigan Press.

(1994). "The Significance of the Probabilistic Voting Theorem," *Canadian Journal of Economics* 27: 433–45.

(1995). *The Uneasy Case for Equalization Payments.* Vancouver: Fraser Institute.

van Velthoven, Ben (1989). *The Endogenization of Government Behavior in Macroeconomic Models.* New York: Springer-Verlag.

van Velthoven, Ben, and Frans A. A. M. van Winden (1991). "A Positive Model of Tax Reform," *Public Choice* 72: 61–86.

van Winden, Frans A. A. M. (1983). *On the Interaction Between State and Private Sector: A Study in Political Economics.* Amsterdam: North-Holland.

(1997). "On the Economic Theory of Interest Groups: Towards a Group Frame of Reference in Political Economics," invited paper, European Public Choice meetings (April, Prague).

Vining, Aidan R., and David L. Weimar (1988). "Information Asymmetry: A Policy Framework," paper presented at the Public Choice Society (March, San Francisco).

Vogel, Robert C., and Robert P. Trost (1979). "The Responses of State Government Receipts to Economic Fluctuations and the Allocation of Counter–Cyclical Revenue Sharing Grants," *Review of Economics and Statistics* 61: 389–400.

von Furstenberg, George M., Jeffrey R. Green, and Jin–Ho Jeong (1986), "Tax and Spend, or Spend and Tax?" *Review of Economics and Statistics* 68: 179–88.

von Hagen, Jurgen (1991). "A Note on the Empirical Effectiveness of Formal Fiscal Constraints," *Journal of Public Economics* 44: 199–210.

Wagner, Richard E. (1976). "Revenue Structure, Fiscal Illusion and Budgetary Choice," *Public Choice* 25: 45–61.

(1985a). "Tax Reform through Constitutional Limitation: A Sympathetic Critique," *Cumberland Law Review* 15: 475–97.

(1985b). "Normative and Positive Foundations of Tax Reform," *Cato Journal* 5: 385–400.

Warskett, George, Stanley L. Winer, and Walter Hettich (1998). "The Complexity of Tax Structure in Competitive Political Systems," *International Tax and Public Finance* 5: 127–55.

Webber, Carolyn and Aaron B. Wildavsky (1986). *A History of Taxation and Expenditure in the Western World.* New York: Simon and Schuster.

Weingast, Barry R. (1979). "A Rational Choice Perspective on Congressional Norms," *American Journal of Political Science* 23: 245–62.

(1996). "The Political Foundations of Democracy and the Rule of Law," A. Breton, G. Galeotti, P. Salmon, and R. Wintrobe (Eds.), *Understanding Democracy: A Social Science Perspective.* Cambridge: Cambridge University Press.

(1997). "Democratic Stability as a Self–Enforcing Equilibrium," in A. Breton, G. Galeotti, P. Salmon, and R. Wintrobe (Eds.), *Understanding Democracy: Economic and Political Perspectives.* Cambridge: Cambridge University Press, pp. 11–46.

Weingast, Barry R., and William J. Marshall (1988). "The Industrial Organization of Congress; or, Why Legislatures Like Firms Are Not Organized as Markets," *Journal of Political Economy* 96: 132–63.

West, Edwin G., and Stanley L. Winer (1980). "Optimal Fiscal Illusion and the Size of Government," *Public Choice* 35: 607–22.

Whalley, John (1984). "Regression or Progression: The Taxing Question of Incidence Analysis," *Canadian Journal of Economics* 17: 654–82.

White, H. (1980). "A Heteroscedasticity-Consistent Covariance Matrix Estimator and a Direct Test for Heteroscedasticity," *Econometrica* 48: 817–38.

White, K. J., S. D. Wong, D. Whistler, and S. A. Haun (1990). *SHAZAM User's Reference Manual Version 6.2.* New York: McGraw-Hill.

Wicksell, Knut (1896). "A New Principle of Just Taxation," in Richard Musgrave and Alan Peacock (Eds.), *Classics in the Theory of Public Finance.* New York: Macmillan, (1958).

Wildasin, David E. (1984). "On Public Good Provision with Distortionary Taxation," *Economic Inquiry* 22: 227–43.

Wildavsky, Aaron (1988). "Keeping Kosher: The Epistemology of Tax Expenditures," *Journal of Public Policy* 5: 413–31.

Wilson, John D. (1989a). "An Optimal Tax Treatment of Leviathan," *Economics and Politics* 1: 97–118.

(1989b). "On the Optimal Tax Base for Commodity Taxation," *American Economic Review* 79: 1196–1206.

(1990). "Are Efficiency Improvements in Government Transfer Politics Self-Defeating?" *Economics and Politics* 2: 241–58.

Winer, Stanley L. (1983). "Some Evidence on the Effect of the Separation of Spending and Taxing Decisions," *Journal of Political Economy* 91: 126–40.

Winer, Stanley L., and Walter Hettich (1988). "The Structure of the Sieve: Political Economy in the Explanation of Tax Systems and Tax Reform," *Osgoode Hall Law Journal* 26: 409–22.

(1989). "Tax Expenditures and the Democratic Process," in Neil Bruce and Jack M. Mintz (eds.), *Tax Expenditures and Government Policy.* Kingston, Ontario: John Deutsch Institute, Queen's University, pp. 379–405.

(1991a). "Debt and Tariffs: An Empirical Investigation of the Evolution of Revenue Systems," *Journal of Public Economics* 45: 215–42.

(1991b). "Political Checks and Balances and the Structure of Taxation in the United States and Canada," in A. Breton, G. Galeotti, P. Salmon, and R. Wintrobe (Eds.), *The Competitive State.* Dordrecht: Kluwer, pp. 39–56.

(1992). "Explaining the Use of Related Tax Instruments," working paper, Sonderforschungsbereich 178, serie II, nr. 189, Faculty for Economics and Statistics, University of Konstanz, Germany (September).

(1993). "Optimal Representative Taxation, Information and Political Institutions," paper prepared for the International Seminar in Public Economics (August, Linz, Austria).

(1997). "Analyzing the Collective Power to Tax: Models and Policy Issues," in Rick Krever (Ed.), *Tax Conversations: A Guide to the Key Issues in the Tax Reform Debate – Essays in Honor of John G. Head.* The Hague: Kluwer Law International, pp. 49–95.

(1998). "What Is Missed if We Leave Out Collective Choice in the Analysis of Taxation," *National Tax Journal* 51: 373–90.

Winer, Stanley L., and Thomas Rutherford (1993). "Coercive Redistribution and the Franchise: A Preliminary Investigation Using Computable General Equilibrium

Modelling," in A. Breton et al. (Eds.), *Preferences and the Demand for Public Goods*. Dordrecht: Kluwer, pp. 351–75.

Wintrobe, Ronald (1990). "The Tinpot and the Totalitarian: An Economic Theory of Dictatorship," *The American Political Science Review* 84: 849–72.

Wiseman, Jack (1989). *Cost, Choice and Political Economy*. Cheltenham, UK: Edward Elgar.

   (1990) "Principles of Political Economy: An Outline Proposal, Illustrated by Application to Fiscal Federalism," *Constitutional Political Economy* 1: 101–24.

Witt, Ulrich (1992). "The Endogenous Public Choice Theorist," *Public Choice* 73: 117–29.

Witte, John F. (1985). *The Politics and Development of the Federal Income Tax*. Madison: University of Wisconsin Press.

Wittman, Donald (1987). "Elections with *N* Voters, *M* Candidates and *K* Issues," in Manfred Holler (Ed.), *The Logic of Mutiparty Systems*. Dordrecht: Kluwer, pp. 129–36.

   (1990). "Spatial Strategies When Candidates Have Policy Preferences," in J. Enelow and M. Hinich (Eds.), *Advances in the Spatial Theory of Voting*. Cambridge: Cambridge University Press, pp. 66–98.

   (1995). *The Myth of Democratic Failure: Why Political Institutions Are Efficient*. Chicago: University of Chicago Press.

Wood, Louis A. (1924). *History of Farmers' Movements in Canada*. Toronto: Ryerson Press.

Woolley, John T. (1984). *Monetary Politics: The Federal Reserve and the Politics of Monetary Policy*. Cambridge: Cambridge: University Press.

Yablon, Jeffrey L. (1994). "As Certain as Death – Quotations about Taxes," *Tax Notes* (November 14): 897–911.

Yang, C. C. (1995). "Endogenous Tariff Formation Under Representative Democracy: A Probabilistic Voting Model. *American Economic Review* 85: 956–63.

Yitzhaki, Shlomo (1979). "A Note on Optimal Taxation and Administration Costs," *American Economic Review* 69: 475–80.

Zodrow, George R. (1985). "Partial Tax Reform: An Optimal Tax Perspective," *Canadian Journal of Economics* 18: 345–6.

   (1988). "Eliminating State and Local Tax Deductibility: A General Equilibrium Model of Revenue Effects," in Harvey Rosen (Ed.), *Fiscal Federalism: Quantitative Studies*. Chicago: University of Chicago Press, pp. 177–214.

   (1997). "On the Transition to Indirect or Direct Consumption-Based Taxation," in Rick Krever (Ed.), *Tax Conversations: A Guide to the Key Issues in the Tax Reform Debate – Essays in Honor of John G. Head*. The Hague: Kluwer Law International, pp. 187–219.

Name Index

Subject Index

ability to pay, 100–101
administration costs; *see also* sorting
  equilibrium; tax administration; tax
  structure; tax systems: and political
  influence, 80–83; with self-selection
  constraints, 86–9; in sorting equilibrium
  tax, 72–83; tax structure designed to reduce,
  49–53; in tax system, 51–2; in treatment of
  taxpayers, 269; variation in, 196
advertising, political, 134–7
agenda control in median voter model, 15, 25
applied general equilibrium: benchmark data
  set as, 161–8; and calibration of political
  influence weights, 167–8, 181–2, 190–2;
  and cardinalization of utility, 171–2; and
  counterfactual simulations (1973 and 1983
  economies), 182–7; and GEMTAP model,
  156, 160, 163–8; importance of, in study of
  political economy, 172–81; and model with
  competitive political sector, 160–71;
  probabilistic voting in, 157–9

bargaining: collectively about expenditures
  and taxes, 123; in cooperative game theory
  model, 22–3; Lindahl process, 123–5
benefits, political: marginal, 46–7; in political
  equilibrium, 46–8
Blueprints for Basic Tax Reforms (1977), 109
borrowing: as revenue source in Canada
  (1871–1913), 246–7, 251, 255, 257–8; as
  substitute for current taxation, 217; as tax
  on future, 34–6, 246

calibration of political influence weights,
  181–2, 191–2
Canada: borrowing as revenue source in
  (1871–1913), 246–7, 251, 255, 257–8;
  discretionary tax policy in, 276–7;
  economic influences on tax system of,
  270–1; evolution of revenue system in,
  237–61; federal grants in budget in, 281–2;
  hypotheses related to effect of structural
  competition in, 271–83; influence of
  interest groups (1871–1913) in, 248–9, 255;
  interdependence in federal system in,

281–2; Pension Plan in, 276; Royal
  Commission on Taxation (1966) in, 58n13,
  101n4, 109; tax process in parliamentary
  system of, 267–9; tax system in
  parliamentary system of government in,
  265–6
capital flows, cross-national, 266
coalitions in cooperative game theory model,
  22, 29
collective choice: comparative treatment of, in
  tax models, 24–5; in predictive models,
  11–23; standard of reference to judge
  outcomes of, 121–5; tax policy as
  equilibrium outcome of, 1
collective choice analysis, 285–6; and
  influence on study of taxation, 122;
  integrated into policy analysis, 291; view of
  public policy emerging from, 290–1
competition; *see also* political competition;
  structural competition; tax competition:
  effect of, on political parties, 124–5;
  intragovernmental, 265; among political
  units, 218–19, 234
computable equilibrium. *See* applied general
  equilibrium
Condorcet equilibrium (median voter model),
  13, 15
constant elasticity of substitution (CES),
  77–82, 171
constitution: checks and balances in written,
  265; as constraint on Leviathan, 22; to limit
  government's power to tax, 106–13, 117–18
consumers: in applied general equilibrium
  model, 168–9; and welfare loss from
  taxation, 134–40
continuity of expected vote function, 28
convergence of policy platforms, 67–8, 94
cooperative game theory: in comparison with
  other models 23–34; as model of tax policy,
  37; in tax system formation, 11, 22;
  unresolved concerns about, 31
coordination among policy makers in choice
  of tax systems, 131–4
cost, political: marginal, 46–7; of raising tax
  rates to finance expenditures, 57